MARCO⊕POLO

FLORIDA

D0191551

www.marco-polo.com

Sightseeing Highlights

»Fun in the Sun« – one of the many slogans used by advertisers to attract attention to the **»Sunshine State«**.
And it's true: nowhere in the USA does the sun shine more than in St. Petersburg, nowhere in the USA are there as many beautiful beaches as in Florida and nowhere in the USA are there as many amusement parks as in Florida. And Florida also has the oldest city in the USA!

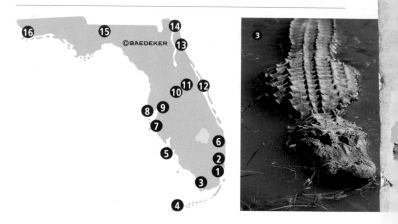

❶ ✶✶ Miami
Florida's hot metropolis has its own unique flair: on the one hand Latin American (thanks to the many exiled Cubans and other immigrants), on the other hand cool business sense – with Spanish and English (»Spanglish«) spoken in between.
page 240

❷ ✶✶ Miami Beach
Hot parties – with stars like Jennifer Lopez and Britney Spears – as well as the pastel colours and neon lights of Art Deco, the special trademarks of the brilliant city on the sea. **page 261**

❸ ✶✶ Everglades National Park
Truly a »river of grass«, the Everglades presents itself as ever green with its many varieties of fauna.
page 158

❹ ✶✶ Key West
Key West almost seems like a Caribbean island, and is only 90 miles/150 kilometres away from Cuba. **page 211**

❺ ✶✶ Sanibel & Captiva
This place has the most beautiful seashells and some of the most beautiful beaches in the USA.
page 342

Do You Feel Like ...

... Florida the way you like it? Maybe these tips will help.

INDIAN HERITAGE

Crystal River ▶
Crystal River Archeological Site protects Native American cultic mounds, which were made long before the first Europeans arrived here. **page 149**

• **Fort Myers**
In Cayo Costa State Park shell mounds commemorate the once flourishing Calusa Indian culture. **page 191**

• **Miami**
The Historical Museum of Southern Florida specialises in the Native American settlement of Florida before the European conquest. **page 247**

MANATEES

◀ **Crystal River**
The affectionate manatees favour the delta of the Crystal and Homosassa Rivers. **page 150**

• **Fort Myers**
Manatees swim in Manatee Park in the eastern part of town undisturbed by motor boats. **page 187**

• **Tampa**
The warm waters around Big Bend Power Station is another favourite haunt of manatees. **page 370**

ENJOYING ART
St Petersburg ▶
The Salvador Dali Museum is one of the world's most important exhibition sites for the Catalan surrealist artist. **page 335**
- **Winter Park**
Wonderful craft items by Louis Comfort Tiffany is displayed in the Charles Hosmer Morse Museum of Art. **pag 291**
- **Miami**
The Miami Art Museum exhibits the crème de la crème of modern American art. **page 247**

STONE CRABS
◀ **Miami Beach**
Stone crab season begins in mid-October. Joe's Stone Crab is always full then.
page 272
- **Sarasota**
The name says it all at Moore's Stone Crab Restaurant on Longboat Key. Freshly cooked crabs are served here.
page 347

PADDLING
Everglades National Park ▶
See the Everglades from a new angle in a canoe.
page 160
- **Cedar Key**
Dolphins often accompany tours around the island.
page 144
- **Ocala/Silver Springs**
Huge fresh water springs bubble to the surface here. There is great canoeing on the streams they form. **page 284**

BACKGROUND

ENJOY FLORIDA

Seafood in all shapes and sizes: »Floribbean Cuisine«

A Saturn Ib Rocket at Kennedy Space Center

Art Deco in Miami Beach

Dark Clouds over Miami Beach

PRACTICAL INFORMATION

PRICE CLASSES
Restaurants
(main course)
$$$$ = over $30
$$$ = $20 – $30
$$ = $12 – $20
$ = up to $12
Hotels (doube room)
$$$$ = over $250
$$$ = $180 – $250
$$ = $100 – $180
$ = up to $100

BACKGROUND

Important information on nature, landscape and climate, history, economy and culture, about the people and everyday life, of course also about alligators, Mickey Mouse and rockets – all of it is in this section.

Fun in the Sun

So much to do – so little time: this phrase can be heard again and again, sighed out loud by visitors to Florida. Rightly so, as the variety of activities and entertainment on offer is overwhelming. It's impossible to see everything within a single visit! And to spend the entire holiday at the beach or in theme parks is not recommended. Florida is – of course – more than just sun, sand and Mickey Mouse.

First there was the disputed evaluation of the ballots cast during election of George W. Bush as president. Then came the terror attacks of 11 September 2001, the shock waves of which led to a fall in tourism even in Florida, which is consistently well-visited. And just when the most important branch of the state's economy had recovered from these record-breaking losses, the summer of 2004 brought a quartet of hurricanes that caused destruction, once again reducing the number of bookings to Florida to the levels seen after September 11th. Florida sure didn't have it easy! But despite damage running into billions – the tourist areas along the west coast were worst affected – the Sunshine State declared »business as usual« within the same year: most holiday areas, including Miami and the Florida Keys, remained largely untouched by the tropical storms, and in Orlando, Disney World and the others opened their doors the very next day as if nothing had happened. The beaches of the western part of Florida's panhandle suffered a further setback in 2010 when they were afflicted by the oil spill from the oil rig Deepwater-Horizon.

TRUE LIES

Nobody worried that the guests would stay away permanently even though Florida was deeply affected by the real estate and financial crisis that began in 2007 and the oil spill in 2010. Florida stands for lazy holidays beneath the palms, expeditions to see alligators in the Everglades, pink flamingos and cocktails on the beach. Ever since the cult crime series Miami Vice, Miami has been synonymous with suntanned bodies and pastel sunsets, and means hot nights and beautiful people at MTV awards

Enchanting underwater world of the Florida Keys

Mickey Mouse: children's best friend in Disney World

parties. Florida means swimming with the dolphins just like Bud and Sandy Ricks did with Flipper, hanging out at breezy beach bars like »Papa« Hemingway, America's hard-drinking author, who threw wild parties and caught swordfish down in Key West, and while at it, wrote some of his best novels. And no string of clichés would be complete without mentioning Florida's – no exaggeration – gigantic theme parks, from Disney World in Orlando to the Kennedy Space Center in Cape Canaveral. Put bluntly, everyone thinks of enjoyment in tropical temperatures. The variety of amusement on offer in Florida is as massive as the cumulus clouds floating above the Keys.

RELAXED IN THE HERE AND NOW

Those staying for longer will, most of all, learn to appreciate Florida's carefree lifestyle. Nowhere else on the continent does the sky seem to be so blue, the sand so soft and the heat so pleasant as it does here. It provides the best possible conditions for a tropical version of the »American way of life«, mixing freedom and free time, sand and sun, candour and optimism into a very tempting cocktail. Inevitably, it's impossible to be completely alone on the palm-fringed beaches, on the hot sand and the tropical islands. Meanwhile, 75 million visitors come to Florida each year. But the »Sunshine State« is more than just a tourists' paradise. Those in the know argue that Florida is one of the least understood areas in the USA. With up to 1,000 immigrants per day, it is still a long way away, politically and socially, from being a »complete« state.

BOREDOM? NO THANKS!

It is indeed often just a frisbee-throw from the rows of bronzed sunworshippers to an idyllic beach known only to nature lovers. Islands that are otherwise the preserve of bird watchers offer great coral reefs for snorkelling. And untouched forests, lakes and huge swamps with alligators and other primitive creatures can be found at the borders of modern cities. Anyone who gets bored in Florida, an American newspaper wrote recently, should be locked up.

Facts

Nature and Environment

What are the Everglades? Where are the mountains in Florida, and where are the coral reefs? What are the main sectors of the economy and in which regions do the most people live?

FLAT PENINSULA

With an area of 151,670 km2 (58,560 sq mi) Florida is bigger than England. Located on a **peninsula** between the Atlantic Ocean and the Gulf of Mexico, on the same latitude as North Africa, the »Sunshine State«« is the southernmost state in the continental USA and its south-eastern extremity. The southern tip of the peninsula **reaches all the way to the tropical belt**. It is only 145km/90 mi from Key West to Havana on the Caribbean island of Cuba, and only 100km/60 mi from Miami Beach to the Bahamas in the Atlantic. The greatest distance between north and south – from Pensacola to Key West – is 834 mi/1342km. To the north, Florida shares a border with Georgia. In the north-west, the flagpole-like extension known as the Panhandle borders the state of Alabama.

Encompassing 58,560 sq mi/151,670 sq km – about 10% larger than England – the Sunshine State ranks as the 22nd largest state in the US. The coast is 1900mi/3000km long (800mi/1280km of which is beach), and even inland, the sea is never further than 60mi/100km away.

Location and size

The Florida Peninsula is largely flat. The highest »mountains« are the merely 100m/330ft-high **Iron Mountain** near Lake Wales and, at 113m/371ft above sea level, **Lakewood**, near DeFuniak Springs in the north-west. Only the **Panhandle** in the north-west is a gently rolling hill landscape, with a **Gulf coast** in the west interspersed with extensive swamp areas. The **Atlantic coast** in the east, with its shallow bayous and lagoons, is mainly protected by offshore sand banks and islands, known as the Barrier Islands. Inland, the peninsula is dotted with around 7,800 lakes.

Around 250 million years ago, at the end of the Palaeozoic Era, after the super-continent of Pangaea broke up, Florida was still a small part of Gondwana, the huge continent in the southern hemisphere. The dissolution of Gondwana, accompanied by intense

A look at the geology

A trip through the amphibian landscape of the Everglades in an airboat is exciting

volcanic activity, took place during the Mesozoic era, from 230 to 65 million years ago. Similarities in the rock structure show that the present-day south-eastern corner of the USA was once joined to West Africa. Along with the present-day Caribbean islands, Florida and the eastward-lying Bahamas were once a group of volcanic islands.

With the **Tertiary period**, which began around 65 million years ago, the land sank gradually into the ocean. Over this time, rivers displaced huge masses of quartz sand, marl and clay from the Appalachians to the sea, creating enormous deltas in what is now the north of Florida. To the south, the **Florida Platform** (Florida Plateau) was formed. This layer of limestone and dolomite, 3,800–5,400m/12,500–17,700ft thick, pushed the bedrock even deeper into the earth. Only in the late Tertiary period, around 20 million years ago, did an opposing force take effect: Florida was the last area of the continental USA to be pushed up above sea level.

During the **Ice Ages**, which began around two million years ago, enormous masses of water were frozen. This led to a **sinking of sea levels** by up to 120m/400ft. The receding of the oceans exposed the ground near to the coasts. For a time the Florida Peninsula – measured by its surface area – was twice the size it is today. Rivers and wind transported tremendous amounts of sand onto the exposed shelf. Between the Ice Ages the sea levels rose again, in places to above the present-day levels, as terraces and previous beach-lines show. At the end of the last Ice Age, around 12,000–10,000 years ago, waves and currents distributed the sand-masses along the coasts. Huge sand banks and rows of dunes were formed. Expansive islands of sand arose, separated by lagoons of varying width, some of which exist to this day.

Thick layers of chalk formed in the warm, salty water. **Coral** created **reefs** in the clear, oxygen-rich water. Along the shallow coasts off the estuaries of North Florida, wetlands with mudflats, salt marshes and swamps were created. Since then, belts of mangrove have surrounded the southern tip of Florida, with their network of roots protecting the low-lying areas from flooding during storms.

Groundwater pressed into the porous layers of limestone on the mainland. The carbonic acid dissolved in the water leads to the **corrosion of the stone**. Fissures and cracks in the rock spread to form crevices and caves, even entire systems of caves. And when advanced erosion leads to the collapse of the cave roofs, funnels are formed, which are then suddenly filled with water. The **groundwater**, which is under pressure in many places, comes to the surface in rapidly-flowing **springs**. The present-day appearance of the Florida Peninsula is largely a result of the erosive power of water. The karst formation of the limestone shelf, which is often only a few metres above sea level, has led to widely differing landscapes.

NORTH FLORIDA

Almost half of Florida, particularly the area north of the Tampa–Orlando line, is covered with forests and swamps and is sparsely populated. In the shadow of the mega-sized theme parks in and around Orlando, Florida's four national forests – Apalachicola, Choctawhatchee, Ocala and Osceola –offer a quite different experience. Canoe tours through **cypress swamps**, walking tours through largely unspoiled **subtropical forests**, swimming in crystal-clear **spring waters** and nights spent in rustic huts or magnificently-situated campgrounds can put sandy beaches and Mickey Mouse far from the mind. This is also where the most important of Florida's 34 mostly quite short rivers flow. Some of the **estuaries on the Gulf Coast** are the last refuge of the endangered manatee (sea-cow): they are particularly at home in the swampy delta of the Crystal River. In North Florida's hinterland, all roads lead to Gainesville. Half of the 80,000 residents are students at the local University of Florida, which guarantees lively nightlife. But the nearby Paynes Prairie Preserve State

Forests and wet zones

Picturesque karstic spring ponds are typical of northern Florida

Park is much more worth visiting. Its **diverse forests in swampy marshes** are a reminder of how large parts of the inland once looked before they were drained. »The Ridge«, which runs from Lee in the north, through central Florida, down to Sebring in the south, with rows of hills rising up to 100m/330 feet, is used for agriculture: to this day it is the largest citrus-growing area in the world. That nature, progress and entertainment can coexist is demonstrated by North Florida's Atlantic coast: the **Canaveral Peninsula** is not only where rockets are launched into space. It is also a place where migratory and marsh birds, as well as wildcats, various types of sea turtles and other rare species live in the nature reserves of Canaveral National Seashore and Merritt Island National Wildlife Refuge.

SOUTH FLORIDA

Subtropical holiday paradise

South of this line Florida really lives up to its cliché. The **Coastal Lowlands**, reaching up to 90km/55mi inland, make dreams of a holiday spent lazing in a hammock come true. While the expansive northern areas are used for farming and grazing, it seems the only reason for the existence of the populated places along the coast is tourism: every town has a pier, a restaurant with a view, and at least one motel. Where the dry coastal areas were too narrow, such as in Naples, swamp areas were drained. Within a few decades, this former fishing village grew into the tourist centre of the south-west coast. The most densely populated area is the south-east coast. Miami and Fort Lauderdale have merged into a metropolitan area with over four million inhabitants. Nevertheless, the south-east coast more than makes up for all the urban bustle with its fabulous beaches and an exceptional array of culture. Just how much life in Florida is concentrated on the coasts can be seen in Naples. Directly beyond the city limits begins the expansive swamp areas of **Big Cypress Swamp** and the **Everglades**. There are no settlements to be found in this primeval landscape at the peninsula's southern corner. Lying just a foot or two above sea level, the Everglades are a succession of **freshwater marshes**, **swamp areas and grasslands** occasionally interspersed with **hammocks** (hardwood groves). The fact that this is actually a river, 50mi/80km wide but only 6in/15cm deep, is not visible to the naked eye. This **»river of grass«** is the largest subtropical wetland in North America, the habitat for hundreds of animal species, including in particular the famous alligator, the »mascot of the Everglades«, and pelicans, herons and ibises. Their future is far from secure. The highly sensitive ecosystem is subject to many threats, among them are dry spells and tropical storms. But the biggest threat is from people. Ever increasing areas are drained to create farmland, or water is diverted for irrigation. Whether or not the conservation projects

In the south the Florida Keys gradually disappear into the sea

initiated by the government and private groups will be effective remains to be seen. For now, the remains of this unique landscape are protected at various nature protection areas, including Everglades National Park and Big Cypress National Preserve, which was devised as a buffer between the inhabitants and the swamps. Last but no least: the **Florida Keys**. This chain of islands, which on the map reaches out into the Gulf of Mexico like a hook, is a 137mi/220km long arc, beginning half an hour's drive south of Miami and ending where the Dry Tortugas disappear into the Gulf of Mexico. The tiny islands – some smaller than a football field – are ridges of the world's third largest coral reef, which was formed over the last 150,000 years. Today, it attracts snorkelers and divers from around the world.

CLIMATE

The most south-eastern state of the United States of America is influenced by two climate zones. While the north of Florida lies in the subtropical to temperate zone, the southern part of the peninsula is entirely subtropical. To the extreme south, the periodically wet tropical climate of the Caribbean is noticeable.

Climate zones

MARCO ⊕ POLO INSIGHT

Hurakán

The inhabitants of the West Indies called them hurakán, the Spanish conquistadors adopted the expression and the English followed them. These tropical whirlwinds sweep across the Florida peninsula between June and October every year.

Okeechobee 1928

FLORIDA

Jacksonville •

Number of hurricanes in the last 100 years

- 0–9
- 10–19
- 20–32

• New Orleans

Labor Day 1935

Gulf of Mexico

Wilma 2005

Tampa •

Andrew 1992

Katrina 2005

• Miami

Hurricane scale
Wind speed in km/h (mph)

- **5** > 250 (150)
- **4** 210–249 (125-150)
- **3** 178–209 (106-124)
- **2** 154–177 (92-105)
- **1** 119–153 (71-91)

Donna 1960

• Havana

CUBA

▶ **How hurricanes form**
Hurricanes form most often in the Atlantic over water near the equator with a temperature on the surface of at least 26°C/78°F, in a place where there are already extremely high thunderclouds.

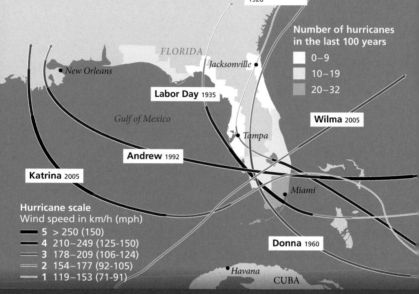

1 Rising air
2 Rain
3 Thunderclouds form
4 Low pressure zone develops

5 Rising air builds up the storm system
6 The earth's rotation causes the storm to start turning

The worst hurricanes in Florida

Florida is devastated regularly by hurricanes. While there are fewer fatalities due to improved warning systems the damage to property is exploding. The storm of the century Katrina (2005) was an especially destructive hurrican

Okeechobee	Sep. 6, 1928
Peak winds	260 kmh
	156 mph
Damage	$100 mil.

🧍🧍🧍🧍🧍🧍🧍🧍🧍🧍🧍🧍🧍🧍🧍🧍🧍🧍🧍🧍
🧍🧍🧍🧍🧍🧍🧍🧍🧍🧍🧍🧍🧍🧍🧍🧍🧍🧍🧍🧍
🧍🧍🧍🧍🧍🧍🧍🧍🧍🧍🧍🧍🧍🧍🧍🧍🧍🧍🧍🧍
🧍🧍🧍🧍🧍🧍🧍🧍🧍🧍🧍🧍🧍🧍🧍🧍🧍🧍🧍🧍

4.000 fatalities

Labor-Day	Aug. 29, 1935
Peak winds	260 kmh
	156 mph
Damage	$6 mil.

🧍🧍🧍🧍🧍🧍🧍🧍🧍🧍

500 fatalities

Donna	Aug. 29, 1960
Peak winds	260 kmh
	156 mph
Damage	$3 bil.

🧍🧍🧍🧍🧍🧍🧍

360 fatalities

Andrew	Aug. 16, 1992
Peak winds	280 kmh
	168 mph
Damage	$26 bil.

🧍

26 fatalities

Katrina	Aug. 23, 2005
Peak winds	280 kmh
	168 mph
Damage	$100 bil.

🧍🧍🧍🧍🧍🧍🧍🧍🧍🧍🧍🧍🧍🧍🧍🧍🧍
🧍🧍🧍🧍🧍🧍🧍🧍🧍🧍🧍🧍🧍🧍🧍🧍🧍🧍

1800 fatalities

Wilma	Okt. 15, 2005
Peak winds	295 kmh
	177 mph
Damage	$29 bil.

🧍🧍

70 fatalities

Speeds

Hurricanes move in speeds between 15 and 40 kmh (9 and 25 mph). Within the storms speeds up to 250 kmh (50 mph) can develop.

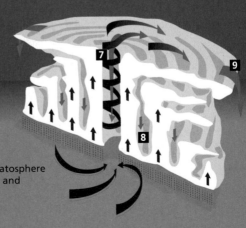

7 Cloudless eye of the storm: windless, cold and dry air

8 When the air reaches the stratosphere it is forced back into the eye and between the rain bands

9 Other air moves outward and is forced away there

Seasons The four seasons of the year are clearly definable in the north of Florida. Rainfall can also be expected practically all year round. In southern Florida, by contrast, there are practically only two seasons. The warm water, high **humidity** and high evaporation rates contribute to **sweltering** summers, which can be oppressive between May and October. However, the season from November to April is constantly cool and characterized by three to five months of little precipitation.

Temperatures and rainfall From **June to September** it is rather hot throughout the entire peninsula. The highest temperatures are found around the Florida Keys as well as in the drier inland areas. Several weeks of hot spells with daytime **temperatures of up to 40°C/104°F** or even more are not uncommon. In the south-eastern USA, temperatures of up to 35°C are considered normal. During summer, heavy storms can be expected practically every day, bringing not only hail, but occasionally also dangerous tornados. The months of March, April and May, as well as October and November are very pleasant. Temperatures rise to summer levels, mostly with plenty of bright sunshine. From **December to February**, it can get noticeably cool in northern and central Florida. Heavy gusts of cold air from the north can also bring **frosts**, which do enormous damage to the citrus and vegetable crops. The southern tip of Florida is free of frost. Average winter temperatures here rarely sink below +6°C. The highest rates of precipitation are measured in the north of the state in the area of the Florida Panhandle, where sometimes well over 1500mm/60in of rain fall annually. It is drier in the Keys, with 1000mm/40in, only two thirds of the rainfall levels in the north.

Hurricane season Every year, Florida can expect several tropical storms to pass through or pass by, usually occurring in the time from June to September. Hurricanes can not only reach enormous magnitudes, they can also develop a tremendous potential for destruction. No-one has forgotten Hurricane »Sandy«, which left a trail of destruction along Florida's Atlantic coast beaches, including the beaches at Fort Lauderdale, in late October 1992.

> **?** *Warm water from the Gulf*
>
> MARCO ⊕ POLO INSIGHT
>
> The phenomenon of the Gulf Stream was first described by Ponce de León in 1513. At that time the Spanish made use of the warm current, which flows from the Gulf of Mexico towards Europe, on their homeward journey from the West Indies.

The Gulf Stream, an important component of the circumplanetary weather system, has a major influence on the weather conditions in western and central Europe. As the Florida Stream, **warm surface waters** flow from the Gulf of Mexico through the Florida Strait where, off Florida's east coast, they meet the equally warm Antilles Stream, from the area of the West Indies. 30mi/50km wide on average and up to 1000m/3,300ft deep, the Gulf Stream continues up along the American east coast, before flowing north-east towards western Europe. Up to 55 million cubic metres of water per second are transported north-eastwards.

FLORA

The transition from the pine forests of the temperate zone to the lush vegetation of the subtropical and fringe of the tropical zone is typical of Florida. Many varieties of pine thrive in northern and central Florida, and **Sabal palms** make up the underwood of the **pine forests**, which are not dense. From north to south, the number of **palms** increases, particularly coconut, date and dwarf palms. Majestic king palms also grow here and there in large numbers. Among the most impressive trees are the evergreen **live oaks**, which have dense underwood and branches hung with whole beards of the bromeliad known as **Spanish moss**. In the wetlands, **cypresses** are the typical tree.

Forests

To the south, the forests give way to grasslands and wetlands, in which numerous tropical plants thrive. The characteristic plants of these zones are swamp cypresses, a large variety of grasses, epiphytes, ferns, lianas, as well as all kinds of orchids. Numerous vines and bromeliads can also be found. In the actual swamp areas, many reeds, sedges, rushes, water lilies, and especially water hyacinths can be spotted. Those who know where to look can also find many varieties of orchid.

Grasslands and swamps

Florida's wetlands feature a large number of **hammocks**, or hardwood groves, with palm, mahogany, oak and magnolia trees. Sabal palms, palmettos and many climbing plants make up the impenetrable underbrush.

Hammocks

Southern Florida, where the mainland gradually sinks to below sea level, is also home to extensive mangrove coasts. Due to their highly specialized nature, these mangrove forests are home to only a few varieties. The predominant species is the red mangrove, the tannin of which lends the water a reddish shimmer. In addition, there are white and black mangroves. These salt-loving plants with their thick, evergreen leaves live in the amphibious bush forests. Stilt roots and pneumatophoric roots hold the plants up.

Mangroves

Florida is famous for its citrus fruit farming. Extensive citrus plantations along the Indian River, in central Florida and on the Gulf Coast

Citrus fruits

There's lots to do: orange harvest in central Florida

primarily grow oranges and grapefruits, but also tangerines and lemons. These fruits are mainly processed into juices and juice concentrates. Florida also has its own characteristic citrus fruit: the Key lime, a green to yellowish, thin-skinned fruit, the acidic juice of which is used for cooking. Essential oils are produced from the citrus rinds.

FAUNA

Diversity of species Despite the massive impact of humans upon the natural habitat of the Florida Peninsula, a number of protected areas give an idea of just how diverse the region's fauna once must have been. This impression is confirmed when reading descriptions by naturalists such as Muir or Audubon.

Bird life A colourful variety of bird life can be found in Florida, especially in the area of Merritt Island (near Cape Canaveral) on the Atlantic coast, and in the mangrove coasts of south-western and southern Florida, where hundreds of species mate and nest in the largely unspoiled marshes as well as in the swamp areas. Among them are grey herons, little blue herons, **egrets**, little egrets, green-backed herons as well as white and **brown pelicans**. Wood storks, **darters** (anhingas), roseate spoonbills, various woodpeckers and vultures can also be seen. Very often it is possible to spot **ospreys**, also known colloquially as fish eagles or seahawks, which are common in South Florida. The American national emblem, the bald eagle, soars among them over bays and swamps. Keen ornithologists will also spot limpkins, cormorants, glossy ibises, skimmers and little owls. A number of flamingos still live in the wild.

Around one million **alligators** have their home in Florida's waterways and swamp areas. They can be found in the Everglades and in the canals surrounding the space station at Cape Canaveral. They turn up in the greenery around big shopping malls, on golf courses, in gardens, and at night it's not an uncommon occurrence to see a »gator« crawling across the highway. The **American crocodile** is a far rarer sight. This reptile is in danger of extinction as a result of extensive hunting and poaching. The important sanctuaries for these reptiles are the Everglades as well as the swamp areas along the Bay of Biscayne and Florida Bay, where a few dozen crocodiles still live. Several **species of turtle** are also in danger of extinction. They include the Florida soft-shell turtle, the slider turtle and a variety of sea turtles, whose sandy nests are sometimes discovered by hungry alligators or destroyed by careless tourists.
The palmetto undergrowth of hammocks and other dry biotopes is a refuge for poisonous and often highly aggressive diamond **snakes** and ground rattlers. The cottonmouth, the coral snake and the North Florida native copperhead are life-threatening to humans. Alongside these dangerous reptiles, Florida is home to numerous less poisonous snakes, as well as various colubrid snakes, including the garter snake and the yellow rat snake. Recently **pythons** have been brought in and have multiplied, and now pose a threat to local fauna.

Reptiles

Numerous mammals live in Florida, including some endangered species. Raccoons are often spotted, as are bobcats, **white-tailed deer** and other deer species. Coyotes, foxes, wild boars, minks and armadillo can also be seen, and **opossums**, marsupials resembling rats, are quite common. Despite strict protective measures, the **Florida panther's** chances of survival are decreasing. Very few of these lithe big cats live reclusively in southern Florida's Everglades National Park and Big Cypress Preserve. **Manatees** (sea cows) are also in danger of extinction. These bulky yet cute mammals live in shallow coastal waters and feed on the water plants that thrive there. During the colder times of year they leave the cooler waters and head inland towards the relatively warm waters emerging from springs, or canals heated with effluent water from power plants and factories. Their worst enemies are careless recreational motorboat captains, who kill dozens of manatees each year.

Mammals

Endangered Species

It's true in Florida too: wherever people have spread out, the habitat of wild animals gets reduced. Of more than 100 endangered species in Florida more than two dozen have become extinct in the past decades, including the dusky seaside sparrow, the Caribbean monk seal and the Florida red wolf.

▶ **Animal/species**
where they can still be seen

Florida puma
c. 100
C

American crocodile
c. 1.600
A

Roseate spoonbill
100,000–250,000
H

Manatee
c. 3,500 **E**

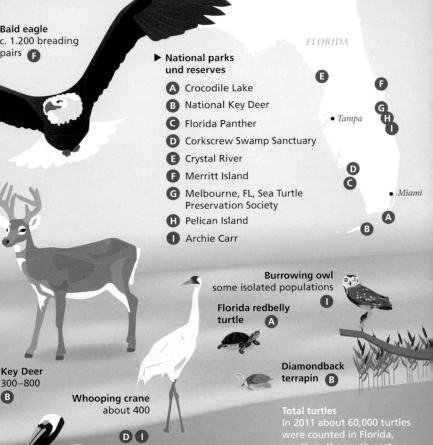

Bald eagle
c. 1.200 breading pairs **F**

FLORIDA

▶ **National parks und reserves**

E

F

A Crocodile Lake
B National Key Deer
C Florida Panther
D Corkscrew Swamp Sanctuary
E Crystal River
F Merritt Island
G Melbourne, FL, Sea Turtle Preservation Society
H Pelican Island
I Archie Carr

G
H
I

• *Tampa*

D
C

• *Miami*

A
B

Burrowing owl
some isolated populations **I**

Florida redbelly turtle **A**

Diamondback terrapin **B**

Key Deer
300–800
B

Whooping crane
about 400

D I

Total turtles
In 2011 about 60,000 turtles were counted in Florida, mostly in the south-east of the state.

Brown pelican **H**
650,000

Sea turtle
G

Dolphn
some thousand

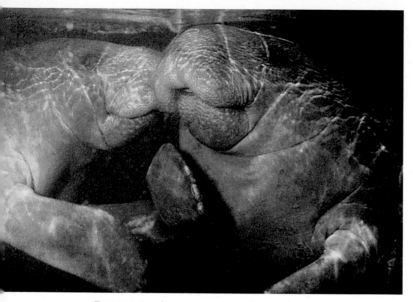

Two manatees in a warm water spring pond

In Florida it is not only possible to see **dolphins** in captivity, but above all, in the wild. They are often spotted in the coastal waters off of south and south-western Florida. Dolphins often accompany boating excursions, and can be encouraged to perform photogenic jumps in the air.

Fish The waters around the Florida Peninsula are home to a large number of **sharks** of various species, among them tiger sharks and hammerhead sharks as well as gigantic whale sharks. **Stingrays** are a danger to beachgoers and swimmers. Particularly in summer, these fish venture into the shallow waters of beaches and swimming areas to reproduce. They bury themselves in the sand and mud with only their eyes and tails exposed. Anyone stepping on such a fish usually comes away with a serious injury as a result of the ray's poisonous stinger.

Insects During the hot, humid summers, time spent in the open air (especially when near standing water) can be torturous. Myriads of **mosquitoes** and flies, which can transmit dangerous diseases such as meningitis, are a plague for people and animals alike in many areas of the Florida Peninsula. Ticks, as well as fleas and **spiders** represent a further nuisance. It is also advisable to beware of poisonous **scorpions**.

ENVIRONMENTAL ISSUES AND ECOLOGY

Protection of the environmental is no longer a low priority in the US. It is not just the increase in fuel prices that has led Americans to use their cars less. The greenhouse effect, the hole in the ozone layer, destruction of coral reefs and ecology are common themes in the US media. The biggest cause for concern is global warming. The predicted rise in sea levels threatens Florida as much as the increase in **tropical storms (hurricanes)**.

Effects of climate change

Water pollution is not the only problem along the coast. In addition, the increased temperature of coastal waters has led to a dramatic decrease in the diversity of marine flora and fauna. The worst-affected areas are the coral banks of the Florida Keys, which react to the slightest of temperature changes in their ecosystem. Studies have shown that as much as 10% of the coral dies each year: if **coral destruction** continues at this pace, most of Florida's reefs will have vanished within a short time. The immense water consumption of the cities and the fruit and vegetable plantations has led to a dramatic sinking of groundwater levels in many areas. This has a negative effect upon the remaining swamp areas: they are gradually drying up. Yet another environmental issue is the contamination of plants and animals by **fertilizers and insecticides**.

Water pollution

The State of Florida reacts to these threats to its nature with laws, regulations, public awareness campaigns. Environmentalists hand out bumper stickers reading »Save the Manatees«. The environmental awareness of Florida's citizens has never been higher. At two national parks, four national forests and at over 100 state parks, Florida's nature is protected or its use is restricted. These protected areas have their own management, with rules that are strictly enforced by park rangers. Visitor centres serve as points of reference and provide information to the public. At the same time, many good programmes have fallen victim to political wheeling and dealing. In the last four years alone, the federal government in Washington has cut funding for wastewater reclamation programs; the »Clean Water Act« to limit pollution from industrial farming has been weakened by making exceptions; and an end has been imposed upon the protection of 300,000 acres of wetlands. With Washington's approval, Florida's powerful sugar industry has delayed the long-agreed timetable to stop the disposal of waste in the Everglades. And the federal government has made an inventory of all potential offshore oil and gas reserves – an act that not only environmentalists suspect will inevitably lead to drilling in the Gulf of Mexico, with incalculable consequences for flora, fauna and people. The memories of the oil spill in 2010 when an oil platform exploded still horrify.

Laws and regulations

Population · Politics · Economy

With a population of more than 19 mil. Florida has one of the highest population densities in the USA. The »Sunshine State«, where 85% of the population has a high school diploma and 26% has at least a B.A., and which has a GDP of almost US$800 billion, is economically the fourth largest state in the USA.

POPULATION

Dynamic growth

The favourable climate and economic opportunities have led to extraordinary population growth in America's south-eastern peninsula. In 1830, only around 35,000 people lived in the then undeveloped area. Today the figure is over 19 million – with hundreds more arriving each day. The development after the end of World War II, when only 2.7 million people lived in Florida, was particularly dramatic. Strong impulses for growth came from the tourist industry, as well as the space programme and the relocation of related high-tech industries. In the 1960s and 1970s came the huge amusement parks, which brought further tourists and migrants to the state. Florida is also a magnet for retired persons and pensioners wishing to live out their twilight years in leisure, and for sun-hungry residents from the cooler northern regions, who spend their winters here.

Florida is growing, especially in the south. Whereas one hundred years ago only five per cent of Florida residents lived in the south, it is now home to forty per cent of the population. The most densely populated area is the **megalopolis on the south coast**, a continuously settled area of well over five million people, spanning from Miami all the way to West Palm Beach. Miami itself is today the hotspot of one of the most financially powerful areas of the USA, as well as an important trade and transport hub between North and South America on the one side, and Europe on the other. The second large conurbation is Tampa, combined with St Petersburg and Clearwater. 2.7 million people live here. Further important, densely populated areas are Orlando, with 1.7 million inhabitants, and Jacksonville, with 1.35 million.

Multicultural Florida

When it comes to the make-up of the population, Florida's proximity to the Caribbean and to Latin America is unmistakable. Nearly a third of the residents are of African-American or Hispanic origin, and nearly one quarter speak a language other than English at home. In greater Miami alone, Hispanics, or Latinos, many of them Cuban exiles, make up over sixty per cent of the population. Other numeri-

Multicultural Sunshine State

cally strong ethnic minorities are Filipinos, Vietnamese, Chinese and Thais. The daily influx of several hundreds of mostly young, qualified professionals is at odds with Florida's image as America's favourite refuge for seniors and retired persons. At the same time, this hardly decreasing flow of immigrants from the south is a reminder of Florida's historic relationship with the Caribbean and Latin America. Today in Miami, Spanish is heard more commonly than English, the Cuban community exerts considerable political influence and the Creole-speaking districts of Miami often make their voices heard. Florida, where English, Spanish and Creole is spoken, is a prime example of the American melting pot. But not all is well. There is a shortage of housing, there are too few schools and poverty is on the increase. The low rate of taxation in Florida, intended to stimulate growth, also leads to difficulties in funding public services. A high rate of infant mortality among the very poorest and street crime are the consequences. Under such conditions, it doesn't take much for the ethnic tensions bubbling beneath the surface of this multicultural society to boil over.

African-Americans

One sixth of the population are black. In addition, there are many **black immigrants from the Caribbean region** (boat refugees). As a result of years of institutionalized racism and a continuing lack of employment opportunities and education, a disproportionate percentage of the black population remains in extreme poverty.

Native Americans

After reaching a low in the 1950s, the Native American (Indian) population is growing once again, and is currently at around 50,000. This is due to the influx of Native Americans from other parts of the USA, who come seeking economic opportunities in Florida. The approximately 3,000 **descendants of the Seminole and Miccosukee** live not only on the reservations in the Everglades and in Big Cypress

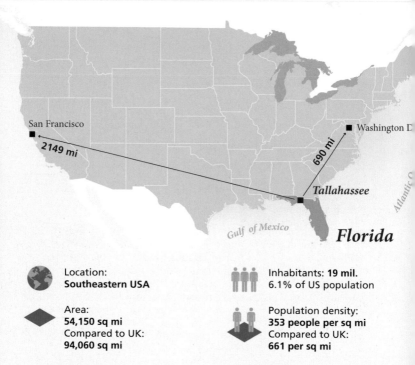

San Francisco
2149 mi

Washington D[

690 mi

Tallahassee

Gulf of Mexico

Atlantic C

Florida

Location:
Southeastern USA

Inhabitants: **19 mil.**
6.1% of US population

Area:
54,150 sq mi
Compared to UK:
94,060 sq mi

Population density:
353 people per sq mi
Compared to UK:
661 per sq mi

▶ **Urban areas**

Miami/Ft.Lauderdale/Palm Beach:
5.5 mil. residents

Tampa/St. Petersburg/Clearwater:
2.8 mil. residents

Raum Orlando:
2.6 mil. residents

Jacksonville:
1.4 mil. residents

▶ **Languages**

English and Spanish

▶ **Religion**

Catholics **30 %**
Protestants **65 %**
Jews **4 %**
Other (including Muslims) **1 %**

▶ **Ethnic groups**

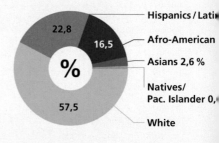

Hispanics / Lati◾

Afro-American

Asians **2,6 %**

Natives/
Pac. Islander 0,

White

22,8

16,5

%

57,5

▶ **Administration**

Capital City **Tallahassee**
67 Counties
Several Indian reservations

▶ Economy

Per capita income 2011
Florida: **39,636 US$**
UK: **39,049 US$**
Poverty rate: **13,8 %**

Agriculture:
Citrus fruits, vegetables,
sugar, cattle and horse
breeding, dairy

Industry:
Food, air and space, electronics, electrotechnology,
machine building, printing,
media

Service industry
Tourism, banking and
insurance, transport

Tourism: Tourism: about **80
mil.** visitors annually, of these
6 mil. from overseas, of these
1.5 mil. from the UK

▶ Climate in Miami

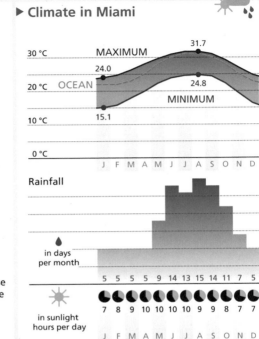

▶ Florida – God's Waiting Room

Many US pensioners live in Florida, which has consequences for demogra-
phic figures. Here are the average ages of the cities with the oldest
population as compared to the city with the youngest population.

**Percentage of
population aged over 65**

Florida **17.6 %**
USA **13 %**

Tallahassee **26.0**
The Villages **68.9**
Sun City **72.2**
Venice City **66.7**
North Fort Myers **62.5**
Bonita Springs **54.3**
Naples **63.9**

Reserve: many of them have adopted the mainstream American way of life and live inconspicuously in various cities in Florida.

Religion The largest religious groups in Florida are **Christians** (Roman Catholic around 30%, Baptists around 30%, Methodists around 15%, Presbyterians about 7% and Anglicans around 5%), about 4% are **Jews**. There has been a recent increase in **Muslims** and followers of various natural religions.

STATE AND SOCIETY

The State of Florida Florida joined the union of the United States of America in 1845. The state government is headed by a **governor**. As at federal level, there is a **congress** comprised of a **senate** and a **house of representatives**. Both houses of congress hold session at the **Capitol** in the **capital city of Tallahassee**. The governor is politically important, though the holder of the office remains subject to the resolutions of Congress. A veto of a congressional resolution by the governor can be overturned by a simple majority vote of congress. The authority of the governor to reinforce the state police with units of the National Guard in the case of civil disturbance is a significant power. Anyone travelling through Florida will come across many examples of the state's **independence** in everyday life: the state regulates the traffic code (i.e. speed limits, blood alcohol limits) and licensing laws for the sale of alcoholic beverages, and determines police policy, voting regulations and the school system. Florida has its **own constitution**, written in 1885 and revised in 1968. The **judicial system** is organized on four levels. The basis is a system of county courts. Above these are the circuit courts and the district court. The highest instance is the Supreme Court, with judges appointed by the governor. At the US Capitol in Washington D.C., Florida is represented by two senators and 25 representatives.

Local government Florida is divided into **67 counties**, each with its own county seat or centre of county administration, which have much more power than comparable European ones. The **Indian Reservations** are governed by the residents themselves, and are not liable to taxation.

ECONOMY

Economic history Florida's economy has developed very dynamically since the end of the 19th century. The decisive impulse was the **construction of railways**. On the one hand, agricultural products could be transported faster to key markets in the north; on the other, the tourist potential of the sunny peninsula was unlocked.

The **role of the military** in the development of the state should not be underestimated. Thousands of Americans went through training camps before and during the two world wars, or worked in the factories of the armaments industry. They spread the reputation of the »Sunshine State«, and so encouraged tourism from north to south. The economy has boomed particularly since the end of World War II.

A strong impulse came from the **US space station at Cape Canaveral**. The rocket builders jump-started the establishment of new industrial and service enterprises.

Additionally, in the past decades, **mega-amusement parks** such as SeaWorld, Walt Disney World, EPCOT, Universal Studios etc. have shot up, contributing not only to an increase in tourism, but also to the creation of many new jobs.

Mining

Florida is the source of a number of mineral resources, including the metals **titanium** and **zirconium**. When it comes to non-metallic resources, Florida produces huge quantities of **chalk**, **phosphate** (around a third of world production) and **high-quality clay**. Large amounts of phosphates are mined in western Florida. The chalk deposits gave rise to a significant cement industry. Off the south-west coast of Florida there are **oil and gas reserves**, but their exploitation is controversial.

Fishing

An important role is played by **oyster beds** (especially in Apalachicola Bay) as well as the **shrimp and prawn catch** (in the area of Amelia Island, amongst others). In addition, each year a great quantity fish for everyday consumption is brought ashore. **Sponge diving**, too, is a source of income. It was immigrants from Greece who first recognized the wealth of natural sponges off the coast of Florida. **Fresh-water fishing** in Florida's inland waters is also worth mentioning. The main catches are catfish, carp, eel and various sunfish.

Forestry

Some regions in the north of Florida are known for their wealth of forests. Over 7 million ha/17 million acres of land are used for forestry operations, especially in northern Florida. The wood is mainly processed for the **paper and cellulose industry**. For many years, **turpentine** has been extracted from the pine forests. The original profusion of hardwoods has been vastly diminished. In order to meet the demand from the timber processing industry and the construction industry, reforestation programmes were implemented as early as the 1920s.

Agriculture

One of the most important branches of agriculture by far is the extensive **citrus production**. Primarily in central and eastern Florida (along the Indian River), each year around five million tons of oranges, two million tons of grapefruits, as well as large quantities of tangerines and lemons are harvested. Despite the costly heating of fruit crops, cold winter spells regularly lead to crop failure.

The **vegetable crop** is also significant. The most commonly planted vegetables are potatoes, cucumber, tomatoes, onions, celery, green beans, melons, pumpkins, eggplant, avocados and much more. These crops also regularly suffer from frosts.

After Hawaii and Louisiana, Florida now takes third place in the USA when it comes to the cultivation of **sugar cane**. The crops now cover around 100,000 ha/25,000 acres of land. Huge sugar cane fields can be found in the Clewiston-Belle Glade area, created by the diking of Lake Okeechobee and the draining of swamp and reed areas.

More recently, **cultivation of flowers and tree nurseries** have been established as new commercial sectors. All kinds of cut flowers, palms and decorative trees are grown, mainly in subtropical southern Florida.

Large amounts of land are taken up by **cattle grazing**. Currently, around two million head of cattle are kept, around 10% of which are milk cows. The successful crossing of robust European cattle breeds with Indian zebus has contributed to this development.

Only relatively recently established in Florida, **horse breeding** is also successful. Numerous studs have proven highly effective at breeding full-blooded Arabians.

Industry   The **food industry** and **tobacco manufacture** were the first industries of note. At the beginning of the 20th century there were more than a hundred cigar factories in Tampa alone, whereas today there are only around two dozen in all of Florida. In contrast, the **citrus industry**, the raw materials of which come from orange and grapefruit plantations, has prospered. There are companies that produce juices and juice concentrates, as well as those that pack and preserve fruit, juices, concentrates etc. This sector also includes companies that specialize in the processing of citrus rinds for the production of oils, preservatives, cosmetics and cleaning solutions.

A conspicuous feature of northern Florida are the huge **paper and cellulose factories** that process the local softwood. Here and there **sawmills**, where hardwoods are cut to size for the construction industry and for building boats, can be seen. The **chemicals industry** has arisen from the lumber industry. One of its most important raw materials is the turpentine that has been extracted from Florida's forests for many years. The **fertilizer industry** processes local raw materials such as chalk and phosphate.

A further important sector of the economy of Florida is the **construction industry**, which profits highly from booming tourism. New holiday complexes, retirement settlements, shopping centres and the likes are being built on every reasonably attractive stretch of coastline. These are followed by amusement parks, marinas, roads, sewage plants and other infrastructure building. Annually, Florida sees well over twenty billion dollars' worth of new construction.

With the building of the space station at Cape Canaveral, many companies related to the **aerospace industry** as well as **electronics** and **technology** have emerged. All of the well-known American aircraft manufacturers, machinery firms and computer giants have offices in the »Sunshine State«. As a result of the aerospace boom, many highly specialized service industries have also been established.

»They came with a twenty-dollar bill and a T-shirt and never changed either of them ...« This cutting remark refers to the tourists of bygone days, who came with a healthy sense of adventure in rickety automobiles to spend the winter in the largely unexplored, still provincial Florida. Today, tourism is a pillar of the economy. Each year, about **80 million people** spend their holidays in the »Sunshine State«. One in five visitors to the US from overseas spend at least part of their stay in Florida. In good years, around six million tourists from overseas come to Florida. Highlights such as the fabulous beaches on the Atlantic and Gulf coasts, the mega-amusement parks of the Orlando area, the US Space Station at Cape Canaveral, Miami and Miami Beach as well as the Everglades and the Keys are magnets for an endless flow of visitors. In the meantime, over two million jobs in the »Sunshine State« are directly or indirectly related to tourism. This so-called »white industry« brings in revenues of around 65 billion dollars annually.

Each year, over **four million cruise passengers** dock in Florida's harbours. Most cruise passengers board in Miami. Other important cruise-liner ports include Port Everglades, Port Canaveral, Tampa and Key West.

Tourism

Florida's appeal as a winter domicile for the wealthy, its industrial growth and its proximity to attractive tax havens (i.e. the Bahamas) has led to more and more financial services opening branches here. Miami, the hub between North, Central and South America, is today one of the world's leading financial centres. The glittering facades of the banking palaces along Miami's Brickell Avenue emphasize this in a most impressive manner.

Financial markets

Other sectors of the economy are currently enjoying rapid growth in Florida: the **software industry**, **biotechnology** and **medical technology**, **research** as well as highly qualified services (health, trade, finance and law). Florida's research centres alone see an annual investment of over 500 million dollars. The Orlando area is booming as a centre of high technology.

Future technologies

Welcome to Everyday Life

Where can you meet »real Floridians«? Usually away from the tourist areas, but sometimes right in the middle of the tourists. Here are some tips.

ART DECO

The largest ensemble of Art Deco buildings in the USA located in one area, around 800 of them, is in Miami Beach. The not for profit Miami Design Preservation League holds walks through the quarter every day, which are led by informed »locals«. They start out at the Art Deco Welcome Center.

Info: Miami Design Preservation League, Art Deco Welcome Center, 1001 Ocean Dr./10th St., www.mdpl.org, ticket US$20

TASTE FRESHLY PRESSED ORANGE JUICE

At Al's Family Farm in Vero Beach on the Atlantic coast oranges, grapefruit and mandarin ornages are picked and processed. From mid-December until Easter it is possible to take part in a tour (reservations required) through the processing plant on Tuesdays, Wednesdays and Thursdays at 10.30am and to taste freshly picked fruit or orange juice pressed here. The tour costs US$5, with lunch at the Mexican-American Red Barn Grill the cost is US$10.

Info: Tel. 1-772-460-0556 www. alsfamilyfarms.com

ENDANGERED ANIMAL WORLD

The Marine Science Center at Ponce Inlet not far from Daytona Beach concentrates on research and information on the living conditions in Florida's coastal regions. Here there are not only many kinds of fish and crabs, but also injured sea turtles, which are treated and released. Right next door, Mary Keller Seabird Rehabilitation Sanctuary cares for injured sea and water birds. In a summer camp 4 to 10 year olds can learn about sea and coastal inhabitants while playing.

Infos: Marine Science Center,
Tel. 1-386-304-5545,
http://marine sciencecenter.com/
activities.htm
www.marinesciencecenter.com/seabird/

SWIMMING WITH DOLPHINS

The Dolphin Research Center, which researches the living conditions of dolphins and sea lions, also offers a »trainer for a day« programme on ist grounds in the Florida Keys. Spend a day with a professional trainer and have close interaction with a dolphin. Visitors with different special needs can take part in various programmes as well.

Info: Dolphin Research Center,
58901 Overseas Hwy., Grassy Key,
www.dolphins.org

From Paleo-Indians to the Space Shuttle

For some Florida's history begins with Mickey Mouse and Walt Disney. But on the sunny peninsula in the south-eastern USA, humans can be traced back for at least 12,000 years.

PALEO-INDIAN SETTLEMENTS

12th–10th century BC	Fishermen, hunter-gatherers come to the peninsula of Florida.
7th century BC	First settlements are established.
1492	Christopher Columbus discovers America.
16th century AD	About 100,000 Native Americans live on the Florida Peninsula.

It is believed that about 30,000 to 10,000 years ago – at the end of the last Ice Age – the Native Americans of North America crossed from North Asia into North America over the Bering Strait. Groups of different ethnic backgrounds immigrated in several waves and developed their own cultures. About 12,000 to 10,000 years ago, the first **nomadic fishermen and hunter-gatherers appeared** on the Florida Peninsula. Numerous springs, lakes and rivers full of fish, shallow lagoons, bays full of shellfish and other marine life, lush vegetation and a rich game population provided favourable living conditions all year round.

Advances in several waves

The oldest human traces were discovered south of Sarasota, near Warm Mineral Springs, and can be dated to an age of 10,000 years. Close to Titusville is evidence of an approximately 8,000-year-old camp. About 9,000 years ago, Paleo-Indians founded first settlements near springs and streams. Findings such as potsherds, copper, iron ore and maize seeds suggest trade relations with the peoples along the Mississippi and in Mexico. Villages with palisade walls were established. The tribal communities were hierarchically organized. The dead of a higher status were buried in hills of earth up to 30m/100ft in height, or **mounds**.

Oldest finds

In the early 16th century, when the first explorers from Europe came to the peninsula, around 100,000 Native Americans lived here. They

Native Americans

Relic of Spanish colonial times in St. Augustine

Indian settlement protected by palisades at the time of the first European conquerors

were divided into several peoples. In North Florida, the **Apalachee** and the **Timuacan** lived as farmers.

The south-west coast was the territory of the martial **Calusa**, who lived mainly from fishing and hunting. They managed to get as far as Cuba in their canoes. The south-east coast was settled by a number of smaller tribes, among them the **Tequesta, Mayaimi and Jeagas**. They lived by fishing in the Atlantic Ocean and hunting in the swamps.

Demise of the Native Americans During the 16th and 17th centuries, the Native American population was largely decimated by the Spanish, French and English, who were advancing into the New World. Many Native Americans fell prey to the illnesses (especially influenza) brought over by the Europeans. In the 18th century the last sizeable groups of Timucuans and Apalachee left Florida when the Spanish retreated to Cuba.

SPANISH, FRENCH AND BRITISH

1492	Columbus discovers America.
1513	Ponce de León claims the peninsula, which he names »La Florida«.
1563/1564	French colonists attempt to settle without success.
1586	Sir Francis Drake completely destroys St Augustine.
1763	The Treaty of Versailles returns Florida to Spain.
1817/1818	First Seminole War
1821	Spain cedes Florida to the USA.

Soon after the discovery of the New World by **Columbus** in 1492, **Giovanni Caboto (John Cabot)** also set off for America in the service of the English king, Henry VIII. It is assumed that he at least saw the peninsula at the end of the 15th century, and possibly mapped it as well. A Spanish map of 1502 marks the outlines of a peninsula resembling Florida. Probably the first European on Florida's shores was the Spaniard **Juan Ponce de León**. On Easter Sunday 1513 he sighted the coast, landed six days later near St Augustine and claimed the land for the Spanish crown. During his second journey in 1521, he was mortally wounded by a Native American arrow at the Gulf Coast, but by then he had already paved the way to Florida for the conquistadors. Now they, too, looked for gold in Florida. In 1528 **Pánfilo de Narváez** landed in Tampa Bay and pushed northwards with his soldiers, murdering and plundering, but without success. In 1539, with a thousand soldiers, **Hernando de Soto** at first followed Narváez' route. He was lured on by the tales told by frightened Native Americans of immeasurably rich towns in the north. He travelled 3,750mi/6,000km through Georgia, Tennessee, South Carolina, Arkansas and Mississippi. In 1542 he succumbed to fever on the Mississippi. The remains of his force, nearly annihilated by hostile Native Americans, pushed through the country until finally reaching Mexico. After another disastrous expedition led by **Tristán de Luna**, who intended to found a settlement in Pensacola in1559, sank in a storm, the Spanish crown lost interest in Florida temporarily.

Columbus and his consequences

> **?** **MARCO ◉ POLO INSIGHT**
>
> *Pascua Florida*
>
> Juan Ponce de León named the new land that he sighted on Easter Sunday in 1513 »La Florida«, in reference to the Spanish Easter celebration, Pascua Florida.

Strategically, Florida remained important. Spanish fortresses here helped to defend the fleets transporting gold from Mexico. For this reason, Madrid was unwilling to accept the presence of the French Huguenots, who under **Jean Ribault** built Fort Caroline along the St John's River in 1564. One year later a Spanish expedition under **Pedro Menéndez de Avíles** destroyed the fort. Afterwards, Menéndez began to line the coast with a chain of well-defended forts, including St Augustine, and to construct missions along the northern border. In 1570, Florida was already a providence of New Spain, but in comparison with the other providences, among them Mexico and Venezuela, it was considered a poor backwater. In 1586 **Sir Francis Drake** burnt down St Augustine. The Spanish responded by building the defiant Fort San Marcos, which exists to this day. Renewed conflicts with the French were settled without bloodshed: New Spain allowed French settlements in Mobile and New Orleans. In return, the Bourbons agreed not to send any naval forces to the Gulf of Mexico.

Competition between Spain and France

Spanish missions

Although the Spanish were able to sustain their governance over Florida for more than two centuries, few new settlers were willing to settle outside Spanish military posts or fortified missions. For this reason, the Spanish began in 1565 to build missions. A row of settlements was intended to stretch from **St Augustine** northwards across the settling area of the Timucua to the northern borders of the Spanish sphere of influence. Another spread from St Augustine westwards into the area of Apalache, as far as **Pensacola**. One of the most important missions, **San Luis de Talimali**, was constructed in 1656 along the periphery of the present-day Capitol of Tallahassee. Here, as well as at other missions, the local Native Americans and the Spanish Franciscan monks and military lived together peacefully. Next to a Christian church and a town hall was a Native American village with an assembly hall and a field for ritual ball games.

The Treaty of Paris and its consequences

The British were more serious rivals. In 1762 they took Havana. In 1763, they were able to dictate conditions to the French, who had been defeated in the Seven Years' War, in the **Treaty of Paris**. The treaty stipulated that they must surrender all interests in North America forever. Spain was side-lined as Florida became British. The new rulers kept the colony under control, but acted much like the Spanish: for ease of administration, they first all divided the peninsula into East Florida (capital: St Augustine) and West Florida (capital: Pensacola). Afterwards, the governor promoted the immigration of families from Europe and the 13 colonies in the North. Along the navigable rivers, **cotton, indigo and sugarcane plantations** were farmed by **slaves**. Tropical timber was shipped to South Carolina. For the first time, Florida achieved modest wealth.

Second Spanish period

20 years later, political events hit the British settlers all the more painfully. In 1783, with the **Peace of Versailles**, the English king ceded his subjects, who had remained loyal and faithful to the crown during the American War of Independence, not to the newly-founded USA, but to Spain, which had already reconquered Pensacola two years earlier. But the Spaniards were not able to enjoy their success. First of all, the British settlers left in droves. Then **Seminole**, displaced by the Americans, crossed the border and settled in Florida. Aside from the disputed border in the north and general lawlessness in the south, which was not bound by the colonial administration, American-Spanish relations were soon threatened by the practice of Native Americans giving refuge to runaway African slaves. Because of this, the American government laid claim to certain parts of Florida, and American slaveholders were able to pursue their »possessions« with impunity. The Spanish colonial administration came under more and more pressure. In 1817–18 the **First Seminole War** began when **General Andrew Jackson** destroyed numerous Native American

villages between Pensacola and Suwanee River, killing or dispersing their inhabitants, and eventually attacked Spanish settlements. General Jackson had a clear aim: the humiliation of Spain and the occupation of Florida. In 1821, Spain ceded Florida to the USA for five million dollars.

FLORIDA BECOMES PART OF THE USA

1835	Osceola, leader of the Seminole, begins a guerrilla war against units of the US Army.
1855–58	Third Seminole War
1861	Florida sides with the Confederacy during the American Civil War.
1865	End of the Civil War, victory for the Union; abolition of the slavery
1881	The Disston Purchase begins the methodical development of Florida.
1886	Flagler's railway reaches St Augustine.

Settlers and infrastructure were lacking in the new US territory, and furthermore, the Seminole were hostile. Washington decided to levy a series of taxes to fill up Florida's coffers. At the same time, planters from Georgia began to settle on the most fertile farmland of Florida. They founded huge cotton and indigo plantations between the Suwannee and Apalachicola rivers in the north-west. Already by 1840, Florida, with a feudal-agrarian upper class, was a **part of the old South** and tightly bound to the other southern states. In contrast, the sandy ground of central Florida was occupied by many small farmers, the »Florida Crackers«, a nickname for poor white people. Towns – or anything deserving the name – hardly existed. However, American settlements like Jacksonville and the **new capital Tallahassee** soon overtook the Spanish military settlements of Pensacola, St Augustine and Key West.

Cotton barons and »Florida Crackers«

Until the Civil War, Florida remained the least industrialized region of the South: the **timber industry and tar and turpentine production**, the most important sources of income next to the **plantation economy**, had no railway to bring their products to the northern markets.

7,000 **Seminole** also stood in the way of development in central and southern Florida. Several attempts to relocate them to reservations were futile. Skirmishes with settlers were a regular occurrence. In 1832, when a group of elders agreed upon the relocation of the tribe to Oklahoma in the **Treaty of Fort Gibson** without any consultation

Seminole Wars

with the chiefs, a young Seminole named **Osceola** put himself at the forefront of the resistance. In 1835 he began a guerrilla war which pinned down the American army for many years. Heavy casualties were inflicted in the **Dade Massacre**, where Major Francis Dade and 110 soldiers were killed in an ambush between Tampa and Ocala, among others. The government tightened the noose around the Native Americans with a ring of small forts – Fort Lauderdale, Fort Myers, Fort Meade and Fort Pierce were built as military bases during the Seminole War. Bounties were offered, and Seminole villages were razed.

Osceola's end   In 1837, Osceola was lured to peace talks with false promises and arrested. He died in prison a year later. The surviving Seminole escaped to the swamps. But even there they were not safe. White trappers and fishermen begrudged them their livelihood, leading once more to confrontation. Around 1840, while the plantation economy in northern Florida blossomed, the south was a war zone. When Florida became a federal state in 1845, a special unit of the US-army combed the swamps hunting for Native Americans. A ceasefire with **Billy Bowlegs**, the leader of the Seminole, didn't hold for long. The **Third Seminole War** lasted from 1855 until 1858; again bounties were offered for men, women and children. Only when Bowlegs' family was also captured did the last leader of the Seminole capitulate. He was deported with his following to Oklahoma. The way was freed for the development of the south of Florida.

End of slavery   However, the Civil War delayed the leap forward. The owners of the plantations were the lords of Florida. More than half of the 140,000 inhabitants were black slaves: in early **1861, Florida joined the Confederate States**. In the following years, the Confederate armies were supplied with meat from Florida. The peninsula was mainly spared the ravages of war. Union troops blockaded the harbours and shipping routes. Only in 1864 was there a major **battle at Olustee** east of Lake City. Outside the village of Olustee, the Confederates were able halt the invasion by Union troops and pushed the northerners back to Jacksonville. Nonetheless, **in 1865 the Civil War ended with victory for the Union**. The **abolition of slavery** declared by President Lincoln in 1863 was now enforced in Florida too. A third of the 15,000 men who went to the war did not come back.

Disston Purchase   After the Civil War ended, towns were filled with investors from the north. They boosted Florida's economy, but also instigated a reorganization of the structures of ownership, which to this day is still a sore point. In 1881, **Hamilton Disston**, a rich manufacturer from Philadelphia, set the course for the future: with the so-called **Disston Purchase** he acquired four million acres of land between the Kissi-

During the Civil War Unionists and Secessionists paid a high price in blood

mee Basin, the Gulf Coast and the Everglades, drained the swap and sold it in parcels to farmers, investors and wealthy east coast notables. Practically overnight, new towns and agricultural regions appeared, among them the citrus-growing areas. Already in 1884, several hundred tourists, among them the inventor **Thomas A. Edison**, spent their winter on the Gulf Coast.

The »Disston Purchase« put Florida in the sights of the railway barons. **William D. Chipley**, with his **Pensacola & Atlantic Railroad**, connected the timber industry of the Panhandle with the markets in the north. The **South Florida Railroad** of **Henry B. Plant** connected Sanford, on the St John's River, with the Gulf Coast, turning this unimportant fishing town into a port overnight. Convinced of Florida's potential for tourism, Plant built hotels, notably the fine Tampa Bay Hotel, with rooms that already cost 100 dollars per night 120 years ago. **Henry M. Flagler**, the most dazzling of these »railway barons«, connected New York and St Augustine with his **East Coast Railroad** in 1886. St Augustine was thereby transformed into a winter destination for tourists, so Flagler extended his railway even further south. It reached Palm Beach in 1894, and Miami in 1896. From 1904 to 1912, he built his railway over the Keys and the open sea all the way down to Key West.

Railway era

FLORIDA IN THE 20TH CENTURY

From 1868	Cuban War of Independence: numerous refugees come to Florida.
1914–18	World War I: Florida's dockyards flourish.
After 1920	Florida land boom. Famous architects follow their visions.
1930s	Florida suffers from the consequences of the stock market crash of 1929.
1939–45	World War II: Florida is a training and recreation area for the US army.
1950	Begin of the rocket testing programme in Cape Canaveral
1959	Castro takes power in Cuba. Many thousands of Cubans escape to Florida.
1961	Launch of the first US manned space flight
1969	Apollo 11 lifts off to the moon.
1971	Walt Disney World opens its gates.
1981	The first space shuttle, Columbia, takes off into space.

Tobacco and tourism

Cuba had been suffering unrest since the breakout of its war for independence in 1868. Many **Cuban refugees** had settled in Tampa, bringing with them the manufacture of tobacco as a profitable economic activity. More and more **celebrities built luxurious villas** in places such as Fort Myers, St Petersburg and Palm Beach. The first **automotive tourists** rolled in on brand-new highways. World War I made Florida's dockyards flourish.

Unparalleled building boom

From 1920, the sunny state experienced the »**Florida land boom**«: hundreds of thousands came, saw and purchased. Famous architects, above all **Addison Mizner**, created dreams in pink that sprang up out of the dunes. Visionaries created islands and towns: **George Merrick** built Coral Gables, **Carl Fisher** constructed a dike facing the offshore dune. Shortly thereafter, Miami Beach became »the« seaside resort of America. Less wealthy Americans became a new type of tourist, the so-called »**tin canner**«. These early motorized tourists camped in trailer parks on the outskirts of the resorts to enjoy the sand, beach and sun.

Economic crisis and the World War II

In 1926, Florida's **overstretched real estate market** had a massive meltdown. The **stock market crash of 1929** and the disastrous hurricane of 1935, which destroyed Flagler's railway over the Keys, worsened the economic chaos in Florida. Not until the reforms of the **New Deal** was the state revived.

Then **World War II** pushed Florida's **war industry** forward. Huge **training camps** were established, particularly for the US Air Force. The invasions of Italy and France were rehearsed on the beaches of St Petersburg and Daytona.

The Fifties ...

After 1945, decades of unfettered growth began. The **development of juice concentrates** led to the expansion of acreage for oranges and grapefruits. In 1950, the beginning of the **rocket development programme** on **Cape Canaveral** signalled the birth of Florida's aerospace industry and related futuristic sectors. And, of course, **tourism**! The introduction of the two-week paid holiday from now on brought millions of people to the south each year. Most of all, the south-east coast experienced an unparalleled **building boom**. Up until the middle of the 1950s, in Greater Miami alone, more hotels were built than in all the other states combined. Gigantic highway projects, among them the **Sunshine Skyway** over Tampa Bay and the **Florida Turnpike**, helped bring together the different regions of Florida. By 1959, the Sunshine State already boasted 5 million inhabitants.

Cuban missile crisis

In 1959, Fidel Castro came to power in Cuba. Thousands of Cubans left their homeland and settled in Florida. In Miami, **Little Havana** emerged. In 1961, the so-called Sugar War broke out between the USA and Cuba, culminating in the breakdown of diplomatic relations between the two countries. In a new wave, thousands of Cubans once again came to Florida. The **Cuban missile crisis** (1962) nearly caused a Third World War. The USSR, at that time allied with Cuba, began to build a marine and air force base and a missile launching site on the Island. The USA perceived this as a direct threat and imposed an air and naval blockade against Cuba. Finally the Soviets backed down. But to this day, massive sanctions are imposed by the USA against the Caribbean island-state. From 1965 to 1973, as part of the **Freedom Flights**, thousands of Cubans were flown out of their home and into Florida. During the 1980s, the Cuban government allowed more than 120,000 people to immigrate to the USA. Most of them chose Greater Miami as their new home. By 1990, the number of Cubans living in Florida had increased to well over 650,000.

Armstrong and Aldrin on the moon

As early as 1961, the **first manned American space mission** was launched from Cape Canaveral. In following years, Cape Canaveral was to become the American space base. From here, the successful Mercury, Gemini, Apollo and Skylab missions were launched. In 1966, the first »soft« moon-landing was launched from

Cape Kennedy. US space travel suffered a major setback in 1967, when three astronauts lost their lives due to a fire that broke out aboard Apollo I.

On 21 July 1969, the Apollo 11 astronauts Neil Armstrong and Edwin Aldrin became the first human beings to set foot on the moon. 1986 was year of the **Challenger catastrophe**: all seven astronauts died aboard the space shuttle Challenger. All manned space travel was cancelled for the period of around two and a half years. In 1988, the Kennedy Space Center prepared for a new series of manned space flight. The space shuttle Discovery was launched into the earth's orbit.

In 1971, a new era began in Florida with the **opening of Walt Disney World in Orlando**. This mega-amusement park set new standards in entertainment and tourism. Other similarly designed attractions, like Universal, SeaWorld and recently Legoland Florida, followed.

Flourishing economy
In the shadow of the tourist industry, Florida's traditional economic sectors such as phosphate mining, fishing, vegetable and citrus plantation also blossomed. New economic sectors such as technology for space travel and the military, biotechnology and software development led to constant structural change in the economy. More and more pensioners chose Florida as a place to enjoy retirement.

Its relative proximity to the Caribbean and Latin America also happened to make Florida the Promised Land for **refugees arriving by boat** from the Caribbean. Cohabitation between the most varied of ethnic groups is not always peaceful: more than once social tensions have been aired violently. The gang warfare in Miami, drug-related crime – Miami was a key hub of drug trafficking in the 1980s and 1990s – and the armed robbery of tourists, including even the murder of some visitors, has to be seen within this context.

In 2000 **the scandalous procedures during the election of the new US president** polarized Florida. Protest against the election results were loudest of all in Greater Miami. Prior to that, Secretary of State Katherine Harris had halted the counting of all cast

Family fun Disney World

votes, declaring her Republican colleague George W. Bush the winner in Florida. At this point, Bush was ahead of his Democratic opponent Al Gore by less than 1,000 votes. This and the allegation that road-blocks, which were illegally installed by police, had kept potential Gore-voters – above all African Americans – away from the ballot box, threw light on questionable practices in US politics.

FLORIDA IN THE EARLY 21ST CENTURY

11 September 2001	Terrorist attacks in New York and Washington affect Florida's tourism.
Late summer 2004	An entire series of hurricanes leaves enormous damage.
2007–2012	The real estate and financial crisis puts great strain on Florida's economy.
20 April 2010	After the explosion of an oil platform huge amounts of crude oil flow into the Gulf of Mexico and along Florida's northwestern coast.
2011	Last planned launch of a space shuttle into outer space

On 11 Septeemer 2001 President George W. Bush was visiting a school in Sarasota, Florida, when he heard the news about the terror-ist attacks in New York and Washington. The consequences of those events were soon noticeable in the Sunshine State. The tourist sector, which had to cope with a decline in tourism, was strongly affected.

A consequence of climate change: the Florida Peninsula has been struck more and more often by **disastrous tropical storm**s. In the late summer of 2004, a series of four hurricanes caused damage amounting to at least 30 billion US dollars.

From 2007 to 2012 the **real estate and financial crisis** put great strain on Florida's economy. Tourism was not spared either.

In 2010, after the **explosion of an oil platform**, crude oil flowed into the Gulf of Mexico for months. The waters along Florida's northwest-ern coast as well as the beaches became polluted.

The **shuttle programme** ended with the last mission of the space shuttle »Endeavour« in July 2011. What the future of US manned space flight will look like is uncertain

The future of Florida tourism raises hopes. In 2013 more than 94 mil. tourists visited the Sunshine State.

Art and Culture

Modern Art and Architecture

Don't worry: Florida not only brings comic figures to life, it also has some of the best art museums and galleries in the USA. The way to get to know Florida's special architectural style is beneath the open sky – at best in the late afternoon, when the sun begins to work its magic.

VISUAL ARTS

Miami Vice, CSI Miami and Universal Studios, Kennedy Space Center and Disney World are what first spring to mind when Florida is mentioned. But the Sunshine State not only has »fun & sun«: it also has »real« culture. Aside from the craftsmanship of the Native Americans –the patchworks and weavings of the Miccosukkee are well-known – it has been painters and photographers who have taken Florida as their theme since the 16th century.

The earliest pictures originate from the Frenchman **Jacques le Moyne de Morgues** (1533–88), who accompanied the French Expedition Laudonnière as an illustrator and painter in 1564. Whereas his interests were more of scientific nature, a romantic enthusiasm for the landscape and its hidden allure was the main emphasis of the painters and photographers of the 19th and early 20th centuries. There are a number of impressive landscape paintings by the Bostonian painter **Winslow Homer** (1836–1910). The photographer **Walker Evans** (1903–75) also worked in Florida from time to time, especially in the years from 1928 to 1941. The natural beauty of the Everglades and the views of St Augustine, the oldest town of continental USA, were popular motifs for painters and photographers. Views of St Augustine, alongside those of Niagara Falls, were the most common decoration in American living rooms for quite some time. The activity of rich collectors was what finally gave Florida a real taste for the arts: the Gallery of Fine Arts, established by **Ralph Hubbard Norton** (1875–1953) in West Palm Beach, and the Museum of Art, founded by **John & Mable Ringling** in Sarasota laid the foundations. **A. E. »Bean« Backus** (1906–90) of Fort Pierce made a name for himself with naturalistic landscape pictures. **Hiram D. Williams** (1917–2003) from Gainesville painted his way to an established position among the American Impressionists, and the painter **Doris Leeper** (1929–2000) from New Smyrna Beach was, as an en-

Painting and photography

Nowhere else as noticeable: Art Deco in Miami Beach

vironmentalist, instrumental in the founding of the Canaveral National Seashore. In the 1970s, Floridan artistic activities received some support from the state's highest-ranking guardian of culture: Secretary of the Interior **George Firestone** (born in 1931), who endeavoured to turn Florida into a »State of the Arts«, raised financial support for young artists by an unbelievable 3200 per cent during his term in office. In addition, established modern artists such as **Robert Rauschenberg** (born in 1925) in Captiva, and in Aripeka, the pop-artist **James Rosenquist** (born in 1933) each took new talent under their wings. »Bean« Backus was a mentor to the **»Highwaymen«**, a group of African-American painters around **Alfred Hair** (1941–70) who sold nearly 200,000 pictures with tropical motifs for American living rooms in the 1960s and are currently experiencing a renaissance nationwide. Photographers also fell for the same tropical landscapes. Two excellent contemporary photographers document this: the detail-obsessed **Clyde Butcher** (born in 1942) from Ochopee records threatened nature for generations to come, and the Gainesville-based **Jerry N. Uelsmann** (born in 1934) captivates his audience with abstract, dreamlike montages.

Contemporary sculpture In many public spaces, parks, transportation buildings and cultural facilities in Florida, sculptures by contemporary artists have been displayed to an increased extent since the 1970s. Among them are works by **Claes Oldenbourg, Isamu Noguchi, Nam June Paik, Edward Ruscha** and many others. The intention is to upgrade the quality of life and to emphasize the identity of the community.

In front of the Center for the Performing Arts in Miami Beach, for example, the sculpture Mermaid by **Roy Lichtenstein** catches the eye. The artist quotes the local art deco style in this work. In collaboration with his wife **Coosje van Bruggen**, **Claes Oldenbourg** designed a fountain at the hypermodern Metro-Dade Government Center. The work is entitled *Dropped Bowl with Scattered Slices and Peels* and is meant to symbolize the multicultural diversity of Florida's metropolis, a city which, according to Claes Oldenbourg, is »in a state of constant development and whose system of organization is based upon the disorder of its urban development, which doesn't go according to plan ...«.

ARCHITECTURE

Mediterranean influences Over 200 years of Spanish colonialism did not fail to leave its mark on Florida's buildings. Combining Spanish and Italian influences, the **Mediterranean style** emerged at the end of the 19th century as an increasingly popular architectural style alongside the strict Victorian and the symmetrically-orientated Colonial style.

An example of the Mediterranean style: the luxury hotel
The Breakers in Palm Beach

Today – much simplified – it is the predominant form for domestic
building in Florida. The characteristics of the Mediterranean style are
curved arches, terracotta-tiled roofs and sand-coloured stucco walls
with adornments painted in pastel colours, emulating the light so
typical to Florida. Italian and Spanish influences are often clearly recognizable on expensive villas and buildings designed to impress.
While Italian-inspired buildings, in their love of detail – balustrades,
doors and windows are elegantly decorated – appear more feminine
and commonly make use of brick walls, Spanish-inspired houses ab-
stain from too much ornamentation and seem therefore more mas-
culine. This style, also known as the **Mizner style**, had its heyday
during the1920s. Impressive examples of »Mediterranean« architecture can be found not only in the area around Miami (above all in
Coral Gables, Coconut Grove, Miami Beach), but also in Palm Beach,
Naples and Tampa. Miami Beach even developed the architectural
style known as **Mediterranean Revival**, a southern variation of the
»Colonial Revival« in New England. Pretty details with the appeal of
Spanish, Italian and Moorish forms adorn the buildings of the Mediterranean Revival style. The local **coquina limestone** was often chosen as a construction material.

When visiting Miami Beach, it is impossible to miss the Art Deco   Art Deco
Historic District (▶MARCO POLO Insight p.268/270). Nowhere else
are there so many different examples of this eclectic architectural
style, which unites streamlined forms and motives from all epochs

und cultures. Since the 1970s, many famous citizens have mobilized for the conservation of the approximately 600 art deco buildings in Miami Beach. Beautifully renovated houses can mainly be seen along promenades such as Ocean Drive, Collins Avenue and Española Way.

Conch houses

Another specialty awaits travellers to the Florida Keys: Conch houses, which are suited to the tropical climate. Built on stilts for better ventilation, their tilted metal roofs reflect the heat and conduct rainwater into water butts. Blind-like shutters keep out the heat and provide protection from hurricanes. Balconies and surrounding verandas offer shade and protect from too much heat. Some particularly attractive old Conch houses can be admired in Key West.

Architecture after 1945

During the booming years after the World War II, especially along the Atlantic coast between Miami Beach and Palm Beach, skyscraper **hotels and apartments** sprung up like mushrooms. In Miami Beach, these huge tourist hotels threatened to overpower the art deco architecture that been built since the 1930s. Along with a lot of unattractive »boxes«, a few architecturally interesting new buildings were designed. One of them is the **Fontainebleau Hilton** in Miami Beach, a hotel complex and typical example of the flamboyant architecture of the 1960s. In recent years, huge **postmodern skyscrapers** have been constructed around Miami. On the one hand they put all previous buildings in the shade, and on the other hand, they quote the architectural forms and design elements of art deco. During the 1970s and 1990s, Downtown Miami developed at a breath-taking pace along Biscayne Bay. The new skyline and above all the flashy banking palaces on Brickell Avenue show very impressively how the city is the second most important financial and service industries centre in the USA. A prime example is the **Centrust Tower**, completed in 1987 and designed by America's most famous contemporary architect, I. M. Pei in collaboration with Spillis Candela & Partners. **Atlantis** (see above) is a creation of the architectural group Arquitectonica and caused a furore with the hole in its facade containing a red staircase, a palm tree and a swimming pool.

> ! **MARCO POLO INSIGHT**
>
> *Coquina limestone*
>
> Coquina limestone, which was already appreciated by the Spanish colonial builders as it was simple to work, is mainly made of fossil shells and coral.

Contemporary architecture

In recent times there an increased orientation towards tradition, by using construction methods of the Native Americans and quoting stylistic elements of the colonial period.

Architectural forms that are spread throughout the Caribbean area, as well as those of Anglo-American monumental architecture are apparent. The impact of the huge skyscrapers of banks, insurance com-

Spectacular Miami: the 20-storey apartment building Atlantis with a hole in the façade

panies and other big enterprises is alleviated by the influence of post-modernism. Nowadays successful contemporary architecture can be seen everywhere in Florida. Hotels like pyramids and shopping malls like oriental towns, houses like medieval castles, statues and fountains: in the theme parks of Florida, America's architects are allowed to let off steam. **Entertainment architecture** is intended to inspire, stimulate the imagination and, quite simply, just amuse. A classic example is the Swan & Dolphin Hotel at Walt Disney World. The roofs of the 2500-room hotel are decorated with statues; playful fish and swan sculptures suggest buoyancy and a sense of humour. Monumental wall paintings with tropical motifs and postmodern-style pastel interiors provide relaxation.

The new **holiday-home settlements** of Seaside, Grayton Beach and Seagrove Beach along the Gulf coast are also remarkable. The completely new holiday resorts which are appearing here represent a step away from massive and bulky concrete architecture toward a filigree, individualized architecture quoting all kinds of styles.

Famous People

NEIL ALDEN ARMSTRONG (1930 - 2012)

A native of Wapakoneta, Ohio, the astronaut Neil Armstrong, as a   Astronaut
member of the Apollo 11 mission, launched from Cape Canaveral,
became **the first man to set foot on the moon, on 21 July 1969**.
Armstrong was a US-Navy pilot during the Korean War. Later he
studied aircraft engineering, then worked as a test pilot for NASA before becoming an astronaut in 1962. He made his first flight into space
in 1966, as part of the Gemini 8 mission. As a commander, he was in
charge of the first coupling manoeuvre between two spacecraft. From
1971 to 1979 he worked as a lecturer in aerospace engineering at the
University of Cincinnati. After that he was a member of various
boards. Later he put his energy into promoting new moon and Mars
missions. Armstrong died on August 25, 2012 in Cincinnati.

JOHN JAMES AUDUBON (1785–1851)

The son of a tradesman, the illustrator and ornithologist Audubon   Ornithologist
was born in Les Cayes (Haiti). He came to the USA in 1805, settling   and painter
near Philadelphia. At first he worked as a businessman with limited
success, but Audubon was an exceptionally **gifted illustrator**. His
copper engravings and drawings displaying flora and fauna made
him famous. Between 1827 and 1838 he produced the Birds of America atlas. Many of his impressions were collected during his expeditions to Florida, which also led him to the Keys. Beside his drawing
activities, he also authored articles introducing Florida's birds. America's oldest nature conservation organization, the National Audubon
Society (NAS), founded in 1905, bears the name of this great illustrator.

JIMMY BUFFETT (BORN 1946)

The Grateful Dead have the »Deadheads«; Jimmy Buffett has the   Musician
»Parrot Heads«: His fans, who always appear in colourful Hawaiian
shirts and wearing fanciful headgear, turn every Buffet concert into
a happy beach party. The lively bard has been singing about nothing
other than the lightness of being under Florida's palm trees for 30
years – becoming one of the state's cultural assets. Hits like Why
Don't We Get Drunk, Margaritaville and Come Monday have made
Key West's best-known son famous. Today Jimmy Buffett is to Florida what the Beach Boys are to California.

**Andrew Jackson, seventh president of the United States,
on the 20 dollar bill**

»Scarface« Al Capone

AL(FONSO) CAPONE (1899–1947)

Alfonso Capone, originally from the southern Italian city of Naples, grew up in Brooklyn, New York. In 1920 he moved to Chicago, where he became a redoubtable underworld legend. As the boss of the local mafia syndicate, he controlled gambling, alcohol smuggling and prostitution, among other things. Furthermore, he exerted considerable influence on the work of the police. He became enormously wealthy. Although he was suspected of initiating many brutal murders and robberies, no one dared to bring him to trial, for fear of reprisals. Finally, in 1931, he was sentenced to eleven years in prison for tax evasion. He served part of his sentence on the notorious prison island of Alcatraz, near San Francisco. He was released early due to ill health. In 1939 he moved to Florida (Deerfield Beach) and died in Miami in 1947.

RAY CHARLES (1930–2004)

Musician On his death, a newspaper adoringly wrote: »Heaven gets some blues«. Ray Charles, who was also at home with soul and pop, spent the first 18 years of his life in Florida. He went blind at the age of seven, and first attended the Florida School of the Deaf and Blind in St Augustine. Here he learned Braille – and to play the piano. At the age of 15 he earned his first money in the bars of Jacksonville, Tampa and Orlando. At the age of 18 he moved to Seattle, and the rest is history. With songs like Georgia on my Mind and What I'd Say he captured hearts of a worldwide following.

THOMAS A. EDISON (1847–1931)

Inventor When, on the advice of his doctor, Edison began to spend the winter in Florida, he was already a famous man and had invented the electric light bulb. **From 1901 on, he came every winter to Fort Myers to recuperate.** He did not come up with any epoch-making inventions there, but the reputation of this genius resident attracted further prominent figures, above all the automobile manufacturer Henry Ford. In order to thank the native Floridians for their hospitality, he planted 200 Cuban palm trees along the streets of Fort Myers.

GLORIA ESTEFAN (BORN 1957)

Singer

For over two decades – and she still has plenty of rhythm in her blood – the Latino icon Gloria Estefan has had international success in the music business. She eventually gained recognition with her English speaking album Unwrapped. She speaks out for prisoners on Cuba and supports the Ladies in White, an oppositional women's group in Castro's state. Born in Havana and raised in Miami, the future singer of Miami Sound Machine became famous for songs in Spanish. Her two albums Mi Tierra and Alma Caribena are unforgotten. Hardly any other star of the music scene has her ability to **combine catchy pop with salsa rhythms and elements of soul**. She came to world-wide fame when the song Reach from her 1996 album Destiny was chosen as the official song of the Olympic Games in Atlanta. That Gloria Estefan still has very strong charisma is proven by the success of much younger colleagues such as Jennifer Lopez and Shakira, who have adopted her as a role model and learned much from her.

Latin icon Gloria Estefan

HENRY MORRISON FLAGLER (1830–1913)

In the »Sunshine State« the co-founder of Standard Oil made the impossible possible. In 1878, due to the illness of his wife, Flagler came to the peninsula and recognized its tourist potential. By merging the railway companies of Florida into Eastcoast Railroad, he linked the East Coast towns of the North with Miami, and finally with the Keys. In 1912 his railway reached the treacherous bridges of Key West. Flagler was also prominent in the hotel sector: In

St. Augustine he built the Ponce de Léon Hotel, and in Palm Beach the Royal Poinciana Hotel. However, he rejected the request of the people in Biscayne Bay to name their town Flagler. Instead, he suggested Miami.

JOHN GORRIE (1803–55)

Doctor Scientist, humanist, politician, doctor: Gorrie, born in the Caribbean, had many talents. But his monument at the National Statuary Hall in Washington D.C. is in honour of his study of tropical diseases. Shortly after his arrival in Apalachicola, he recognized that his patients recovered from yellow fever more quickly in chilled rooms, and invented – with a machine producing artificial ice, thereby effectively lowering the temperature in the hospital wards – the prototype of the air conditioner.

ERNEST HEMINGWAY (1899–1961)

Writer When Ernest Hemingway settled in Florida in 1928, he was already well known as a writer. Key West, at that time still a backwater town of smugglers and adventurers, inspired him to write some of his best works, including Death in the Afternoon and The Snows of Kilimanjaro. For twelve years, when he wasn't travelling he lived in his house at 907 Whitehead Street. He worked in the mornings, spent the afternoons deep sea fishing and he frequented the bars in the evenings. Today Ernest Hemingway is as much a part of Key West as the sunsets on Mallory Square, and his face smiles from the T-Shirts at Sloppy Joe's, his favourite bar.

The »old man« at the sea

ZORA NEALE HURSTON (1903–60)

Her most important novel angered both sides: blacks, who accused her of accepting financial support from whites, and whites, because she challenged the stereotypes of black Americans that was accepted at the time. In Their Eyes Were Watching God (1937), Hurston, one of the most important African-American authors, portrayed her black fellow-citizens simply as normal people. In doing so, she was far ahead of her contemporaries. Raised in Eatonville, near Orlando, she first studied ethnology. In New York she joined a group of African-American artists who became known as the Harlem Renaissance. Later she travelled back and forth across Florida and Mississippi, collecting old African-American stories. Following her death, her work faded into obscurity. She was rediscovered in the 1980s and since then her books have become required reading at American universities.

ANDREW JACKSON (1767–1845)

Jackson, a lawyer and plantation owner from Waxhaw, South Carolina became a judge at the Supreme Court of the State of Tennessee in 1798, but he gained fame for his service as a major general. In January 1815 he defended New Orleans against the British. Afterwards he participated in military campaigns against the Seminole and against Florida, which was still under Spanish control. In 1817–18 he took the town of Pensacola. His bold course of action led to tensions between Spain and England. The Seminole even called him »Devil«. He found support within the American government. In 1821 Jackson became the first governor of both of the territories of West and East Florida. Three years later he ran for office as a presidential candidate, but was defeated. However, he went on to win the elections of 1828, and then 1832. As US president he represented the interests of common citizens and was known as liberal and anti-monopolistic. Although he caused a serious financial crisis with the divestiture of the National Bank, and despite his controversial resettlement of Native Americans, he enjoyed a high reputation throughout his life.

General, 7th President of the USA (see picture on page 58)

GEORGE EDGAR MERRICK (1886–1942)

As a small boy, Merrick dreamed of castles in Spain. He came to Florida with his parents in 1898. In 1922, now grown-up and a lawyer, Miami real estate agent, businessman and aesthete, he began to make his dreams of Spain a reality. In 1924 he built his »**City Beautiful**«, a romantic, aesthetic ensemble of wide, palm-fringed streets, hacienda-like villas, fanciful swimming pools and golf courses. That same year, Coral Gables was declared the most beautiful suburb in America. Despite financial setbacks Merrick stayed in the real estate business until 1940.

Businessman and town planner

ADDISON MIZNER (1872–1933)

Architect

Mizner was Florida's **leading architect during the 1920s** and a darling of high society. Influenced by Spanish and Mediterranean architecture, in Palm Beach alone he designed over 50 exclusive residences with playful ornamentation for the likes of Irving Berlin, Oscar Hammerstein and the Vanderbilts – even though he never studied architecture and could not draw plans. Even his first house in Palm Beach, El Mirasol, had 37 rooms, an illuminated pool and an underground garage for 40 cars. There was nothing he liked less than soulless houses. His credo was that a house has to look as if it had fought its way from ugly duckling to beautiful swan, and to this end he encouraged his workers to break roof tiles to make them look older. The Depression thwarted his ambitious plans for Boca Raton and ruined him. Mizner died in poverty, but the unconventional »Mizner Style« had already made its mark on Florida's architecture.

OSCEOLA (ABOUT 1800–1838)

Leader of the Seminole

The son of a white settler and a Native American, Osceola Nickanochee was born in the north of Georgia. When he was four years old his mother left Georgia with him in order to escape discrimination by the whites, taking refuge in Florida. Osceola became a leading figure among the Seminole. In 1812 and 1818 he fought against General Andrew Jackson and **declined to sign any treaties with white people**. His attacks against white settlers and army patrols were among the reasons for the outbreak of the second Seminole War. The American Army was unable to achieve any victory against the guerrillas of the Seminole. There were attempts to negotiate. But in 1837 Osceola, his family and a few of his adherents were arrested during peace talks, although he had been promised free passage beforehand. He died of malaria one year later in Fort Moultrie, South Carolina. Afterwards, his head was exhibited as a circus attraction.

JUAN PONCE DE LEÓN (1460–1521)

Spanish conquistador

Ponce de León was the first Spanish conquistador to set foot upon North American soil. This took place on Easter Monday (Spanish: »Pasqua de Flores«) in 1513. On behalf of the Spanish crown he founded the colony La Florida, which reached from the swamps of the Gulf of Mexico to Labrador. In addition, it was Ponce de León who first recognized the phenomenon of the Gulf Stream. The Spaniard accompanied Columbus on his second trip to America in 1493. From 1502 to 1504 he took part in the conquest of Higüey on the

Antilles island of Hispaniola. From 1509 to 1512 he was governor of the neighbouring island of Puerto Rico. In 1513 he left for the first recorded expedition to present-day Florida. He landed in the area now known as Ponte Vedra Beach, believing he had discovered another large island. In 1521 he made another expedition to Florida, deeply driven by the wish to find the fountain of youth. As he examined one of the many springs he was hit by the poisoned arrow of a Native American. He died on his way back to the Caribbean. Ponce de León was buried in the Cathedral of San Juan on the Caribbean island of Puerto Rico.

HERNANDO DE SOTO (ABOUT 1500–42)

After studying at the University of Salamanca, Hernando de Soto served in Central America from 1519 to 1532. In 1532–33 he took part in the conquest of Peru and the capture of Atahualpa, the last ruler of the Inca. After disputes with Pizarro, he returned to Spain a wealthy man in 1535. In 1537, he was appointed governor of Cuba and the royal representative in Florida. On 25 May 1539 he landed near the present-day harbour of Charlotte. He spent the next month on an **unsuccessful search for the riches of Florida**. During his march through the swamps he met the Spaniard Ortíz, a survivor of the failed Narvaez expedition, who from then served as an interpreter. With his help, De Soto gathered valuable knowledge about the south of the USA. His scouts reached as far as Carolina and Tennessee. He himself headed south in Alabama, where he again reached the Gulf of Mexico near Mobile. Here he waited in vain for supply ships. In 1541, during his westward march, he crossed the Mississippi, and spent the winter of 1541–42 in the present-day Arkansas. In April 1542 he returned to Florida. Constant attacks by Native Americans, fever and the disappointment of not finding any treasure demoralized De Soto. He died the same year.

Spanish
Conquistador

ENJOY FLORIDA

Which culinary delights does Florida offer? Where can we
take our children? Where is the best shopping? Where can
we stay? What kinds of sports can we do? Find the answers
on the following pages.

Accommodation

From Campgrounds to Penthouse Suites

Camping on a wooden platform in the Everglades? No problem. Holiday in a penthouse suite with your own butler and a view of the Atlantic? Not really a problem either if you're not counting the cost. Tennis players or golfers can stay in club-like facilities only a few steps from their favourite sports pitch, and passionate anglers can see the fishing pier from their room.

Anyone who loves nostalgic charm books in a **bed & breakfast** inn that is furnished with antiques and lit with Victorian crystal chandeliers. Theme hotels in Walt Disney World near Orlando create the illusion of a holiday in Polynesia, in the Rocky Mountains or in darkest Africa.

There are very reasonable deals at **motels** on the edge of larger cities and along highways or interstates.

Even if you prefer to sleep underwater there is palace for you: the Jules' Undersea Lodge at Key Lago lets you watch through a porthole as divers bring you your breakfast in a watertight container.

There are chic **boutique hotels** with good chances of seeing celebrities, especially in Miami and Miami Beach; there are hotels with a rainbow banner at the door, showing that they prefer gay guests; and there are family resorts with large playgrounds and especially expansive pool areas.

Isolated hotels on small islands that are only accessible by boat and naturally mega-resorts with endless daily programmes of entertainment and sports are also available.

Campers with tents can explore the »Sunshine State« in a car; anyone who prefers a mobile home can choose between everything from a VW minibus, a pick-up truck to an expandable 32-foot luxury motor home.

The variety and quantity of accommodations with completely different levels of comfort, prices and interests in Florida is unique to the whole world. More than 400,000 hotel rooms and about 700 campgrounds with 100,000 places for tents and caravans await the more than 80 million annual guests.

In the USA there is a price per room, which usually applies no matter if one, two, three or even four people are staying in it. **A rough rule**   Prices

World famous: the luxury hotel »The Breakers« in Palm Beach

Luxury Beach Resorts

Whoever wants to spend his beach holiday in Florida in luxurious surroundings can find the right selection on every coast.

Own beach or direct access to the beach, several pools, gourmet hotel restaurants available, diverse sports facilities and a spa with fitness and wellness areas are all part of it. There are often attractive entertainment programmes for children, where the children often eat together too – so that the parents have a bit more time to themselves.

Popular Resorts

Insider Tip

Omni Amelia
Island Plantation
6800 1st Coast Hwy.
Fernandina Beach, FL 32034
Tel. 1-904-261-6161
www.omnihotels.com
The elegant hotel complex with several villas in addition offers pure luxury on 1350 acres right on the Atlantic. All 404 rooms have an ocean view; sportive guests can putt a total of 54 holes on several golf courses or swing tennis rackets on 23 hard courts. Hiking trails and kayak courses lead through nature; children have their own programme. 12 restaurants leave hardly a culinary wish unfulfilled.

Boca Raton Resort & Club
501 E. Camino Real
Boca Raton, FL 33432
Tel. 1-561-447-3000
www.bocaresort.comThe pink building was built in 1926, the heyday of the legendary investor and planner Addison Mizner. It has been renovated and brought to modern luxury standards; the guests will find rooms that each decorated differently with Venetian canopy beds or cultured modern luxury. The Club House includes three fitness and one tennis centre as well as an expansive spa with a Turkish bath and rejuvenating treatments of all kinds. The restaurants are among the best in Florida.

Acqualina Resort & Spa
17875 Collins Ave., Sunny Isles
Miami Beach, FL, 33160
Tel. 1-305-918-8000
www.acqualinaresort.com
The resort has three pools and lawns right next to the well-cared for beach at Sunny Isles north of Miami Beach. The generous rooms are furnished with all modern conveniences; the baths have the best of everything. A wonderful spa offers every treatment possible in a relaxed atmosphere. The Italian restaurant »Il Mulino New York« is one of the best in town. Complete children's programme.

South Seas Island Resort
5400 Plantation Rd.
Captiva, FL, 33924
Tel. 1-239-472-5111
www.southseas.com
The grounds have more than 325 acres and there are 106 rooms and 365 suites; all of this takes up the whole northern end of Captiva Island and is faces water on three sides. The hotel's own beach (4km/2.4mi) borders on sand du-

nes. Woods, mangroves and dunes host birds and small animals. Luxury sailboats and yachts are tied up in the marina, an excursion boat takes guests to nearby islands. Anyone who doesn't want to leave the resort can shop at the mini-shopping centres. There are also a small zoo, fitness centre, rental bikes, sailing school, tennis courts and the recreational possibilities are practically endless.

Disney's Grand Floridian Resort & Spa

4401 Floridian Way
Magic Kingdom Resort Area
Lake Buena Vista, FL 32830
Tel. 1-407-934-7639
http://disneyworld.disney.go.com/resorts/

The beach on the shores of the Seven Seas Lagoon turns the Victorian style hotel into a beach resort. The five-storey high lobby is covered by a colourful glass dome. The elevator with brass facings, the opulent verandas and the red tile roofs are reminiscent of the golden age of the great railway hotels 100 years ago. Guests can drink after-noon tea in the lobby while listening to live piano music. Luxuriously appointed rooms, several pools and a private pier are part of the superior character. The restaurant »Victoria & Albert's« belongs to the hotel.

Hawks Cay Island Resort *Insider Tip*

MM 61 OS, 61 , Hawks Cay Blvd.
Duck Key, FL 33050
Tel. 1-305-743-7000
www.hawkscay.com

Located on Duck Key, about half-way to Key West, and surrounded by turquoise blue water. A bridge connects the Overseas Highway to this private little island. The guests live in Caribbean-style, large rooms, suites or villas. There is a lot for children to do: own pool, a pirate ship with water cannons and a Kids' Club. Kiting, diving and snorkelling, tennis, angling, kayaking and more are available for the sports-minded. The »Dolphin Connection« offers swimming with dolphins. Seven restaurants and bars offer top quality culinary variety, the »Calm Waters Spa« offers relaxation and beauty treatments.

Caribbean atmosphere: Hawks Key Island

of thumb for the price of a room for one night would be: first-class, luxury more than $150; comfortable, middle class more than $80; budget more than $40.

Most hotels and motels generally do not include breakfast in the price of the room, unlike B & Bs. If a complimentary breakfast is offered, it is usually quite frugal. But the breakfast in a B & B is usually generous.

Additional charges: Taxes and local charges will be added to the price of the room and can amount to 15% of the net rate. Many hotels charge extra for parking and the use of the safe.

Weekend rates: Many hotels and accommodation away from the tourist centres offer reduced weekend rates.

Dorms **Insider Tip**

During the school holidays the rooms in the university dormitories in Florida's university towns (including Miami, Tampa, Gainesville) are rented out for quite affordable rates. The local tourist offices and university administrations have information.

Reserving a room

Reserving a room in advance by telephone or e-mail is especially recommended during the main travel times. Accommodation guides are available at the local tourist office and also on the internet.

Youth hostels

The US youth hostel organization Hostelling International – American Youth Hostels (HI-AYH) is a member of the International Youth Hostel Association and its houses are furnished according to their standards. The prices run from $15 to 40 per night. **Caution!** Among the youth hostel operators there are some black sheep who do not meet HI standards and are not members of this association. The authentic youth hostels have the triangle-shaped HI logo with the usual house-and-tree symbol.

YMCA · YWCA

Young people can stay at the YMCA (Young Men's Christian Association) and YWCA (Young Women's Christian Association) in larger cities.

Camping in the wild

Camping outside of campgrounds is prohibited in the USA. Permission for exceptions must be obtained from the local authorities.

HOTEL CHAINS
Best Western
Tel. 1-800-780-7234
www.bestwestern.com

Choice Hotels
Tel. 1-877-424-6423
www.choicehotels.com

Days Inn
Tel. 1-800-225-3297
www.daysinn.com

Hilton
Tel. 1-800-445-8687
www.hilton.com

Holiday Inn
Tel. 1-800-181-6068
www.ichotelsgroup.com

Howard Johnson
Tel. 1-800-446-4656
www.hojo.com

Hyatt
Tel. 1-800-591-1234
www.hyatt.com

Marriott
Tel. 1-800-236-2427
www.marriott.com

Motel 6
Tel. 1-800-466-8356
www.motel6.com

Quality Inn
Tel. 1-877-424-6423
www.choicehotels.com

Radisson
Tel. 1-800-181-4442
www.radisson.com

Ramada
Tel. 1-800-272-6232
www.ramada.com

Sleep Inn
Tel. 1-800-424-6423
www.choicehotels.com

Super 8 Motels
Tel. 1-800-454-3213
www.super8.com

Travelodge
Tel. 1-800-525-4055
www.travelodge.com

BED & BREAKFAST *Insider Tip*
Florida Bed & Breakfast Inns
Tel. 1-877-303-3224
www.florida-inns.com

American Historic Inns
Tel. 1-949-481-6256
www.iloveinns.com

YOUTH ACCOMMODATION
Hostelling International USA Florida Council
Tel. 1-888-520-0568
www.hiusa.org

YMCA/YWCA
Tel. 1-888-477-9622
www.ymcainternational.org

CAMPING
Florida Association of RV Parks & Campgrounds
Tel. 1-850-562-7151
www.farvc.org

Kampground of America (KOA)
Tel. 1-888-562-0000
Tel. 1-406-255-7402
www.koa.com

Children in Florida

Holiday Dreams for Children

Playing in the sand, splashing in the ocean, seeing favourite cartoon characters in person, canoeing through remote natural scenery, seeing giant rockets and real astronauts, looking into an alligator's mouth, swimming with comical manatee. There's a lot in store for children who travel to Florida with their parents. Hardly any holiday venue offers as many attractions, and boredom doesn't have a chance!

Many resorts and hotels offer **entertainment packages for children**, so that parents, of course, have time for their own interests. Florida is world famous for **sunny beaches** on the long peninsula coastlines. There are about 1,800km (1,080mi) of sand and shell beaches in all, enough place to dig, play ball or swim in the refreshing Atlantic or the somewhat warmer Gulf of Mexico. No admission is charged to the beaches.

Unfortunately this is not true for the mega-amusement parks in the hinterland that are so attractive to children. Families with several children need to think well about which theme parks to visit so that the hole in the holiday budget doesn't get too big. But admission to »Magic Kingdom«, »Epcot Center«, »Animal Kingdom«, »Universal Studios«, »Islands of Adventure«, »Busch Gardens«, »SeaWorld« or »Legoland« includes in each case all of the attractions within the park. But that's not all. Water parks like »Wet'n Wild« or »Typhoon Lagoon« offer endless swimming and splashing fun with exciting waterslides and artificial waves.

Amusement parks

Anyone interested in space travel should not miss Kennedy Space Center, which offers exhibits with much to experience for young and old including das a simulated flight with a space shuttle, real rockets and a chance to meet astronauts.

Kennedy Space Center

Nature also has spectacular experiences to offer from canoeing in the Everglades, swimming in the ponds and lakes of giant karstic springs in the middle and north of the peninsula. Meeting manatees, chubby sea cows, which can be seen at Homosassa Springs and many other places, is a special experience.

Nature

Especially children have lots of fun in the mega-amusement park Universal Studios in Orlando

Top Tips for Families with Children

No other region of the USA has as much to offer families with children as the Florida Peninsula. Nowhere else are there so many mile-long beaches with fine sand, so many amusement and theme parks and so many holiday facilities with children's programmes. Florida's natural setting has something to offer children as well.

Indeed, a trip to Florida leaves a lasting impression on most children and teens; many families come back every year.

Popular Beaches

The super beaches of the two islands off Fort Myers, Sanibel and Captiva, are a real paradise for small children. The reason: the flat sand beaches are covered with sea shells of all sizes and shapes. Children are occupied here for hours with collecting and sorting the varied and colourfully shimmering shells. In the evening it's an effort for parents to get the children off the beach again.

Super-wide beaches that are great for children have been reserved on many beaches along the Florida coast especially for building sand castles. Especially worth mentioning here are the wonderful beaches on the Atlantic at St. Augustine and on Amelia Island as well as the family beaches on the Gulf coast by St. Petersburg, where the sun shines 365 days a year, and further south by Naples. The beaches on the Florida Panhandle, like Panama City Beach, Seaside, Destin Fort Walton and Pensacola are also ideal for children. The best yet: many of these beaches have other attractions for children like carousels, water slides, ball playing

fields etc. and of course ice cream sellers, family restaurants, toy shops and much more.

Underwater Adventure

Parents of older children or teens can introduce them to underwater adventures. The Atlantic coast and especially the Florida Keys offer great places for snorkelling and diving. Some resorts and other facilities offer underwater courses or programmes especially for children and teens. A trip on the glass bottom boat in John Pennekamp Coral Reef State Park is recommended especially; the children won't be able to get enough of the fish in all sizes shimmering in all colours as they dart in and out of the coral reefs. Florida Keys Eco-Discovery Center in Key West also has great programmes for children. They will learn all about the ecosystem of a coral reef and its water fauna world. They also learn all about shipwrecks from the Spanish colonial period that lie on the bottom of the ocean off the Florida coast.

Nature Experiences

Children of all ages also love the other nature areas, like Everglades National Park. Here just as in Corkscrew Swamp Sanctuary further to the north near Naples and in J. N. »Ding« Darling National Wildlife Refuge there are plank walks with observation points, which are easy to follow, from which dangerous alligators and many other kinds of wildlife can be observed, including wood storks and flamingos.

Kids will love the manatees, which can be seen at Crystal River, Homosassa Springs or Lee County Manatee Park on the Orange River.

Many children of all ages are interested in the turtles that build their nests in some of Florida's beaches. »Turtle Watch« programmes are held on the Atlantic coast in Sebastian Inlet State Park near Melbourne, in John D. MacArthur Beach State Park near Palm Beach, in Gumbo Limbo Nature Center near Boca Raton as well as on the Gulf coast in the Mote Marine Laboratory & Aquarium near Sarasota.

Swimming with dolphins is also a big hit. This is offered in the Florida Keys in the Dolphin Research Center near Marathon, in the Dolphin Facility on Key Largo and in Wild Dolphin Encounter in Key West.

Swimming with dolphins is possible in several places in Florida

Festivals · Holidays · Events

Lively Feast of Festivals

The best cowboys on broncos and unpredictable bulls meet at the »Silver Spurs Rodeo« in February and in June to measure their strength and agility. At the »Winter Park Sidewalk Art Festival« more than 250 artists display their work in the suburb of Orlando and compete for prizes. At the »Fiesta of five Flags« in June the turbulent history of the city of Pensacola with five different national governments is celebrated with parades, concerts and a re-enactment of the landing of the first Spaniards in 1559. In October thousands of motor bikers come to Daytona from all over the USA and Canada on their heavy machines for »Biketoberfest«, a huge family festival.

Florida's population is composed of immigrants or descendants of immigrants from the whole world; they keep up their history, traditions and culture until today.

This calls for lots of celebrations, for example the Cuban »Calle Ocho Festival« in March in Miami's Little Havana. Florida's own if comparatively short history after the first landing of European conquerors is another reason for festivals or re-enactments like Civil War battles in Olustee Battlefield State Park. There are also harvest festivals like the Strawberry Festival in Plant City and the Citrus Festival in Winter Haven, cultural festivals like the International Film Festival of Miami, sports events like the NASCAR race in Daytona or festivals just to celebrate like the parades in Walt Disney World or the Fun ´n´ Sun Festival in Clearwater.

Things that are usually taken for granted, like sunset, are reason enough to celebrate in at least two places on the Florida peninsula: in Key West and Clearwater. Live bands, artistes, craftsmen who sell their wares and a party every evening.

Festive dancing pleasure in Orlando

Calendar of events

NATIONAL HOLIDAYS
1 January: New Year's Day
3rd Monday in January: Martin Luther King Jr. Day
3rd Monday in February: President's Day
March/April: Good Friday (only regional)
Last Monday in May: Memorial Day
4 July: Independence Day
1st Monday in September: Labor Day
2nd Monday in October: Columbus Day
1st Tuesday in November (only in election year!): Election Day
Veteran's Day: 11 November
Thanksgiving Day: 4th Thursday in November
Christmas Day: 25 December

HOLIDAYS ONLY IN FLORIDA
Shrove Tuesday (regional mainly in the panhandle and in Miami, Little Havana): Mardi Gras
26 April: Confederate Memorial Day
31 October: Halloween (only in some areas)

JANUARY
Key West
Key West Literary Seminar
Literature event in honour of the authors Ernest Hemingway, Thornton Wilder and Tennessee Williams

Miami Beach *Insider Tip*
Art Deco Weekend
Events in the Art Deco District in South Beach

Tarpon Springs *Insider Tip*
Greek Epiphany (6 January)
Celebrated by Greek immigrants

FEBRUARY
Daytona Beach
Speed Weeks (February/March)
Auto and motorbike racing freaks meet at the Daytona Speedway.

Fort Myers
Edison Festival of Lights (3rd week in February)
Festival of lights with parades through the illuminated centre of town in honour of the great inventor.

Miami, Coconut Grove
Coconut Grove Arts Festival (mid-February)
Young artistic talents exhibit in Peacock Park.

Palm Beach
ArtiGras
Mixture of art festival and carnival with horse racing and birthday party for Henry Flagler.

Tampa *Insider Tip*
Fiesta Day (late February)
Street festival for exiled Cubans in historic Ybor City; in Hillsborough Bay sailboats accompany the notorious pirate ship; street festivals and parades on land.

MARCH
Jacksonville
Riverside Art Market
(March – Dec every Sat 10am – 4pm)

More than 160 artists display their works, live performances, food and drinks

Miami Downtown
Carnival Miami (1st week in March)
Exuberant street festival with carnival background

Miami
Jazz in the Garden (early March)
World's best jazz performers meet in Downtown Miami

Miami
Miami Film Festival (early March)
Most recent American and international productions

Miami, Calle Ocho
Calle Ocho Festival (2nd week in March SW 8th Street)
Folk festival of the exiled Cubans in Little Havana

APRIL
Key West
Conch Republic Independence Celebration (4th week in April)
Party on Mallory Square to commemorate the Keys' declaration of independence in 1982 (not to be taken seriously)

MAY
Fort Lauderdale
Lauderdale Air Show (late April)
US Air Force and Navy perform flying feats

JUNE/ JULY
Fort Walton Beach
Billy Bowlegs Festival
Re-enactment of the conquest of the city by pirates (1779)

Miami, Coconut Grove
Goombay Festival (1st week in June)
Carnival-like parties with lots of music by Bahaman immigrants

Daytona Beach
Pepsi 400 (1st week in July)
Highly respected NASCAR race

Key West
Hemingway Days (2nd and 3rd week in July)
Readings and live music in honour of the great writer

Miami Downtown
America's Birthday Bash (4th July)
Street festivals with music and fireworks celebrate Independence Day

Pensacola Beach
Blue Angels Air show
World famous stunt flyers

AUGUST
Miami
ID Festival (1st week in August)
Wild electro music festival

OCTOBER
Daytona Beach
Biketoberfest (3rd week in October)
Biker and motorbike Oktoberfest

Miami
Columbus Day Regatta (2nd week in October)
Florida's largest sailing regatta

DECEMBER
Miami Beach
Art Basel Miami Beach
One of the most important art trade fairs in the USA

Spaniards, Pirates, Sounds of Battle

»The weekend early September on the Battle of Crystal River will include a re-enactment of some tactical skirmishes, parades, a meeting of the brigade officers as well as the whole brigade. All actors are welcome: Union soldiers, Confederates or civilians.« This text announces the re-enactment of a battle on the western coast of Florida during the Civil War.

The American soft spot for re-enacting the comparatively short history of the USA since the arrival of European conquerors in annual festivals can be seen in Florida too. Hardly a military event, like a raid on a farm and repelling the attackers, is too unimportant to be investigated and re-enacted every year. Old uniforms and weapons are sold or traded at fairs. The groups involved in dramatizing historic events meet during the year to exchange ideas. The landing of the Spanish conquistadors from the early 16th century, the struggle for the control of Florida, the Seminole wars, the Civil War between the Union and the seceded Confederate states, the flight of runaway slaves to the north or tens of thousands of Cubans from their home island not far from Florida are the reason and subject of annual small and large celebrations, which have often left their historic cause and turned into street festivals.

Gasparilla Festival

This harbour festival in late January in Tampa the Spanish pirate José Gaspár is the centre of attention; his violent trade held the western coast of Florida in a grip of fear in the late 18th/early 19th century. Info: www.gasparillapiratefest.com

Battle of Okeechobee

Despite the high casualty rate the later US president Colonel Zachary Taylor was promoted to general after winning the battle against the Seminole Indians on Christmas Day 1837. The conflicts on the northern end of Lake Okeechobee are re-enacted every spring by actors wearing old military uniforms.
Further info:
www.okeechobeebattlefield.com

Big Cypress Shootout

In late February battles between Indians and the US cavalry during the Seminole Wars are re-enacted on the grounds of Big Cypress Reservation.
Info: www.bcshootout.com

Fiesta Day

In February a street festival in honour of the settlement of Ybor City by exiled Cubans at the turn of the 20th century is held in Tampa. There are concerts and many stalls by local businesses and organizations along 7th Avenue.
Further information:
http://ybor.org/node/1419

Battle Re-enactment

On the anniversary of the Battle of Olustee in February 1864 the battles are re-enacted by actors wea-

Musicians on Fiesta Day in Tampa

ring historic uniforms. In the original battle each side had 5,000 soldiers, of which almost 3,000 lost their lives.
Info: www.olusteefestival.com

Fiesta of Five Flags

A festival is held during the first two weeks of June in Pensacola which commemorates the landing of the Spanish conquistador Don Tristan de Luna. He founded the first Spanish colony in North America in 1559. The landing of the Spanish nobleman on the beach is re-enacted. More recently parades, races, dancing and cooking contests have been added to this event.
Further info:
www.fiestaoffiveflags.org

Drake's Raid 1586

In June St. Augustine rolls out the cannons to commemorate the raid by the British privateer who was licenced by the crown, Sir Francis Drake, on the Spanish possession San Agustin. The historic old city is part of the setting of the event.
Further info: www.drakesraid.com

First Weekend Union

On the grounds of Fort Clinch on Amelia Island on the first weekend of every month actors in historic uniforms show what life was like in the garrison at the time of the American Civil War around 1864. Cannons are fired, soldiers march, the kitchen and washing house are open.
Further info: www.floridastateparks.org/fortclinch/

Food and Drink

Florida's Cuisine

Anyone who is open for culinary discoveries and who loves fresh ingredients will immediately feel at home in Florida. Sun and good water makes almost everything that the cooking pot, plate and heart desires thrive in fields, on bushes and trees: tomatoes, zucchini, salads, cabbage, beans, okra, paprika, oranges or grapefruit. South of Orlando is beef country; cattle graze under palm trees there. Fish and seafood lovers also have their dreams come true here. Grouper, swordfish, tuna, dorade jump at the bait or into the net; Florida lobster and stone crabs wait in traps and delicate oysters are bred near Apalachicola.

For continental Europeans American cooking can take some getting used to. This starts with the hearty American breakfast with bacon and eggs and does not end with the cotton wool-like bread or the weakly brewed coffee. But hamburgers, ketchup, hot dogs and crisps are not the only originally American foods – on the contrary: many American restaurants now serve light and healthy meals. As a classic land of immigrants, the USA also has countless **ethnic restaurants** to choose from. Cuban, Mexican, Brazilian, Thai, Indian, Arab, Italian, French: in Florida you can eat your way around the world. There are also kosher and vegetarian restaurants. The numerous **seafood** restaurants, which offer many specialties, are also worth trying. Don't miss the chance to try the extremely palatable Florida wines, and for dessert a **Key lime pie**.

From hearty to exotic

MEALS

Breakfast is best eaten in a coffee shop or a fast food restaurant near the hotel or motel. American breakfast includes a glass of grapefruit or orange juice, coffee, eggs (poached, fried sunny side up or scrambled or an omelette), fried bacon or sausages, hash browns, pancakes with maple syrup and of course toast with butter and jam. Many breakfast buffets have cornflakes and milk, fresh muesli, fruit and flavoured yogurts.

Breakfast

Brunches are very popular on Sundays and holidays (combination of breakfast and lunch), when generous buffets await hungry guests from 11am to 3pm.

Brunch

Florida's delights

Lunch A light meal is usually eaten at noon (lunch), for example a salad, chicken sandwich or grilled meat and vegetables.

Dinner The main daily meal is eaten in the evening (dinner). It consists of meat or fish with all sorts of accompaniments and side dishes. An appetizer and dessert is usually included. In some restaurants dinner shows entertain the guests.

Prices Many chain restaurants serve reasonably priced meals (e.g. Burger King, Kentucky Fried Chicken, McDonald's, Pizza Hut, Taco Bell). Better chain restaurants, including the family restaurants »Denny's« or »Applebee's«, can be found in larger tourist areas. In the dressed up historic town centres, on the marinas as well as near luxury hotels there are very good, but often also very expensive restaurants

Meat dishes T-bone steaks, Porterhouse steaks and sirloin steaks are the main meat dishes in Florida as well, along with the ubiquitous burgers. A barbecue (BBQ) practically has a ritual of its own, where all sorts of meat are grilled on a charcoal grill. But chicken (chicken fingers are baked fingers of chicken breast) and pork (prime rib) are also popular. They are served with a baked potato with sour cream or French fries. The traditional food on Thanksgiving Day is turkey.

Excellent fish dishes There is not only seafood from the Atlantic and the Gulf of Mexico, but also fresh-water fish from rivers and lakes. Crab, shrimps, clams, lobster, crawfish, bass and snappers are popular. The native stone crabs, conches from the Keys and oysters from the oyster banks near Apalachicola are also valued as delicacies.

Desserts Cheese cake and above all Key lime pie made with juicy limes and cream are popular desserts.

Fruit, vegetables Fresh fruit and vegetables are available all year in Florida. This applies especially to citrus fruits and vegetables that are easy to prepare, like cucumbers, tomatoes and avocados.

Coffee American coffee is not as weak as it used to be. New chains like Starbuck's have taken care of that and have popularized cappuccino, caffè latte etc. In areas where many exiled Cubans and immigrants live, coffee is usually drunk as a strong espresso or cafe Cubano from little cups. In the tourist areas the number of street cafés in the southern European style is growing.

Wine Wine is grown in some parts of Florida, as around St Augustine, but the restaurants mostly serve Californian and imported wines, generally chilled.

Best seafood is served in Florida

Beer in the USA is always chilled and frequently has noticeably less alcohol than European beer. Bars generally have a variety of bottled and draft beer on hand. In Florida US brands (Budweiser) are preferred. Import beers (like the Mexican Corona) are also popular, but considerably more expensive. In the past few years an increasing number of **small or local breweries** have been able to prevail against the established large breweries. The »local brews« generally use traditional brewing methods and have already gained a good share of the market.

Beer

Fruit juices made from local oranges, grapefruits or pineapples are available everywhere. Soft drinks and root beer, which is made from water, sugar, colouring and spices, as well as iced tea are popular thirst quenchers.

Juices, soft drinks

A glass of water is served with every meal, but be warned: it is usually tap water with crushed ice. Anyone who wants real table water should order »sparkling water« (carbonated table or mineral water) or »mineral water« (often uncarbonated mineral water).

Water

Popular alcoholic drinks, which can only be bought in **liquor stores** and in bars only at certain times, include whiskey (Bourbon, Scotch, Canadian, rye, Irish, blended), gin, vodka, brandy, rum, vermouth and cordials. **Drinks based on rum, whiskey or tequila** are often mixed in bars. The favourites are mojito, daiquiri, planter's punch and caipirinha, mixed drinks that are made with rum or sugar cane liquor imported from the Caribbean or Brazil.

Spirits (liquor)

Floribbean Cuisine

This is the new magic word in the south-eastern United States. Spicy food with an emphasis on fresh ingredients like fish and seafood, poultry, fruits and vegetables is strongly influenced by immigrant cooking from places like the Caribbean, Asia and of course by the many tourists from all over the world.

Grouper, like snapper, are reef fish that live in the ocean close to the coastline. Because they are so delicious they are one of the most popular fish for eating in Florida. Grouper taste especially good when stuffed with a filling of, celery, sour cream and lemon and baked in the oven. A fish weighing about 2 kilos (2lbs 6 oz) takes about 45 minutes to bake at 180° C (350° F); with side dishes it is enough for six people.

Stone crabs, more precisely their pincers, are among the tastiest food that Florida waters have to offer. Many gourmets prefer the taste of the delicate pink seafood to lobster tails. With a little lemon butter and white wine your evening meal will become a feast. The best yet: only one pincer is removed from the crab and then it is thrown back into the sea. Within two years the pincer has grown back.

The **palmetto palm**, also called sabal palmetto or swamp cabbage, is Florida's official state tree and under nature protection. The **tender hearts of the palm** when grown domestically is sold, rarely fresh, most often frozen or conserved. It can be salted and sautéed as a vegetable or – better – sliced and served as salad with a spicy dressing.

The best-known Spanish dish, **picadillo**, is known in many different variations from the Philippines to Mexico. The Cuban variety with ground beef came to Florida with refugees from Cuba. Beefsteak is the base. Add onions, green peppers, garlic, tomatoes, olives, chili, capers, oregano and a little brown sugar. Let it simmer for 45 minutes. It tastes great with rice or tacos.

The sweet and sour **key lime pie** is loaded with calories. Prepare a pie pastry with butter. Then mix lime juice, sweetened condensed milk and egg yolks. Put it in the pie and top with a meringue of egg whites and sugar. Bake until the meringue is golden brown, and then Florida's official state cake is done. It will change your life!

Insider Tip

Southern Fried Chicken and More

Actually all of Florida's cooking comes from immigrants who settled here because they were looking for political freedom or fleeing economic troubles. All of them brought their own traditions along, including their food and the dishes of their home culture.

Northern Florida is closely connected to the American South in culture and economy. Until the Civil War in the middle of the 19th century it was common for plantations to be worked by slaves.

Soul food refers to the hearty food that was not only meant to strengthen the body but also to pamper the soul. Grilled pork with **okra** or **southern fried chicken** with grits, cole slaw or sweet potatoes can be enjoyed today by their descendants as free citizens. And it's still »finger licking good.« Soul food restaurants can be found all over the state from Tallahassee to Key West.

Spanish Influence

The first Spanish conquistador to arrive on the Florida coast was Ponce de Leon in 1513. The contact with Hispanic culture, to Spain itself or to the colonies and later the independent states in the Caribbean and Latin Americas has not been broken since then. Cubans sailed to Key West in 1830 already; about 50 years later they started producing tobacco goods in Tampa and the business grew from then on. Many Hispanic dishes belong, at least in the southern half of the state, to standards in any kitchen and restaurant, and they can be found in Cuban or other Hispanic restaurants in the Sunshine State. Various vegetables and fruits, like plantains, manioc, guavas, avocados, mango or breadfruit are usually associated with the Caribbean, but some of them actually originate in other Spanish or British colonial regions, or from Africa, the home continent of the slaves.

Thanks to Cuban immigrants and refugees who have settled in Florida, the Cuban version of Hispanic cooking is already part of everyday life. Like **tostones relleno**, filled green plantains with various side dishes, »potaje de frijoles negros«, black bean soup or **pollo y arroz amarillo**, chicken with yellow rice. As dessert caramel cream, called **flan de leche** and in any case a strong **café Cubano**.

Latino Influences

Other Latin American eateries, Peruvian restaurants that serve spicy seafood dishes, Argentinian ones with grilled specialties and many Mexican ones with tacos, enchiladas or filled green chili peppers, **chile poblano**, can be found especially in the southern part of the peninsula. In Miami Beach and at other beaches many restaurants serve **nuevo Latino** cuisine, modern interpretations of Latin American recipes and often combined with culinary influences from other cultures.

Kosher Cooking

In south-eastern Florida there is a large Jewish community, including many senior citizens from the northern United States who have retired in the warm sub-tropical climate. So **chicken livers, bagels** or various **cabbage dishes** are often found on menus here. In Florida there are more than 100 restaurants that keep the strict religious regulations and serve kosher food.

Greek Influence

Many of the residents of Tarpon Springs on the Gulf coast and the Keys are descendants of Greeks from the Dodecanes Islands, who came here to work as sponge divers. They brought Greek Island recipes with them. Salads with **feta cheese** and olives, moussaka, souvlaki or in **lamb marinated** in lime juice, olive oil, oregano and garlic is on the menus of many Greek restaurants, especially along the western coast of Florida.

Native American Food

The Native Americans' love of **fish** and **clams** has been preserved, and is documented by clamshell mounds that exist until today. Occasionally hearty **alligator stew** can be found on a menu, made from the usually tasteless meat of the giant lizard.

Seafood in all shapes and sized can be enjoyed in Florida

Shop´ Until You Drop...

This saying could have been created in Florida. Endless and tempting – provided there is a favourable exchange rate and some cash to spare – the selection in the malls, city shopping centres or in museum and national park shops.

Shopping is one of the most popular pastimes while on holiday. At last, a chance to browse through shops without being under time pressure and to buy that designer shirt, trainers or the knock-out bikini at a bargain. Needless to say, the selection in the countless shop in the holiday paradise Florida is appropriate.

Shopping temptations are waiting around every corner and hardly anyone is immune to the subtle skills of advertising and salespeople. »After all, you deserve it!« Anyone who rightly assumes that the not exactly bargain admission prices for one of the large theme parks in Orlando, like Walt Disney World, Universal Studios or Busch Gardens in Tampa, is all there is to pay will realize in face of the endless selection of often decorative odds and ends and other souvenirs, that was just the beginning.

Shopping temptations

Shopping in Miami

Anyone looking for a bargain will need to keep his eye on the exchange rate. But local and regional products that are only available in Florida can be both appealing and a bargain. These include citrus fruits, Native American crafts and creations by American designers. Anyone looking for colourful and unique fashions will find it, for example, on Key West, in Naples, on Sanibel, in the Fashion District of Miami or along St. George Street in St. Augustine. Or anyone who wants to impress the people back home with especially unique seashells from the beach, but did not find any himself, can stop by the Shell Factory in Ft. Myers and pick the right one from their overwhelming selection.

Smokers will appreciate cigars that were traditionally hand rolled by Cuban immigrants, for example in Tampa's Ybor City.

Sponges in all shapes and sizes are sold along the Gulf Coast

Mega Outlets

The mall, a conglomeration of often several hundred shops of all kinds, is the magic word. The large department stores and chains, like Abercrombie & Fitch, G-Star Raw, Hollister, Victoria's Secret, Bloomingdale's or J. C. Penney have specials all year round. Factory outlet malls, shopping centres with brand name shops turn even non-consumers to shopaholics with their reductions of up to 70% on last season's goods.

The attractive labels in the outlet malls do the rest. Fashion labels and outdoor products are traditionally among the most visible items, Van Heusen, Armani, Calvin Klein, Dior, DKNY, Tommy Hilfiger, Diane von Furstenberg, Boss or Jimmy Choo. Shoes, like Cole Haan, Bally or Timberland, fashions for kids like GAP or OshKosh B'gosh, bags and luggage by Samsonite or Gucci, watches by Skagen or TAG Heuer.

These tempting shopping traps are mostly located on the roads leading out of the largest holiday areas and cities, like Orlando, Miami and Tampa, Sarasota/Bradenton or Fort Myers and announce their best buys miles before on the correct exit ramp on billboards along the interstates.

Some mega malls like Sawgrass Mills near Fort Lauderdale offer shuttle busses free of charge from the hotels, others have large multiplex cinemas, bowling alleys and dozens of reasonable restaurants for tired shoppers for diversion and recuperation before the next round of shopping.

The best Outlets

Aventura Mall, Miami
19501 Biscayne Blvd., Aventura
Tel. 1-305-935-1110
www.aventuramall.com

Mon – Sat 10am – 9.30pm,
Sun 12pm – 8pm
The gigantic mall with about 250 shops from Apple to Louis Vuitton is located in the north of Miami and Miami Beach.

Sawgrass Mills, Fort Lauderdale *Insider Tip*
12801 West Sunrise Blvd., Sunrise
Tel. 1-954-846-2300
www.simon.com/mall
Mon – Sat 10am – 9.30pm,
Sun 11am until 8pm
One of the world's largest outlet malls with more than 350 shops is located west of Fort Lauderdale on Interstate 75.

The Gardens Mall, Palm Beach
3101 PGA Blvd.
Palm Beach Gardens
Tel. 1-561-622-2115
www.thegardensmall.com
Mon – Sat 10am – 9pm, Sun 12pm until 6pm
More than 160 shops, including Nordstrom, Saks Fifth Avenue, Bloomingdale's, Macy's and Sears can be found in this luxury shopping centre a few miles north of Palm Beach.

Florida Mall, Orlando
8001 S. Orange Blossom Trail (west of Orlando Int. Airport)
Orlando
Tel. 1-407-851-6255

www.simon.com/mall
Mon – Sat 10am – 9pm, Sun 12pm until 6pm
Huge mall with Dillard's, J.C. Penney, Macy's, Nordstrom, Saks Fifth Avenue and 250 other shops. In addition there are 30 restaurants and fast food shops for hungry shoppers.

Premium Outlets, Orlando

4951 International Drive, Orlando (near Universal Studios)
Tel. 1-407-352-9600
www.premiumoutlets.com/orlando
Mon – Fri 11am – 11pm, Sat 10am until 11pm, Sun 11am – 9pm
Reduced goods by popular designer labels, like J.Crew, Kenneth Cole, Lacoste, Neiman Marcus, Polo Ralph Lauren, Saks Fifth Avenue Off 5th, Victoria's Secret and another 180 shops.

Tyrone Square Mall, St. Petersburg

6901 22nd Ave N, St Petersburg
Tel. 1-727-347-3889
www.simon.com/mall/?id=135
Mon – Sat 10am – 9pm, Sun 10am until 7pm
More than 170 shops and diverse snack and grill restaurants await shoppers on the mainland not far from Treasure Island off the coast.

Premium Outlets, Ellenton

5461 Factory Shops Blvd., Ellenton
Tel. 1-941-723-1150
www.premiumoutlets.com/outlets/
Mon – Sat 10am – 9pm, Sun 10am until 7pm
Republic, Calvin Klein, Coach, J.Crew, Kenneth Cole, Lacoste, Lucky Brand, Nike, Saks Fifth Avenue

Off 5th are among the roughly 130 shops not far from Sarasota and Bradenton.

Miromar Outlets, Ft. Myers

10801 Corkscrew Rd., Estero
Tel. 1-239-948-3766
www.miromaroutlets.com
Mon – Sat 10am – 9pm, Sun 11am until 6pm
Upmarket shops in a Mediterranean style centre on the edge of Fort Myers with 140 shops from Aeropostale to Worth.

Fashion designer Niki Taylor in the mega-outlet »Sawgrass Mills« checking the quality

Cigars Made in Florida

Lonnie Herman of »Historic Walking Tours« has a lot to relate when showing guests around Ybor City, the former Cuban quarter of Tampa. He knows about the city's history, about the arrival of Vincente Ybor and other Cubans, who fled the Spanish colonial rule on their home island via Key West 125 years ago, about the Mafia who later controlled street life and many shops in the area, and especially about the cigar factories started by Cuban immigrants in their new homeland.

For a long time Tampa was considered to be the North American capital of cigars, where up to 40,000 workers rolled cigars, »Clear Havanas«, for half a continent. The best torcedores, cigar rollers, could make up to 200 cigars a day. The exclusive and very much appreciated specialists earned good money, had medical insurance and were kept informed on daily events in the production halls by a person who was employed to read to them from newspapers and books.

New Times

The heyday of the cigar is long past, and the cigarette that followed it has also passed its zenith. But the art of rolling a good cigar has not. In Miami with its large Cuban population around Calle Ocho and Maximo Gomez Park, in Tampa and several other Florida cities the best hand-rolled cigars can still be bought at in part newly established factories and shops.

Best Cigar Shops

JC The Cuban Roller
162 St George St., St. Augustine
Tel. 1-904-808-1523
www.jccubanroller.com
Daily 11am – 5pm, sometimes later

Julio Cordero, exiled Cuban and trained »Cuban Roller«, rolls every cigar by hand. He opened his shop in St. Augustine in 2007.

El Sol Cigars Insider Tip
4951-B E. Adamo Dr., Suite # 230, Tampa
Tel. 1-813-248-5905
www.elsolcigars.com
Mon – Sat 10.30am – 5.30pm
The oldest producer of cigars moved out of his small shop in Ybor City into a more modern location.

Hand Rolled Cigars & Wine
4058 Tampa Rd., Suite 2, Oldsmar
Tel. 1-813-818-7175
Mon – Sat 10am – 11pm, Sun 10am until 9pm
For more than twenty years the best tobaccos from the Dominican Republic have been hand-rolled in Oldsmar between Tampa and Dunedin into Jose de Valle cigars. Other brands and accessories are also for sale.

Little Havana Cigar Factory Insider Tip
1501 SW 8th St., Miami
Tel. 1-305-541-1103
www.lhcfstore.com
Mon 10am – 6pm, Tue – Sat 10am until 8pm, Sun 10am – 6pm
The shop with its warm wooden panelling has an overwhelming se-

lection of cigars of various quality brands. In a lounge with heavy leather armchairs the toros and torpedos can be smoked at leisure. A short tour shows how El Credito's La Gloria Cubana and other stogies are made.

El Titan de Bronze
1071 SW 8th St., Miami
Tel. 1-305-860-1412
www.eltitandebronze.com
Mon – Sat 9am – 5pm
This elegant cigar shop is named after a general in the Cuban war of independence against Spain. Newcomers to cigars are given good advice. Five different kinds of cigars are made in the house-own manufacture.

Cuban Crafters
3604 NW 7th St., Miami
Tel. 1-305-573-0222
www.cubancrafters.com
Mon – Sat 9am – 9pm
Everything necessary to enjoy a good cigar is available here. House-brand cigars and other quality brands, ashtrays, cigar trimmers, lighters and wines that fit well to cigars. You can even have your shoes polished while smoking a cigar.

Cigars & Tobacco Shopping
310 Duval St., Key West
Tel. 1-305-295-9283
www.cigars-tobacco-shopping.com
Hand-rolled cigars made from Cuban tobacco, more precisely from tobacco that was grown from the seeds of Cuban tobacco plants and cultivated in Nicaragua, Honduras and the Dominican Republic. »La Liga« is the house brand, which is sold or shipped in five variations.

A torcedero (cigar roller) at work

Sport and Outdoors

Sporting Activities

Diving, snorkelling, hiking, biking, tennis, golfing, horseback riding, Nordic walking... Anyone who only thinks of beaches and visiting amusement parks by Orlando when in Florida is way off. Holidaymakers who love sports will find – with the exception of mountain climbing and snow skiing – an abundance of the best opportunities for a sporting holiday.

The only coral reef off the North American mainland stretches from the south-east coast to the southern Keys and offers superior **snorkelling and diving conditions** in many places, which are mostly accessible by boat. Cave divers can explore central and northern Florida's underworld through karstic springs and caverns with a guide, an unusual adventure.

Spoiled for choice

The Ocala National Forest and other wooded regions north of Orlando can be explored by **canoe or kayak**.

The island world west of Florida is a great place for sea kayaking, especially around Pine Island Sound between the islands Sanibel, Captiva and Cayo Costa and the mainland, also around the Everglades from Marco Island to Key Largo. Former railway lines and lumber trails have been converted to biking trails all over the peninsula as part of the »Rail to Trail« programme.

Insider Tip

Beginners at **golf** are spoiled for choice. They get to pick the right course for themselves from more than 1,000 golfing facilities.

The situation for **tennis** players is similar with about 7,000 facilities available, from public community tennis courts to exclusive resort facilities. Several tennis academies, the best known are by Nick Bollettieri near Bradenton, by Chris Evert in Boca Raton and by Jimmy Evert in Fort Lauderdale, are located in Florida. Sanibel Harbour Marriott Resort & Spa on the outskirts of Ft. Myers even has a tennis stadium with 5,500.

The Florida Sports Foundation has a complete overview on its website (►p.109) on all the ways and places for doing sports in Florida or for watching athletes – amateurs as well as professionals.

BEACHES

About 1,900 kilometres of sand beach along the long coast along with warm weather present ideal conditions for a successful beach holiday.

The most beautiful beaches

Healthy sports on the soft sand of Miami Beach: Nordic walking is very popular in Florida

No matter where in Florida the next beach is never far away. But all beaches are not equal. The barrier islands off the panhandle in the north-west have fine and in places brilliant white sand beaches. Shell collectors will find petrified shark teeth on the beach at Venice on the Gulf Coast; further south on Sanibel Island or Lovers Key the selection of shells that are constantly being washed ashore is practically overwhelming.

Child-friendly, wide beaches that slope gently into shallow waters are available almost everywhere, on the islands off the coast by Sarasota, near Fort Myers Beach or also on Anastasia Island on the southern edge of St. Augustine. Surfer will find their personal hotspots in several places, on Siesta Key on the west coast or variously on the Atlantic coast, near Cocoa Beach, on Sebastian Inlet or near Dania Beach. But anyone looking for action and beach life will not be disappointed by Panama Beach and Ft. Myers Beach on the Gulf coast or Daytona Beach, Miami Beach and Key West.

Still one of Florida's most popular beaches: South Beach at Miami Beach

At **South Beach** in the south of Miami Beach between 5th and 21st Street not just the broad beach, but also the beach life counts, seeing and being seen. At 12th Street the gay community has its meeting point. Stylish holiday-makers on roller blades glide along Beach Boulevard. There are usually fashion photographers around making use of the decorative background created by Art Deco hotels and bars along with the nightlife that spills out into the streets.

The waves breaking on the beaches at **Sebastian Inlet State Park** on the Atlantic just south of Melbourne attract surfers. At Monster Hole, in the very south, the long ground swell offers the best conditions for long rides on the waves. The 24 mi/38 km long lonely beaches of Canaveral National Seashore are located between Kennedy Space Center in the south and Daytona Beach in the north. Here there are no giant apartment complexes to block the view and only occasionally do rockets take off nearby. In June and July it pays to be careful as the protected loggerhead sea turtles lay their eggs in the sand at that time.

Bahia Honda State Park is located 12 mi/19 km south of Marathon on the Florida Keys. There is a wonderful beach here, turquoise-coloured water and behind the beach there are restful hiking trails. The remains of a bridge that was once part of the railway line from Miami to Key West is a popular photo motif.

Caladesi Island State Park covers the whole island. Caladesi is one of the few remaining »uncivilized« islands Florida, with mangroves and marshes on the side facing the mainland and undisturbed sandy beaches on the Gulf of Mexico. The island is only accessible via ferry from Honeymoon Island or a private boat.

Insider Tip

There is a postcard beach in **Fort DeSoto State Park** on the southernmost tip of Pinellas Peninsula, not far from St. Petersburg and its equally attractive beaches. There are just about 8 mi/13 km of fine sand beaches on the group of five connected islands that cover about 400 ha / 980 ac. On Mullet Key historic Fort De Soto guards the entrance to Tampa Bay.

Lovers Key State Park lies immediately south of bustling Ft. Myers Beach. The brilliant over 3km/ 2mi long shell beaches not only attracts romantic couples but also quite normal sunbathers.

St Andrews State Park with snow-white beaches and dunes covered with sea grass lies south of Panama City. The light forests of this protected roughly 400 ha /980 ac area is even home to foxes and deer. Hard to believe that vibrant Panama Beach is only a few minutes away.

Gulf Islands National Seashore is a protected national park that stretches along almost the whole Florida Panhandle to Pensacola. The many fine sanded beaches with almost white quartz sand are bordered by dunes.

Baywatch on Florida's Atlantic coast

Siesta Key Beach on a narrow island with the same name off Sarasota has a public beach with fine sand that is more than one kilometre (0.6 mile) long. Surfer feel at home also because of the high waves.

OTHER WATER SPORTS

Snorkelling, diving

The flat lagoons between the mainland and barrier islands or fringing reefs off the coast, which are often covered with sand dunes, are well suited to snorkelling and diving. Here is a colourful and diverse microcosm with a **large number of fish, corals, molluscs and crustaceans**. The waters are, for the most part, still very clean and offer excellent conditions for observing, photographing and filming. There are also shipwrecks – including some Spanish silver transports – on the ocean bottom that attract treasure hunters.

The best **diving** is in the Florida Keys. There are well-equipped diving stations on Big Pine Key and Cudjoe Key, in Islamorada, on Key Largo, Key West and Looe Key and in Tavernier. Along with the marine zone of Key Biscayne National Park the Key Largo Coral Reef Preserve, John Pennekamp Underwater Park and the coral limestone islands between Marathon and Key West are especially interesting. The Gulf Island National Seashore also offers good diving on the gulf coast of the Panhandle. The main diving stations are in Destin, Fort Walton Beach, Panama City and Pensacola. The many **spring basins** inland are also good places to dive. There are diving stations here as well (including Live Oak, High Springs).

Almost all larger tourist sites and beach hotels rent sailboats, motor-boats, water scooters, water-skis, jet skis, surfboards, water sports and diving equipment for a minimal charge. But water sports equipment may only be used in the areas outside of the swimming areas.

Surfing, water-skiing etc.

There are numerous **marinas** in Florida, where boats can be rented for sailing trips with and without crews. There are many sailboats in the waters between Miami and the Bahamas, also around the Florida Keys as well as parts of the Gulf coast (including Fort Myers – Punta Gorda, Tampa Bay, Panama City, Destin – Fort Walton Beach, Pensacola). **Island hopping** by sailboat around the Keys as well as in the barrier islands off the east coast and the northern Gulf coast is also popular.

Sailing, canoe, kayak, houseboat

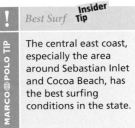

! *Best Surf* **Insider Tip**

MARCO POLO TIP

The central east coast, especially the area around Sebastian Inlet and Cocoa Beach, has the best surfing conditions in the state.

Anyone who likes kayaking, canoeing and other sports boats or travelling by house-boat is in the right place in Florida. More than 1,600km/960mi of waterways are ideal for canoeists and kayakers. The **Atlantic and Gulf coast** as well as numerous waterways and lakes inland make all sorts of activities possible. It is possible to boat around Florida's peninsula on the **Intracoastal Waterway** or across it on the **Okeechobee Waterway**. Adventurous routes through mangrove swamps offer the chance to see diverse reptiles, birds and insects up close, and to visit coral islands and lagoons.

Fishing is one of the most popular American hobbies. But in Florida the fishing season is strictly regulated. To fish in rivers, lakes and waters close to the coast, it is necessary to acquire a fishing licence (for a fee). They can be acquired at the local government revenue offices, in many marinas as well as in some of the shops that sell fishing equipment.

Fishing

Deep sea fishing or big game fishing for large fish is possible from many ports. Fully equipped boats both with and without crews can be chartered there. Swordfish, sharks, barracuda, tuna are among the fish that can be caught off the coast of Florida.

Surf fishing requires robust equipment, since heavy weights and the appropriate rods are necessary to cast long distances and the fish that bite are generally strong. The line should be at least 150m/500ft long.

Mecca of Golf

Golfers can choose between 1,250 golf courses. The palette extends from small 9-hole courses to extensive and sophisticated 18-hole courses, which will satisfy even the most demanding pros. There are many public courses that are run by local communities, as well as exclusive and correspondingly expensive private golf clubs. But even here guests are often welcome, provided the guest can play golf and is a member of his local golf club.

Golf can be played all year round in Florida, with the most moderate season being the winter from November until April. In the hot and humid summer courses tend to be less frequented. Many hotels have their own courses or offer packages with local golf courses.

Popular Golf Courses

Disney's Osprey Ridge
3451 Golf View Drive
Lake Buena Vista
Tel. 1-407-939-7675
http://disneyworld.disney.go.com
This spectacular course, one of around 170 in the Orlando area, with artificially raised tees and greens, has nine ponds and 70 well-placed bunkers.

Metro West Golf Course
2100 S. Hiawassee Rd., Orlando
Tel. 1-407-299-1099
www.metrowestgolf.com
This course was designed by von Robert Trent Jones Jr. to satisfy the most demanding golfers and has been used for qualifying tournaments for the PGA Tour and the US Open. The course winds along water hazards and expansive bunkers, has changes in elevation of more than 30 metres (100 feet) and is suitable for enthusiastic golfers of various levels.

Diplomat Country Club
501 Diplomat Pkwy, Hollywood
Tel. 1-954-883-4000
http://florida.twoguyswhogolf.com/resorts/diplomat.html
This course has an excellent layout with many small lakes and bunkers to thrill golfers of all levels of experience. It is located between Miami Beach and Ft. Lauderdale.

Blue Monster at Doral Golf Resort & Spa
4400 NW 87th Ave, Miami
Tel. 1-305-592-2000
www.doralresort.com/golf/
A PGA tournament is held on this famous course every year– and there are four more on the grounds. Anyone who wants to master the long fairways and tricky bunkers should not have just started playing golf.

Miromar Lakes Golf Club
18520 Miromar Lakes Blvd. W.
Fort Myers
Tel. 1-239-425-2340
www.miromarlakes.com
Hedges and slopes make this golf course near the west coast less visible for others. Firm grass makes it possible to putt year round. The generously designed greens are well suited for beginners.

Ocean Course Hammock Beach Resort
Insider Tip

200 Ocean Crest Drive, Palm Coast
Tel. 1-386-447-4611
www.hammockbeach.com
Jack Nicklaus was one of the designers for this course on the Atlantic coast. Six holes are hidden in the dunes. The expansive grounds of the resort include woods and lakes as well as the challenging Conservatory Course.

World Golf Village – King and Bear

1 King and Bear Drive
St. Augustine
Tel. 1-904-940-6088
www.golfwgv.com
When the two designers Arnold Palmer and Jack Nicklaus work together, something good (usually) happens, as this beautiful course between pine and oak forests show. It is part of the grounds of the World Golf Hall of Fame.

Bloomingdale Golfers Club

4113 Great Golfers Place, Valrico
Tel. 1-813-685-4105
www.bloomingdalegolf.com
The most famous and probably best golf course around Tampa is located east of the city in wooded and beautifully planned grounds. No wonder that several top pros call it home.

Copperhead Course – Westin Innisbrook Golf Resort

36750 U.S. 19 North, Palm Harbor
Tel. 1 727 9 42 20 00
www.innisbrookgolfresort.com
The Chrysler Championship of the PGA Tour is held on the Copperhead Course of this famous resorts south of Tarpon Springs, where there are three more golf courses. But the walk for golfers through the course is about seven kilometres (4 miles) amongst ponds, lakes, pine and oak woods in varied terrain.

Florida – Mecca of Golf – and obviously not without reason

NATIONAL PARKS · STATE PARKS

Protected areas

Many parts of Florida are under nature protection. These are divided into parks or nature reserves (national or state parks, national or state forests, national or state wildlife refuges or preserves, national seashores etc.), areas under monument protection (national or state monuments, historic sites, archaeological sites) and recreational parks (national or state recreational area). Land use is restricted in these areas and visitors are subject to follow strict regulations. The protected areas are supervised by specially trained personnel (park rangers). Anyone who wants to explore one of these areas on his own can only do so with permission of the park ranger. Admission is charged at most of the protected areas (3 to 25 US$ per person or vehicle!).

> **MARCO ◉ POLO TIP**
>
> ! *America The Beautiful Pass* **Insider Tip**
>
> For people who want to visit more than one national park should consider buying an America The Beautiful Pass. The price is currently $80 and allows free entry into all national parks for one year. The pass can be purchased at park entrance gates or in the visitor centres.

Adventurous canoe trip through the mangrove swamps in Everglades National Park

Many of the national parks and state parks have motels, lodges and cabins. There are usually also camp grounds and places to park caravans along with the necessary facilities (water and electricity, waste disposal etc.). Make sure to make reservations in time.

Accommodation

Leaving the marked trails and roads is not allowed in the protected areas. Camping and making campfires is only allowed in specially marked areas. Rubbish is not to be taken along or disposed of properly and wild animals may not be fed. Hunting is not allowed, angling only with a licence. It is understood that plants and even animals may not be taken out.

Rules

NATIONAL PARKS
National Park Service
Headquarters
1849 C Street NW
Washington, DC 20240
Tel. 1-202-208-3818
www.nps.gov

Biscayne National Park
9700 SW 328 Street
FL 33033-5634
Tel. 1-305-230-7275
www.nps.gov./bisc/

**Everglades
National Park**
40001 State Road
Homestead, FL 33034-6733
Tel. 1-305-242-7700
www.nps.gov/ever/

**Canaveral National
Seashore**
212 S. Washington Avenue
Titusville, FL 32796
Tel. 1-321-267-1110
www.nps.gov/cana/

**Dry Tortugas
National Park**
P.O. Box 6208
Key West, FL 33041

Tel. 1-305-242-7700
www.nps.gov/drto/
www.fortjefferson.com

**Gulf Islands National
Seashore**
1801 Gulf Breeze Parkway
Gulf Breeze, FL 32563-5000
Tel. 1-850-934-2600
www.nps.gov/guis/

**Timucuan Ecological &
Historic Preserve**
12713 Fort Caroline Rd.
Jacksonville, FL 32225
Tel. 1-904-641-7155
www.nps.gov/timu/

STATE PARKS,
WILDLIFE REFUGES
Florida Department of Environmental Protection
3900 Commonwealth Blvd.
Tallahassee, FL
Tel. 1-850-245-2118
www.dep.state.fl.us

US Forest Service
325 John Knox Road
Tallahassee, FL 32308
Tel. *1-800-832-1355
www.fs.fed.us

That's fun: flying in a biplane

A bird's eye view Getting a bird's eye view of Florida doesn't take magic. There are many smaller airports where **double-decker airplanes with open cockpits** as well as other small aircraft take off for fascinating flights. Some also have **skydiving schools** that offer tandem jumps, among other things. A ride in a **hot air balloon** is also exciting.

SPECTATOR SPORTS

Baseball Baseball is the most popular sport in America, but for the uninitiated it is difficult to follow. The top teams in Florida that play in the pro leagues are the **Florida Marlins** and the **Tampa Bay Devil Rays**. Baseball fever breaks out in spring. At that time many pro teams come to Florida for their spring training and for test games in the **Grapefruit League**.

American football American Football, game with a fascinating rhythm and tactics, is gaining a growing number of fans in Florida. The best teams include the **Miami Dolphins**, the **Jacksonville Jaguars** and the **Tampa Bay Buccaneers**. American football is especially popular in the colleges. The **Miami Hurricanes**, the **Gainesville Gators** and the **Tallahassee Seminoles** have all made a name for themselves. The college teams compete for important trophies every spring.

Basketball Thanks to superstars like Kobe Bryant, LeBron James and Dirk Nowitzki, basketball fans flock to the National Basketball Association (NBA) arenas. The American Airlines Arena on the Miami Bayfront was built a few years ago in record time and became the new home of the **Miami Heat**. **Orlando Magic** plays in Orlando.

SPORTS GENERAL
The Florida Sports
Foundation
2930 Kerry Forest Parkway
Tallahassee, FL 32309
Tel.1-(850-488-8347
www.flasports.com
This organization publishes
directories and brochures on
various topics like golf (Florida
Golf Guide), fishing and boating
(Fishing & Boating Guide) as well
as a guide to baseball spring
training camps (Baseball Spring
Training Guide).

GOLF
The Florida State Golf
Association
12630 Telecom Drive
Tampa, FL 33637
Tel. 1-813-632-3742
www.fsga.org
Find out anything you want to
know on golf and golf courses in
Florida here.

CANOE AND KAYAK TOURS
Florida Department of
Environmental Protection
3900 Commonwealth Blvd.
Tallahassee, FL 32399-3000
Tel.1-850-488-3701
www.dep.state.fl.us
Get the very informative brochure
Florida Canoe Trails here.

Florida Paddlesports
Association
Tel. 1-941-494-1215
www.paddleflausa.com
More information here

HOUSEBOATS
Holiday Cruise Yacht
Charters
www.houseboatrentalcenter.com
Offers from about two dozen
houseboat renters all over Florida.

Marinatown House Boating
Tel. 1-888-454-8825
www.houseboating.org
Houseboat rentals on Sanibel and
Captiva as well as on the
Caloosahatchee River

River Adventures
Tel. 1-866-687-2628
www.riveradventuresinc.com
Houseboats for St. Johns River
and Lake George

HIKING AND BIKING
Florida Department of
Environmental Protection,
Office of Greenways & Trails
3900 Commonwealth Blvd.
Tallahassee, FL 32399-3000
Tel. 1-850-245-2052
www.dep.state.fl.us
This office coordinates the
protection of the Everglades.

Florida Trail Association
5415 SW 13th Street
Gainesville, FL 32608
Tel. 1-352-378-8823
www.florida-trail.org
Both institutions have info
material on hiking, biking and
canoeing.

TOURS

Along the Atlantic or the Gulf coast? A visit to Cape canaveral,
the mega-amuseuments parks or the alligaotors in the Everglades?
This muchis certain: Florida has something for everyone!

Tours through Florida

The attractions of the »Sunshine State« in the south-east of the USA are not only the climate and beautiful beaches, spectacular amusement parks, high tech and rocket parks, but also large areas of protected nature. See the dolphins, manatees, alligators, sea eagles not only in a zoo, but also in their natural habitat and up close. The following pages have suggestions and tips for interesting excursions. The three suggested routes can easily be combined into a big Florida tour, which would however take several weeks.

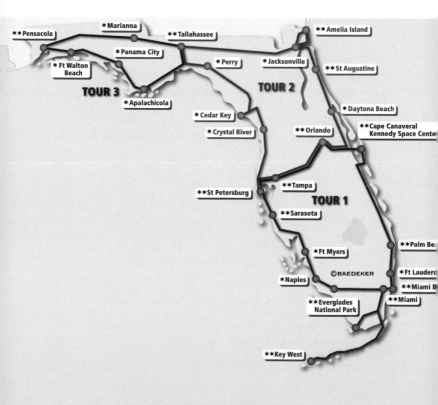

Tour 1   **South Florida**
This circular route goes to some of the main attractions in Florida. Miami and Miami Beach are included, as are Cape Canaveral's rocket launching pads and the mega-amusement parks in Orlando and Tampa. The swamps of the Everglades, Florida Keys and Key West have not been left out.
►page 115

Tour 2   **North Florida**
This tour also includes some highlights, like the big amusement parks in Orlando and the US space centre Cape Canaveral, but also St Augustine, the oldest city in the USA, and Tallahassee, Florida's capital. There are great beaches on Amelia Island, and places to see manatees include Crystal River and a few spring basins.
►page 119

Tour 3   **Florida Panhandle**
Florida's panhandle also has spectacular sights and great beaches. The mysterious spring basins near Tallahassee should not be left out, nor the U.S. Naval Aviation Museum near Pensacola and the miles-long beaches of fine-grained sand at Fort Walton and Panama City. And the fishing town Apalachicola has oysters galore.
►page 122

Travelling in Florida

The sunshine state in south-east USA is one of the regions that continues to enjoy massive and growing numbers of holiday-makers despite »nine-eleven« and the financial crisis, and deservedly so. The peninsula, which has been blessed with a pleasant climate, has a great deal to offer: wonderful **white beaches** which are not paved with beach towels; **lots of nature** including adventures with alligators, manatees, sea turtles, dolphins and colourful coral as well as **great cities** and **mega-amusement parks**, with lots to enjoy. Florida has lots to offer in the way of **culture** as well. The art deco architecture in Miami Beach and the Dalí museum in St Petersburg are examples.

Fun in the sun

Most holiday-makers and tourists use a **rental car** to explore Florida or a **camper**. The excellent network of multi-lane highways

By car

and two-lane state roads, county roads and local roads make driving around Florida easy. In the metropolitan areas (Miami/Fort Lauderdale/Palm Beach, Jacksonville, Orlando, Tampa/St Petersburg/Pinellas Coast) it is easy to get lost because of the many over- and underpasses, intersections and one-way streets. In areas where there is little traffic, like the Everglades, in the forested areas in northern Florida and on the Lost Coast the road system is well-developed. But be careful when you need petrol, since the stations are less frequent here. Tourists in campers are well catered-for in Florida. Everywhere – in the national parks and state parks as well – there are well-equipped campgrounds and trailer parks. The campsites are mostly much bigger than in Europe.

Many tourists travel around Florida by bus, either in a package tour or independently. In all larger tourist centres there are travel agents who offer tours on comfortable and air conditioned buses, vans and limousines. Most cities and tourist centres in Florida can be reached on well-equipped **Greyhound buses**, which also makes travelling comfortably on your own possible throughout the USA.

> **!** *Greyhound »Discovery pass«*
>
> MARCO ⊕ POLO TIP
>
> The economical »Discoverypass«, available for 7 to 60 days, can be recommended for travelling around Florida and the neighbouring states. But this pass can only be bought outside of the USA (▶p.403). **Insider Tip**

By public transport It is a little more difficult to explore Florida only on public transport (except for Greyhound buses). It works well in the metropolitan areas like Miami/Fort Lauderdale/Palm Beach and Orlando, where there is a good network of **bus routes**. Even though Florida's history and the history of tourism are inseparably connected to the railway, the rail passenger service only plays a minor role today. Passenger service has been stopped on some routes because it is no longer profitable.

Amtrak trains only run on the route New York – Charleston – Jacksonville –Orlando – Miami or Tampa. Metropolitan Miami can also be reached on the **»Tri-Rail« regional express**. In the less populated areas the standard of bus service varies greatly, so it can take a long time to get from one place to another.

In some places citizens have started initiatives to reactivate and operate old railway lines as **museum trains or dinner trains**.

By houseboat A unique way to explore Florida is by houseboat. Sail around the entire Florida peninsula on the **Intracoastal Waterway** that runs between the barrier islands and the mainland. Some waterways, like St John's River, can be travelled well into the interior.

South Florida

Tour 1

Starting and ending point: Miami
Length of tour: about 930mi/1500km
Duration: at least 8 days

This tour introduces Florida's highlights. These include the twin cities of Miami and Miami Beach, the rockets at Cape Canaveral or Kennedy Space Center, the mega-amusement parks of Orlando and Tampa, the swamps of Everglades National Park and of course the Florida Keys island chain.

The tour begins and ends in Florida's metropolis ❶****Miami** with its interesting sights. Don't miss Bayside Marketplace, the Miami Art Museum, Villa Vizcaya and the Miami Seaquarium. Little Havana as well as the suburbs of Coconut Grove and Coral Gables are worth a visit. Then go to ❷****Miami Beach** with its world famous Art Deco District, its celebrity-filled South Beach and the excellent Bass Museum of Art. Anyone who has time should try out the nightlife, and maybe even see Madonna or Gloria Estefan. When you have had enough of Miami and Miami Beach, follow highway A1A north. It follows the Atlantic coast to ❸***Fort Lauderdale**, where the high-

Atlantic coast

World famous bar in Key West

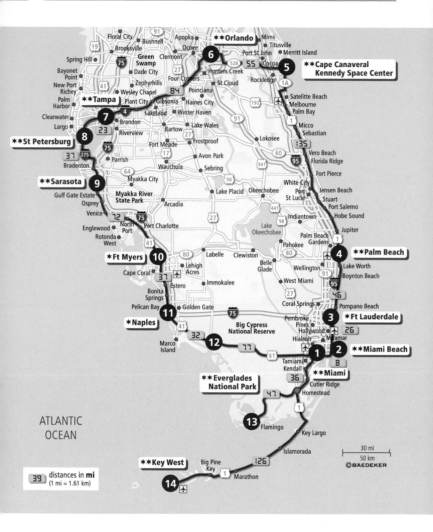

light is Las Olas Boulevard with its Museum of Art. Continue north on A1A through famous oceanside resorts like Pompano Beach, Deerfield Beach, Boca Raton, Delray Beach and Boynton Beach to sophisticated ❹ **Palm Beach**, where old and new money meets. Take some time to stroll along the breathtakingly expensive Worth Avenue or even have tea at the luxurious hotel The Breakers. After Palm Beach the Atlantic coast quiets down.

Via Jupiter, Port St Lucie, Fort Pierce and Vero Beach drive on to the so-called Space Coast with its wonderful beaches. From there it is not far to ❺** **Cape Canaveral/Kennedy Space Center**, the US space centre, which is well-visited all year round, with its rocket launching pads and its excellent exhibitions and hands-on activities. There is accommodation in Cocoa Beach, Melbourne or Titusville.

To the US space center

From Cape Canaveral it takes about one hour to get to the »world capital of amusement« in central Florida ❻** **Orlando**. It would take weeks to visit all the attractions here. The best are SeaWorld, Discovery Cove and Universal Studios. 20 minutes by car to the west is the mega-park Walt Disney World with its different theme parks.

Nothing but fun

From Orlando or Disneyworld follow highway I 4 straight to ❼** **Tampa**, where the nicely renovated Ybor City, the Florida Aquarium and the Henry B. Plant Museum await interested visitors. Then relax in the amusement park Busch Gardens or just beyond Tampa Bay in ❽** **St Petersburg**, where the sun shines especially long and where there are wonderful beaches on the Gulf coast. Other highlights in »St Pete« are the Pier and the Dalí Museum. Then follow the spectacular Sunshine Skyway (toll!) across the mouth of Tampa Bay to the south along the Gulf coast. The next stop is ❾** **Sarasota** with the imposing residence and the rich art collections of the circus king John Ringling and his wife Mable. There are beautiful beaches around Sarasota. From here take a worthwhile detour to Myakka River State Park. The relatively new highway I 75 and the older US 41 continue southwards past Venice and Port Charlotte, and finally reach the growing city of ❿* **Fort Myers**, where the legendary inventor Thomas A. Edison and the automobile manufacturer Henry Ford had their winter homes. From here make a worthwhile side trip to the beautiful beach at Fort Myers Beach or to the wonderful seashell-covered beaches on Sanibel and Captiva islands. The next part of the tour goes to the luxury ocean resort ⓫* **Naples** with its impressive Dockside and a long pier. Here again there are superb beaches like Vanderbilt Beach with its luxurious Ritz-Carlton Hotel. Nearby there are several interesting nature reserves, like Corkscrew Swamp Sanctuary. A side trip to Marco Island with its beaches is also charming.

From the interior to the Gulf coast

Naples is the western gateway to ⓬** **Everglades National Park**. This swampy landscape between Naples and Miami is crossed by the Tamiami Trail (US 41), which was built with great effort at one time and today is a broad highway. Stop in Everglades City, where park rangers conduct boat trips, or visit the Miccosukee Indian village and gain insight into their everyday life and their arts and crafts. **Tamiami Trail** (US 41) leaves the Everglades in the far suburbs of Miami and ends at Calle Ocho (SW 8th Street) downtown ❶** **Miami**.

Into the swamp

Sidetrip to the Keys

The last part of the route is a side trip via the Florida Keys down to ⑫****Key West**. En route another detour leads to ⑫****Everglades National Park**. At the southern edge of the Miami metroplex, near Florida City, County Road 9336 turns off into the Everglades, passes the administrative headquarters with its visitor centre and ends in the coastal landscape of ⑬**Flamingo.** The **Overseas Highway** (US 1) starts in Homestead or Florida City; it follows a railway line that runs to the coral islands of the Florida Keys and was destroyed in a hurricane in 1935; it ends in ⑭****Key West**. Right at the beginning of the Overseas Highway, on Key Largo, is the turn-off to the north for an enjoyable side trip into the marine nature preserve **Biscayne National Park** and a bit further to the south on Key Largo to **John Pennekamp Coral Reef State Park**. Don't fail to take a tour on a glass-bottomed boat or a snorkelling trip to the colourful world of the coral reefs. Beyond Marathon the Seven Miles Bridge crosses the ocean; a little way beyond it lies Bahia Honda with its wonderful beach. At Spanish Harbour is the boundary of the National Key Deer Refuge, where efforts are being made to protect the cute but endangered little key deer. The final destination is ⑭****Key West** with its pretty old city, where Ernest Hemingway felt at home. Visit not only the home of the winner of the Nobel prize for literature but also the exhibition of the legendary treasure hunter Mel Fisher, which shows what he salvaged from sunken ships of the Spanish gold and silver fleet. When spending the night in Key West, don't miss the fabulous sunsets at Mallory Square. The ever popular Sloppy Joe's Bar is the classic place to end the day.

Tour 2   North Florida

Starting and ending point: Orlando
Length of tour: about 850mi/1370km
Duration: at least 6 days

The second tour of Florida explores the north and north-east. There are spectacular things to see here, too, starting with the mega-amusement parks of Orlando and the rockets of Kennedy Space Center and ending at the mysterious spring basins near Florida's capital, Tallahassee, and Crystal River, which is inhabited by manatees.

US space center and northern Atlantic beach

The trip begins in ❶****Orlando**, the »world capital of amusement« with its giant theme parks, which were already mentioned in Tour 1. From here drive eastwards to reach the US space centre ❷****Cape Canaveral/Kennedy Space Center**, which was also already mentioned

Wall paintings in Tampa's historic Ybor City

in Tour 1. After the visit follow US 1 north to New Smyrna Beach, which was founded by Greek immigrants, and on to ❸*Daytona Beach with its famous auto beach and equally famous speedway for auto and motorcycle races. From Daytona Beachfollow Highway A1A north along the coast and its wonderful beaches (including Flagler Beach). A few minutes north of Palm Coast is Marineland of Florida with its interesting dolphin shows. A short distance later at the mouth of the Matanzas River the historic little Fort Matanzas is worth a short stop. Pass the beautiful Crescent Beach and St Augustine Beach to the next destination ❹**St Augustine, the oldest city in the USA that was founded by Europeans with many interesting historic sights. North of St Augustine, Highway A1A follows beautiful beaches to Jacksonville Beach, the recreational area of the city of ❺*Jacksonville, where this part of the tour ends. In Jacksonville there are several interesting museums to see. Do not miss making a detour to ❻**Amelia Island, Florida's historic northernmost island with its beautiful beach, the picturesque island capital of Fernandina and the historically interesting Fort Clinch.

Back in ❺*Jacksonville follow the I 10 westwards. En route stop in the pretty town of **Lake City**, from where there is a side trip to Osceola National Forest. Continue through the forested north of Flori-

Pine forests and giant spring basins

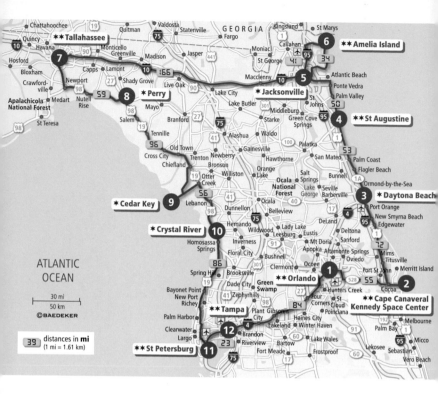

da to **7 **Tallahassee**, Florida's historic capital with the old and new state capitol building, the Museum of Florida History and the San Luis Archaeological Site. From Tallahassee a detour into the surrounding area is also worthwhile, to Apalachicola National Forest or to the sub-tropical karstic spring region of **Wakulla Springs**, which was made famous by Tarzan actor Johnny Weismuller, and to St Marks National Wildlife Refuge with its interesting animal world. From Florida's capital follow State Road 363 south to St Marks, where it crosses US 98. Follow US 98 south-east to **8 *Perry**, which proudly calls itself the »Tree Capital of the South«. Do not miss the local outdoor museum. A few miles south-east of Perry the detour to **Lost Coast** the lonely Keaton Beach and the quaint fishing village Steinhatchee is rewarding. About an hour away cross the **Suwannee River**, a good place for boating and kayaking. Just before Chiefland, State Road 230 turns off westwards to Manatee Springs, where you will see manatee gliding through the water. From Chiefland CR 345 runs south to **9 *Cedar Key**, which used to be an important wood export port. After a stop in Cedar Key and maybe a canoe tour through the delta of the Suwannee River, follow State Road 24 back to US 19/98 and this in turn south to ⑩＊**Crystal River**, the last stop on this part of the tour. Here the river itself is the attraction, since about 200 manatees live in it. There is also an old Indian religious site here. From Crystal River follow US 19 south for a few miles to the wildlife park of **Homosassa Springs**, which is located on a natural spring pond. 22 mi/35 km further south the spring basin of **Weeki Wachee Springs** has been turned into a tourist attraction with acrobatic »mermaids« performing their feats under water.

The sponge-diving town of Tarpon Springs is on the Pinellas Peninsula with its beautiful swimming beaches. The next stop is ⑪＊＊**St Petersburg** with its lively pier and interesting Dalí Museum. From there cross Tampa Bay to ⑫＊＊**Tampa**, where the nicely decorated old neighbourhood founded by the tobacco industrialist Vincente Ybor, the Florida Aquarium, the Henry B. Plant Museum and of course Busch Gardens are all worth visiting. Leave Tampa on the I 4 going north-east and in one hour you will reach Walt Disney World and a little later ❶＊＊**Orlando**, the starting point of the trip.

Brilliant beaches and interesting cities

Florida Panhandle

Tour 3

Starting and ending point: Tallahasee
Length of tour: about 440mi/710km
Duration: 3–7 days

The third tour explores Florida's northwest, also called the Florida Panhandle. It leads through a region that, unlike south Florida, is not known well in Europe, but which has natural and cultural charms of its own. The fantastic beaches along the Gulf coast and historical sites like Tallahassee and Pensacola show this.

❶＊＊**Tallahassee**, the state capital of Florida, has much to see, like the old Capitol building, the Florida Museum of History and the San Luis Archaeological Site. The new Capitol building deserves a look, too. From Tallahassee follow US 319 south along the eastern edge of the **Apalachicola National Forest** down to Apalachicola Bay. A side trip to **Natural Bridge** and a Civil War battlefield on the way are worthwhile. **Wakulla Springs**, the setting of Tarzan movies with Olympic swimmer Johnny Weismuller, should not be missed; neither should a side trip to **San Marcos de Apalachee** and the eponymous nature reserve.

Places rich in history

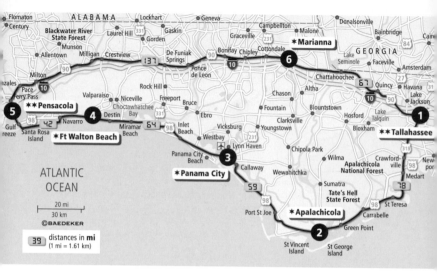

Fishing towns and holiday beaches

A few miles beyond the bridge over the **Ochlockonee River**, which is popular with canoers and kayakers looking for excitement, US 319 merges with US 98, a panoramic road along the Gulf coast of the Florida Panhandle. It leads to the friendly port of ❷***Apalachicola**, which proudly calls itself the »world capital of oyster fishers«. Anyone who has never had fresh oysters can make up for it here. Off the coast of Apalachicola **St George Island**, a narrow barrier island, has beautiful beaches. A few miles west of Apalachicola, State Road 30 leads to St Joseph Peninsula, which extends like a hook into the Gulf, and more excellent beaches. Via Port St Joe US 98 leads north-west along a beautiful coast to ❸***Panama City** and **Panama City Beach**, a densely populated holiday resort that is already lively in spring. Further north-west are the super South Walton Beaches, where new holiday villages line up one after the other. **Seaside** with its innovative holiday architecture is worth seeing. Nearby is the relaxing **Grayton Beach** and the castle-like residence Eden Garden. A sand bar leads to **Destin**, the »world capital of sports fishermen«. From here cross Choctawhatchee Bay to ❹***Fort Walton Beach**, where there are remains of old Indian cultures and a museum on the US Air Force attract visitors. Right after Fort Walton Beach the **Gulf Islands National Park** begins with Santa Rosa Island, which is very narrow but nevertheless known for its wonderful beaches (Navarre Beach, Pensacola Beach). Just before crossing to the historic port of ❺****Pensacola** the Gulfarium and historic Fort Pickens are worth a visit. Pensacola itself has renovated historic neighbourhoods. The U.S. Naval

Aviation Museum is one of Florida's most interesting technical museums.

From Pensacola follow US 90 north-east. This and the interstate highway I 10 cross the hilly, forested and in part dried-out hinterland of the Florida Panhandle. **Blackwater River** with the forest of the same name, is very popular among kayakers; it is a part of the original north Florida landscape. Via Crestview and De Funiak Springs the route reaches the legendary Ponce de León Springs and a little while later the pretty town of ❻＊**Marianna**, where the caves of the **Florida Caverns** make an interesting excursion. Then drive southeast towards the border to Georgia. Near Chattahoochee is the **Apalachicola River** and Jim Woodruff Dam, which dams up Lake Seminole back into Georgia. The restful **Three Rivers State Park** was established here. From here it takes about an hour to get back to ❶＊＊**Tallahassee**.

Karstic interior region

SIGHTS FROM
A TO Z

Fabulous white sand beaches and pastel-coloured seaside resorts, adventurous swamps and historic fortresses, glittering cities and world-famous amusement parks – there's much to discover and to experience in Florida!

Amelia Island

✦ H 2

Region: Central East
Elevation: 0 – 7m/23ft above sea level

This paradise has been discovered already, but it is still possible to get away from the mainstream to enchanting white beaches and historic settlements: the island is barely an hour's drive north of ▶Jacksonville and offers a special mix of beach life and culture.

Wonderful beaches and historic buildings

The Ritz-Carlton usually means an expensive and somewhat snobbish holiday site. But the one on Amelia Parkway is refreshingly relaxing: guests walk through the lobby in shorts, and the personnel are not nearly as intense as in this luxury chain's other hotels. The same applies to Amelia Island: relaxed, informal and in parts still left in its natural state. What with the miles of beaches, dense forests of evergreen oak, red maple, cedars, pine, magnolia and palmetto brush, this is not surprising. The ecologically conscious islanders, including many endearing eccentrics, won't have it any other way either. History may have helped, too. When Flagler's East Coast Railroad passed by in the early 20th century, it brought tourism: steam ships brought tourists until then, and the town of Fernandina, a Victorian gem, flourished as a transhipment port for wood and phosphate. Then the whole island seemed to fall asleep, and only the international tennis tournaments kissed it awake again in the 1970s. With them came the uniformity of golf courses, tennis courts and luxury resorts, above all in the south of the 20km/12mi-long and about 5km/3mi-wide island. But fishing has remained the most important source of income along with tourism; Fernandina, however, has been spared the effects of building developers. And the beaches … aah, the beaches!

WHAT TO SEE ON AMELIA ISLAND

*Fernandina Beach Historic District

The houses reflect every building style used from 1870 to 1910, from whimsical Queen Anne to aristocratic Beaux-Arts. But the compact old city, which is has preserved monument status, is much older. There was a Spanish fort here in 1696.

In the 18th century the island went back and forth between England and Spain. In 1811 the Spanish officially founded the town and named it after King Ferdinand VII: Fernandina was the last town that Spain founded in North America and was intended to stop US American expansion to the south. But then pirates and freebooters took

Picturesque: Spanish colonial architecture in the Fernandina Beach historic district

over until it was occupied by American troops in 1817 and incorporated into the newly acquired state of Florida in 1821. In 1853 the city shifted to the south but the chequerboard pattern of the old city, which had Spanish origins, remained. The streets that branch off from Centre Street lead to picturesque residential areas with beautiful homes. Fairbanks House (7th St., Italian Style), Fernandina Beach Courthouse (Atlantic Ave. corner of 5th St., Victorian Style) and Villa Las Palmas (304 Alachua St.; Spanish Mission Style) are especially worth seeing.

The main street of the old city is **Centre Street**, which continues to the east as Atlantic Avenue. The town's fishing fleet docks at the west end of the historic district in Fernandina Harbor Marina. Nearby is the Palace Saloon (117 Centre St.) of 1878, one of Florida's oldest saloons. If you see a ghost here, it won't be because of the alcohol: »Good ol' Charlie« Beresford, who was the bartender here for 54 years, has been walking here since 1960. At least that's what they claim on the ghost tours organized by the **Amelia Island Museum of History**. The exhibition also presents the varied history of the island in an interesting and serious manner.

Amelia Island Museum of History: 233 3rd St., Mon – Sat 10am – 4pm, Sun 1pm – 4pm, admission US$7, http://ameliamuseum.org

Amelia Island

INFORMATION
Amelia Island Tourism Development Council
102 Centre St.
Fernandina Beach, FL 32034
Tel. 1-904-277-0717
www.ameliaisland.org

WHERE TO EAT
Brett´s Waterway Café $$$
1 S. Front Street
Fernandina Beach
Tel. 1-904-261-2660
Eat and enjoy the view of the bay; fish and seafood as main dishes, but also tasty sandwiches.

Bright Mornings Café $
105 S. 3rd St, Fernandina Beach
Tel. 1-866-739-2117
This ist he place for breakfast lovers. Salads and homemade burgers for lunch.

WHERE TO STAY
Elizabeth Point Lodge $$$$
98 S. Fletcher Ave.   **Insider Tip**
Tel. 1-904-277-4851
www.elizabethpointlodge.com
This lovely B & B in New-England-style brick with 24 rooms and a cottage as well as a beautiful terrace with rocking chairs is right on the beach at the end of Atlantic Avenue.

The Hoyt House $$$
804 Atlantic Avenue
Fernandina Beach, FL
Tel. 1-904-277-4300
www.hoythouse.com
Romantic B & B in the historic district of Fernandina Beach; the ten guest rooms in a tidy frame house are furnished stylishly with historic furniture. An opulent breakfast is served in the morning.

Beaches   The main street (Centre St. or Atlantic Ave.) ends at the Atlantic to the west. Beyond the high dunes is Main Beach, with showers, toilets and parking. Adjacent to the south is **Peters Point Beach Park, a wonderful beach that also has its own amenities, and American Beach. It is part of the beach community that was founded by Afro-American Life Insurance in 1935. American Beach flourished in the 1950s, when Ray Charles, Duke Ellington and Count Basie performed in the legendary nightclub Ocean Rendezvous. Wedged between the luxury resorts of the Ritz-Carlton Amelia Island and Amelia Island Plantation, the remaining 30 families have refused to sell to developers and golf course builders to date. The result is a section of beach that is free of apartment blocks and hotels.

**Fort Clinch State Park   From Main Beach a 5km/3mi-long walk leads to Fort Clinch State Park. In the fall whales can be seen here. The nature reserve includes dunes, the densely forested northern point of the island and beautiful beaches with shells and driftwood. The long pier is not only popular among anglers, but also among lovers – because of the wonderful sunsets. The park is named after a fort, which was begun in 1847, occupied by Union troops in 1862 and finally abandoned in 1898. The main attraction of the fort are the communicative »re-enactors«; dressed in Yankee and Confederate uniforms they present living history and give informative guided tours on the first weekend of every month. They even sleep in the fort in order to be as authentic as possible.

❶ 2601 Atlantic Ave., daily 8am to sunset, admission: pedestrians US$2, vehicles US$6, Living History performance an additional US$2, www.floridastateparks.org/fortclinch/

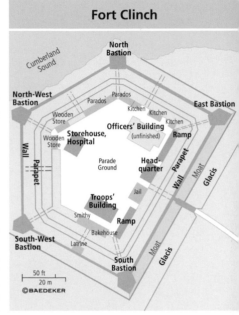

There is a nature reserve at the southern tip of Amelia Island, where the special conditions of a barrier island can be studied. Here there are also traces of **settlements of the Timucuans**, the Indians who lived in north-eastern Florida when the Spanish first came.

✶ Apalachicola

⟡ E 3

Region: North-west
Elevation: 0 – 6m/20ft above sea level
Population: 2,200

Until the fateful Deepwater Horizon oil spill (2010) about 80% of all oysters harvested in the Sunshine State come from the banks in Apalachicola Bay. The »Oyster Capital« also profited from the stream of tourists that flowed into this part of the Gulf coast.

The fact that in 1850 Apalachicola had the third-largest harbour on the Gulf, an opera and a racetrack is no longer evident today. Only about 200 old houses, many encircled by verandas, remain as a reminder of the plantation owners who exported cotton from here. When the railway came, its tracks bypassed the flourishing port. The increasing size of ships made it impossible for them to dock in the

From exporting cotton to growing oysters

Apalachicola

INFORMATION
Apalachicola Bay Chamber of Commerce
122 Commerce St.
Apalachicola, FL 32320
Tel. 1-850-653-9419
www.apalachicolabay.org

WHERE TO EAT
The Boss of Oyster $$ **Insider Tip**
123 Water St.
Tel. 1-850-653-9364
Fried, steamed or au gratin: in this rustic restaurant on the waterfront oysters are available in every variation with more than two dozen different toppings.

WHERE TO STAY
The Gibson Inn $$
51 Ave. C
Tel. 1-850-653-2191
www.gibsoninn.com
Charming Cracker-style inn with 30 rooms with rocking chairs on the veranda, where you can enjoy the breeze from the Gulf with a drink in the evenings.

Oysters galore in Apalachicola

harbour, which was located in a shallow, lagoon-like bay. Apalachicola managed to live on sponge diving and the trade in cedar wood for a while, but in the 1930s it declined for good. It was only the oysters and tourism that brought money in again. Today the quiet town is especially popular among young families from the cities. They are presently transforming Apalachicola into a pretty and, for its size, quite cosmopolitan town.

WHAT TO SEE IN AND AROUND APALACHICOLA

Historic downtown The speed is slow and a breath of Gone with the Wind blows through the streets: hardly any other place in Florida has as many beautiful old wooden houses standing between the gnarled, moss-hung oaks. The ones worth noting include the Cotton Warehouse (1838; Water St. and Chestnut St.) and the Sponge Exchange (Commerce St. and Chestnut St.). Trinity Episcopal Church was designed in the Greek Revival style in 1837 in New York and all of the building materials were shipped around the Keys. The John Gorrie Museum is housed in a simple bungalow and worth a visit; its display includes the ice-maker designed by the famous physician (▶Famous People).

Trinity Episcopal Church: 6th and Chestnut Sts., daily 9am – 5pm, free admission, donations requested, www.mytrinitychurch.org

John Gorrie Museum: 6th St., Thu – Mon 9am – 5pm, admission US$2, www.floridastateparks.org/johngorriemuseum/

In Apalachicola's harbour and along US 98 there are many restaurants that serve fresh oysters – fried, steamed or in gratin, with or without spicy cocktail sauce. Note: unlike many Europeans, few Americans slurp fresh oysters right out of the shell!

Harbour

The 24km/14mi drive east on US 98 is not too far to see this 15km/9mi-long beach, which many consider to be Florida's most beautiful. In Eastpoint turn right and cross the bridge. It connects the mainland with St George Island 6km/4mi off the coast. The island is only a few hundred yards wide but 45km/27mi long; as a barrier island it protects the coast. The state park itself is located at the eastern tip and preserves dunes, salt water marshes and 15km/9mi of the finest sand beach from construction. The first 7km/4mi are accessible by car, and the rest can be explored on foot.

St George Island State Park

Insider Tip

❶ 1900 E. Gulf Beach Drive, St. George Island, daily 8am until sunset, admission: pedestrians US$2, vehicles US$6, www.floridastateparks.org/stgeorgeisland/

Another beach regularly gets one of the top places in beach rankings. A few miles west of Apalachicola, FL 30 turns off US 98 onto a hook-shaped pencil-thin spit of sand. Past Cape San Blas, through sparse pine forests on sand and dunes, the road turns north again. The bare northern point is protected by the state park. Along with undisturbed sunbathing and swimming, it is a place to watch the pelicans glide over azure-blue waters.

St Joseph Peninsula

❶ 8899 Cape San Blas Rd., Port St. Joe, daily 8am until sunset, admission: pedestrians US$2, vehicles US$6, www.floridastateparks.org/stjoseph/

21mi/34km west of Apalachicola, US 98 reaches Port St Joe (population 3,600), which was founded in 1835. The first constitutional assembly of the state of Florida met here in 1838. The Constitutional Convention Museum commemorates this event.

*Apalachicola National Forest

❶ Thu – Mon 9am–noon and 1pm– 5pm, admission US$2, www.floridastateparks.org/constitutionconvention/

?

Animal conservation

Marshes, dunes, impenetrable brush: that is what the barrier islands in the Gulf once looked like. St Vincent is one of the last refuges for alligators, sea eagles, wolves and sea turtles. But the island is only accessible by boat (Mon – Thu 10am – 3.30pm). The Apalachicola Chamber of Commerce has information on excursion boats, tel. 1-850-653-9419.

This large nature reserve starts one hour's drive north of Apalachicola. It has been a national forest since 1936, and its oaks, cedars and cypresses have recovered from exploitation. With savannahs, wetlands and rivers suitable for canoeing, it offers a wonderful alternative to the usual tourist activities.

Fort Gadsden After the park entrance a road turns off to Fort Gadsden State Historic Site. A few overgrown trenches and a plaque point to the exciting history of the site. In 1814 the British built the fort in order to recruit Indians and runaway slaves for the war against the Americans. Two years later it was destroyed by American troops, but during the First Seminole War it served as an American supply base.

❶ daily 8am – 6pm, admission: pedestrians no charge, vehicle US$3, www.fs.usda.gov/apalachicola

✴ # Boca Raton

✦ J 6

Region: South-east
Elevation: 0 – 6m/20ft above sea level
Population: 86,000

The name is Spanish and means »rat's mouth«; Spanish sailors who anchored in this bay in the 17th century described the sharp-edged reefs off the coast with this term.

Sophisticated resort Boca Raton is one of Florida's wealthiest ocean resorts today and it can be assumed that the current residents did not name their thoroughly perfect paradise after a rodent. Smiling people in fashionable holiday clothing and armed with cream-coloured shopping bags under palm trees; uniformed personnel parking customer cars at supermarkets, and yuppies with constantly peeping cell phones driving their golf clubs around in jeeps set the scene: Boca Raton is rich and beautiful, and efforts are being made to keep it that way. This includes extremely strict building regulations: even McDonald's was forced to adjust its logo to fit. Whoever builds here has to have red tiles on the roof and arched entries for the house, office building or restaurant. Since star architect Addison Mizner (▶Famous People) used this style and was creative here in the 1920s, nothing but his Mediterranean Style (▶Arts and Culture) has been allowed. Mizner had ambitious plans for Boca Raton, including canals with gondolas and a cathedral for his mother, but they were given up with the Florida Land Bust in 1926. A few of his projects were completed however. His Boca Raton Hotel (now: Boca Raton Resort & Club), a pink, Moorish-style beach palace, is now the town's trademark.

WHAT TO SEE IN BOCA RATON

All roads lead to Mizner Park. It was built in the 1990s and has an overflowing calendar of events; its lawns are bordered by cobblestones and it is more than a chic mall for enthusiastic shoppers.

*Mizner Park

Boca Raton

INFORMATION
Greater Boca Raton
Chamber of Commerce
1800 N. Dixie Hwy.
Boca Raton, FL 33432
Tel. 1-561-395-4433
www.bocaratonchamber.com

WHERE TO EAT
Cap's Place $$$
2765 NE 28th St./Court Lighthouse Point
Tel. 1-561-941-0418
The address for excellent seafood since the 1920s. Take the launch from Cap's Dock in the marina of Lighthouse Point to the restaurant, an old shack where US President Roosevelt and gangster boss Al Capone once ate.

Brewzzi $$
2222 Glades Rd.; Tel. 1-561-392-2739
Great variety of imaginative fish, poultry

and pasta dishes; the sandwich and burger variation are also recommended. There is also beer from the house brewery.

WHERE TO STAY Insider Tip
Boca Raton Resort & Club $$$
501 E. Camino Real
Tel. 1-888-543-1277
www.bocaresort.com
Boca Raton's pride and joy has been expanded several times since 1926 and as the perfect resort it has more than 963 rooms and suites, 120 villas as well as two golf courses, tennis courts and fitness rooms, five pools and ten restaurants.

Ocean Lodge $$
531 N. Ocean Blvd.
Tel. 1-561-395-7772
Clean, two-storey motel. 11 of the 18 rooms have kitchenettes. Pool and terrace; beach across the street.

Very photogenic: beach life in Boca Raton

The modern, pink museum is one of the best of its kind in the southern USA. The most interesting artists in Florida exhibit here. There is also a small collection of 19th and 20th-century masters, including Picasso, Degas and Matisse.

❶ Mizner Park, Tue -- Fri 10am – 5pm, Sat, Sun noon–5pm, admission US$8, www.bocamuseum.org

*Boca Raton Hotel

Not only a hotel, but also a tourist attraction: guided tours through this pink palace explain how Addison Mizner managed to make the wood floors look so old (by having the construction workers apply their hobnailed shoes), who has slept in the ornate rooms and what happened there – both the important and the piquant (501 E. Camino Real).

❶ 501 E. Camino Real, reservation required for tours, www.bocahistory.org/tour/tour_hotel-asp

*Gumbo Limbo Environmental Complex

Not artificial but original: the forest region between the Atlantic and Intracoastal Waterway was named after a native tree and protects one of the last original coastal regions in Florida. A boardwalk runs through hammocks (wooded islands) and mangrove islands, and ends at an observation tower with a beautiful view of the Atlantic. The residents of this biotope include rare brown pelicans, diverse amphibians and manatee, which can be seen with a little luck

❶ 1801 N. Ocean Blvd.; Mon – Sat 10am – 2pm, Sun noon to 4pm, free admission, donations requested, www.gumbolimbo.com.

Some of the most beautiful beaches in the area are protected as state parks. In Boca Raton this includes South Beach Park (400 N. Ocean Blvd.) and Spanish River Park Beach a bit further to the north. Here trails lead through dense vegetation to an observation tower. Delray Public Beach (Ocean and Atlantic Boulevards).

*Beaches

❶ Beach access daily 8am until sunset

AROUND BOCA RATON

This wonderful traditional Japanese garden confuses many a visitor geographically. The peaceful site is 16km/10mi north-west of Boca Raton in Delray Beach and commemorates a group of Japanese farmers, who were settled here around 1900 by the East Coast Railway to grow tea and rice. The experiment failed. Only George Sukeji Morikami stayed and successfully switched over to pineapples. He later left his estate to the county.

*Morikami Museum & Japanese Gardens

❶ 4000 Morikami Park Rd., Delray Beach; Tue – Sun 10am – 5pm, admission US$13, www.morikami.org.

The 60,000ha/148,000-acre wilderness is located 20km/12mi west of Delray Beach and is the northernmost point of the Everglades. It consists mainly of swamps and creepy cypress groves, and is home to thousands of alligators, varieties of cranes, wood ibis and more than 250 other bird species. The best way to explore this area is on the water: miles of canoe trails provide great photo motifs. Approach the swamp on foot via the short boardwalk trail which begins at the visitor's centre.

*Loxahatchee National Wildlife Refuge

❶ 10216 Lee Rd., Boynton Beach; daily 6am until sunset, admission pedestrians US$1, vehicles US$5, www.fws.gov/loxahatchee

✱✱ Cape Canaveral · Kennedy Space Center

✦ J 4

Region: Central East
Elevation: 0 – 10m/33ft above sea level

Take-off point into space: a visit to America's space port is a great experience – not just for rocket fans. The hangars and launching pads on the Atlantic coast document the unbroken optimism of a nation as well as man's unquenchable thirst for new challenges.

Cape Canaveral

INFORMATION
John F. Kennedy Space Center
Kennedy Space Center, FL 32899
Tel. 1-877-436-9660
www.kennedyspacecenter.com

Florida's Space Coast Office of Tourism
430 Brevard Ave.
Cocoa, FL 329622
Tel. 1-877-572-3224
www.visitspacecoast.com

Cocoa Beach Regional Chamber of Commerce
400 Fortenberry Rd.
Cocoa Beach, FL 32952
Tel. 1-321-459-2200
www.cocoabeachchamber.com

WHERE TO EAT
Café Margaux $$$
220 Brevard Ave., Cocoa, FL
Tel. 1-321-639-8343

Creative French cuisine with Mediterranean and Asian touches, excellent wines

The Cape Codder $$
2690 S. Atlantic Ave., Cocoa Beach, FL
Tel. 1-321-868-2560
A popular fish restaurant dedicated to New England cooking: Especially delicious: Bill's homemade New England clam chowder

WHERE TO STAY
Hampton Inn Cocoa Beach $$
3524 N. Atlantic Ave., Cocoa Beach, FL
Tel. 1-321-799-4099
www.hamptoninncocoabeach.com
Modern hotel with 150 rooms and suites, swimming pool and fitness centre

Apollo Inn & Motel
4125 S US 1, Cocoa, FL
Tel. 1-321-636-8511
Friendly family-run business with well-furnished rooms

History   Hundreds of successful space trips began here, including the Apollo missions to the moon, the Spacelab project and the space shuttles that were launched into orbit here. During the Apollo missions in the 1960s up to 25,000 people were employed here.

America's space port was founded after World War II as a testing area for long-range missiles. In 1949 US President Harry S. Truman had Cape Canaveral, which reaches far into the Atlantic, closed off; at that time it was still unspoilt, even though city-dwellers from Miami and Jacksonville often went there. It was a good choice. Tests could be made over the Atlantic without endangering anyone and the weather was good almost all year. The tests began the next year, first on modified V-2 missiles from German stocks, which could fly as high as 16km/10mi. Under the coordination of the German expert Wernher von Braun, rockets of increasing power were developed in the following years, including the Redstone and Polaris rockets for the army and navy. But it was the Sputnik shock in 1957 that really set the American space industry in motion. The success of the Russian Sputnik 1 space probe made Washington aware of the fact that Moscow was building better rockets. So in order to bundle American ambitions or »for the peaceful use and exploration of space« the space agency NASA (National Aeronautics and Space Administration) was founded on 1 October 1958. Soon the entire coast between Fort Pierce and Daytona Beach had a new name: Space Coast. On 31 January 1958 the team of Werner von Braun's colleague Kurt Debus put the 13.6kg/22lb satellite Explorer 1 into orbit. But while NASA was still being established, the Soviets put the first man in space. On 12 April 1961 the cosmonaut Yuri Gagarin went into orbit. Less than a month later the USA responded, by sending **Alan Shepard** on board **Mercury 1** into space on 5 May. In the

On 20 July 1969 Neil Armstrong became the first human to walk on the moon

same month US President John F. Kennedy announced that within ten years manned expeditions would be sent to the moon. With that the Apollo programme was born. Merritt Island to the west became the launching pad for the gigantic **Saturn V rockets** and was named John F. Kennedy Space Center (KSC) after the president who was murdered in 1963. While unmanned rockets continued to be launched from Cape Canaveral, the KSC served as the take-off point for the moon. In 1966 the Apollo programme started and reached its climax with Apollo 11: on 20 July 1969 **Neil Armstrong** became the first human to walk on the moon. Other moon expeditions followed. Apollo 13 went down in history as a near-catastrophe. Shortly before reaching the moon and about 386,000km/240,000mi from the earth, one of the oxygen tanks on the mother ship Odyssey exploded. The landing on the moon was cancelled and the crew managed to save themselves through daring manoeuvres. In December 1972, Apollo 17 the last expedition to the moon to date, started. Financially constrained, NASA then concentrated on the – cheaper – exploration of space from earth's orbit. On 14 May 1973 a Saturn V rocket brought the space lab **Skylab** into orbit. Until fall of 1973 three research teams spent a total of 513 days on board, conducting research on the sun and earth, and on the long-term effects of

America's Spaceports

The first rocket was launched on July 24, 1950 from Cape Canaveral Air Force station. It was followed by the first US satellite, Explorer, innumerable other satellite launches and the manned Mercury and Gemini missions. NASA built a separate launch complex for the giant Saturn V moon rockets, and all of the missions have been launched there ever since.

Height: c. 110m/330ft
- Rescue tower
- Apollo command capsule
- Apollo service module
- Lunar module (under the cover panel)
- Instrument unit
- Third stage fuel tank
- Third stage booster rocket Thrust: 890 kN
- Second stage fuel tank
- Five second stage booster rockets Thrust: 5155 kN
- First stage fuel tank

▶ Space shuttle and Saturn V moon rocket

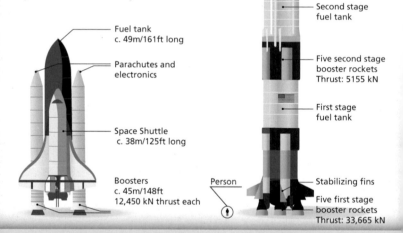

- Fuel tank c. 49m/161ft long
- Parachutes and electronics
- Space Shuttle c. 38m/125ft long
- Boosters c. 45m/148ft 12,450 kN thrust each

Person

- Stabilizing fins
- Five first stage booster rockets Thrust: 33,665 kN

▶ History of US manned space flight

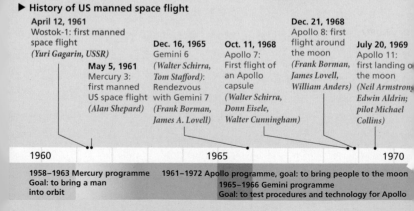

April 12, 1961
Wostok-1: first manned space flight
(Yuri Gagarin, USSR)

May 5, 1961
Mercury 3: first manned US space flight
(Alan Shepard)

Dec. 16, 1965
Gemini 6
(Walter Schirra, Tom Stafford):
Rendezvous with Gemini 7
(Frank Borman, James A. Lovell)

Oct. 11, 1968
Apollo 7:
First flight of an Apollo capsule
(Walter Schirra, Donn Eisele, Walter Cunningham)

Dec. 21, 1968
Apollo 8: first flight around the moon
(Frank Borman, James Lovell, William Anders)

July 20, 1969
Apollo 11: first landing on the moon
(Neil Armstrong, Edwin Aldrin; pilot Michael Collins)

1960   1965   1970

1958–1963 Mercury programme
Goal: to bring a man into orbit

1961–1972 Apollo programme, goal: to bring people to the moon
1965–1966 Gemini programme
Goal: to test procedures and technology for Apollo

Lunar Module

Height	7m/23ft
Diameter	9,4m/31ft
Weight	14,696kg/32,331lbs
Room inside	6,7m³/236ft³
Crew	2

http://grin.hq.nasa.gov/
subject-space.html

▶ First men on the moon
»One small step for a man, one giant leap for mankind.« Neil Armstrong's words went down in history. Twelve men in all walked on the moon. The second one was »Buzz« Aldrin, as photographed here by Armstrong.

Landing sites and lengths of stay
Apollo 11–17

Fra Mauro
33 h, 30 min.

Hadley Rima
41 h, 54 min.

Taurus-Littrow
74 h, 59 min.

Sea of Tranquility
21 h, 36 min.

Descartes
71 h, 2 min.

Oceanus
Procellarum
31 h, 31 min.

15
17
12 14
11
16

500km/310mi

Dec. 7, 1972
Apollo 17: last
moon landing
*(Eugene Cernan,
Harrison Schmitt;
pilot Ronald Evans)*

April 12, 1981
First space shuttle
launch
(Columbia)

Jan. 28, 1986
Challenger disaster,
all seven crew
members are killed

Feb. 1, 2003
Columbia disaster,
all seven crew
members are killed

May 14, 1973
Launch of
Skylab

until 1986
21 missions
with satellite
transports

July 21, 2011
Last space shuttle
mission (Atlantis)

1970   1980   1990   2000   2010

1973–1974
Skylab project

1970–2011 Space shuttle era
Goal: a reusable spaceship

weightlessness. When Skylab burned up in late summer 1979 in the earth's atmosphere, NASA had already publicly presented the reusable **space shuttle Columbia**. The shuttles, which were carried into space piggy-back on rockets but land like airplanes, were supposed to operate often and cheaply, and carry cargo like satellites and spare parts. On 12 April 1982 the space shuttle Columbia made its maiden voyage with two astronauts on board. During the following two decades a total of five shuttles carried 61 satellites, transported about 700 pilots, crew members and passengers and flew over 700 million air kilometres (420 million miles). When the International Space Station »ISS« was being built in 1998 they acted as transports. But the space shuttles did not achieve the original goal of reducing flight costs: instead of the predicted 10 to 20 million US dollars, every trip cost about 500 million. Moreover two tragic accidents overshadowed the shuttle programme: on 28 January 1986 **Challenger exploded** 73 seconds after taking off. On 1 February 2003 Columbia burned up when it re-entered the earth's atmosphere. After this NASA stopped the shuttle flights. Only on 26 July 2005 did the space shuttle Discovery start on another trip to space. After more than 30 years of space travel and more than 130 missions the last space shuttle flight was launched in Juli 2011. The retired shuttles can be seen in the Visitors Complex of Kennedy Space Center (Atlantis), in Chantilly, VA (Discovery), in New York (Enterprise) and in Los Angeles (Endeavour). But rockets are still launched into space from Cape Canaveral with satellites for military and civilian purposes.

WHAT TO SEE ON CAPE CANAVERAL

An expansive collection of flat white buildings with green areas and two artificial lagoons is probably the most interesting visitor's centre in the USA. It is easy to spend a whole day here. The history of American space travel from the first satellites to the Mercury, Gemini and Apollo missions and the shuttle programme is presented in a number of buildings in a style that is exciting and simple to understand for the uninitiated. Two IMAX movie theatres show a rotating programme of spectacular space documentaries. NASA offers visitors a programme that can be booked in advance, including an Astronaut Training Experience, which gives the participants a first impression into the arduous work astronauts, as well as Lunch with an Astronaut (reservations: tel. 1-866-737-5235), an opportunity to meet personally an astronaut who has actually been in space. The simulator Shuttle Launch Experience shows the start of a space transport and arrival in orbit with a

**John F. Kennedy Space Center, KSC Visitor Complex

Insider Tip

The last space shuttle was launched into space on Cape Canaveral on July 8, 2011

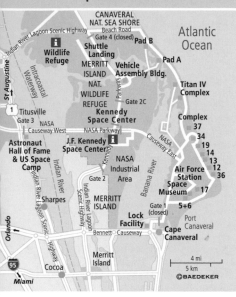

Space Coast

magnificent view back to earth. The Redstone, Atlas and Titan rockets in the so-called Rocket Garden are also worth seeing. The space shuttle Atlantis, which was last used in the summer of 2011, can also be viewed. Complete information is available at the Visitor Center.

❶ Visitor Center: tours daily 9am–7pm, tickets US$50; www.kennedyspacecenter.com

Bus tours: Buses run to various sites including the launching pads, construction hangars and rockets. Note: to avoid long lines come very early in the morning. The 90-minute KSC Up-Close vehicle Assembly Building Tour goes to A/B Camera Stop, which gives a view of the shuttle launching pad; visits the Launch Control Center and ends at Apollo/Saturn V Center, where original spaceships and moon landing modules are on display.

❶ Tours: Info and reservations tel. 1-866-737-5235, ticket US$27

Launch dates   The start of a satellite booster rocket makes a lasting impression. Launch dates available at the Visitor Center of the Kennedy Space Center and in the internet. The **NASA Causeway Launch Viewing Transportation Admission Package** (price US$61) includes admission to the Space Center as well as transport to an observation point near the launching pad. Incidentally, Kennedy Space Center is closed during a rocket launch. Find out the latest information before visiting. If KSC is closed, go to the observation points on the causeways leading to Merritt Island.

Launches can also be seen well from Jetty Park at the eastern end of Port Canaveral (off George King Blvd.).

❶ www.nasa.gov/missions/index.html

Astronaut   About 6 mi/10 km east of Titusville the Astronaut Memorial com-
Memorial   memorates the 24 astronauts who lost their lives.

Astronaut Memorial: NASA Parkway (6 mi/10 km east of Titusville), daily 9am – 5pm, admission only as part of a tour booked at the Kennedy Space Center, www.kennedyspacecenter.com

AROUND CAPE CANAVERAL

Progress has its ecological side, too: NASA has turned over land that it does not use to nature reserves. In the north lies Canaveral National Seashore, a barrier island with untouched dunes, hammocks and saltwater marshes that is about 21km/13mi long and a few hundred yards wide. Thousands of varieties of plants and more than three hundred varieties of birds have been seen here, including sea eagles, falcons and ibis. With a little luck you can see manatee and sea turtles in Mosquito Lagoon between the island and mainland. Get to the South Beaches via FL 3 about 13km/8mi east of Titusville and to the North Beaches via New Smyrna Beach in the north. Sun worshippers take note: the wonderful Playalinda Beach in the southern part is – again – one of the most beautiful beaches in Florida. ***Canaveral National Seashore**

❶ daily 6am – 6pm, in the summer until 8pm, admission pedestrians US$1, vehicles US$5, www.nps.gov/cana/

This beautiful nature reserve borders on the south. In 1963 it was established as a buffer zone by NASA and has marshes, dunes, pine forests as well as palm and oak hammocks. More than 500 species of animals, including 15 endangered ones, live in this highly individual habitat, including manatee, sea eagles and alligators. The varied animal world can be observed on hiking trails 2mi/3.5km to 5mi/8km long. The 11km/7mi-long, unpaved Black Point Wildlife Drive offers nice views for photographers. Information is available at MINWR Visitor Center east of Titusville. ***Merritt Island National Wildlife Refuge**

❶ Tue – Sat 10am – 4.30pm

The two towns of Cocoa and Cocoa Beach south of the rocket area grew along with Kennedy Space Center and have a population of about 17,000. The beach is popular among surfers because of its regular groundswell; it is 6mi/10km long and divided into several recreational parks. Ron Jon's Surf Shop is a point of entry into the world of surfing; this retail cathedral for all followers of the cult is shaped like a sandcastle. The beach on the 270m/300yd-long Cocoa Beach Pier is dotted with fish restaurants and is a mecca for surfers with a lively clientele and all the necessary facilities. **Cocoa Beach**

Insider Tip

❶ Ron Jon's Surf Shop: 4151 N. Atlantic Ave., www.ronjonsurfshop.com

Port Canaveral, a super-modern cargo and cruise port, grew up from the 1960s about a stone's throw from the space port. Cruise ships embark from here every day on excursions to the Bahamas and the Caribbean. Moreover many shrimp fishers and charter boats for big game fishing leave from Port Canaveral. **Port Canaveral**

❶ www.portcanaveral.com/cruising/

Titusville Located in the hinterland of the Space Coast on Indian River, the town of Titusville (population 40,000) owes its development from a small fishing port to a rapidly growing industrial centre to the events in the nearby US space port. In the **Astronaut Hall of Fame** on NASA Parkway the impact of space travel on technical progress is portrayed comprehensively. In Space Camp children and teenagers can experience how astronauts are trained, what weightlessness is and what a space flight simulator feels like (hours: daily 9am–6pm).

❶ NASA Pkwy., daily 12noon – 6pm, admission US$27, mostly included in the price of a KSC ticket

✳ **Cedar Key**

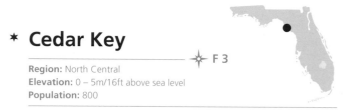

✦ F 3

Region: North Central
Elevation: 0 – 5m/16ft above sea level
Population: 800

The most beautiful side trip in Florida: the sleepy fishing village on the Lost Coast of the Gulf of Mexico is not only at the end of the road, but also on an island. This guarantees character and tranquillity, as well as pleasant encounters in places where the locals eat.

Cedar island Old Florida lies three miles off the coast. Connected to the mainland by a causeway, FL 24 from Gainesville ends at Cedar Key – the island, however, is called Way Key. It was settled in the 1840s and began to flourish when the railway arrived from Fernandina (▶Amelia Island). This brought tourism and opened the markets in the north for the lumber industry. In 1865 Eberhard Faber Inc. built a sawmill and a pencil factory here. At one time Cedar Key was the second-largest city in Florida. But when the forests were used up, the income dried up, too. A hurricane in 1896 put an end to Cedar Key. The people who stayed anyway went back to the original sources of income: fishing and oysters. Enterprising city dwellers soon rediscovered this town on the largest barrier island in the Gulf. In the past years many run-down houses have been restored and occupied. A handful of nice restaurants, two interesting little museums and beautiful wilderness areas only accessible by boat are good reasons to spend a couple of quiet days here.

WHAT TO SEE IN AND AROUND CEDAR KEY

*Historic Cedar Key The remote location and the warm, humid climate take the hurry out of one's step. Cedar Key means quiet meandering on the covered

Cedar Key

INFORMATION
Cedar Key Area Chamber of Commerce
2nd St., Cedar Key, FL 32625
Tel. 1-352-543-5600
www.fws.gov/cedarkey

Cedar Key National Wildlife Refuge
16450 NW 31st Place
Chiefland, FL
Tel. 1-352-493-0238
www.fws.gov/ cedarkeys

Manatee Springs State Park
11650 N.W. 115th St.
Chiefland, FL
Tel. 1-352-493-6072
www.floridastateparks.org/
manateesprings

WILDERNESS TOURS
Kayak Cedar Keys **Insider Tip**
Downtown Marina
1st & A Sts., Cedar Key, FL
Tel. 1-352-543-9447
www.kayakcedarkeys.com
See dolphins, sea turtles and cranes up close during guided kayak tours

WHERE TO EAT
The Island Room at Cedar Cove $$
192 E 2nd St.
Tel. 1-352-543-6520
Good pasta, seafood and steaks with a beautiful view of the bay towards the south.

Coconuts of Cedar Key A
590 Dock St.
Tel. 1-352-543-6390
Classic sports bar; serves hot dogs, sandwiches etc., but also fish soup and a raw bar with oysters.

WHERE TO STAY
Cedar Key B & B $$
810 3rd St., Cedar Key, FL
Tel. 1-352-543-9000
www.cedarkeybandb.com
Pretty inn with a large garden, friendly guest rooms and very good breakfast.

Cedar Inn
410 2nd St., Cedar Key, FL
Tel. 1-352-543-5455
www.cedarinnmotel.com
12 simple rooms, Southern-style accommodation in the middle of Cedar Key. Pretty terraces with a view of the Gulf and Main Street.

sidewalks of Second Street, the main street, and strolling through the few side streets where pretty old wooden houses with verandas typical of the south pose under palm trees. The town's highs and lows are documented in the Cedar Key Museum and the Historical Society

The Pencil Kings in Florida

»*I much prefer to take up a pencil, with which it is easier to write: For it has happened several times that the scratching and spraying of a quill woke me out of my dreamy compositions, distracted me and thus stifled a little creation at birth.*« *Johann Wolfgang von Goethe wrote this in his work »Poetry and Truth«.*

But what does that have to do with Cedar City? A bit. In 1855 Eberhard Faber, the industrious son of the already world-famous pencil dynasty from Stein near Nürnberg, bought cedar forests around Cedar Key and had a sawmill built here. The wood was cut into boards here and transported to Germany for further processing. The cedar wood, which was optimal for the production of pencils was combined with the best Siberian graphite and turned into the coveted writing implements that soon began to conquer the world. Thus Eberhard Faber contributed to the economic growth of Cedar Key, which reached its height in 1885 to 1888.

Cedar Key around 1884

Faber in America

A. W. Faber had already opened a sales branch in New York in 1849. Until then the American demand had been supplied by English and French products, for the most part. A. W Faber was the first German company to be established in the USA and soon presented good sales figures. The New York branch was taken over by Eberhard Faber. Since foreign products were charged protective duties in the USA, it was to his advantage to produce the wooden pencils in the USA.

Eberhard Faber went to work in Cedar City. In 1861, with the help of the German mother company, he started his own business in Brooklyn. In the 1890s the American company separated from A. W. Faber

Faber pencil advertisement

and became independent. Then there were two Faber companies, who went separate ways for awhile: A. W. Faber and Eberhard Faber. After World War I A. W. Faber was confiscated as enemy property, but Eberhard Faber Company continued to exist as an American company. In the mean time it was being run by the sons of Eberhard Faber. In 1988 Faber Castell Corporation took over the Eberhard Faber Company. Since then the two companies with a common origin have been united again.

The permanent exhibit of the Cedar Key State Museum, which was opened in 1962, depicts the work of the Faber company in northern Florida. Along with old photographs there are pencils, cases, as well as medals for outstanding Faber products on display here.

Seeds from Florida in Franconia, Germany

The older brother of Eberhard Faber, Baron Lothar von Faber, not only made himself a name as a producer of pencils, but also as the founder of the »Nürnberger Lebensversicherung AG« (life insurance) as well as the co-founder of the »Vereinsbank Nürnberg« (bank). He was also interested in progress in agriculture and forestry, and especially in the introduction of new agricultural crops. Thus he had his younger brother send him cedar seeds, which he was able to grow successfully in Stein. The Faber cedar woods near Nürnberg flourished, but it was destroyed during the Second World War.

Museum. The former has a remarkable exhibition of all shells that can be found in the Gulf and reminders of the heyday of the pencil centre founded by the German »pencil king« Eberhard Faber. The exhibitions in the Historical Society present artefacts of the Timuacan and Seminole Indians.

Cedar Key Museum: 12231 SW 166 Court, Thu – Mon 9am – 5pm, admission US$2, www.foridastateparks.org/cedarkeymuseum/
Historical Society Museum: D and 2nd Sts., Sun – Fri 1 – 4pm, Sat 11am until 5pm, admission US$2, www.cedakeymuseum.org

Cedar Key National Wildlife Refuge

West of Cedar Key a dozen islands have been under strict nature protection since 1929. The varieties of birds that live here include ibis, brown pelicans and varieties of deer as well as sea eagles and buzzards. Migrating birds rest here in March and April as well as in August and September. Rattlesnakes lurk in the dense thicket of the island interiors. The refuge can only be reached by boat from Cedar Key; various companies offer tours and rent kayaks. Exploring the island alone is restricted from March to July because of the brooding time, and is not recommended anyway because of the rattlesnakes.

❶ Arrive from Cedar Key via SR 345, from Chiefland via US 19 and SR 345, admission daily 8am until sunset, www.fws.gov/cedarkeys/

Manatee Springs State Park

From Chiefland on US 19/98, FL 320 runs about 5mi/8km west to the nature reserve on the lower Suwannee River was established in 1955 and famous for its karst spring basin, which shimmers in every shade of green and blue and is surrounded by cypresses and hardwood islands; its waters flow into the Suwannee River. Bathers and snorkellers enjoy the pleasant water temperatures. Divers explore the extensive cave system of this richly flowing spring. In the fall and winter manatee can be watched in the temperate waters, with a little luck. The park's services include a campground, canoe rental and a small shop.

❶ 11650 NW 115th St., Chiefland, FL, daily 8am until sunset, admission pedestrians US$2, vehicles US$6, www.floridastateparks.org/manateesprings/

✱ Crystal River

✳ G 4

Region: Central West
Elevation: 0 – 2m/7ft above sea level
Population: 3,500

How do you protect hundreds of manatee from hundreds of thousands of tourists? The blessings and curses of manatee tourism can be studied well around the town of Crystal River in the sparsely populated Big Bend or on the Nature Coast.

Crystal River is the name of the town and the river. Both are about a two-hour drive from ▶Tampa on Highway 19. The quiet town is a popular place to retire to when the Tampa Bay area becomes too noisy. Before the area was settled by Europeans in 1840, pre-Columbian Indians lived here, probably Timuacan. The pensioners and the natives were attracted by one thing above all: the – for once literally – crystal-clear waters of Crystal River, which is fed by several karst springs and flows into King's Bay at the end of its short course.

Holiday resort with history

WHAT TO SEE IN AND AROUND CRYSTAL RIVER

From about 200 BC until the 15th century there was an important Indian religious and cultural centre at Crystal River. Six massive hills have been identified, which probably served as sanctuaries and burial sites. In one of the burial sites more than 450 graves have been

*Crystal River Archaeological Site

Crystal River

INFORMATION
Citrus County Visitor & Convention Bureau
9225 W. Fishbowl Dr.
Homosassa, FL 34448
Tel. 1-352-628-9305
www.visitcitrus.com

Crystal River National Wildlife Refuge
Refuge Manager
1502 SE Kings Bay Dr.
Crystal River, FL
Tel. 1-352-563-2088
www.fws.gov/crystalriver

MANATEE TOURS Insider Tip
Bird's Underwater Manatee Tours
320 NW US 19, Crystal River, FL
Tel. 1-352-563-2763
www.birdsunderwater.com

Crystal Lodge Dive Center
525 NW 7th Ave.

Crystal River, FL
Tel. 1-352-795-6798
www.manatee-central.com

WHERE TO EAT
Charlies Fish House Restaurant $$
224 NW US 19, Crystal River, FL
Tel. 1-352-795-3949
Tasty fish dishes, fresh salads; the stone crab claws are excellent.

WHERE TO STAY
Best Western Crystal River Resort $$$
614 NW US 19, Crystal River, FL
Tel. 1-352-795-3171
www.crystalriverresort.com
Very comfortable mid-range hotel with bright rooms, a swimming pool and a nice restaurant named Cravings Cantina right on the water. It also includes a marina for sailing enthusiasts.

found. Steles, which are usually not found in North America, point to connections with the civilizations of Mexico or Central America. The little museum in the visitor centre for the archaeological site and the Indian culture is very informative.

❶ outdoor area daily from 8am, museum Thu – Mon 9am – 5pm, admission pedestrians US$2, vehicles US$3, www.flordastateparks.org/crystalriverarchaeological/

Crystal River National Wildlife Refuge

The reserve consists of 20 islands in Kings Bay. The bay is fed by the Crystal River. Since the water temperature rarely falls below 22°C/72°F during the course of the year; the bay is a good place for about one quarter of all manatees in Florida to winter. But what attracts the manatees, who are sensitive to cold, also attracts fishers, divers, snorkelers and tourists. Diving shops, marinas etc. in Crystal River owe their existence to the cute water animals. A special corridor for swimmers and divers was established at the spring basin of Kings Springs. The places where manatees come often are marked with warning buoys.

❶ 1502 SE Kings Bay Dr., Crystal River, www.fws.gov/crystalriver/

*Homosassa Springs Wildlife State Park

On US 19, about 7mi/11km south of Crystal River, it is possible to observe manatees without getting wet. They are astonishingly agile in their element – the manatees in this state park were injured and brought here to recover – and can be observed through the large windows of an underwater observatory. The 17m/56ft spring basin is also the habitat of various species of fish. The area around the basin is a birdwatchers' paradise.

❶ 4150 S. Suncoast Blvd., Homosassa, FL, daily 9am – 5.30pm, admission US$13, http://www.floridastateparks.org/homosassasprings/

Yulee Sugar Mill State Historic Site

About 2.5mi/4km south-west of Homosassa Springs the former sugar cane plantation of the railway magnate Yulee is open to the public. The sugar works were built in 1851 and have recently been carefully restored. An educational trail describes in detail the process of making sugar.

❶ SR 490, Homosassa, FL, 8am until sunset, free admission, www.floridastateparks.org/yuleesugarmill/

Chassaho-witzka National Wildlife Refuge

Located south-west of Homosassa Springs this 120,000ha/297,000-acre nature preserve is only accessible by boat. The sensitive ecosystem is a refuge to countless aquatic birds and many wild animal species (including alligators, racoons, turkeys, wild deer, otters, red bobcats).

❶ 1502 SE Kings Bay Drive, Crystal River, FL 34429, http://www.fws.gov/chassahowitzka/

A manatee in the Crystal River takes a deep breath

44mi/70km south of Crystal River there is a special attraction: Weeki Wachee Springs. Up to 600 million litres (158 million gallons) of water per day bubble out of the natural spring basin, which is more than 80m/260ft deep. There is also an underwater show by imaginatively dressed »mermaids« several times a day, which can be watched through the glass windows of a special underwater room. Around the springs is a regular amusement park with a petting zoo, monkey cage, parrot and reptile show.

❶ 6131 Commercial Way, Spring Hill, FL, daily 9am – 5.30, mermaid shows daily 11am, 1.30pm and 3pm, admission US$13, www.floridastateparks.org/weekiwachee, www.weekiwachee.com

Weeki Wachee Springs

This park near Weeki Wachee Springs attracts families with children above all. There is a water slide here and the river provides real jungle and wild water adventures.

❶ Commercial Way, Spring Hill, FL, late March – Labor Day daily 10am – 5pm, admission US$13, www.weekiwachee.com

Buccaneer Bay Water Park

✴ Daytona Beach

✴ H/J 3

Region: Central East
Elevation: 0 – 5m/16ft above sea level
Population: 61,000

Where fast cars howl and choppers sputter... The trademarks of Daytona Beach are a beach that is always busy, where even cars are allowed, and a world-famous motor raceway. Auto racing fans from all over the world and thousands of motor-bike drivers with their chromed machines meet here; students celebrate their spring break here as well.

It all started with Olds, Chevrolet and Ford

The love affair between Daytona Beach and the car is almost 100 years old! At the beginning of the 20th century Ransom Olds, Louis Chevrolet and Henry Ford raced their latest models on the 40km/25mi-long beach, which the Atlantic had beaten solid. Rich New Yorkers – there were no highways yet – had their horseless carriages shipped here so that they could really step on the gas for once. Speed records were made and broken regularly: in 1931 Sir Malcolm Campbell shot across the sand along the edge of the water at a fabulous 441km/h (274mph), the highest speed ever measured on that

It's spring break at Daytona beach

Daytona Beach

INFORMATION
Daytona Beach Area CVB
126 E. Orange Ave.
Daytona Beach, FL 32114
Tel. 1-386-255-4015
www.daytonabeach.com

DAYTONA International Speedway
1801 W. International Speedway Blvd.
Daytona Beach, FL 32114
Tel. 1-386-254-2700
Tickets: 1-800-748-7467
www.daytonainternationalspeedway.com

EVENTS
NASCAR Speed Weeks

Daytona 500
The auto races in February are the high point of the year. Reserving tickets early is highly recommended.

Bike Week – Daytona 200
Every year in early March way over 300,000 bikers of all ages in black leather outfits with their shiny Harleys, Hondas, BMWs and many other marques come to Daytona Beach for a boisterous meeting that culminates in the famous motorbike race that was first held on the beach in 1942.

Biketoberfest
In October bikers from all over the USA meet in Daytona Beach.

SHOPPING
Daytona Beach is not equipped for strolling and window-shopping. The only exception is Beach Street between Bay Street and Orange Avenue, also called the Riverfront Marketplace. Pretty clothing boutiques, galleries and antique shops can be found here.

Daytona Flea & Farmer's Market
2987 Bellevue Ave., junction I-95/US 92;
Fri, Sat, Sun 9am – 5pm
More then 1,000 stalls sell everything from fruit to clothing.

FISHING
Fishing from Main Street Pier – a relaxing and also social alternative to grilling in the sun. Rods, bait and licenses are available in »bait shops«.

WHERE TO EAT
❶ Anna's Italian Trattoria
304 Seabreeze Blvd.
Tel. 1-386-239-9624
Good Italian cooking. The home-made ravioli is excellent.

❷ Angell & Phelps Cafe
156 South Beach Street
Tel. 1-386-257-2677
Restaurant with delicious American cooking, also good wines.

WHERE TO STAY
❶ Plaza Resort & Spa $$$
600 N. Atlantic Ave.
Tel. 1-386-255-4471
www.plazaresortandspa.com
The best in town has 323 tastefully furnished rooms and suites, a great pool and an impressive lobby.

❷ Shoreline All Suites Inn
2435 S Atlantic Ave., Daytona Shores
Tel. 1-386-252-1692
www.daytonashoreline.com
The holiday resort offers clean and cheery suites and cottages with kitchens.

Daytona Beach

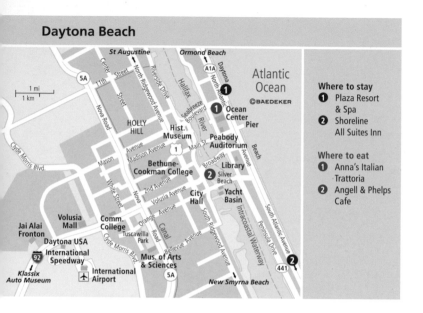

Where to stay
1 Plaza Resort & Spa
2 Shoreline All Suites Inn

Where to eat
1 Anna's Italian Trattoria
2 Angell & Phelps Cafe

beach. The natural surface was soon no longer considered to be safe, but only in 1959 could the National Association for Stock Car Auto Racing (NASCAR) move into the newly built 150,000-seat Daytona International Speedway. Races continue to take place here, including the legendary Daytona 500. But it is still permitted to drive on the beach towards the heat-washed horizon – even if only at a maximum speed of 10 mph (16km/h) and for an admission charge. Cars roll up to »their« place and are parked at a right angle not too close to the water – watch the tides! Then the grill and beach umbrella is set up and the beer comes out of the cooler – that's when you have arrived in Daytona Beach!

A city changes its image Since it was founded in 1872 Daytona Beach has gone through various phases. The last just ended a few years ago. At that time the city fathers decided that the reputation of Daytona Beach, which was strongly marred by the half million students who descended on it every year during spring break to drink and party, needed to be rescued and began an advertising campaign that was aimed at other target groups. The results were questionable: along with teenagers and students, tattooed motorsport fans – attracted by the many car and motorbike races all year – go overboard here. The run-down beach front made up of silo-like hotels and motels was beautified and people interested in culture might even be surprised at what is offered. But it will take some years before Daytona Beach has lost its image as a cheap vacation place!

WHAT TO SEE IN DAYTONA BEACH

People in all shapes, of every age and from every part of the country: the beach is up to 150m/500ft wide and seems to fade into the distance. One look and the world disappears. One of the beach's focal points is the 200m/650ft-long Main Street Pier on wooden piles. Fishermen can buy bait here in »bait shops« before casting their lines at the end of the pier. The Boardwalk, a beach promenade with many bars and t-shirt shops, runs several blocks north to south from the lively end of Main Street.

*Beaches

Beach life is the big thing, but Daytona Beach has some surprising cultural highlights. These include the **Museum of the Arts & Sciences**. The museum presents its varied collection in expansive rooms. It includes African masks, paintings and sculptures of early Cuban artists which were donated by the Cuban dictator Batista as well as the giant skeleton of a pre-historic sloth.
The **Halifax Historical Museum**, in a former bank with a classical portico, offers an exciting look at the speedy history of the city, which is documented by historical photographs.
The story of Afro-Americans in Daytona Beach and surrounding areas is depicted by the **Mary McLeod Bethune Foundation** with memorabilia of the civil rights activist who was born here. Currently closed for renovations.

Museums

> **MARCO ◉ POLO TIP**
>
> ! *Ride a Harley just once ...*   **Insider Tip**
>
> America's largest Harley-Davidson shop is at 290 North Beach Street. The classic motorbikes are not only sold but also leased here (tel. 1-800-307-4464; www.daytona harleydavidson.com).

Museum of the Arts & Sciences: 1040 Museum Blvd., Tue – Sat 9am – 5pm, Sun 11am – 5pm, admission US$13, www.moas.com
Halifax Historical Museum: 252 S. Beach St., Tue – Fri 10am – 4.30, Sat 10am – 4pm, admission US$5, www.halifaxhistorical.org
Mary McLeod Bethune Foundation: 640 Mary McLeod Bethune Blvd., current information: www.cookman.edu

4mi/6.5km inland is the holy of holies for American car freaks. The oval 3.5mi/5.5km-long racetrack is 13m/42ft wide and the curves have a steep incline (31%!), to make high speeds possible. Races are held on 10 weekends every year, with stock cars at up to 300km/h (180mph), motorbikes at speeds up to 270km/h (160mph) and go-karts with speeds up to 200km/h (120mph). Many other events take

**Daytona USA

Race cars on a hot track at Daytona

place here apart from the races. Tickets sell out quickly. Reserving early is recommended, especially for the Daytona 500. Local racing history is presented in the **World Center of Racing Visitor Center** in multimedia presentations (Daytona 500 Experience east of the Speedway).

❶ 1801 W. Speedway Blvd., tours 10am – 3pm on the hour, ticket US$23, www.daytona internationalspeedway.com

AROUND DAYTONA

Ormond Beach   About 6mi/10km north of Daytona lies Ormond Beach, which is characterized by modern apartment buildings and resorts and has a population of almost 40,000.

After Flagler's East Coast Railroad came and the Ormond Hotel was built in 1887 with its golf course, the town became a sophisticated oceanside resort where the American plutocracy of the day – Vanderbilt, Rockefeller etc. – met in the winter months. Incidentally: the first auto race in the area took place in 1902 not in Daytona, but on the beach at Ormond.

Further to the north a road leads off to the ruins of a plantation that was founded in 1821 by Major C. W. Bulow. Until it was destroyed in the Second Seminole War, cotton, sugar cane and indigo were cultivated here. Only the foundations of the manor house are left. A footpath passes by the former slave quarters to the ruins of the sugar mill. The history of the plantation is displayed on plaques on the grounds.

*Bulow Plantation Ruins State Historic Site

❶ 3165 Old King Rd., Thu–Mon 9am–5pm, admission US$4 per car or US$2 per person, www.floridastateparks.org/bulowplantation/

About 10mi/16km south of Daytona Beach the red brick lighthouse of 1887 rises to a height of 50m/165ft. Its platform offers a fantastic panoramic view. The former house of the lighthouse keeper has an exhibition on local seafaring history.

*Lighthouse

❶ 4931 S. Peninsula Dr., daily 10am–6pm, admission US$5, www.ponceinlet.org

Learn everything about local flora and fauna just a few steps from the lighthouse. Wounded sea turtles and sea birds are also treated at the station. The latest attraction is a pool where a stingray can be touched.

Marine Science Center

❶ Ponce Inlet,100 Lighthouse Dr., Tue–Sat 10am–4pm, Sun 12noon–4pm, admission US$5, http://marinesciencecenter.com

New Smyrna Beach (population 23,000), just 12mi/20km south of Daytona, is protected by a barrier island. In the second half of the 18th century Greek immigrants under the leadership of a Scots doctor tried to start a plantation here. The Scotsman named the location after the birthplace of his wife in Asia Minor.

*New Smyrna Beach

On the west side of town is the ruins of the New Smyrna Sugar Mill, the centre of a large sugarcane plantation from 1830 to 1835. After the army failed to move all of the Seminole Indians to the west of the Mississippi, Indians attacked the colony at New Smyrna in 1835, stole the cattle and slaves and set the plantation on fire. This was the start of the Second Seminole War.

New Smyrna Sugar Mill

This town about 25mi/40km west of Daytona has been spared from tourists so far. A New York manufacturer of Stetson hats, Henry De-Land, wanted to built a modern Athens in Florida in the 1870s and donated money to found a private university here in 1886. On the university campus an art gallery and a mineral collection can be viewed. The Museum of Florida Art on Woodland Boulevard has ro-

DeLand

tating exhibitions by famous artists. The Indian section has attractive basketwork and ceramics.

❶ 600 Woodland Blvd., Tue. – Sat 10am – 4pm, Sun 1pm – 4pm, admission US$5, http://museumoffloridaart.org/

De León Springs
About 5mi/8km north of De Land is the De León Springs State Recreation Area. On the property of a former sugarcane plantation there is a »fountain of youth« (a warm spring for bathing), diving, snorkelling, canoeing and a nature trail for hiking.

❶ daily 8am until sunset, admission: pedestrians US$2, vehicles US$6, www.floridastateparks.org/deleonsprings/

Spring Garden Ranch
A few miles north of De Land, on US 17, several hundred horses are raised on one of the largest stud farms in Florida. The racetrack on the ranch holds top-quality races in the winter half of the year.

❶ 900 Spring Garden Ranch Rd., De Leon Springs, Mon – Fri 8am – 3pm, admission by appointment only, tel. 1-386-985-5654, http://springgarden-ranch.com

✦✦ Everglades National Park

✦ H/J 7

Region: South-east
Elevation: 0 – 5m/16ft above sea level
Area: 5,661sq km/2,186sq mi

As is often the case, the prettiest name is the one the Indians gave to this region: they called the giant wetlands »Pa-hay-okee«, »Grass River«.

Always in flux
They also showed their excellent powers of observation. For, to be exact, the Everglades are not a swamp but a river that flows so slowly that the current can barely be perceived by the naked eye: the water in the 80km/48mi-wide but only knee-deep »river« takes more than a month to cross south Florida. The Everglades used to cover about one third of Florida, but in the north and east were drained to create farmland. Along its eastern border the land is cultivated right up to the boundary of the national park in places. At first sight this flat swamp and marsh landscape seems monotonous, lost, even boring. But its truly incomparable charm can only be seen up close. The most

Appears lethargic but is still wide awake:
alligator in a well-tempered natural pool in the Everglades

Everglages National Park

INFORMATION
Everglades National Park
40001 State Rd. 9336
Homestead, FL 33034-6733
Tel. 1-305-242-7700
www.nps.gov/ever/
Admission: pedestrians US$5, vehicles
US$10
Camping fees: US$16 – US$30

Everglades Area Chamber of Commerce
P.O. Box 130
Everglades City, FL 34139
Tel. 1-239-695-3941
www.evergladeschamber.com

SEASON
The best time for a visit to the Everglades are the dry winter months (Nov–
April), when the animals and migrating
birds collect near the water (brackish
lakes, canals, etc.). In the rainy summer
(May–Oct) the reed prairies are under
water. The migrating birds are gone, but
there are myriads of mosquitoes!

CAUTIONARY MEASURES
Caution absolutely must be taken when
hiking away from the permanent trails,
when camping or picnicking. Poisonous
coral snakes, black water moccasin
snakes and diamondback rattlesnakes
live here along with a type of dwarf rat-
tlesnake. Beware of the alligators at all
times, but also of the »cute« racoons
that love to inspect or beg for leftover
food. Feeding the animals in the park is
not allowed. There are poisonous plants
as well, like poison ivy (rhus radicans) or
poisonwood (metopium toxiferum), a
relative of the staghorn sumac. Physical

contact with these plants, especially
their sap, can cause serious illness. Insect
repellent is absolutely necessary.

ACTIVITIES   Insider Tip
In the national park canoes and kayaks
are the ideal mode of transport, and the
only way to see the animal residents up
close. The lengths of the canoe trails
vary from a one-hour trip to an expedition of several days. Everglades City and
Flamingo are good starting points. Canoes or kayaks can be rented for reasonable prices at the marina in Flamingo.
Other tour operators:

Everglades National Park Tours
815 Oyster Bar Lane, Everglades City
Tel. 1-239-695-2591
www.evergladesnationalparkboat
toursgulfcoast.com

Ivey House Boat Tours
107 Camellia St., Everglades City
Tel. 1-239-695-3299
www.iveyhouse.com
Ivey House B & B organizes paddle tours
through the mangrove forests of Ten
Thousand Islands, which are guided by
biologists and outdoor experts.

Shark Valley Tram Tours
daily 9am – 4pm
www.sharkvalleytramtours.com
Experts accompany the two-hour
tours from Shark Valley in off-road
vehicles.

WHERE TO EAT
Oyster House Restaurant $$
Chohoiloskee Causeway, Hwy. 29 S

Everglades City, FL
Tel. 1-239-695-2073
Seafood of all kinds is served in this old-fashioned fish restaurant on the Gulf of Mexico.

Camellia Street Grill $$
202 Camellia St.
Everglades City, FL
Tel. 1-239-695-2003
Nice little eatery on the canal; tasty sandwiches, salads and seafood, vegetarian dishes. Take the homemade key lime pie for dessert.

El Toro Taco A
1 S. Krome Avenue Homestead
Tel. 1-305-245-8182
Homemade tortilla chips, fajitas and burritos, attentive service.

Joanie's Blue Crab Café
39395 Tamiami Trail
Ochopee, FL
(about 500m/550yd past the Ochopee Post Office)
Tel. 1-239-695-2682
daily 9am–5pm
Classic swamp café, with stuffed owls and walls decorated with postcards from all over the world. The specialties are gator nuggets and seafood sandwiches.

WHERE TO STAY
Accommodations in or near the park are scarce and also simple. Near the park there are accommodations in Everglades City and Homestead.

Ivey House B & B $$
107 Camellia St.
Everglades City; FL
Tel. 1-239-695-3299
www.iveyhouse.com
Certified »green hotel« with 29 pretty rooms with tropical decor.

Travelodge Florida City $$
409 SE 1st Ave/US 1
Florida City, FL
Tel. 1-305-248-9777
www.travelodge.com
This well-run motel with 88 clean rooms is a good base from which to explore the Everglades.

Captains Table Lodge & Villas A
102 E. Broadway
Everglades City, FL
Tel. 1-239-695-4211
www.captainstablehotel.com
Simple accommodations with several clean rooms and apartments (kitchenettes for self-catering).

fascinating aspect is that minimal differences in elevation have produced completely different ecosystems. While mangrove thickets extend along the coast, inland there are salt grass steppes, where hardy cacti flourish. Wherever there is fresh water classic wetlands evolved, with hammocks as the only features on the horizon. These tree islands consist of mahogany trees, strangler fig and gumbolimbo trees. Only a few inches deeper, reed grasses up to 3m/10ft high, called saw grass here because of their indented edges, form an impenetrable thicket. In the north there are endless, spooky cypress swamps.

DRIVE THROUGH THE EVERGLADES NP (FL 9336)

In a different world

Everglades National Park is located one hour's drive west of Miami and was founded by US President Harry S. Truman in 1947. It is the only sub-tropical protected area in North America. Its animal world is just as varied as its flora: alligators and the endangered American crocodile live here. Wild cats hunt deer, and dolphins disport themselves in the mangrove swamps. Moreover there are 345 different species of birds. The road FL 9336, which begins a bit south of Homestead and ends in Flamingo on Florida Bay, offers a good overview. At the entrance to the park the **Ernest F. Coe Visitor Center** with exhibits, brochures and mosquito spray is a good place to prepare for the tour. It is the first of five visitor centres in the national park, which are each located in a different biotope.

❶ 40001 SR 9336, Homestead, FL 33034, daily 9am–5pm, free admission, www.nps.gov/ever/planyourvisit/coedirections.htm

Trails

Insider Tip

Several walking and hiking trails start after 2 mi/3 km. The 800m/2,600ft-long Anhinga Trail is a boardwalk through a sawgrass marsh where alligators, turtles, anhings (also called darters) and cranes can be watched. The Gumbolimbo Trail winds through a thicket of royal palms and gumbolimbo trees.

The **Pineland Trail** (11km/7mi west of the park entrance) runs through a fairytale-like palmetto thicket.

The **Pahayokee Overlook Trail** (21km/13mi west) ends at an observation platform over the »River of Grass«.

The **Mahogany Hammock Trail**, a walkway through a jungle of mahogany trees, begins 32km/19mi after the park entrance.

Just before Flamingo about a dozen beautiful trails begin. The 1km/0.6mi-long **West Lake Trail**, located in the transitional zone to the coast, winds through a mangrove forest on the shores of West Lake, a brackish lake.

The 2.6km/1.5mi-long **Snake Bight Trail** leads through a jungle of dozens of tropical hardwood trees, a paradise for bird lovers.

Flamingo with the **Everglades Flamingo Marina** is located at the end of the road and 60km/36mi beyond the park entrance: a restaurant and a hotel were not rebuilt after being destroyed by a hurricane. It almost seems as if more was going on here a hundred years ago. At that time Flamingo was a fishing village with three dozen houses on stilts: it is said there were so many mosquitoes that they blotted out the light of the lanterns. That no longer happens today, and those who come here want to »get swamped«. Excursion boats, kayaks and canoes are available for this, especially those at the marina in Flamingo (▶p.160). In fact paddling along one of the eight canoe trails around Flamingo is the best way to see the Everglades and its inhabitants up close.

Flamingo Visitor Center: daily 9am – 4.30pm, free admission,
Tel. 1-239-695-2945, www.nps.gov/ever/planyourvisit/flamdirections.htm
Everglades Flamingo Marina: Mon – Fri 7am – 7pm, Sat, Sun 6am – 7pm,
tel. 1-239-695-3101, http://www.nps.gov/ever/planyourvisit/flamdirections.
htm

THE TAMIAMI TRAIL (US 41)

The road across the southern tip of Florida was a cooperative meas- **The quick**
ure. In 1928 the two cities of "Miami and "Naples decided to build a **Everglades**
road through the »River of Grass«. The results was Highway US 41, **tour**
better known as the Tamiami Trail. Where once prisoners, immigrants and day labourers built the road through the swamp under the
protection of alligator hunters, the drive along the northern edge of
the national park takes three or four hours and leaves plenty of time
for sightseeing.

**There's much to see on a boat trip with the
park ranger through the amphibious landscape of the Everglades**

Important note: Along the Tamiami Trail airboat owners try to sell trips into the swamps of the Everglades. But in the national park itself, as in Big Cypress National Reserve to the north, trips on these fast and deafening propeller boats are not allowed.

*Shark Valley First stop: the Shark Valley Visitor Center. A 15mi/24km-long paved trail starts here and runs far into the seemingly endless freshwater marsh. On a bus tour guided by park rangers (▶p.160) alligators, otters, raccoons and countless varieties of marsh birds can be seen. But the view from the top of the observation tower at the highest point along the road is worth turning off for.

Alligator show in Miccosukee Village

❶ 36 000 SW 8th St., daily 9.15am – 5.15pm, free admission, www.nps. gov/ever/planyourvisit/svdirections. htm

In contrast the popular Indian village a few miles further west leaves rather mixed impressions. Miccosukee Indians sell pretty crafts at a few souvenir stands and picturesque workshops. Visitors are invited to ride the airboat into the swampy wilderness. And then muscular young Indians wrestle with alligators for the tourists and their cameras.

❶ Alligator shows daily 11am, 12.30pm, 1.30pm, 3pm, 4pm, free admission, donations requested, airboat ride US$10, www. miccosukee.com/indian_village/

A few minutes drive to the west is ***Big Cypress National Preserve**, the ecological continuation of Everglades National Park. Numerous endangered species of birds and animals live here, including wood storks, Florida panthers and snowy egrets. About halfway between Miami and Naples the Big Cypress Swamp Welcome Center at Oasis has information on ecology and the latest information on environmental protection   .

❶ 33 000 Tamiami Trail East, daily 9.30am – 4.30pm, free admission, www.nps.gov/bicy

Endangered Everglades

Since the 1920s large parts of the northern Everglades, which at that time still reached up to today's Lake Okeechobee, were drained in order to gain land for agriculture, especially for growing sugar cane. These measures have proven to be disastrous. The currents and the ecological balance of the »River of Grass« were effectively damaged.

For a long time the cultivation of this swamp wilderness was praised as a great technical feat by the U.S. Army Corps of Engineers. It was considered possible to fence in the rest and protect it in this way. But this point of view changed in the 1990s. The current faith in technology had overlooked the fact that this wetland lives from flowing water. Diking, channelling and above all overdraining are endangering the national park until today, as are the fertilizer and insecticides that seep in from the surrounding farmlands. Moreover the partial draining of the swamp has caused an imbalance in the regional climate: in Florida temperatures have dropped noticeably because flat land used for agriculture does not hold heat as well as wetlands.

Current Conditions

Efforts have been made for years to restore the current conditions and the ecological balance of the Everglades, for example by retention basins in neighbouring pasturelands. In 2008 the state of Florida wanted to buy up tens of thousands of acres of farmland between ▶Lake Okeechobee and Everglades National Park for about 2 billion dollars in order to renature it. In recent times new laws were thought up to protect the Everglades. The federal government contributed 89 million dollars from the Wetlands Reserve Program in July 2010 to renature agricultural land. This land is located in a corridor that has been marked for renaturing, which would in the future connect central Florida with Everglades National Park. This measure is supposed to improve the water quality in Lake Okeechobee and in the Everglades.

Uncertain Future

However, results are not living up to expectations: the politicians in Tallahassee and Washington are caught between ecologists on the one hand, and agriculture and real estate developers on the other. Half-hearted measures and laws that are modified later to benefit political lobbies are the result. Moreover the real estate and financial crisis of 2007 to 2012 have caused further setbacks in efforts to save the Everglades. Meanwhile more land has been bought up south of Lake Okeechobee for 1.75 billion US dollars, in order to more or less restore the natural currents. Influential circles, including well-known land developers, cal this a waste of the taxpayers' money. The bitter conflicts around the restoration of the Everglades continue.

*Ochopee Post Office	Near Ochopee, a town scattered through an area of bush, there is a different kind of attraction: the little white house on the edge of the road with a huge American flag flying next to it is the smallest post office in the USA. Tourists love to send their postcards from here. The staff keep the 900 or so Indians, hunters and fishers who live here in touch with the rest of the world. ❶ 38 Tamiami Trail East, Mon–Fri 10am–12noon and 1pm–4.30pm, Sat 10am–11.30am, free admission
*Fakahatchee Strand Preserve	To the west of Copeland lies a wonderful nature preserve, where dissolving limestone left long ridges (»strands«), which were transformed in the course of time to **extremely photogenic cypress swamps**. The main entrance to this preservation area is a few minutes' drive to the west on the Tamiami Trail. A narrow half-mile-long planked walkway leads through the almost tropical jungle to an observation point, from where alligators, turtles and many kinds of birds can be seen. ❶ 137 Coastline Drive, Copeland, daily 8am until sunset, free admission, www.floridastateparks.org/fakahatcheestrand/
Everglades City	Everglades City (population 500), the self-appointed »Gateway to the Ten Thousand Islands«, is located to the south. The small hamlet surrounded on the north-west boundary of Everglades National Park is a good starting point for expeditions into the park. Boat trips through the **Ten Thousand Islands**, the mangrove labyrinth to the west, are on offer here. Canoes and kayaks bring you even closer, with or without a guide. However, choose wisely among the many tour guides! ❶ Gulf Coast Visitor Center, 815 Oyster Bar Lane, Everglades City, FL 34139, mid April–mid Nov 9am–4.30pm mid Nov–mid April 8am–4.30pm: free admission, www.nps.gov/ever/planyourvisit/gcdirections.htm

* Florida Keys

—————————————— ✦ H/J 7/8

Region: South-east
Elevation: 0 – 3m/10ft above sea level
Population: 80,000

Off the southern coast of Florida the USA ends in the form of an archipelago of droplets, the Florida Keys. There are over 400 islands, 30 of which are connected by the spectacular Overseas Highway. The Keys are a world of their own. The spirit of the Keys can already be breathed in on the spectacular road over the ocean. But anyone who wants to inhale it deeply has to go to the Back Country, to the islands that are only accessible by boat with their wonderful, tropically colourful underwater world.

Highlights Florida Keys

Juan Ponce de León, in 1513 the first European known to have visited these shallow waters, will hardly have noticed the brilliant reef
dwellers. As a devout Catholic he named the coral islands that rise
out of emerald green water »Los Martíres«: they reminded him –
probably at a distance – of suffering people. During the next 300
years the Keys – the word derives from the Spanish word »cayo« for
a reef or cliff – were a refuge for pirates. Only around 1800 did settlement begin on the larger islands. Fishing and »wrecking«, i.e. salvaging and hocking goods from ships that broke up on the reefs, brought
money in – so much that Key West was the richest city in the USA
for a short time around 1850.

*Reefs and
cliffs in
emerald-
green water*

Up to the 20th century the Keys were accessible only by ship; then
came **Henry Flagler**. »All we have to do«, the railway mogul is supposed to have said, »is to set one cement pylon after another, and
we'll get to Key West in a hurry.« It wasn't that simple, but on 22
January 1912 the East Coast Railroad brought its 83-year old boss to
Key West. For the next 20 years »Flagler's Folly« connected the Keys
to the rest of the world. In 1935 a hurricane destroyed the causeway,
but the islanders' new isolation did not hold long. Two and a half
years later, on the ruins of the Flagler railway, US 1, a 113mi/182km-
long **Overseas Highway** with 42 short or long bridges, was opened.
And the tourists soon followed. The »Conches«, as the islanders are
called, still live from tourism. Millions of tourists follow the highway
every year to the Keys – with consequences for the animal world. Sea
turtles, manatee and coral reefs are endangered by sailors; the delicate Key deer, which exist only here, by drivers of cars. The greatest
danger, global warming, remains invisible for the present. It will take
a few years before the rising level of the ocean visibly starts to gnaw
at the islands. Until then the Keys will remain a paradise for water

sports, fishers and loafers, and Key West, the southernmost city of mainland USA, will remain America's most liberal venue for artists and drop-outs.

For a trip to the Keys from Florida's main city ▶Miami, allow at least three days. The directions are child's play: the Overseas Highway is the only through road. It begins in Florida City and ends in ▶Key West. Little green markers on the right-hand edge of the road, called mile markers (MM), show the remaining distance to Key West.

UPPER KEYS

The Upper Keys are the islands furthest to the north of the entire chain. The largest – Key Largo, Tavernier and Islamorada – are a weekend venue for many people from the Miami area for diving and fishing, and are pretty well overrun by tourists. However, there are also worthwhile sights here.

The island of Key Largo has an area of 31 sq km/12 sq mi and a population of 10,500. The main town has the same name and a few hotels and motels.

Key Largo

John Pennekamp Coral Reef State Park is run very professionally. It was established in 1963 and named after an editor of the Miami Herald who fought for the protection of the Keys, and is the first underwater nature preserve in the USA; it includes the coral reef that reaches to Key West. The millennia-old coral deposits are home to a colourful hodge-podge world of tropical underwater flora and fauna. These can be seen from glass-bottom boats or on diving or snorkelling tours. The mangrove forests in the nature preserve are best explored in a kayak or canoe.

**John Pennekamp SP

❶ Key Largo, MM 102.5, daily 8am until sunset, Visitor Center daily 8am – 5pm, admission US$8 per car or US$2 per person, www.floridastateparks.org/pennekamp/

MARCO ⊕ POLO TIP

! *For diving honeymooners* **Insider Tip**

Room service, pizza delivery and the daily newspaper in the morning: nothing special in a hotel. But in Emerald Lagoon off Key Largo all of this is available several feet underwater. Jules' Undersea Lodge, an underwater research station from the 1970s, has two comfortable bedrooms and a salon, and it is especially popular among divers on a honeymoon. Diving lessons are available, too, of course. Address: 51 Shoreland Drive, Key Largo, tel. (305) 451-2353, www.jul.com

Wonders of modern engineering: both the old Overseas Highway (right) and the modern Seven-Mile-Bridge (left)

Upper Keys

INFORMATION
Key Largo Visitor Center
Milemarker 106
Key Largo, FL 33036
Tel. 1-305-451-4747
www.keylargo.org

Islamorada Visitor Center
Milemarker 82.5
Islamorada, FL 33036
Tel. 1-305-664-4503
www.islamoradachamber.com

ACTIVITIES WITH DOLPHINS
Along with the boating, diving and snorkelling tours that the park administration offers there are numerous tour companies in Key Largo that offer programmes with dolphins.

Florida Bay Outfitters
MM 104, tel. 1-305-451-3018
www.kayakfloridakeys.com
Tours through John Pennekamp Coral Reef State Park

Theater of the Seas
Theater of the Sea MM 84.5
Tel. 1-305-451-1993
www.theaterofthesea.com
Swimming with dolphins.

Dolphins Plus
31 Corrine Place, Key Largo
Tel. 1 305 4 51 19 93
www.dolphinsplus.com
Swimming with dolphins

BOATING AND FISHING TOURS
Boating is the most popular activity here. Dozens of rental agencies at Robbie's Pier in Islamorada as well as along the Overseas Highway hire out boats of every size and type. Twice a day the glassbootim boat »Key Largo Looker« starts from Pilot House Marina.

WHERE TO EAT
Whale Harbor Seafood Buffet $$$ **Insider Tip**
MM 83,5, Islamorada, FL
Tel. 1-305-664-4955 Ext. 205
Oysters, crabs, lobster, shrimp, clams and fish soup with cold and warm appetizers.

Harriette's Restaurant
MM 95.7, Key Largo, FL
Tel. 1-305-852-8689
Harriett likes to greet her guests personally in her simple canteen. Good breakfast, hearty lunches, fine dinner.

WHERE TO STAY
Holiday Inn Key Largo
MM 100
Key Largo; FL
Tel. 1-305-451-2121
www.holidayinnkeylargo.com
Beautiful holiday hotel with 130 rooms and suites, its own marina and extensive selection of water sports.

Banana Bay Resort & Marina $$$
4590 Overseas Highway
MM 49.5
Tel.1-305-743-3500
www.tavernierhotel.com
Nice accommodation, also for families with children, many banyan trees and palms; wonderfully kitschy restaurant.

Isn' it beautiful? A nice place near Islamorada.

Tavernier

At the edge of Tavernier, a village of 2,000 nestled sleepily among palmetto and hibiscus brush on the island of the same name, the **Florida Keys Wild Bird Rehabilitation Center** is a little difficult to spot. Wounded wild birds are kept here after altercations with cars or motorboats and nursed by volunteers. Take a stroll through Tavernier's restored old city, which goes back 100 years to the time of the pineapple plantations, and a coffee break in the pink Tavernier Hotel, which started life as a cinema and was the hospital for hurricane victims in 1935. Not far away is Harry Harris Park (MM 92.5), a pretty site with a beach, picnic grounds and live music on the weekends. Florida Keys Wild Bird Center: MM 93.6, daily 8am until sunset, free admission, www.fkwbc.org

Islamorada

Beyond Tavernier the Keys Plantation, Windley, Upper and Lower Matecumbe are usually known under the combined name Islamorada and have a population of 7,000. If sports fishing is popular in the

Florida Reef Tract

The Florida Reef Tract off the southeastern coast of Florida is the world's third largest barrier coral reef after the Australian Great Barrier Reef and the Central American Belize Barrier Reef. Ther reef banks reach from Biscayne Bay near Miami to the south-west for 240km/140mi and include the Florida Keys and the Dry Tortugas. The Florida Reef is the home of unusually colourful and varied sealife including alone 30 different kinds of coral.

▶ **Coral polyp**
The individual skeletons are branched like plants. There are often colourful polyps at the ends of the branches. The corals feed on microscopic plankton and other materials and trace elements that are carried on the ocean currents

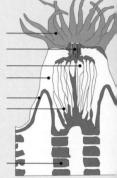

Tentacle
Mouth
Gastric area
Body shell
Ectodermic layer
Endodermic layer

Calcium skeleton

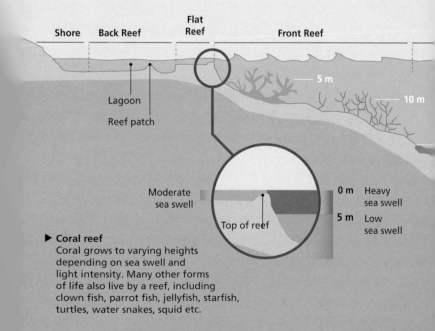

Shore   Back Reef   Flat Reef   Front Reef

Lagoon
Reef patch

5 m
10 m

Moderate sea swell

Top of reef

0 m   Heavy sea swell
5 m   Low sea swell

▶ **Coral reef**
Coral grows to varying heights depending on sea swell and light intensity. Many other forms of life also live by a reef, including clown fish, parrot fish, jellyfish, starfish, turtles, water snakes, squid etc.

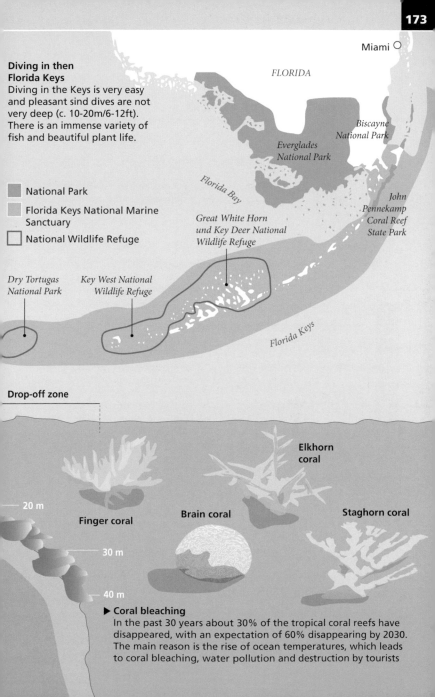

Miami ○

FLORIDA

Diving in then Florida Keys
Diving in the Keys is very easy and pleasant sind dives are not very deep (c. 10-20m/6-12ft). There is an immense variety of fish and beautiful plant life.

Biscayne National Park

Everglades National Park

Florida Bay

■ National Park

■ Florida Keys National Marine Sanctuary

□ National Wildlife Refuge

John Pennekamp Coral Reef State Park

Great White Horn und Key Deer National Wildlife Refuge

Dry Tortugas National Park

Key West National Wildlife Refuge

Florida Keys

Drop-off zone

Elkhorn coral

— 20 m

Finger coral

Brain coral

Staghorn coral

— 30 m

— 40 m

▶ **Coral bleaching**
In the past 30 years about 30% of the tropical coral reefs have disappeared, with an expectation of 60% disappearing by 2030. The main reason is the rise of ocean temperatures, which leads to coral bleaching, water pollution and destruction by tourists

rest of the Keys, it is omnipresent in this 32km/19mi-long part. Islamorada, the self-proclaimed »sports fishing capital of the world«, seems to consist of marinas, boat ramps and tackle shops. Motorboats (the kind with a seat and safety belt in the back) as well as fishing tackle with and without a skipper can be rented everywhere. The coveted prizes are swordfish or marlin, which decorate billboards, cups and t-shirts.

Theater of the Sea
Inevitably all of the sights on land have some connection with the ocean. The Theater of the Sea has put on dolphin and sea lion shows for over 50 years and also offers swimming with the dolphins.

❶ MM 84.5, daily 9am – 5pm, admission US$32, Swimming from US$175 on, www.theaterofthesea.com

Robbie's Pier
Probably the cheapest – and a quite unusual– attraction on the Keys is **tarpon feeding** at Robbie's Pier (MM 77.5). Ever since a compassionate shop owner named Robbie Reckwerth took in and fed a wounded tarpon 20 years ago, 80 to 100 of these fish, which can get up to 2m/6ft long and weigh up to 100kg/220lb, circle like minisubs under the water's surface and wait to jump for the herring that the tourists offer them. Robbie's Pier is also the starting point for tours to Indian Key and Lignumvitae Key, which have been left in their natural state and are protected as state parks. Florida can be experienced here as it was before the Europeans came. For loafing and swimming there is Anne's Beach (MM 73), a long, gently sloping beach with a beautiful picnic area.

> **!** **MARCO❋POLO TIP**
>
> *Relax!*
>
> By all means avoid travelling around the Keys on Friday afternoon or on Sunday evening! That is the only way to avoid the heavy traffic caused by holiday-makers from the metropolitan Miami area.

MIDDLE KEYS

*Marathon
Pelicans glide by at eye-level; the mini islands have wonderful Shangri-La-like holiday resorts. The Overseas Highway fades into the blue mist on the horizon: between Duck Key and Bahia Honda the drive over the ocean becomes almost surreal. But a turtle hospital and other interesting sights keep tourists on the ground.

Indians, pirates, white settlers from the Bahamas, Flagler's railroad workers, hobby captains and tourists: the happenings in the 10,000-strong town on Vaca Key during the last 200 years are documented in the **Crane Point Museum & Nature Center** in refreshingly critical studies. A sub-tropical area of woodland is also part of the museum and can be explored via a path of wooden planks. Other

Great catches can be brought ashore on the Florida Keys

residents of the Keys are protected in a former striptease bar: animal-loving motel owners converted Fanny's Bar into the **Hidden Harbor Turtle Hospital** in 1986 and care for sick or injured turtles. In the **Dolphin Research Center** care that is appropriate to the species is important: 15 dolphins live in a saltwater lagoon; they can be petted under supervision. The best spot for a picnic is Sombrero Beach, a beautiful, palm-lined beach with picnic benches and toilets.

Crane Point Museum & Nature Center: 5550 Overseas Hwy., MM 50.5, Mon – Sat 9am – 5pm, Sun 12noon – 5pm, admission US\$14, www. cranepoint.net

Harbor Turtle Hospital: 2396 Overseas Hwy., MM 48,5, tours daily 10am until 4pm every hour, tickets US\$18, www.turtlehospital.org

Dolphin Research Center: MM 59, Grassy Key, daily 9am – 4.30pm, admission US\$22, www.dolphins.org

Seven Mile Bridge, Pigeon Key

The 7mi/11km-long bridge from Vaca Key to Bahia Honda Key (pho-to ▶p.168) was completed in 1982 at a cost of US\$45 million. The

Middle Keys

INFORMATION
Greater Marathon Visitor Center
Overseas Hwy, MM 53.5
Marathon, FL 33050
Tel. 1-305-743-5417
www.floridakeysmarathon.com

WHERE TO EAT

Herbie's $$
MM 50.5, Marathon
Tel. 1-305-743-6373
Nice old-fashioned neighbourhood
meeting place for over 30 years: oyster
bar, fresh lobster, fresh fish.

Barracuda Grill $$$
MM 49.5 Marathon
Tel. 1-305-743–3314
Pretty bistro-style restaurant. »New«

American cuisine, with good fish dishes
and steaks.

WHERE TO STAY
Hawk's Cay Resort $$$
MM 61, Duck Key
Tel. 1-305-743-7000
www.hawkscay.com
Holiday paradise on its own island with
177 rooms, 230 suites, spa and 3 restau-
rants, all types of water sports, swim
with dolphins programme

Lime Tree Bay Resort Motel $$
US 1, MM 68.5
Tel. 1-305-664-4740
www.limetreebayresort.com
Nice rooms, suites and cottages be-
tween Marathon and Islamorada or on
the border to Long Key Recreation Area.

feeling when driving high over the ocean really is intoxicating. The
view of the old bridge built by the railway magnate Flagler, the middle section of which was torn down – it featured in the Schwarzeneg-
ger action movie *True Lies* – might inspire a side trip to Pigeon Key.
The island is accessible by bus (from Pigeon Key Visitor Center, MM
47) across the old bridge and until 1935 served as a camp for railroad
workers. Further information: www.pigeonkey.net

LOWER KEYS

****Bahia
Honda State
Park**

*Insider
Tip*

Too far away for weekend trips from the mainland and only a half-
hour drive from Key West, the islands between Bahia Honda Key and
Coppitt Key have had only a slight brush with tourism. This makes
them the best place to see flora and fauna. Paths through tropical
hammocks with palms, rare plants and exotic birds, mangrove forests
and the most beautiful beach in the Keys: right after Seven Mile
Bridge is a piece of postcard Caribbean. Boats, windsurfing boards,
diving and snorkelling gear can be rented at Bahia Honda Marina.
❶ 36850 Overseas Hwy., 8am until sunset, admission US$8 per car or US$2
per person, www.floridastateparks.org/bahiahonda/

Key deer live here. The somewhat shy miniature deer with a maximum height of two feet at the shoulder do not get much bigger than an Alsatian dog; in the thicket of the nature preserve they are difficult to see. Along the side of the road there is a better chance of finding one – i.e. one that was hit by a car. With about 800 deer the population has recovered well – when the refuge was established in 1957 on Big Pine Key there were only 27 of them. To find out the best places to observe the deer, ask at the refuge office.

**National Key Deer Refuge

Via Cudjoe Key, where US American TV programmes are transmitted to the Caribbean and Cuba by means of Fat Albert, a dirigible that is anchored high above the island, as well as via Sugarloaf Key and the naval air station Boca Chica the road continues on to ►Key West.

National Key Deer Refuge: 28950 Watson Blvd., Big Pine Key, FL 33043, tel. 1-305-872-2239, www.fws.gov/nationalkeydeer/

* Fort Lauderdale

✦ J 6

Region: South-east
Elevation: 0 – 3m/10ft above sea level
Population: 176,000

With more than 260km/160mi of mostly palm-lined canals, Fort Lauderdale rightly and proudly calls itself the »American Venice«. Countless artificial canals criss-cross the city and connect the Finger Islands, the exclusive residential areas with tropical gardens and private piers, which have been copied by many other towns in Florida meanwhile.

The times when hordes of unleashed college students turned the town upside-down during the spring break are over. Today the city at the centre of the Gold Coast represents the classic example of a successful integration of city and beach. There are plans to build several new resort hotels in the next years. Fort Lauderdale's port, Port Everglades, has now become one of the most-visited cruise destinations in the world. Greater Fort Lauderdale currently includes 30 towns and communities with a total population of about 1.7 million. The metropolitan area extends from Pompano in the north to Hallandale Beach in the south.

Centre of the Gold Coast

During the Second Seminole War in 1838 a fort was built here and named after its commanding officer. But the actual founder was a businessman called Frank Stranahan, who started a trading post and a bank here in the 1890s and built the first road to Miami. In 1896 Flagler's railroad came, in the 1920s the land boom. During this time Charles G.

City history

Highlights Fort Lauderdale

Rodes, an architect and fan of Venice, transformed the swamps into canals that ran parallel through the city. They form the basic pattern of today's canals, which criss-cross the urban area. Colleges all over the USA discovered Fort Lauderdale after World War II as the place to hold their swimming competitions. In 1960 this »youth movement« culminated in the teen movie Where the Boys Are, which put Fort Lauderdale on the map as a »party town«. Recently the city has become a popular holiday venue for families and financially fit Best Agers.

City and orientation
Many miles of palm-lined canals traverse the city. They not only connect exclusive residential areas, but also the office buildings downtown, the galleries and boutiques on Las Olas Boulevard as well as museums, theatres and nightclubs on Riverwalk. All the streets are numbered. Only the main streets that run through, like the large east-west streets between the beach and downtown, have names. The city centre is three miles (five kilometres) inland on New River and has excellent museums and an old city that is well worth seeing. Las Olas Boulevard reflects the zeitgeist with numerous small ateliers and boutiques. On the other side of the Intracoastal Waterway, Ocean Boulevard follows the white palm-lined beach for seven miles (eleven kilometres).

WHAT TO SEE IN FORT LAUDERDALE

Downtown
Even if the beach is irresistible, there are a few attractions between the sober office buildings downtown. A pedestrian promenade on

**Welcome to Fort Lauderdale: canals, marinas
and apartment buildings**

New River, the River Walk connects the Museum of Discovery and
Science with the IMAX 3D cinema with the Broward Center for the
Performing Arts, the city's modern cultural centre and theatre. The
museum, which is specially attractive to children, has hands-on presentations on ecology and high-tech. Where else could you programme a robot yourself?

Museum of Discovery & Science: 401 SW 2nd St., Mon – Sat 10am – 5pm,
Sun 12noon – 6pm, admission US$13, with IMAX US$18, www.mods.org

The oldest house is hardly older than the city's oldest residents. Frank
Stranahan built the house that was named after him in 1901 and used
it first as a trading post for the Seminole trappers. A little exhibition
depicts this time

❶ 335 SE 6th Ave., tours daily 1pm, 2pm, 3pm, ticket US$12,
http://stranahanhouse.org

**Frank Strana-
han House**

The main shopping street, between the art museum and the Atlantic, is
nicely decorated. Nostalgic gaslights, chic boutiques, galleries, antique
shops and countless restaurants, bars and nightclubs set the scene. At
the beginning of this boulevard, which is equally frequented by tourists
and locals, is the **Museum of Art**, a shrine to modern art with works
by such artists as Henry Moore, Pablo Picasso und Andy Warhol, a collection of paintings by the American Impressionist William Glackens
and many key works of the European CoBrA movement.

Museum of Art: 1 E. Las Olas Blvd., Mon – Sat 10am – 5pm, Thu until
7pm, Sun 12noon – 5pm, admission US$10, www.moafl.org

****Las Olas
Boulevard**

Fort Lauderdale

INFORMATION
Greater Fort Lauderdale CVB
100 E. Broward Blvd. Suite 200
Fort Lauderdale, FL 33301
Tel. 1-954-765-4466
www.sunny.org

AIRPORT
Fort Lauderdale/Hollywood International Airport is integrated well into the network of North American airlines and can be reached from Europe daily. The airport is served by city buses (Broward County Transit/BCT) and commuter trains (Tri-Rail). Many hotels and car rental agencies have their own shuttle buses.

CITY TOUR BY BOAT
Water Taxi
Tel. 1-954-467-6677
www.watertaxi.com
These water taxis run daily from 10am to all important attractions.

Carrie B. Harbor Tours
Ft. Lauderdale Dock
440 N New River Drive
Tel. 1-212-209-3370
www.carriebcruises.com
June – Oct Thu – Mon, Nov – May daily 11am, 1pm, 3pm, ticket US$23
www.carriebcruises.com
These boats run to movie settings and the villas of the rich and beautiful.

Jungle Queen Riverboat
Seabreeze Blvd., near Bahia Mar Shopping Center
Tel. 1-954-462-5596
www.junglequeen.com
Daily 9.30am and 1.30pm from Bahia Mar Shopping Center
This paddle wheeler runs daily through Fort Lauderdale's canals on tours with live commentary.

PROMENADES
The Beach Promenade between Sunrise Blvd. and SE 17th Street is the ideal place for strollers, the Beach Bar & Grill in the Sheraton Beach Hotel (321 N. Beach Blvd.) a good place for **Insider** people-watching. The River Walk **Tip** meanders along with the New River and is another mecca for strollers, as is Las Olas Boulevard.

SHOPPING
Las Olas Boulevard
Hard-core shoppers will find more than 100 luxury boutiques here.

Gallery at Beach Place
www.galleryatbeachplace.com
This shopping centre on Beach Boulevard has mainly ready-to-wear fashion (Gap, Banana Republic etc.).

Sawgrass Mills
12801 W. Sunrise Blvd.
Sunrise, FL 33323
www.simon.org
Mon – Sat 10am – 9.30pm, Sun 11am – 8pm
One of the top shopping addresses is a giant outlet shopping mall on the north-western edge of Fort Lauderdale with about 300 factory outlets and boutiques of famous designers (including Calvin Klein, Jockey, MCM, Nike, Sergio's). There are also diverse attractions for young and old, food courts

where delicacies from all over the world can be bought, and several restaurants.

Swap Shop
3291 W. Sunrise Blvd.
www.floridaswapshop.com
Mon – Thu 9am – 5.30pm, Fri – Sun 8am – 6.30pm
Largest indoor flea market in southern Florida with a giant selection from more than 2,000 sellers.

EVENTS
Las Olas Art Festival
Every year usually in January an art festival takes place on Las Olas Blvd. with artists from all over the USA.

NIGHT LIFE
❶ The Strip
The nightly entertainment route starts at the eastern end of Las Olas Boulevard and runs to Sunrise Boulevard on the beach. Here there are many restaurants, cafés, nightclubs, discos.

❷ Seminole Hard Rock Café & Casino
1 Seminole Way
Hollywood, FL 33314
Tel. 1-866-502-7529
www.seminolehardrockhollywood.com
The Indian reservation near Hollywood has lots to offer: there is a casino with a hotel, several restaurants, nightclubs and piano bars, which play everything from live jazz to rock'n roll.

WHERE TO EAT
❶ Johnny V's $$$$
625 E. Las Olas Blvd.
Tel. 1-954-761-7920
Rustic gourmet cuisine, e.g. pheasant

nachos or grilled bream with lobster and mango-cranberry chutney.

❷ Mai-Kai $$$
3599 N. Federal Highway
Tel. 1-954-563-3272
Kitsch from the pre-Mickey-Mouse era: a restaurant decorated like a Polynesian village, with hula dancers and fire-eaters

❸ Floridian $$
1410 E. Las Olas Blvd.
Tel. 1-954-463-4041
24-hour diner, called »the Flo«, for more than 60 years the best source for calorie-rich American breakfast

WHERE TO STAY
❶ Riverside $$$
620 Las Olas Blvd.
Tel. 1-954-467-0671
www.riversidehotel.com
The oldest hotel in the city (built in 1936) was recently given a thorough renovation and has an infectious Old Florida charm. It has 217 comfortable rooms and suites.

❷ Best Western Pelican Beach $$$
2000 N. Atlantic Blvd.
Tel. 1-954-568-9431
www.pelicanbeach.com
This popular beach hotel has 180 large rooms and suites.

❸ Tropi Rock Resort $$
2900 Belmar Street
Tel. 1-954-564-0523
www.tropirock.com
Nice hotel frequented by younger guests (30 rooms); only a 2-minute walk to the beach.

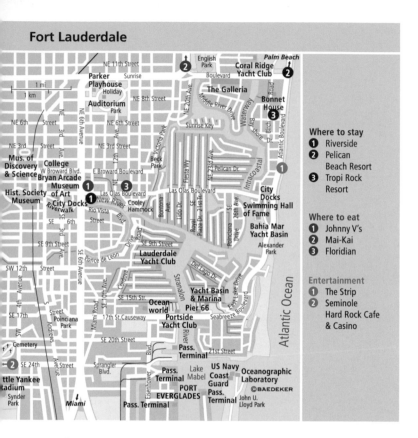

Fort Lauderdale

Where to stay
❶ Riverside
❷ Pelican Beach Resort
❸ Tropi Rock Resort

Where to eat
❶ Johnny V's
❷ Mai-Kai
❸ Floridian

Entertainment
❶ The Strip
❷ Seminole Hard Rock Cafe & Casino

*Bonnet House Museum

This house that is surrounded by box-like hotels gives an idea of what Fort Lauderdale looked like 80 years ago. Built in 1921 by the eccentric artist Frank Clay Bartlett in plantation style in a luxuriant garden on the ocean, it now houses excellent animal sculptures.

❶ 900 N. Birch Rd., Tue – Sat 10am – 4pm, Sun 11am – 4pm, admission US$20, www.bonnethouse.org

Int'l Swimming Hall of Fame & Aquatic Complex

All the big names in swimming are here, the Tarzan actor Johnny Weismuller as well as the swimming star Mark Spitz, who won seven gold medals at the Olympic Games in Munich in 1972. It includes an arena for swimmers, high board divers and scuba divers.

❶ 1 Hall of Fame Dr.; Mon – Fri 9am–5pm, Sat, Sun 9am – 2pm, admission US$8, www.ishof.org

Where students used to hold drinking binges and bikini contests during spring break, recent improvement efforts have transformed the place. Now skaters, bikers, joggers, Nordic walkers, volleyball players and above all families with children play here. Moreover street cafés, restaurants and boutiques attract strollers.

*Beachfront Promenade

SOUTH OF FORT LAUDERDALE

Port Everglades, the port of Fort Lauderdale, south of the city, is the deepest seaport between Norfolk and New Orleans. It was only completed in 1989 but since then has developed into the second most important cruise port in Florida (after Miami) with well over two million passengers every year. In the northern part of the port the modern Convention Center (1950 Eisenhower Blvd./S.E. 17th St.) with hotels and a large shopping centre was opened in 1991.

Port Everglades

South of Fort Lauderdale and the airport lies the town of Dania (population 30,000), which is divided by the A1A; it was founded in 1896 by Danish immigrants. Today Dania is a popular ocean resort with a beautiful beach. Dania's Main Street is well known for its many antique shops. And Dania's fishing pier is popular all year round with hobby and sports fishers waiting for a big catch. Everything worth knowing about big game fishing can be found out at the IGFA Fishing Hall of Fame (300 Gulfstream Way; hours: daily 10am–6pm).
❶ 300 Gulfstream Way, Mon – Sat 10am – 6pm, Sun 12noon – 6pm, admission US$10, www.igfa.org

Dania

MARCO ⊕ POLO TIP

! *Blue Jeans Blues Club* **Insider Tip**

Whether music lovers wear expensive Armani suits or worn-out jeans – if they love jazz and blues they meet here: 3320 NE. 33rd St., tel. 1-954-306-6330).

This resort was only established in the 1930s, but it developed explosively after World War II and today has a population of far more than 140,000. New buildings have changed its appearance markedly in the last years. The downtown area has been revived and now has many galleries, boutiques and sidewalk cafés. On the brand new Broadwalk along the beach the athletic, young and beautiful skate and bike.

Hollywood

In north-west Hollywood, on Seminole Way, there is a little Indian village. Here souvenirs and textiles that the Indians made themselves are sold, and Indian food can be tasted. A few older women demonstrate traditional crafts and young men show how to handle alligators and poisonous snakes. In order to earn money the Indians have built an ultra-modern entertainment complex: Seminole

*Seminole Okalee Indian Village & Museum

Hard Rock Hotel & Casino with a casino, several restaurants and a few clubs, which is popular among nighthawks from the whole region.

❶ Seminole Okalee Indian Village: Wed – Fri 9.30am – 5.30pm, Sat 12noon – 9pm, Sun 10am – 7pm, admission US$12, www.semitribe.com

**Flamingo Gardens

In the suburb of Davie south-west of Fort Lauderdale all Florida clichés have been put together in Flamingo Gardens: flamingos, alligators, a luxurious exotic plant world with beautiful orchids, Everglades swamp and orange trees. Pine Island Ridge Hammock is covered by ancient oaks with Spanish moss hanging from them and the Everglades Museum displays Seminole artefacts. A traffic museum displaying the typical Florida airboat and swamp buggy as well as a few old-timers is attached.

❶ Davie, 3750 S. Flamingo Rd.; hours: daily 9.30am–5pm, June – Oct closed Mon, admission US$18, www.flamingogardens.org.

A bird's eye view of the Fort Lauderdale beachfront

NORTH OF FORT LAUDERDALE

Not far to the north lies the popular ocean resort of Pompano Beach (population 100,000). The many canals are characteristic. Hotels, motels and other holiday complexes are strung out along the long beach. The 330m/1,000ft-long Fisherman's Wharf on the beach promenade is popular.

Pompano Beach

Further to the north Ocean Boulevard (A1A) crosses Hillsboro Inlet with its many boats. From Fish City Marina boats go out for big game fishing. On the other side a lighthouse of 1906 marks the entrance to the harbour. Numerous luxury villas line the beach.

Hillsboro Inlet

Butterfly World west of Pompano Beach is worth a visit. The gardens with roses and orchids are trying to preserve various endangered butterfly species. With a little patience thousands of colourfully glittering butterflies and other insects can be seen. Hummingbirds also dart around.

**Butterfly World

❶ Tradewinds Park, Coconut Creek, 3600 W. Sample Rd.; Mon – Sat 9am – 5pm, Sun 11am – 5pm

✳ Fort Myers

✦ **H 6**

Region: South-west
Elevation: 0 – 5m/16ft above sea level
Population: 65,000

Fort Myers is located at the broad mouth of the Caloosahatchee River in the Gulf of Mexico; it is the rapidly growing centre of south-west Florida. Anyone for whom the Gold Coast has become too crowded lives, works and invests here. Fort Myers became famous because the inventor Thomas Alva Edison once had his winter home here. Fort Myers does not yet have the class of its more sophisticated neighbours Naples, Sanibel and Captiva. Not yet.

Only 30 years ago, those who landed in Fort Myers had to carry their baggage across sun-dried grass to a shack of an »arrival hall«. In 1983 100,000 people flew to Fort Myers. Meanwhile Southwest Florida International Airport registers more than 5 million passengers. They go on to Fort Myers and a few other towns that only sprouted out of the ground in the last two decades. Not bad for a city that started life as a fort during the Second Seminole War; it only saw its first settlers after the Civil War and in 1885 had a pop-

How to become a »City of Leisure«

Fort Myers

St Petersburg, Tampa

Civic Center
Fairgrounds

Charlotte
Harbor

Gator
Slough Canal

41

75

Matlacha Pass

Buren Store Road

Bayshore

Diplomat Parkway

Bayshore Road

Tice

Pine Island Road

Convention
Center

i

Palm Beach Boulevard

Island Road

Boulevard

Del Prado Boulevard

Th.A.Edison
Winter Home

Anderson
Ave.

Hist. Museum

Pine

Matlacha

Trafalgar
Pkwy

Santa Barbara Boulevard

Club Blvd.

Henry Ford
Winter Home
Ecology
Park

2

Calusa Nature
Centre & Planetarium

Little
Pine
Island

Chiquita
Blvd.

Cape
Coral

Cleveland Avenue

Fort
Myers

Colonial

Blvd.

Page
Field

75

Flamingo
Bay

Boulevard

Surfside

Caloosahatchee

McGregor Boulevard

Ortiz Loop Road

Cape Coral Parkway

Cape Coral
Bridge

Daniels

Road

Pine
Island

Lakes
Park

Southwest Florida
Regional Airport

Gladiolus Dr.

41

St James
City

867

Alico

Road

Punta
Rassa

York
Island

Intracoastal Waterway

San

Carlo Bay

865

San Carlo
Park

Sanibel Causeway
(Maut)

J.N. »Ding« Darling
Nat. Wildlife Refuge

Periwinkle Way

Ft Myers
Beach

Estero Boulevard

Estero

Captiva

W. Gulf Drive

Sanibel
Lighthouse

Estero
Island

Mound
Key

Koreshan State
Historic Site

75

Sanibel
Island

1

Carl E. Johnson
Recreation Area

Naples

Gulf of Mexico

3 mi

5 km

©BAEDEKER

41

Bonita
Springs

Naples

Where to stay
1 The Outrigger Beach Resort   **2** Holiday Inn Downtown Historic District

Where to eat
1 Veranda

Fort Myers

INFORMATION
Lee County VCB
2201 2nd St.
Suite 600
Fort Myers, FL 33907
Tel. 1-239-338-3500
www.fortmyers-sanibel.com

EVENT
Edison Festival of Lights
A festival of light is held from late January to mid-February in honour of the great inventor.

WHERE TO EAT
❶ *Veranda* $$$$
2122 2nd Street
Tel. 1-239-332-2065
Right in the centre of town with very good, Mediterranean-style cooking

WHERE TO STAY
❶ *The Outrigger Beach Resort* $$
6200 Estero Blvd.
Fort Myers Beach
Tel. 1-239-463-3131
www.outriggerfmb.com
Friendly Sixties-style beach hotel with 155 rooms and suites and an informal Tiki Bar at the pool.

❷ *Holiday Inn Historic District* $$
2431 Cleveland Ave.
Fort Myers, FL 33901
Tel. 1-239-332-3232
www.holidayinn.com
Centrally located and yet pleasant accommodation with 122 cheery rooms and suites

ulation of about 350 people, who raised tomatoes and sold their cattle to Cuba. But everything changed in 1885. Thomas Alva Edison (1847–1931) went ashore here during a cruise – and fell under a spell. From then on, the famous inventor whose doctor had advised him urgently to get a change of climate, spent every winter here. Other prominent people, including the automobile manufacturer Henry Ford, followed him. In the 1920s the railway and the newly opened Tamiami Trail made tourism available to all classes in the south-west. Building continued here even during the Depression. It was only slowed down by the »Florida Land Bust«, and the town's growth continued immediately after World War II. During the 1980s it grew out of all proportion. But only a few of the houses are higher than the palms that Edison once had planted.

WHAT TO SEE IN FORT MYERS

Efforts are being made here to preserve historic buildings. An example of the style at the end of the 19th century is **Burroughs Home** (2505 First Street) In Peck Street Station there is now an **Historical Museum**. The part dedicated to the Calusa Indian culture and a his-

Downtown

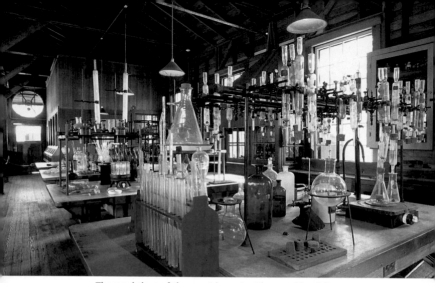

The workshop of the great inventor Thomas Alva Edison

torical model of the town are worth seeing. The museum staff also offer city tours (Wed, Sat, 10am).

Burroughs Home: 2505 First St., tours upon request, tel. 1-239-337-0706, ticket US$12, www.burroughshome.com

Historical Museum: 2300 Peck St., Tue – Sat 10am – 5pm, admission US$9.50, city tours Jan – April Wed and Sat 10am, ticket US$5, www.swflmuseumofhistory.com

**Edison &
Ford Winter
Estates

Fort Myers' main attraction is »Seminole Lodge«, Thomas Alva Edison's home at McGregor Road (no. 2350). Edison (1847–1931) came to Florida in the 1880s because his doctors had told him to spend winters in a warmer climate. At that time he was experimenting with bamboo fibres as the filaments in his new electric light bulbs. Bamboo and reed were abundant in this area so Edison had a holiday home built in 1886 on the Caloosahatchee River, where he spent the next 46 winters. A massive banyan tree marks the entrance with its tangled air roots. This was a gift to Edison in 1925 from his friend, the rubber and tyre manufacturer Harvey Firestone (1868–1938). Edison was not only interested in fibre but also in plants that contained latex, which could be used to produce rubber. The house is furnished as it was when Edison still lived here. The light bulbs are the kind that Edison produced in 1912. Edison developed numerous epoch-making technical devices in the workshop and laboratory. He registered more than 1,000 patents. The highlights of his work can be seen in the museum. Incidentally, the pine building materials for the house which Edison designed himself reached the Gulf Coast by ship. This makes Edison's house the first pre-fab house in America. Edison was responsible for another novelty: the swimming pool in his garden was the first in the southern USA. »Mangoes«, the neighbouring winter quarters of the car manufacturer Henry Ford (1863–1947), is also open for viewing. Ford, who was the first to produce cars on an assembly line, bought the estate in 1916 and spent the winters here near his friend Edison until his death. Ford sold the property in 1945. In 1988 the city of Fort Myers bought the villa and turned it into a museum.

❶ 2350 McGregor Rd., tours daily 9am – 5.30pm, ticket US$12, www.edisonfordwinterestates.org

The trademark of Fort Myers is Palm Alley. Royal palms imported from Cuba line McGregor Boulevard, which leads to the Gulf. The trees were planted in 1900 at Edison's suggestion, as he wanted to beautify the street that ran past his house.   ***Palm Alley**

Manatee Park Manatee Park east of town is a special attraction where several of these massive but peaceful animals can be watched in waterways and ponds.   ***Manatee Park**

❶ 10901 Palm Beach Blvd., daily 8am until sunset, Visitor Center Nov -- Mar 9am – 4pm, admission: pedestrians US$1 vehicles US$3, www.manatee.de/florida-state-parks/manatee-park-fort-myers/

Driving on the famous Palm Alley near Fort Myers

AROUND FORT MYERS

*Fort Myers Beach About 12mi/20km to the south is the Fort Myers' seaside resort on Estero Island. Here, especially around Times Square (intersection of Estero and San Carlos Blvd.), the activity never stops, due to the solid front of motels, fast-food joints and t-shirt stores. En route to the south the scene quietens down and the barrier island, which is 7mi/11km long, but only a few hundred yards wide, has some of Florida's most beautiful beaches. At the southern end a causeway leads to the island Lovers Key, which is still quite undisturbed. The 2.5mi/4km-long beach can only be reached on foot or by bicycle from the parking lot.

Insider Tip

*Koreshan State Historic Site About 16mi/25km south of Fort Myers lies the town of Koreshan on the Estero River, where a religious cult tried to realize its vision of the perfect city over 100 years ago. The members of the »Koreshanity« lived celibate in communes. They possessed no personal property. Their leader Teed planned a city for 10 million people; its broad boulevards were supposed to be 160km/100mi long. When Teed died in 1908 the community that he started sank into oblivion.

❶ Estero, South US 41/Corkscrew Rd., daily 8am until sunset, admission: pedestrians US\$2, vehicles US\$5, www.floridastateparks.org/koreshan/

Brown pelicans in Cayo Costa State Park

North of the Caloosahatchee River delta the town of Cape Coral is spreading out rapidly. It was only founded in 1958 and incorporated in 1970, but today it has a population of over 150,000 already. Cape Coral has the largest area available for development, about 300 sq km/115sq mi, of any city in Florida except ▶Jacksonville. From the very beginning the houses built along the many canals that criss-cross the city were mainly single family homes with yacht moorings. This explains the almost affectionate nickname »Water Wonderland«.

Cape Coral

The islands of Cayo Costa and North Captiva as well as a few neighbouring islands at the entrance to Charlotte Harbor have been made into a state park. These islands are accessible only by boat; they still look as they did when the first Europeans arrived here. Mounds of clam and oyster shells bear witness to thousands of years of Indian settlement. On the Gulf side of Cayo Costa and North Captiva Island there are wonderful seashell sand beaches and dunes. In the summer sea turtles deposit their eggs here. The mangrove swamps on the land side are one of the largest breeding grounds for brown pelicans in Florida. Ospreys, bald eagles and frigate birds also nest here. Tourists can rent simple huts on Cayo Costa; on North (Upper) Captiva Island there is a little holiday resort with a marina that is not part of the State Park.

**Cayo Costa State Park

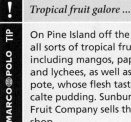

MARCO ⊕ POLO TIP

Insider Tip

Tropical fruit galore ...

On Pine Island off the west coast all sorts of tropical fruits flourish, including mangos, papayas, guava and lychees, as well as black sapote, whose flesh tastes like chocalte pudding. Sunburst Tropical Fruit Company sells them in their shop.

❶ daily 8am until sunset, admission US$2, www.floridastateparks.org/cayocosta/

This island, which has been taken over by wealthy Americans and Europeans, is accessible from the mainland by car from the northern entrance to Charlotte Harbor via FL 771 across a toll bridge. It is not certain if the island was named after a Spanish priest or a notorious pirate. Boca Grande, the main town on the island, is located at the end of FL 771; it has kept much of its original atmosphere. Nice restaurants have been integrated into the historical architecture. Boca Grande's main attraction are the seashell sand beaches as well as the lighthouse, which was built in 1888 at the end of the island.

*Gasparilla Island

This town of 17,000 residents, where Peace River runs into Charlotte Harbor, is the main town in an area that takes its character from cattle raising and fishing. In 1513 Ponce de León sailed into Charlotte Harbor and probably went ashore here. Spanish missionaries were active here in the 16th and 17th centuries; then pirates hid out here. Today's town was incorporated in 1885. Until 1904 Punta Gorda was

Punta Gorda

the terminus of the Florida Southern Railway. From Long Dock ships sailed for ▶Key West, Havana (Cuba) and New Orleans.

In place of the old pier on the banks of Peace River »Fishermen's Village« has sprung up. It is a complex of souvenir shops, restaurants, holiday apartments and entertainment as well as a yacht harbour. In the **Charlotte County Museum** fossils and remains of various mammals from the ice age are on display. At the west end of Marion Avenue Ponce de León Park commemorates the landing of the famous Spanish explorer in 1513.

Charlotte County Museum: 22959 Bayshore Rd., Tue – Fri 1pm – 5pm, Sat 10am – 3pm, admission US$2, www.charlottecounty.com/historical/
Peace River Wildlife Center: daily 11am – 4pm, admission, donation requested, www.peaceriverwildlifecenter.com

Port Charlotte

The area north-west of Punta Gorda was still pastureland until the 1960s. Today almost 50,000 people live in Port Charlotte. The artificial city was conceived for about twice as many, but it was strongly affected by the real estate and financial crisis. About 60km/35mi of natural shoreline as well as 264km/158mi of artificial waterways, most of which open directly into the bay, make Port Charlotte a popular place to live and to holiday for water sports fans. Port Charlotte Beach with its fishing pier extends out from the south-western end of Harbor Boulevard. From Port Charlotte take a boat trip to the islands of Useppa Island, Cabbage Key and Cayo Costa. Interesting boating tours of the waterways in the surrounding areas are also available (Babcock Wilderness Adventures or King Fisher Fleet, among others).

Fort Pierce · Port St Lucie

✦ J 5

Region: Central East
Elevation: 0 – 8m/26ft above sea level
Population: 41,000

The boom in the centres of the Gold Coast appears to have passed by Fort Pierce. The city at the centre of the equally unpretentious Treasure Coast lives from citrus fruits first, and tourists second – despite the yacht harbour right in the centre of town.

A new tourist attraction

Fort Pierce began as a military post during the Second Seminole War and only started to blossom after Flagler's railway came. There was a

Fort Pierce · Port St Lucie

INFORMATION
St Lucie County Chamber of Commerce
1850 Fountainview Blvd.
Port St. Lucie, FL 34986
Tel. 1 772-340-1333   www.stlucie-chamber.org

WHERE TO EAT
Mangrove Mattie's
S. Hutchison Island
1640 Seaway Dr., Fort Pierce
Tel. 1-772-466-1044

Fresh fish and seafood with a view from the terrace onto Fort Pierce Inlet.

WHERE TO STAY
Dockside Harborlight Inn $$
1160 Seaway Dr., Fort Pierce
S. Hutchison Island
Tel. 1-772-468-3555
www.docksideinn.com
Nice place to stay with its own piers, pool and a large selection of water sports nearby.

naval base here during World War II. Modest tourism began in the 1950s – the nice old-fashioned motels and the piers that reach far into the ocean bring back memories of highway cruisers and drive-in-diners. Since then Fort Pierce has developed the atmosphere of a working-class town. The nicely restored centre is unfortunately over-shadowed by the towers of a cement factory and there is a large water filtration plant at the edge of town. But that doesn't matter. There are still things to see on the way across the lagoon called »Indian River« and out to North Hutchison Island, a barrier island off the coast that has remained largely undisturbed.

WHAT TO SEE IN AND AROUND FORT PIERCE

He always said what he thought and was never averse to a fight. A. E. »Beanie« Backus (1906–90) was as rough as his town – and at the same time Florida's most famous landscape painter. Not far from the A1A across Indian River is the **A. E. »Bean« Backus Museum**, which is dedicated to the life and work of the painter who made Florida known throughout the world with his tropical subjects. A few blocks to the south there are free-roaming manatees in Moore Creek at the **Manatee Observation & Education Center**. A guided tour through the marine research institute Harbor Branch Oceanographic Institution, as part of the Florida Atlantic University, gives information on modern aquacultures and occasionally allows a visit to a research ship. The **Fort Pierce Inlet State Park** the southern tip of North Hutchison Island has beautiful beaches. Surfers also appreciate this beach. One of the most unusual museum in Florida is situated in

Fort Pierce

a round white house under palm trees: the **UDT-SEAL Museum** presents the work of the US Navy elite fighting troop as well as their undercover operations in the whole world. From World War II until the Vietnam War the elite units of the US navy were trained here.

A. E. »Bean« Backus Museum: 500 N. Indian River Dr., visits by appointment only, tel. 1-772-465-0630, mostly Sat 10am – 4pm, admission US$20, www.backusgallery.com

Manatee Observation & Education Center: 480 N. Indian River Dr., Jan – Jun and Oct – Dec Tue – Sat 10am – 5pm, Sun 12noon – 4pm, July until Sept Thu – Sat 10am – 5pm, admission US$1, www.manateecenter.com

Harbor Branch Oceanographic Institution: 5600 N. US-1, Mon – Fri 10am – 5pm, Sat 10am – 2pm, free admission, www.fau.edu/hboi/

Fort Pierce Inlet State Park: daily 8am until sunset, admission: pedestrians US$2, vehicles US$6, www.floridastateparks.org/fortpierceinlet/

UDT-SEAL Museum: Hutchison Island, 3300 N. A1A, Tue – Sat 10am – 4pm, Sun 12noon – 4pm, admission US$8, wwwnavysealmuseum.com

*Vero Beach

Vero Beach, a town of 19,000 residents, can be reached via the A1A, which traverses the length of North Hutchison Island, after 14mi/23km. Despite the fact that well-heeled winter residents have added a certain flair, Vero Beach has remained a nice small town with friendly people. Miles of beach on Ocean Drive, especially **South Beach Park** attract sun-worshippers and swimmers.

At the northern end of the island Sebastian Inlet State Park (only open during daytime) also has a surf shop and kayak and canoe rental. The thunder of the regularly breaking waves can be heard from far off. In the **McLarty Museum** exhibitions of remains and salvage from sunken Spanish galleons graphically explain the origin of the name »Treasure Coast«. The **Sebastian Fishing Museum** informs on the local fishing industry.

Sebastian Inlet State Park: 13180 N. A1A, daily 8am until sunset, admission: pedestrians US$2, vehicles US$8, www.floridaparks.org/sebastianinlet/

McLarty Museum, Sebastian Fishing Museum: daily 10am – 4pm, admission same as Sebastian Inlet State Park

Indian River

Still, dark and brackish, mostly only 1m/3ft deep, the so-called Indian River runs about 125mi/200km parallel to the Atlantic coast from New Smyrna Beach in the south to Stewart in the north – always protected by the off-coast barrier islands. The river, which is really more a lagoon, is especially shallow between Vero Beach and Sebastian and forms a labyrinth of marshes and islands, which provide a haven for countless varieties of birds. A channel has been dredged out for boats since Indian River is part of the Intracoastal Waterway. Parts of the lagoon have been reserved for different kinds of water sports.

The Environmental Learning Center (ELC), on Wabasso Island near Vero Beach in the middle of Indian River, reminds its visitors how delicate this biotope is. Open pools let visitors see typical local sea plants and animal life; a boardwalk leads through the thicket.

Wabasso Island

❶ Tue – Fri 10am–4pm, Sat 9am – noon, Sun 1pm – 4pm

Port St Lucie, on the northern branch of the river of the same name, is one of the fastest growing cities in the USA. Where cattle were pastured until 1958 and orange pickers worked, a town sprang up in no time and now has a population of 150,000. In 2007/2008 the housing development with marina, a yacht club as well as a golf course was strongly affected by the real estate and financial crisis.

Port St Lucie

The fishing port of Stuart (population 16,000) 18mi/29km south of Fort Pierce does not hide its reputation as the **sailfish capital of the world**: yachts and sports fishing boats as far as the eye can see. Countless fishers go to sea from this port after sailfish (Istophorus americanus) with its striking back fin. Stuart is also popular because of its historical centre, which has been carefully restored and successfully revived with restaurants, bars, shops etc. The shoreline promenade and the houses along Flagler Avenue and Osceola Street are picturesque.

Stuart

★ Fort Walton Beach · Destin

———————————— ✳ C 2

Region: North-west
Elevation: 0 – 8m/26ft above sea level
Population: 31,000 (metropolitan area: 190,000)

Until the BP oil spill it was true: what a beach! 25 miles/40 kilometres of fine white sand, flat, gently sloping beaches, emerald green water: year after year the readers of lifestyle magazines chose Fort Walton Beach as the most beautiful in Florida. Meanwhile traces of the oil spill have been removed and the beach looks good again.

The best part: 60% of the coast is protected by law from any building whatsoever, which makes the »Emerald Coast« deservedly the most popular section of the Gulf Coast in the panhandle. The consequence has been a boom over recent decades. But since June 2010 more and more lumps of tar and oil slicks from the Deepwater Horizon oil spill washed up on the beach, which had to be removed at great effort.

Tourism and military

All traces of the oil spill have been removed from Fort Walton Beach

However, the town founded in the 19th century by Civil War veterans on the west bank of Choctawhatchee Bay and located on highway US 98, which is unabashedly called the »Miracle Strip«, does not live from tourism alone, but also from **Eglin Air Force Base**, one of the largest air force bases in the world and right on the city limits. Generations of American pilots were trained here, for missions to the Near East and other zones of conflict. But they leave hardly any mark on the city, apart from a few topless bars, pubs and vapour trails in the sky.

History The coast around Fort Walton has been settled for about 10,000 years. In the 5th century BC Mississippi Indians raised the first mounds for religious purposes. During the Civil War the few white settlers who lived in this area formed the »Walton Guards«, who defended the eastern entrance to Pensacola and the Santa Rosa Sound. Some of them returned to the coast after the war and started the settlement Fort Walton Beach.

WHAT TO SEE IN AND AROUND
FORT WALTON BEACH

*Indian Temple Mound & Museum Drivers coming into town on Miracle Strip (US 98) passes a mound that was raised by Indians, probably in the 13th or 14th century, and is crowned by a reconstruction of an Indian cultic hut. The museum

Fort Walton Beach · Destin

INFORMATION
Emerald Coast CVB
1540 Miracle Strip Parkway
Fort Walton Beach, FL 32548
Tel. 1-850-651-7131
www.destin-fwb.com

EVENTS
Destin Fishing Rodeo
Every year in October a large-scale deep-sea fishing competition is held in Destin with lots of prizes. There are also lots of good fish dishes available to taste. Further information: www.destinfishingrodeo.org

WHERE TO EAT Insider Tip
Old Bay Steamer
102 Santa Rosa Boulevard
Fort Walton Beach
Tel. 1-850-664-2795
This restaurant, which is popular with the locals, serves lots of fish and seafood of the best quality.

WHERE TO STAY
Venus by the Sea $$
885 Santa Rosa Blvd.
Tel. 1-850-301-9600
www.venuscondos.com
Decent accommodation in a good location right behind the dunes.

associated with the site provides information on the infiltration of the Gulf Coast by Indian tribes, and displays Indian pottery from several periods.

❶ 139 Miracle Strip Pkwy. SE, Mon – Sat 10am – 4.30pm, admission US$5, www.fwb.org/index.php/visitor-info/

*Air Force Armament Museum

Anyone interested in the air force should go to this museum 6mi/10km north-east of town at the entrance to Eglin Air Force Base (access via FL 85). All of the US Air Force's weapons systems that were used from World War II to the Gulf War and the war in Afghanistan are exhibited here. A »Flying Fortress« from World War II can be seen as well as a B-52 long distance bomber, the legendary spy plane SR-71 »Blackbird« or an F-16 fighter jet. Of course, there are bombs, rockets and cruise missiles to see, too

❶ Eglin Air Force Base (access via FL 85), Mon – Sat 9am – 4.30pm, free admission, www.afarmamentmuseum.com

**Santa Rosa Island

A modern bridge on US highway 98 leads from the centre of town to the fabulously beautiful beaches of the barrier island; its eastern tip, which is outside the entrance to Choctawhatchee Bay, is called Okaloosa Island. Here too lots of new buildings have positively sprung up out of the sand.

*Gulfarium

Beyond the large bridge is the Gulfarium, which attracts many visitors especially in the school holidays and the high season. Here dangerous sharks and moray eels can be observed from a safe distance, as well as peaceful sea turtles and lively dolphins. A few penguins, sea lions and otters also play in the roomy pools.

❶ 1010 Miracle Strip Pwy. SE daily 9am–4.30pm; dolphin shows daily 10.30am, 12.30pm, 3pm; sea lion shows daily 9.30am, 11.30am and 2pm, admission US$20, www.gulfarium.com

*Destin East of Fort Walton Beach another massive bridge on US 98 spans the entrance to Choctawhatchee Bay and after about 7mi/11km it reaches the fishing village of Destin, which is bursting at the seams today; countless yachts bob about in its harbour and marinas equipped with every variety of fishing equipment. The entire spit with the old harbour on its western tip is covered with hotels and holiday apartments today. The main attraction is the History & Fishing Museum off Emerald Coast Parkway (108 Stahlman Ave., US 98). It exhibits a detailed history of fishing (hours: Tue to Sat 10am–4pm).

❶ Tue – Sat 10am – 4pm, in summer also on Mon, admission US$5, www.destinhistoryandfishingmuseum.org

MARCO ⊕ POLO TIP

!

What a deal... **Insider Tip**

8mi/13km east of Destin are the Silver Sands Factory Stores. In the giant designer factory outlet with more than 100 shops there are bargains galore, including articles by Tommy Hilfiger, Nike, Reebok (10562 Emerald Parkway/US 98; March – Dec Mon – Sat 10am – 9pm, Sun 10am – 6pm, Jan, Feb Mon – Sat 10am – 7pm, Sun noon – 6pm; www.silversandsoutlet.com.

Santa Rosa Beach, Sandestin Follow US 98 eastwards and the sand dunes of Emerald Coast will gradually disappear. What follows is a recreational area with an urban character. Massive high-rise complexes, endless shopping malls, broad highways, giant parking lots with golf courses and other sports complexes in between.

The conglomerate with its sugar-white beach is called Sandestin or Santa Rosa Beach; today it takes up most of the spit of land between the Gulf and Choctawhatchee Bay.

South Walton Beaches East of Sandestin about 50mi/80km of more natural beaches where the leisure industry is less obvious. This section is called South Walton Beaches. Here, at Grayton Beach, Seaside and the new towns of WaterColor and Rosemary Beach, which were planned for tourists, lazy holidays for every taste can be had here.

**Grayton Beach About 5mi/8km south-east of Santa Rosa Beach (via US 98) lies Grayton Beach, which is known as one of the most beautiful beaches in the entire USA. As early as 1880 the first wealthy retired persons from New England settled here. There was already a holiday hotel here at the end of the 19th century.

The first of the wooden cottages that are typical of the coast between ▶Pensacola and ▶Apalachicola were built in the 1920s. At the western edge of town comes Grayton Beach State Park with mostly natural beaches and dunes. Native vegetation can be found here, too, including low-growing, long-needled cedars, palmetto brush and magnolias. In the early summer sea turtles deposit their eggs in the sand here. There is a camp ground, a bathing beach with water sports facilities and a nature trail.

❶ daily 8am until sunset, admission: pedestrians US$2, vehicles US$5, www. floridastateparks.org/graytonbeach/

A few miles to the east the artificially planned holiday resort of Seaside is separated from the other resorts only by a narrow strip of green, and is also located on a wonderful beach. It was planned and built in the 1980s with the aim of making an exceptional holiday resort. Around an almost Baroque main square with pavilions, shops, restaurants and business services, holiday accommodation ranging from luxurious to simply rustic is grouped on lots of various sizes. Renowned architects from across the country have proven here that it is possible to build a modern beach resort without high-rises and

**Seaside

The fabulous sand beach at Seaside was only developed for tourism a few years ago

highways that cut everything up. Pastel-coloured, Victorian-style wooden houses with towers, bay windows and other decorations predominate.

Further to the east lies the holiday resort Seagrove; it is similar to but at the same time more modern than Seaside.

*Eden State Gardens

About 3mi/5km north of Seagrove Beach there is another opportunity to experience the atmosphere of the Deep South; on the eastern tip of Choctawhatchee Bay the wood industrialist Wesley built a baronial plantation-style residence in the middle of a park where azaleas and magnolias bloom in spring. The manor house still has its valuable furnishings.

❶ Park daily 8am – 6pm, tours every hour Thu – Mon 10am – 3pm; admission US$2, vehicles US$4, www.floridastateparks.org/edengardens/

*DeFuniak Springs

About 26mi/42km north of Grayton Beach lies the town of DeFuniak Springs (population 6,000) with its Victorian buildings by a romantic spring-fed lake set in the charming hilly landscape of the Florida Panhandle. It was founded in 1881 when surveyors had to find a route for the Louisville & Nashville Railroad. They named the settlement after their boss. The public library of 1887 as well as Hotel DeFuniak from 1920 are nicely restored buildings.

Ponce de León Springs

This nature preserve lies a few miles to the east. A karst spring is the focal point of this park; it bubbles out of the horizontally layered limestone and forms a beautiful pond. The famous conquistador is supposed to have stopped here while searching for the fountain of youth. Swimming, fishing and exciting hikes through landscape full of wild game are possible here.

❶ daily 8am until sunset, admission: pedestrians US$2, vehicles US$4, www.floridastateparks.org/poncedeleonsprings/

Gainesville

✳ G 3

Region: North Central
Elevation: 52m/165ft above sea level
Population: 124,000 (city) 260,000 (metropolitan area)

About 40,000 students give Gainesville the zest that makes it attractive to visitors. Apart from a youthful appearance and pleasant nightlife the university city in north central Florida also has a sense of civic duty: its programmes for fitness at the workplace make it number one nationwide in the battle against obesity.

More than half of the businesses in the Gainesville area take part in a fitness campaign – enough reason for the city fathers to call it the »most liveable city in Florida«. The Seminoles liked it here too: when Gainesville was founded in 1854, they fought bitterly against being relocated. In spite of the Third Seminole War Gainesville started to grow. Kingsbury Academy moved from Ocala to Gainesville in the 1860s and its incorporation into Florida Agricultural College later spurred the city's growth. In 1905 the college became the University of Florida. Science and the cultivation of citrus fruits went hand in hand from then on and remain important pillars of the university.

Oranges and students

WHAT TO SEE IN GAINESVILLE

In the protected Northeast Historic District there are fine examples of architecture from 1880 to 1930. From the courthouse that was built in 1886 on the corner of E. University Ave. and N.E. 1st Street

*Northeast Historic District

Gainesville

INFORMATION
Gainesville/Alachua County CVB
30 E. University Ave.
Gainesville, FL 32601
Tel. 1-352-374-5260
www.visitgainesville.net

SHOPPING
Oaks Mall Plaza
6419 Newberry Road
Largest shopping mall in the area

Tioga Town Center
105 SW 125th St., Newberry
Shops of all kinds are clustered around a new amphitheatre.

WHERE TO EAT
Paramount Grill $$$
12 SW 1st Ave.
Tel. 1-352-378-3398
Pretty restaurant, polyglot kitchen.

The Top Restaurant $$
30 N Main St.
Tel. 1-352-337-1188
Popular eatery, known for delicious fish and steaks

WHERE TO STAY
Magnolia Plantation Inn & Cottages $$$
Insider Tip
309 SE 7th St.
Tel. 1-352-375-6653
www.magnoliabnb.com
5 rooms, 7 cottages, lovingly restored historic house in the Second Empire style.

Sweetwater Branch Inn $$
625 E. University Ave.
Tel. 1-352-373-6760
www.sweetwaterinn.com
Victorian era style inn with 15 rooms

only the bell tower has remained. The classical-style Thomas Center (306 N.E. 6th Ave.) is used for exhibitions and events now. The earlier post office is now a theatre.

*Florida Museum of Natural History

An extremely instructive nature exhibition is located on the university campus in the western part of town. Biotopes typical of Florida (including savannah, mangroves, hammocks) are constructed in dioramas with explanations. The anthropological and ethnographic department of the museum with extensive collections on Caribbean and Central American native cultures.

❶ 3215 Hull Rd., Powell Hall; Mon – Sat 10am – 5pm, Sun 1pm – 5pm, free admission, www.flmnh.ufl.edu

*Samuel P. Harn Museum of Art

The university campus also has one of the largest art collections of the »Sunshine State«. The exhibits emphasize artefacts from pre-Columbian Mesoamerica, West African and Oceanian art, East Asian ceramics and also contemporary American art.

❶ SW 34th St./Hull Rd.; Tue – Fri 11am – 5pm, Sun 1pm – 5pm, free admission, www.harn.ufl.edu

AROUND GAINESVILLE

View into the sinkhole Devil's Mill Hopper

*Devil's Millhopper State Geological Site is located about 4mi/6km north-west of Gainesville. The sinkhole is 37m/121ft deep and 152m/500ft wide; it was formed about 10,000 years ago when the ceiling of a river cave collapsed. Stairs lead down into the sinkhole with its luxuriant vegetation. The deeper you go, the cooler it gets. As a result plants grow in the sinkhole that are actually at home in the Appalachian Mountains further to the north. The visitor centre has detailed information.

❶ Wed – Sun 9am – 5pm, admission: pedestrians US$2, vehicles US$4, www.floridastateparks.org/devilsmillhopper/

A side trip leads from Gainesville to the south (US 441). **Paynes Prairie State Preserve** begins at the city limits, a swampy grassland with several hardwood tree islands. This is what central Florida looked like 150 years ago: grassland spotted with hammocks and swamps and populated by many animal species. Bison, wild horses, wildcats, alligators and more than 270 varieties of birds can be seen here. There are hiking trails through the park and several observation towers.

❶ access: via I-75, exit 374; daily 8am – sunset, admission: pedestrians US$2, vehicles US$6, www.floridastateparks.org/paynesprairie/

With its Victorian houses, this town 11mi/18km south of Gainesville is the perfect example of a rural town in the Deep South. It was named after a Seminole chief and started in 1821 with a post office. Not much has changed since then: Micanopy, dozing under old oak trees, pleases the eye with classic Southern charm – and the wallet with many interesting antique shops.

*Micanopy

About 15mi/24km south-east of Gainesville lies the property where the American writer and Pulitzer prize winner Marjorie Kinnan Rawlings (1896 – 1953) lived from 1928 to 1941. In a typical Cracker-style wooden house under orange and pecan trees she wrote works like *The Yearling* or *Cross Creek*, in which she depicted life in the Florida of the 1930s. Ever since Cross Creek was filmed (1983) Rawlings' estate has become a shrine for her fans.

*Marjorie Kinnan Rawlings State Historic Site

❶ tours: Oct – Jul, Thu – Mon 11am – 4pm, park daily 9am – 5pm, admission US$3 per car and occupants, www.floridastateparks.org/ marjoriekinnanrawlings/

* Jacksonville

—————————— ✳ H 2

Region: North-east
Elevation: 0 – 7m/23ft above sea level
Population: 822,000 (metropolitan area: 1.3 million)
Area code: 904

Heavy industry, paper mills, large banks, harbours, military establishments: this major city in the extreme north-east of Florida has never been a classic tourist magnet. But those who look closer will see that something is going on. Galleries and hotels are opening, millions were invested in museums.

Locals call their city simply »Jax«, but even this nickname sounds anything but hospitable. Anyone who visited the city on the bend of the St John's River in the past, probably drove through quickly on his way to the beaches further east and ignored the anonymous forest of office buildings.

In the bend of a river ..

NORTH BANK

Downtown

The city centre has been renovated at a cost of millions. With new skyscrapers that glisten in the sunshine, including the Wells Fargo Center and the post-modern style 40-storey Bank of America Tower, designed by Helmut Jahn, the city now has a skyline on the North Bank. Several bridges span the St John's River and connect parts of the city on the northern and southern banks. The city's trademark is the Main Street Bridge, which can be raised to let large ships pass.

M Jacksonville Landing

Coffee shops, restaurants, street musicians, jugglers, body painters: this complex of glass, steel and sun umbrellas on the riverbank includes several dozen shops and various restaurants with a view of the river. Along the front of Jacksonville Landing the Northbank Riverwalk is a beautiful promenade from Berkman Plaza to Times Union Center for the Performing Arts.

*Florida Theater Performing Arts Center

East of Jacksonville Landing the Florida Theater Performing Arts Center glows after a refurbishing. It was built as a cinema in 1926–27. Painted terracotta figures and ornamental bands adorn the façade.

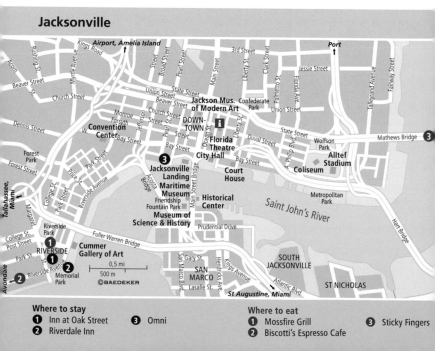

Jacksonville

Where to stay
1 Inn at Oak Street   3 Omni
2 Riverdale Inn

Where to eat
1 Mossfire Grill   3 Sticky Fingers
2 Biscotti's Espresso Cafe

The elaborately decorated theatre with massive beams now holds almost 2,000 guests for cultural events of all kinds.

❶ 128 E Forsyth St., ticket-hotline: tel. 1-904-355-2787, www.floridatheatre.com

Jacksonville

INFORMATION
Jacksonville & The Beaches Convention & Visitors Bureau
208 N. Laura St., Suite 102
Jacksonville, FL 32202
Tel. 1-904-798-9111
www.visitjacksonville.com

SHOPPING
Riverside is known for its urban wear shops. Cool shoes are available especially on Riverside Street between Lomax and Post Street. Avondale is more chic. Prada, Lily Pulitzer and Fantini are in boutiques on St John's Street between Talbot and Pinegrove Street. San Marco Square is a good place to look for antiques, books and CDs.

NIGHT LIFE
Many visitors tend to concentrate on the bend in the river downtown: Jacksonville Landing and Southbank Riverwalk, entertainment areas on opposite sides of the river, are the liveliest places in town evenings and on weekends.

WHERE TO EAT

❶ *Mossfire Grill* $$
Riverside 1537 Margaret Street
Tel. 1-904-355-4434
Spicy Southern food served in an amber-coloured designer ambience.

❷ *Biscotti's Espresso Café* $$
Avondale 3556 St John's Ave.
Tel. 1-904-387-2060

Lively restaurant with creatively designed bistro food and fine desserts

❸ *Sticky Fingers* $
Baymeadows
8129 Point Meadows Blvd.
Tel. 1-904-493-7427
Juicy steaks and ribs – with blues coming from the speakers and pictures of jazz musicians on the walls.

WHERE TO STAY
❶ *Inn at Oak Street* $$$
Riverside, 2114 Oak Street
Tel. 1-904-379-5525
www.innatoakstreet.com
Comfortable inn in historic Riverside. Some rooms have a whirlpool. A masseur is also available.

❷ *Riverdale Inn* $$
1521 Riverside Avenue
Tel. 1-904-354-5080
www.riverdaleinn.com
Beautiful Queen Anne-style residence with eight pretty rooms and a romantic veranda; generous breakfast buffet.

❸ *Omni* $$$
Downtown 245 Water Street
Tel. 1-904-355-6664
www.omnihotels.com
Modern city hotel with 354 rooms, only a stone's throw from the popular Riverwalk, with a heated pool on the roof.

Highlights Jacksonville

► **South Bank River Walk**
Stroll where wharfs and industrial complexes used to be.
►page 207

► **Jacksonville Historical Center**
Important periods in the history of Jacksonville since the first native American settlements are portrayed here.
►page 207

► **Museum of Science History (MOSH)**
Spectacular insights into science and technology for young and old.
►page 208

► **Cummer Museum of Art & Gardens**
Impressive collection with works by Albrecht Dürer, Lucas Cranach the Elder and Peter Paul Rubens.
►page 208

► **Jacksonville beaches**
Well-known seaside resorts with wide beaches – some exclusive, some informal.
►page 210

Prime Osborn Convention Center
West of Jacksonville Landing is the convention centre, built in 1986. This modern structure incorporates Union Station, which was built in 1919 to plans by the New York architect K. M. Murchison. The massive former railway station with its 23m/75ft-high dome serves as the luxurious lobby of the convention centre today.

Museum of Contemporary Art
Contemporary art is exhibited here in an eminently innovative style. International and American artists are represented in the collection, which has works by Helen Frankenthaler and Robert Rauschenberg.
❶ 333 N. Laura St., Tue – Sat 11am – 5pm, Thu until 9pm, Sun noon – 5pm, admission US$8,
www.mocajacksonville.org

LaVilla
When white and black people still lived in different parts of town, LaVilla was the black neighbourhood of Jacksonville. Its cultural centre was the Ritz Theatre, where many famous musicians performed. The Ritz only survived the 1960s passion to replace old with new after a restoration and facelift. The LaVilla Museum relates an interesting part of Afro-American history (829 N. Davis St.; hours: Tue–Fr 10am–6pm, Sat 10am–2pm, Sun 2–5pm).
❶ 829 N. Davis St, Tue – Fri 10am – 5pm, Sat 10am – 2pm, admission US$8,
www.ritzjacksonville.com

Skyline on the river with the city trademark, Main Street Bridge

SOUTH BANK

The south bank of the St John's River has been the site of the South Bank Riverwalk since 1985. This attractive area with top-class hotels, restaurants and three museums is built on a former wharf and industrial property. The promenade offers a great view of the skyline on the North Bank. The focal point of Friendship Park is the fountain, which is illuminated at night and whose water plumes spray up to 36m/118ft high. With a diameter of 200ft/60m it is the largest self-contained fountain in the United States.

**South Bank Riverwalk

The museum at the southern end of Main Street Bridge has displays on important periods in the city's history. The exhibits emphasis the Indian settlements in the city limits as well as the time when Jacksonville was a centre of the film industry.

*Jacksonville Historical Center

❶ 1015 Museum Circle, open by appointment only, tel. 1-904-398-4301, www.jaxhistory.com

Jacksonville Maritime Heritage Center   On the other side of the bridgehead there is another little museum worth visiting, with its exhibits on the history of seafaring in northeast Florida. There are interesting ship models on display here.

❶ Jacksonville Landing, Independent Dr., Tue – Fri 11am – 5pm, Sat, Sun 1pm – 5pm, admission US$5, www.jacksonvillemaritimeheritagecenter.org

**Museum of Science & History (MOSH)   This museum specializes in popular science and gives insight into the world of nature, history, science and technology. Next to the Science Theater and the planetarium the main attractions are the exhibits »Water Worlds« and »Atlantic Tails«, which are about natural history and several endangered species (including dolphins, manatees). The interesting presentation »Currents of Time« is devoted to the 12,000-year history of the settlement of northern Florida.

❶ 1025 Museum Circle; Mon – Fri 10am – 5pm, Sat 10am – 6pm, Sun 1 – 6pm, admission US$10, www.themosh.org.

*San Marco   This neighbourhood is located south of the Southbank Riverwalk and has kept its own charm. Many of the villas, which were built in the early 20th century – in part in art deco style and often right on the waterfront – have been skilfully renovated. The focal point is San Marco Square, where lifestyle and fashion fans will find what they want, as will fans of music clubs, bars and fine dining.

RIVERSIDE AND AVONDALE

*Riverside   Riverside was founded in the 1850s and rebuilt after a fire in 1901. It is located next to Memorial Park and is probably the architecturally most diverse neighbourhood in Florida. Especially around Margaret Street there are wonderful examples of the Mediterranean Revival as well as colonial and neo-classical styles. Riverside Baptist Church, with its elements of Byzantine and Romanesque style, is especially impressive. It was built on Park Street in 1925 to plans by the renowned architect Addison Mizner from Palm Beach.

> **!** *Relax* **Insider Tip**
>
> MARCO ● POLO TIP
>
> Not far to the west of the museum, also on Riverside Avenue, is the pretty Bohemian quarter named »Five Points« with several nice cafés and bistros

The cultural centre of the neighbourhood is this pretty art museum, which is located in a beautiful park on the western end of Fuller Warren Bridge (I-95). It is housed in

**Cummer Museum of Art & Gardens   the late 19th-century baronial villa of a lumber magnate. The collection is based on the art collection of the Cummer family. The spectrum covers everything from pre-Columbian art to Egyptian,

Greek and Roman antiquity and European art of the 15th to 19th centuries. The showpieces are works by Albrecht Dürer, Lucas Cranach the Elder and Peter Paul Rubens (Lamentation of Christ). The collection of Meissen porcelain and the East Asian art objects are also worth seeing.

❶ 829 Riverside Ave.; Tue and Thu 10am – 9pm, Wed, Fri, Sat 10am – 5pm, Sun noon – 5pm, admission US$10 (Thu free admission), www.cummer.org

Riverside Avenue turns into St Johns Avenue further south and after 2.5mi/4km it reaches Avondale. It was designed in 1920 by Telfair Stockton as a neighbourhood for wealthy citizens and is still dominated by a small elite. The upper-class neighbourhood still has the atmosphere of the good old days at exhibition openings etc. ***Avondale**

OTHER ATTRACTIONS IN JACKSONVILLE

The campus of the university, which was founded in 1934, is spread out on the eastern banks of the St John's River. Important facilities include a centre for marine research, the Historic Society Library and especially the **Alexander Brest Museum**, which exhibits pre-Columbian art, ceramics, porcelain and glass from Europe and ivory carvings from the Far East. **Jacksonville University**

Alexander Brest Museum: in the Phillips Fine Arts Bldg., Mon – Thu 9am until, free admission, www.ju.edu/aboutju/pages/alexander-brest.aspx

Jacksonville Zoo lies in the northern part of the city along the Trout River and is worth a visit. Zebras, gazelles and lions roam in the »African Loop«; in the »Great Apes Range« area gorillas, chimpanzees and other primates show off. The animal world of Central and South America can be seen in »Range of the Jaguar«; in the »Wild Florida« there are alligators and manatees. ***Jacksonville Zoo**

❶ 370 Zoo Pkwy; daily 9am – 5pm, admission US$15, www.jacksonvillezoo.com

The production site of the world's largest brewery business is also in the north of Jacksonville. They produce eight million hectolitres (211 million gallons) annually. A large part of southern USA is served from here. **Anheuser-Busch Brewery**

❶ 111 Busch Dr.; tours with tasting (minimum age 21 years): Mon – Sat 10am – 4pm, free admission, taking part in a seminar at the Beer School US$10, www.budweisertours.com/z01/index.php/jacksonville/overview/

About 10mi/16km east of the city a replica of a wooden fort in the Timucuan Ecological & Historic Preserve on the banks of St John's River commemorates the French Huguenots, who built a ***Fort Caroline** base here in 1564 with the permission of the local Timucuan Indians.

Timucuan Ecological & Historic Preserve: daily 9am – 5pm, free admission, www.nps.gov/timu/

Mayport North-east of downtown Jacksonville is Mayport, a small former fishing village. The harbour is a starting point for deep-sea fishing tours. Mayport Naval Station is now one of the largest naval bases on the American eastern seaboard. The aircraft carriers and squadrons of the 6th fleet are stationed here.

Fort George Island, Kingsley Plantation A ferry runs from Mayport to Fort George Island, one of the swampy islands in the mouth of the St John's River.

In the 16th century the Spanish built a mission here. In 1730, when British troops entered Florida, the island got its present name. The governor of Georgia had the fort built. Toward the end of Spanish colonial rule three Americans started plantations here to raise cotton, sugar cane and oranges, including Kingsley Plantation. It is one of the few surviving examples of this type of estate in the south-east United States. The plantation was named after the planter Zephaniah Kingsley and consists of a main house, the cook house and the ruins of 25 of the slaves' quarters. Kingsley, who ran the plantation from 1819 to 1839, was married to a freed slave and business woman. He went with her to Haiti when the USA took over Florida and the slave laws became more restrictive.

BEACHES AROUND JACKSONVILLE

**Jacksonville Beaches South of the mouth of the St John's River there is a line of well-known seaside resorts stretching for 30km/18mi. They have names like Jacksonville Beach, Atlantic Beach and Neptune Beach. Jacksonville Beach, only a 20-minute drive east of downtown Jacksonville, offers all of the benefits of a tourist resort. The Seawalk and Seawalk Plaza, among other places, with their pretty shops and restaurants, grew out of a renovation programme. The 360m/1,180ft Jacksonville Pier, which is illuminated at night, is a popular meeting place for fishers and strollers. Directly adjacent to the south is Ponte Vedra Beach, where exclusive villas and beach houses stand today. Golfers, too, can fulfil their wishes here: the Saw Grass Country Club Course is one of the best of its kind in Florida.

? MARCO ⊕ POLO INSIGHT

La Florida

At South Ponte Vedra Beach, which ends just north of St Augustine, the Spanish conquistador Ponce de León landed and named the newly discovered land »La Florida«. He believed all of his life that he had discovered a large island.

* Key West

————————————————— ✳ H 8

Region: South-east
Elevation: 0 – 7m/23ft above sea level
Population: 25,000

In Key West the Overseas Highway ends between flourishing bougainvillea and pastel-coloured Bahamas architecture. »Mainstream America« ends here too. What remains is a sensual still-life composed of shady verandas, free-roaming chickens and cats, dogs dozing under cars and streets named Caroline or Angela. Even the party zone Duval Street seems more Caribbean than US American.

The first Spaniards to sail by this bone-hard and bone-dry coral island named it Cayo Huesco (Bone Island). When the Americans took over, they misunderstood Cayo Huesco as Key West. The southernmost island of the Florida Keys, only 90mi/145km north of Cuba, is the southernmost point of continental USA and also one of its strategically most sensitive places.

Cayo Huesco used to be a notorious pirates' nest. In 1845 Key West was an important port and the »Conches«, island residents who had come from the Bahamas, lived well from salvaging stranded goods. Around 1870 Key West was Florida's largest and richest city. The stately »Conch« homes today testify to the wealth of the »shipwreckers« and merchant captains. This all changed at the turn of the 20th century. Tourism gradually developed into the most important

From pirates' nest to tourist stronghold

Highlights Key West

▶ **Old Town**
Brightly painted wooden houses dating from the 19th century.
▶page 215

▶ **Sunset on Mallory Square**
Especially beautiful sunsets are still greeted with applause. Acrobats and musicians shorten the wait with lively entertainment.
▶page 215

▶ **Mel Fisher Maritime Heritage Museum**
Bloodthirsty pirate stories brought up from the briny deep.
▶page 215

▶ **Ernest Hemingway Home & Museum**
One of the most famous writers of the 20th century lived, wrote, boxed and drank here.
▶page 216

Key West

INFORMATION
Florida Keys & Visitors Bureau
Key West, FL 33041
Tel. 1-305-296-1552
www.fla-keys.com/keywest/
Key West Chamber of Commerce
510 Greene St., Key West, FL 33040
Tel. 1-305-294-2587
www.keywestchamber.org

ORIENTATION
It's easy to get your bearings here. The cheaper accommodation and fast-food restaurants are along US 1 (Roosevelt Blvd.) on the way into town. The main street, called Duval Street, cuts through the densely built-up Old Town. The better hotels and restaurants are here,

The southernmost point of the continental USA is marked in Key West

most of them in old wooden houses, as well as most of the shops. On Mallory Square at the end of Duval Street people gather every evening to watch the sun go down. Bahama Village, once a hippy neighbourhood on the south side of town, has been up-graded by the appearance of trendy restaurants, but still appears very Caribbean and relaxed. It is best to leave the car in the parking lot, since traffic on Key West is very slow.

CITY TOURS
Pelican Path
This marked path (map and brochure available at the Chamber of Commerce, 510 Green Street) includes 49 historically interesting buildings.

Old Town Trolley
Leaves from Mallory Square: daily 9.30 until 4.30pm
This old-timer bus also runs past all of the interesting spots.

Conch Tour Train
Departures: daily 9.30am – 4.30pm from Front Street; duration about 1.5 hours
Ticket: US$30.45
www.conctourtrain.com
A »train« on tyres following a route that includes all of the most important sights.

ACTIVITIES
Diving, snorkelling, deep sea fishing and »boating« are popular activities on Key West.

Seaduction Dive Center
1605 N. Roosevelt Blvd.
Tel. 1-305-296-9914

www.subtropic.com
Reef and wreck dives are offered here.

Sebago Watersports
201 William Street
Tel. 1 305 2 94 56 87
www.keywestsebago.com
Snorkelling with »Sunset Cruises« are offered here: snorkel during the day, enjoy sunset on a boat.

Angling
Fishers can either rent a boat or join a group. Organizers of fishing tours have their stands around Mallory Square.

BEACHES
Despite Key West's liberal lifestyle, bathing in the nude or topless is prohibited here, too. There are some pretty little sand and pebble beaches for sunbathing and playing in the surf. The largest one, Smathers Beach (S. Roosevelt Blvd.) is where the young people hang out. Fort Zachary Beach (via Truman Annex) offers shade under palm trees. The playground and grills at Higgs Beach make it attractive for families with children.

SHOPPING
Most of the shops are in Duval Street. Really nice shops and chic boutiques can be found above all in Simonton Street and in Caroline Street.

Fast Buck Freddie's
306 William Street
www.fastbuckfreddies.com
Unusual swimwear, many items decorated with flamingos, even vases and furniture

Key Lime Pie Co.
511 Greene Street

www.keywestkeylimepie.com
Great Key Lime Pies are available here, also soaps and candles with lime scent

WHERE TO EAT
❶ Louie's Backyard $$$$
700 Waddell Ave.
Tel. 1-305-294-1061
Fish dishes with a special touch, wild boar and lamb, among the hibiscus and bougainvillea – a feast for the senses!

❷ Garbo's Grill $$ Insider Tip
700 Greene St.
Tel. 1-305-304-3004
This nice and family-friendly Caribbean restaurant was awarded in 2013. Try fish and seafood.

❸ Blue Heaven $$
729 Thomas St.
Tel. 1-305-296-8666
Trendy venue for locals and visitors: Jamaica chicken, curry dishes, lots of fish and homemade granola.

❹ Banana Café $$$
1211 Duval St.
Tel. 1-305-294-7227
Bistro with tropical feeling and creative cuisine. Excellent breakfast.

WHERE TO STAY
❶ Ambrosia House $$$
622 Fleming St., Tel. 1-305-296-9838
www.ambrosiakeywest.com
Nicely hidden near Duval Street. The 22 rooms, 6 suites and 1 cottage are decorated with art by local artists and designers.

❷ Southernmost Point Guesthouse $$$
1327 Duval St.

Tel. 1 305 2 94 07 15
www.southernmostpoint.com
Nicely restored villa, more than 100
years old, with six guest rooms that
come with an opulent breakfast and a
glass of wine in the afternoon.

❸ *The Mermaid and the Alligator
Bed & Breakfast* $$$ **Insider Tip**
Truman Ave.
Tel. 1-305-294-1894
www.kwmermaid.com

Tastefully furnished rooms in a pretty
historic building with a wonderful gar-
den.

❹ *Seashell Motel &
Key West Hostel* $
718 South St.
Tel. 1-305-296-5719
www.keywesthostel.com
Pink youth hostel and motel with 96 beds
and 14 private rooms in the historic town
centre. Snorkelling tours, bicycle rental.

Key West

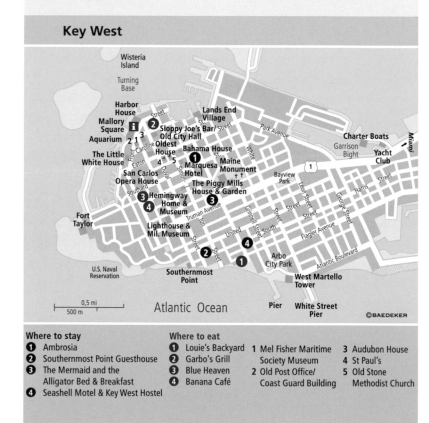

Where to stay
❶ Ambrosia
❷ Southernmost Point Guesthouse
❸ The Mermaid and the
  Alligator Bed & Breakfast
❹ Seashell Motel & Key West Hostel

Where to eat
❶ Louie's Backyard
❷ Garbo's Grill
❸ Blue Heaven
❹ Banana Café

1 Mel Fisher Maritime
  Society Museum
2 Old Post Office/
  Coast Guard Building

3 Audubon House
4 St Paul's
5 Old Stone
  Methodist Church

source of income. Henry Flagler's railway gave this process momentum when it reached Key West in 1912. At that time there used to be a ferry connection to Havana, Cuba. The multi-national background of the residents and the Caribbean lifestyle attracted artists and writers. In the 1930s and 1940s Ernest Hemingway, Tennessee Williams and at times John Dos Passos lived here. Today Key West is one of the most visited tourist attractions in the USA and despite this it is still popular among artists, writers and people who opt out of established society. It is considered to be the most tolerant city east of San Francisco. No one gets excited here when the county commissioner shows up as a drag queen in a bar on Duval Street and sings karaoke, and when other VIPs out themselves as gay or lesbian.

WHAT TO SEE IN KEY WEST

Old Town at the south-western end of the island, with its brightly painted wooden 19th century houses is the main attraction of Key West. Duval Street and its side streets are home to boutiques, art galleries, sidewalk cafés, restaurants and bars. Every evening sundown is celebrated at Mallory Square in lively carnival atmosphere.

**Old Town

Insider Tip

This aquarium has pools for sea turtles, barracudas, mantas and sharks.
❶ 1 Whitehead St., daily 10am–6pm, feedings at 11am, 1pm, 3pm, 4.30pm, admission US$15, www.keywestaquarium.com

Key West Aquarium

Harry S. Truman, 33rd president of the United States, visited Key West several times between 1946 and 1952 and lived in this 19th century wooden villa, the today »Little White House«.
❶ 111 Front St., tours daily 9am–4pm, admission US$17, www.littlewhitehouse.com

Little White House

Spanish gold jewellery, silver coins and other treasures, which the treasure hunter Mel Fisher (d. 1998) salvaged out of the Spanish silver ships Atocha and Santa Margarita are exhibited here. The two ships sank in 1622 in a hurricane off the Marquesas. The museum also has lots of interesting information on underwater archaeology.
❶ 200 Greene St./Whitebread St., daily 9.30am – 5pm, admission US$12,50, www.melfisher.org

**Mel Fisher Maritime Heritage Museum

In 1832 the painter of plants and animals J.J. Audubon (1785–1851) lived in this typical Conch house. Beautiful original etchings and valuable furnishings from the 18th and 19th centuries are displayed here. Sub-tropical and tropical plants bloom in the lush garden.
❶ 205 Whitehead/Greene Sts, daily 9.30am – 5pm, admission US$12, www.audubonhouse.com

*Audubon House & Gardens

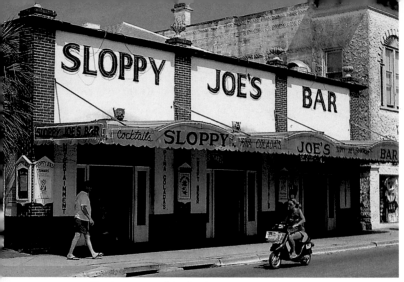
Hemingway used to stop here

*Sloppy Joe's Bar, Captain Tony's Saloon
Captain Tony's Saloon on Greene Street was called Sloppy Joe's Bar from 1933 to 1937. Here **Ernest Hemingway** liked to end the day on the barstool reserved for him. The ceiling and walls of the bar are plastered with business cards that guests left behind. The new Sloppy Joe's Bar is right around the corner in busy Duval Street. Hemingway pictures and Hemingway memorabilia decorate the walls.
❶ 201 Duval St., Mon – Sat 9am – 4am, Sun from 12noon, live music, www.sloppyjoes.com

Fort Zachary Taylor State Historic Site
The fort at the south-west end of the island was built from 1845 to 1866 as part of the US American naval defence system. It played an important role during the Civil War. The Union had a base here and used it to pursue blockade runners. During the Spanish-American War the fort was renovated. It has been a naval base since 1947. Cannons and weapons from the Civil War can be seen in the old fort.
❶ 601 Howard England Way, daily 8am – 5pm, tours daily 12noon, admission: pedestrians US$2.50, vehicles US$7, www.floridaparks.org/forttaylor/

**Ernest Hemingway Home & Museum
Ernest Hemingway's house is one of the most-visited attractions on Key West. The house was built in Spanish colonial style in 1851; Hemingway bought the well-equipped house with a balcony around it in 1931. The Nobel laureate for literature wrote some of his works here until 1961. The lush garden is the home of numerous descendants of Hemingway's cats.
❶ 907 Whitehead St., daily 9am – 5pm, admission US$13, www.hemingwayhome.com

The wreckers of Key West did their best business with the Isaac Allerton: the salvage that washed ashore brought in US$ 50,000. This unique museum documents the exciting, oft morbid history of the salvagers.

Key West's Shipwreck Historeum

❶ 1 Whitehead St., daily 9.40am – 5pm, admission US$15, www.keywestshipwreck.com

At the end of Whitehead Street a large colourful cement buoy (photo ▶ p.212) marks the southernmost point of continental USA. From here Cuba is only 144km/86mi away, closer than Miami! The nearby lighthouse was built in 1847 and is now open as a museum.

*Southernmost Point

The wonderful panoramic view rewards the effort of climbing 90 steps through the narrow stairwell. It was inaugurated in 1848 and marked the beginning of the end of the lucrative wrecking trade. The little museum in the lighthouse keeper's house depicts this inglorious chapter of local history.

Key West Lighthouse Museum

❶ 938 Whitehead St., daily 9.30am – 4.30pm, admission US$10, www.kwahs.com/lighthouse/

Bahama Village: Under siege by tourists, the neighbourhood between Thomas Street, Angela Street and Amelia Street clings to the old spirit of Key West. Most of the chickens live here; the simple wooden houses used to be the homes of cigar makers. Today the residents, mostly descendants of settlers from the Bahamas and Afro-Cubans, still go to church dressed in their Sunday best and love to reminisce about the cockfights that are now forbidden.

Bahama Village

The cemetery in the north of Old Town (Margaret St. and Angela St.) is known for the humorous inscriptions on the gravestones: »Devoted Fan of Singer Julio Iglesias« on one; »I told you I was sick« on another. Monuments for Cuban patriots and sailors who died in the explosion of the »USS Maine« in 1898 in Havana seem almost out of place despite their appropriate earnestness. Because of the hard coral ground and the frequent floods, the dead are »buried« above ground: the caskets are mostly stacked on top of each other and look like a necropolis.

Key West Cemetery

! Sunset Cruise **Insider Tip**

MARCO ⊕ POLO TIP

A special way to enjoy the sunset is on board a sailboat – with a well-filled coolbox and a nice crew. Organizers can be found in Duval Street in Key West.

EXCURSIONS FROM KEY WEST

Excursions from Key West by boat or pontoon airplane to the Marquesas Keys to the west are worthwhile since they form the core of

*Marquesas Keys

The Best Place on Earth

»*This is the best piece on earth that I ever happened on. Flowers, tamarisk trees, guava trees, coconut palms...*« *wrote the author and globetrotter Ernest Hemingway (1899 - 1961) from Key West in 1928 to a friend. The restless writer put down stakes here for six years.*

Key West and especially his villa on Whitehead Street were not only the home base that he returned to from his travels. In Key West's mild winters he wrote his most famous novels and short stories, for example *A Farewell to Arms*, *Snows of Kilimanjaro*, *Green Hills of Africa* and *For Whom the Bell Tolls*.

Journalism

Hemingway grew up with his siblings in Oak Park, an upper class suburb of Chicago. After graduating from high school he became a reporter for the »Kansas City Star«. In 1918 he volunteered for **duty on the Italian front**, where he was wounded seriously. After the war was over Hemingway returned to the USA and worked as a newspaper editor.

Women

In 1921 he married for the first time, **Elizabeth Hadley Richardson**, and they moved to Paris. He wrote the first significant short stories there. They already show Hemingway's famous style, which was characterized by journalism – short, terse sentences.

The marriage to Hadley failed when Hemingway began an affair with **Pauline Pfeiffer**, a friend of his wife. After the divorce Pauline and Ernest Hemingway married in May 1927 in Paris.

New Home on Key West

When the writer John Dos Passos raved about the beauty of Florida, Hemingway and Pauline embarked for Havana in March 1928 and then crossed over to Key West. Most of the residents of Key West had something to do with the sea and Hemingway also became an enthusiastic fisher. Already in April he wrote to his editor Max Perkins that he caught »the largest tarpon that they had seen here this season: 63lbs (29kg).«

907, Whitehead Street

Hemingway and Pauline rented for the first three years, before they bought the Spanish colonial villa at 907 Whitehead Street in spring 1931 with the help of Pauline's Uncle Gus. Pauline had the neglected garden replanted and built the first swimming pool on Key West. The pretty house with its wrought iron balcony all around is Hemingway's poet's garret and his home for the time with Pauline. Today a large colony of cats lives on the grounds, whose ancestors were brought there by Hemingway.

More travels and more marriages

Hemingway did well; he enjoyed his wealth and his fame. In the winter of 1934 he returned with

Hemingway's house in Key West is now a tourist attraction

Pauline from his **first safari in Africa**. He hunted lions, cape buffalo and other large animals at Kilimanjaro. He used some of the experiences there for later literary motifs.

In early 1937 Hemingway went to Spain as a war correspondent to cover the civil war. He met the journalist **Martha Gellhorn** there, whom he had met in Key West when she interviewed him. She became his third wife in 1940.

With the income from his novel *For Whom the Bell Tolls* he bought a finca on Cuba, in order to spend a few summers there. In the early 1940s the two reported on the Second World War from East Asia. He described the liberation of Par-

is and witnessed the battles for the Siegfried Line. His third marriage failed in late 1945 as well.

In March 1946 he married **Mary Welsh** in the Cuban capital Havana. The finca »La Vigia« was to be his home for twenty years. He wrote one of his best works there: *The Old Man and the Sea*, for which he got the **Nobel Prize for literature in 1954**. Hemingway, who had survived war injuries, hunting accidents and two airplane crashes, had no more strength to write. He suffered from severe depression and spoke more and more often about suicide.

On 2 July 1961 Hemingway committed suicide.

One of the pleasant moments in life: an excursion to one of the tiny coral islands off Key West

Insider Tip

the Key West National Wildlife Refuge. Many kinds of birds can be observed in the nature preserve, including terns, egrets, cormorants and pelicans. Snorkelers and divers will see an enchanting underwater world with diverse coral formations and many colourful fish.

Dry Tortugas National Park

About 110km/65mi west of Key West lies the Dry Tortugas National Park, a marine nature preserve that is made up of a group of tiny coral islands and underwater coral reefs. Spanish conquistador Ponce de León discovered them in 1513 and named them after the sea turtles that brood here.

On Garden Key people interested in history can visit **Fort Jefferson,** which was built in 1846 to protect American ships. The brick fort was used between 1863 and 1874 as a prison for prominent political prisoners of the Civil War.

Kissimmee · St Cloud

H 4

Region: Central
Elevation: 19m/65ft above sea level
Population: 55,000

The two towns in the heart of Florida, Kissimmee and St Cloud, are so to speak the gateway to entertainment. From here it is not far to the mega-amusement parks in ►Orlando and ►Walt Disney World.

The picturesque, rural Florida with its lakes and cypress swamps, narrow country roads lined by spreading live oaks with garlands of Spanish moss swaying in the breeze can only be found off the beaten track. In 1878 the first white settlers came to this region. In 1891 the new settlement Kissimmee became the county seat, with a population of only 815. Favourable conditions for fruit and vegetable farming as well as two cigar factories soon attracted more settlers. Its modern development began in 1963 when Walt Disney thought that he had found the ideal conditions here for a perfect, clean amusement park. The rapid development of the Disney world of amusement encouraged other businessmen to set up their own projects in the wake of the Mickey Mouse. Motels, shops and other attractions soon followed. Today the Kissimmee/St Cloud region is an urban area that revolves around the commerce of amusement.

From a farming village to an amusement hotspot

WHAT TO SEE IN AND AROUND KISSIMMEE

The old Main Street and Broadway Boulevard have been nicely renovated. Many little shops dot the scenery. The buildings that are particularly worth seeing are the Osceola Courthouse of 1889, Makinson's Hardware Store of 1895.

Downtown

At Lake Front Park more than 1,000 stones from all of the US states as well as over two dozen countries were used to construct a monument.

Monument of States

The »main street of amusement«, Irlo Bronson Memorial Highway (US 192) runs through Kissimmee from west to east. Along this expansive axis attractions, hotels, motels, restaurants, malls, factory outlets etc. line up. There is a round-the-clock county fair atmosphere. In the **Osceola Center for the Arts** (2411 E. Erlo Bronson Hwy.), which also includes several art galleries, theatre performances and concerts are held.

Irlo Bronson Memorial Highway

Kissimmee · St Cloud

INFORMATION
Kissimmee CVB
1925 E. Irlo Bronson Memorial Hwy.
Kissimmee, FL 34744
Tel. 1-407-742-8200
www.visitkissimmee.com

EVENT
Silver Spurs Rodeo
Every year in early June the largest rodeo east of the Mississippi is held in Kissimmee.

WHERE TO EAT   Insider Tip
Crabby Bills $$
1104 Lakeshore Blvd., St. Cloud
Tel. 1-407-979-4001
In this lakeside restaurant wonderful fish dishes are served; live music and great atmosphere.

Longhorn Steakhouse $$
5351 W. Irlo Bronson Hwy.
Kissimmee

Tel. 1-407-396-9556
Many guests think that the best steaks in the »Sunshine State« are served here. The well-aged meat is prepared just right. Various sidedishes are also served.

WHERE TO STAY
Gaylord Palms Resort $$$
6000 W. Osceola Parkway; Kissimmee
Tel. 1-407-586-0000
www.gaylordhotels.com/gaylordpalms/
1,406 rooms, 115 suites, several restaurants and lounges, spa, convention centre, shopping arcade. In this resort there's something for every taste.

Days Inn Kissimmee-Orlando $$
Main gate east of Disney World
2390 Polynesian Isle Blvd., Kissimmee
Tel. 1-407-396-2199
www.daysinn.com
Nice accommodation with a pool. Close to the mega amusement parks in Orlando.

Old Town   This shopping centre was built in the style of the turn of the 20th century; along with boutiques and restaurants there are also nice rides, like a Ferris wheel from 1928 and a merry-go-round from 1909.
❶ 5770 W Irlo Bronson Memorial Hwy., Kissimmee, daily 10am–11pm, admission, www.http://myoldtownusa.com

*Gatorland   The entrance to Gatorland Zoo between Kissimmee and "Orlando is marked by the giant open mouth of an alligator. Along with various animals from all over the world there are **about 5,000 alligators and crocodiles** here. These animals are raised domestically. Various kinds of snakes can also be seen in the open enclosures. A »Gator Wrestlin' Show« and a »Gator Jumparoo Show« are held every day.
❶ 14501 S. Orange Blossom Trail, daily 9am–6pm, admission US$25, www.gatorland.com

Reptile World Serpentarium   The terrariums of Reptile World Serpentarium in St. Cloud are home to more than four dozen kinds of snakes from all parts of the world.

There are also lizards, turtles as well as alligators to be seen close up. Every day at noon and 3pm staff show the poisonous snakes and demonstrate how the poison is milked from them.

❶ 5705 E. Irlo Bronson Memorial Hwy., Tue – Sun 9am – 5.30pm, admission US$6.75, www.reptileworldserpentarium.com

Forever Florida & Crecent J Ranch This adventure park near St. Cloud covers over 2,000 hectares (5,000 acres). A tour in a safari bus brings guests to animals from various ecosystems. The new EcoPark offers all sorts of adventures; there is an attractive petting zoo and pony rides for children.

❶ 4755 N. Kenansville Rd., daily 9am – 5pm,admission US$135, reservations tel. 1-407-957-9794, www.foreverflorida com

★ Lake City

✳ G 2

Region: North Central
Elevation: 60m/200ft above sea level
Population: 12,500

For many visitors to Florida from US states, Lake City is the entrance to the »Sunshine State«, since it is located at the junction of interstate highways I-10 and I-75. But Lake City is also the starting point for nature lovers, hikers and canoeists who enjoy the nearby Osceola National Forest.

The city developed out of a large Indian village. A chief from this village played an important role in the Dade Massacre (1835), which started the Second Seminole War. The first white people settled here after the hostilities ended. **Forestry** and cattle raising supported the community at first. The discovery of **phosphate** deposits at the Suwannee River helped the economy to grow.

WHAT TO SEE IN AND AROUND LAKE CITY

Historic Districts The city still has several well-preserved buildings from the 19th and early 20th centuries. **Well-restored houses** can be found along Main Street as well as in the Commercial District. There are attractive villas to be admired at Lake Isabella. The Columbia County Historical Museum is also sited here.

Stephen Foster Culture Center Near White Springs, 12mi/20km north-west of Lake City, a cultural centre on the Suwannee River is dedicated to Stephen Foster (1826– 64), who composed and wrote texts for American

Lake City

INFORMATION
Lake City – Columbia County
Tourist Development Council
263 NW Lake City Ave.
Lake City, FL 32055
Tel. 1-386-758-1397
www.springsrus.com

EVENTS
Olustee Battle Festival & **Insider**
Re-enactment **Tip**
www.olusteefestival.com
Every year in February the famous Civil
War battle between Union and
Confederate troops is re-enacted.

Florida Folk Festival
www.floridastateparks.org/folkfest/
This folk festival takes place on the
weekend around Memorial Day in the
Stephen Foster Culture Center State
Park; it offers music, dancing,
storytelling, craft demonstrations as well
as delicious food and drink.

WHERE TO EAT
Bob Evans Restaurant $$
3628 W. US 90
Tel. 1-386-752-8749
www.bobevans.com
Very child-friendly restaurant with tasty
American cooking.

WHERE TO STAY
Best Western Lake City Inn
3598 US 90 West
Tel. 1-386-752-3801
www.bestwestern.com
Comfortable accommodation with 83
spacious and well-furnished rooms,
swimming pool and sauna.

Comfort Suites Lake City $$
3690 W. US 90
Tel. 1-386-755-9028
www.comfortsuites.com
The 104 rooms are pleasantly furnished
and very reasonably priced, pool and
fitness room.

folk songs. His songs *Old Folks at Home* and *Oh, Susanna* became
world-famous.

❶ US 41 W, White Springs, daily 9am – 5pm, admission: pedestrians, US$2,
vehicles US$5, www.floridastateparks.org/stephenfoster/

*Osceola Osceola National Forest to the north-east of Lake City was established
National in 1931 already and with an area of 890 sq km/343 sq mi is the
Forest smallest of Florida's state forests. Expansive cedar forests, countless
lakes, ponds and lagoons as well as cypress swamps, rubber trees and
magnolias characterize the landscape. In the north the forested areas
gradually give way to the Okefenokee Swamp.

An approximately 37mi/60km-long section of the **Florida Trail** runs
through the forest from White Springs on the Suwannee River to the
Olustee Battlefield. One of the most beautiful parts is **Ocean Pond**;
adventurous nature lovers follow the Osceola Trail from the north
shore into the damp hinterlands. Further information: www.
floridatrail.org

Pretty 19th century architecture in Lake City

In 1864 thousands of Union and Confederate troops faced off near Olustee. The Confederates won and secured the supply lines for the South. A museum and an educational trail has more information on the battle.

Olustee Battlefield State Historic Site

❶ 5815 Battlefield Trail Rd., Olustee, daily 9am – 5pm, free admission, www.floridastateparks.org/olusteebattlefield/

The Okefenokee Swamp is ideal for an excursion by nature lovers: the swampy region has an area of more than 2,000 sq km/772 sq mi and is located north of Osceola Forest; it stretches 40mi/64km northwards into the state of Georgia. The »land of swaying ground«, as it was originally called by the Choctaw Indians, is an important store of underground water. A labyrinth of lakes and waterways, cypress swamps and »floating« islands, which might sway when stepped on but which nevertheless carried entire woods and Indian villages, are fed by the Suwannee River, which runs into the Gulf of Mexico after more than 240mi/400km, and the St Mary's River, which runs into

*Okefenokee Swamp National Wildlife Refuge

Many alligators still live in the Okefenokee swamps

the Atlantic about 50mi/80km further east, as well as countless karst springs. The Okefenokee National Wildlife Refuge includes about 90% of the swamp and is a haven for endangered wildlife like black bears and wild cats as well as countless birds. About **10,000 alligators** live in the Okefenokee Swamp at present.

Okefenokee National Wildlife Refuge Office: 2766 Suwanee Canal Rd., Folkston, Georgia Mon – Fri 9am – 5pm, admission US$5, www.fws.gov/okeefenokee/

*Ichetucknee Springs State Park

12mi/20km south-west of Lake City via FL 47 and FL 238 or US–27, Ichetucknee Springs State Park is located in very pretty countryside. Several rich **karst springs** feed the Ichetucknee River. So that future generations can continue to enjoy this natural gem, only 3,000 visitors are allowed in every day. Near the springs traces of **Indian settlement** were found some time ago. The Spanish had a mission station here for a while when they first came to the New World.

● 12087 SW US 27, Fort White, daily 8am until sunset, admission: pedestrians US$2, vehicles US$6, www.floridastateparks.org/ichetuckneesprings/

The Suwannee River flows out of the Okefenokee Swamp and meanders peacefully through northern Florida. It is popular among canoeists and fishers, and the numerous springs around **Live Oak** are ideal for snorkelling and diving. About 14mi/22km north-west of Live Oak, at the **confluence of the Suwannee River and Withlacoochee River**, a bit of Florida's original landscape has been preserved.

Suwannee River State Park

❶ 3631 201st Path, Live Oak, daily 8am until sunset, admission: vehicles US$5, pedestrians US$2, www.floridastateparks.org/suwanneeriver/

* Lakeland

✳ H 4

Region: North Central
Elevation: 67m/200ft above sea level
Population: 90,000

The city halfway between ▶Tampa and ▶Orlando is an ideal base for day trips through rural Florida; it attracted people looking for rest and recreation long before Walt Disney turned his attention to the Sunshine State. Lakeland itself has – apart from water sports on a dozen lakes – a series of pleasantly unspectacular attractions.

In the past decades Lakeland has stubbornly continued to look ahead. There is nothing in this modern small town to recall the high unemployment of the 1980s. Citrus fruits and phosphate mining, Lakeland's two most important income producers, were going through their worst crises ever. The downtown area deteriorated. But then Lakeland changed its perspective. Energetic city fathers attracted new industry and increased their tourism advertising. Commuters who worked in Tampa or Orlando discovered Lakeland as a good place to live and the Detroit Tigers baseball team came here for spring training. Today the city has been comprehensively renovated.

Crisis and progress

WHAT TO SEE IN AND AROUND LAKELAND

The museum in the headquarters of the Experimental Aircraft Association (EAA) at Lakeland Regional Airport shows everything that ever took off. More than 60 flying machines are a source of entertainment, including bizarre homemade contraptions, remote-controlled drones and memorabilia of the aviator and millionaire Howard Hughes.

Florida Air Museum at Sun 'n Fun

❶ 4175 Medulla Rd.; Mon – Fri 9am – 5pm, Sat 10am – 4pm, Sun noon – 4pm, admission US$10, www.sun-n-fun.org/useum/

100% Pure Florida

Florida is one of the world's leading producers and processors of citrus fruits. About 76,000 people are employed by this industry with an annual income of $9 billion. The sandy hills in relatively rainy central Florida offer optimal growing conditions.

▶ **Worldwide production of oranges, 2010, in millions of tonnes**

▶ **Source of vitamin C**
Worldwide production of citrus fruits (2010, in millions of tonnes)

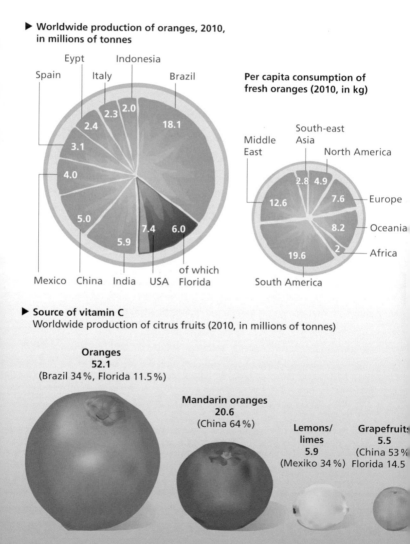

Per capita consumption of fresh oranges (2010, in kg)

Spain — 3.1
Eypt — 2.0
Italy — 2.3
Indonesia
Brazil — 18.1
2.4
4.0
5.0
5.9
7.4
6.0 of which Florida
Mexico — China — India — USA

Middle East — 12.6
South-east Asia — 2.8
North America — 4.9
7.6 — Europe
8.2 — Oceania
2 — Africa
19.6 — South America

Oranges
52.1
(Brazil 34 %, Florida 11.5 %)

Mandarin oranges
20.6
(China 64 %)

Lemons/limes
5.9
(Mexiko 34 %)

Grapefruits
5.5
(China 53 %, Florida 14.5)

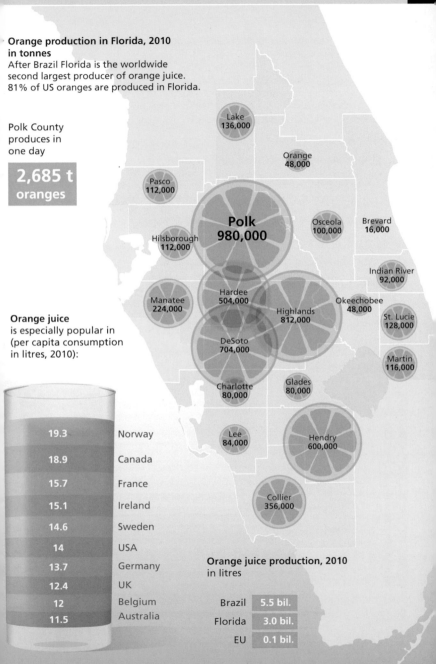

Orange production in Florida, 2010 in tonnes
After Brazil Florida is the worldwide second largest producer of orange juice. 81% of US oranges are produced in Florida.

Polk County produces in one day

2,685 t oranges

Lake 136,000

Orange 48,000

Pasco 112,000

Polk 980,000

Osceola 100,000

Brevard 16,000

Hilsborough 112,000

Indian River 92,000

Manatee 224,000

Hardee 504,000

Highlands 812,000

Okeechobee 48,000

St. Lucie 128,000

Orange juice
is especially popular in (per capita consumption in litres, 2010):

DeSoto 704,000

Martin 116,000

Charlotte 80,000

Glades 80,000

Lee 84,000

Hendry 600,000

Collier 356,000

19.3	Norway
18.9	Canada
15.7	France
15.1	Ireland
14.6	Sweden
14	USA
13.7	Germany
12.4	UK
12	Belgium
11.5	Australia

Orange juice production, 2010
in litres

Brazil	5.5 bil.
Florida	3.0 bil.
EU	0.1 bil.

Florida Southern College
On the grounds of the college south-west of the town centre the architect Frank Lloyd Wright made his mark. The 18 buildings, which are connected by esplanades, embody what Wright called »organic architecture«: embedded in the natural environment and using local natural building materials. Frank Lloyd Wright called the campus his »child of the sun«. The Annie Pfeiffer Chapel and the only planetarium (111 Lake Hollingsworth Drive) that Wright ever designed are worth a look.

*Polk Museum of Art
Small but high-quality: this museum has valuable collections of pre-Columbian art from the Andes Mountains, European and Oriental ceramics as well as 18th and 19th-century American art. It also shows something of Florida's own art scene.

❶ 800 East Palmetto St.; Tue – Sat 10am – 5pm, Sun 1pm – 5pm, Jun til Aug only until 4pm, closed Sun, admission US$5, http://polkmuseumofart.org

Fantasy of Flight
15mi/24km north-east of Lakeland, near Polk City, more than three dozen antique airplanes are on display. The museum's showpieces are a Short Sunderland pontoon boat with four engines, a Grumman Wildcat fighter plane and a Supermarine Spitfire. They also offer flights in a biplane and balloon rides.

Insider Tip

❶ 1400 Broadway Blvd. SE, daily 10am – 5pm, admission US$29, www.fantasyofflight.com

Legoland Florida
About a 20-minute drive east of Lakeland, on the property of the once world famous **Cypress Gardens** near Winter Haven, the **new theme park** Legoland Florida was opened in fall 2011 with copies of famous and unusual buildings – for example the White House – and attractions, mountains and cities, all made from the colourful building blocks from Denmark. There are also a few dozen rides as well as great shows and other attractions, including interactive areas for the whole family.

Another highlight is the first **Legoland Waterpark** with all sorts of exciting slides, pools and wading pools.

❶ One Legoland Way, daily from 10am until 8pm at the latest, admission US$75, with waterpark US$87, parking fee US$12, http://florida.legoland.com

Lake Wales
A half-hour drive south-east, almost exactly in the geographic centre of Florida and nestled in pretty hills, lies Lake Wales (population

Lakeland

INFORMATION
Lakeland Chamber of Commerce
35 Lake Morton Drive
Lakeland, FL 33801
Tel. 1-863-688-8551
www.lakelandchamber.com

EVENT
Sun 'n Fun Fly-in
Pilots' meeting sponsored by the
Experimental Aircraft Association (EAA),
mid-April.

WHERE TO EAT
The Terrace Grill $$$$
329 E. Main Street
(in the Terrace Hotel)
Tel. 1-863-688-0800
Wood-grilled filet mignon and other
American classics are expertly prepared
here.

Harry's Seafood Bar & Grille $$
101 N. Kentucky Ave.
Tel. 1-863-686-2228
Culinary delights from Louisiana are
served here: hearty Cajun cuisine and
pretty spicy Creole cooking.

WHERE TO STAY
Lakeland Terrace Hotel $$
329 E. Main St.
Tel. 1-863-688-0800
www.terracehotel.com
Elegant and tastefully furnished house
from the 1920s with 88 rooms and
suites.

Jameson Inn $$
4375 Lakeland Park Dr.
Tel. 1-863-858-9070
www.jamesoninns.com
Friendly, colonial-style inn with
67 rooms and a pool.

Have fun playing in Legoland Florida

12,000) with its lovingly restored city centre. The pink **Depot Museum** depicts the beginnings of the railway, turpentine production as well as the industrial processing of citrus fruits.

❶ 325 S. Scenic Hwy.; Mon – Fri 9am – 5pm, Sat 10am – 4pm, admission US$2, www.cityoflakewales.com

Bok Tower Gardens A few miles north of Lake Wales aromatic orange plantations surround Bok Tower Gardens. The Dutch publicist **Edward Bok** (1863–1930) made botanical gardens here in the 1920s, which are considered to be the most beautiful in Florida. They were designed by the landscape architect **Frederik Law Olmsted** on the top of **Iron Mountain** (at 90m/300ft one of the highest points in Florida); azaleas, cacti and magnolias bloom here in tropical profusion.

The idyllic setting is dominated by the 60m/200ft-high **Singing Tower**, a daring mixture of Art Deco and neo-Gothic style. The limestone-and-marble tower is poetically reflected in a placid duck pond while a glockenspiel plays (Hwy. 17 A; hours: daily 9am–5pm).

❶ 1151 Tower Blvd., Lake Wales, daily 8am – 6pm, glockenspiel every half hour, longer glockenspiel concerts at 1pm and 3pm, admission US$12, www.boktowergardens.org

Lake Okeechobee
H/J 5/6

Regions: South-east, south-west
Elevation: 3m/10ft above sea level
Area: 1,810 sq km/700 sq mi

The fourth-largest lake in the USA lies in the heart of rural Florida. Endless fields of sugar cane characterize the landscape. Cattle graze on green pastures and there are sleepy villages where the general store is also the post office and petrol station. The lake itself attracts anglers fishing for bass.

Fishing paradise The »Great Water« of the Seminoles in the middle of southern Florida offers a welcome break from the bustle along the coast. People come here especially to fish, since the lake, which is only 15ft/4.5m deep, has more bass than anywhere else in Florida.

The many boat rentals and fishing equipment suppliers as well as campgrounds and trailer parks along the shore in the towns of Clewiston and South Bay testify to this.

Deadly hurricane: The lake, which is quiet most of the year, is part of a broad current of ground water that flows sluggishly between ▶Orlando and ▶Everglades National Park. On a hot Sunday, nothing would seem as impossible as what happened here in 1928. That year 2,400 people died when a hurricane roared over southern Florida and caused heavy flooding here. Afterwards a ring dike and a system of locks and canals were built to control the water level.

Since they were completed the lake has served as a regulator during the hurricane season, and as a fresh-water reservoir. But its natural drainage into the Everglades to the south was blocked off, which has led to a serious conflict between the government and conservationists until today. Ecologists and aquatic engineers are now trying to keep the water around Lake Okeechobee as close to its natural level as possible.

*Lake Okeechobee Scenic Trail

Today the 36ft/11m-high **Herbert Hoover Dike** is the sight of the Lake Okeechobee Scenic Trail, a 176km/109mi-long unpaved trail for hikers, bikers and horseback riders. The trail runs through towns like **Belle Glade**, **Okeechobee** and **Pahokee** and offers nice views of the lake and fields, and constant opportunities to watch waterfowl. The best place to start a tour is **Clewiston** (population 6,500) on the

Lake Okeechobee

INFORMATION
Clewiston Chamber of Commerce
1 Central Ave.
Clewiston, FL 33440
Tel. 1-863-983-7979
www.clewiston.org

ACTIVITIES
Big O Airboat Tours
420 E Del Monte Ave.
Clewiston, FL
Tel. 1-863-983-2037
www.bigofishing.com
Fishing is big here.

WHERE TO EAT
Clewiston Inn Dining Room $$
108 Royal Palm Ave.
Clewiston, FL
Tel. 1-863-983-8151
Best food in town. Spicy southern cuisine can be had here, especially catfish and fried chicken.

WHERE TO STAY
Best Western of Clewiston $$
1020 W. Sugarland Hwy.
Clewiston, FL 33440-2707
Tel. 1-863-983-3400
www.bestwestern.com
Comfortable, motel-like accommodation with 50 spacious rooms and a pool.

! *Take a dive ...* Insider Tip

MARCO ⊕ POLO TIP

The quiet air space in the region and the flat landscape around Lake Okeechobee attracts skydiving fans. Skydiving novices can make a tandem jump here with a professional skydiver. Information at: Skydive Air Adventures, Airglades Airport, Clewiston, ticket US$205, tel. 1-863-983-6151, www.skydivefl.com

southern shore, which calls itself »America's sweetest town« because of the surrounding **sugar cane fields**. Not far to the south of Clewiston, on land belonging to the Brighton Seminole, the modern **Ah-Tah-Thi-Ki Museum** of the Native Americans surprises with many interactive exhibits. An historic Seminole settlement has also been constructed. Tours are also offered.

❶ Wed – Sun 9am – 5pm, admission US$9, www.ahtahthiki.com

* Marianna

——————————————— ✦ **D 2**

Region: North-west
Elevation: 36m/120ft above sea level
Population: 7,000

A scent of the Old South is still in the air: Georgia and Alabama are only a short hop away. Beautiful old residences doze under magnolia trees, and the activity on Main Street is watched closely from shady verandas.

City of Southern Charm

The town that proudly calls itself »City of Southern Charm« was founded in 1829, shortly after Florida joined the USA, by ranchers and cattle breeders from Georgia. Today Marianna is the county seat of rural Jackson County, where everything revolves around peanuts, soy beans and corn, and horse auctions are held regularly. The 19th-century manor houses are worth a closer look, but the real attraction lies outside of town.

AROUND MARIANNA

*Florida Caverns State Park

The main attraction is about 3mi/5km to the north outside of Marianna on FL 167: Florida Caverns. These dripstone caves were discovered by the Spanish in 1693. They were probably a hiding place for Indians, who hid there in 1818 from the approaching troops of US General Andrew Jackson. Only part of the cave system, which was created for the most part by the Chipola River, is open to visitors. In a guided tour wonderful **stalactites and stalagmites** can be seen.

❶ FL 167, tours Thu – Mon 9am – 4pm, ticket US$8, www.floridastateparks.org/floridacaverns/

> **!** **MARCO ⊕ POLO TIP**
>
> *»Trip of a lifetime« for canoeists*
>
> Canoeists can make wonderful trips on the Chipola River. The river is considered to be one of the best waterways for canoeists in Florida!
> **Insider Tip**

Marianna

INFORMATION
Mainstreet Marianna
2880 Green Street
Marianna, FL 32447-0795
Tel. 1-850-482-4353
www.cityofmarianna.com

WHERE TO EAT
Madison's Warehouse $$
2881 Madison St.
Marianna, FL 32446
Tel. 1-850-526-4000
www.madisonswarehouse.com
Only a few steps from Marianna Square

Shopping Center, enjoy tasty steaks and freshly made salads and very moderate prices. Especially delicious: pesci con gamberi.

WHERE TO STAY
Americas Best Value Inn Marianna $
2086 Highway 71
Marianna, FL 32448
Tel. 1-850-526-5666
www.americasbestvalueinn.com
Well-run inn with 74 spacious rooms.

About 20mi/32km west of Marianna there is a natural phenomenon typical of the karst hillscape: Falling Waters. This is the only large waterfall in Florida. A small stream plunges about 20m/100ft into a **rocky gorge** and disappears into a deep cave system. Around it there are other sinkholes, with a difficult path leading to them. Above the waterfall a small lake is an inviting place to cool off. But watch out for alligators.

*Falling Waters State Recreation Area

❶ 1130 State Park Rd., Chipley, FL, daily 8am until sunset, admission: vehicle US$5, pedestrians US$2, www.floridastateparks.org/fallingwaters/

* Melbourne

✳ J 4

Region: Central East
Elevation: 0 – 7m/22ft above sea level
Population: 76,000

The rockets at nearby ►Cape Canaveral and the related development of high-tech businesses caused this town on the so-called Space Coast to expand dramatically in the 1980s. Thanks to the beautiful beaches, tourism has come to stay, too.

The first settlers in the Melbourne area were freed slaves who came here in the 1860s. The town got its name in 1879 from a postmaster who originally came from Australia. In 1894 the East Coast Railway of railway magnate Flagler arrived in Melbourne, which caused an enormous economic boom.

Railway brings growth

Goldrush in the Ocean

On 5 September 1622 a Spanish fleet of 9 ships left Havana harbour. It included the Nuestra Señora de Atocha and its sister ship Margarita, loaded with gold, silver and precious stones. The ships were actually supposed to wait, since there are often severe hurricanes in the Caribbean in September, but fear of robbery made the captains hurry and risk the dangerous journey.

Several days later only a few sailors were still alive. They tried to reach the coast of Florida holding on to planks. The treasures sank to the bottom of the sea. The fate of the two ships, which sank off the coast in a storm, was not unique. On their way home from the New World the ships had no choice but to sail through the **dangerous passage between Cuba and Florida** with its coral reefs and currents.

Blackbeard and Friends

Pirates lurked off the Florida coast as well, for the heavily laden ships were an easy prey here. They could be boarded from lighter ships or lured onto reefs with false lights. The pirate duo **Black Caesar** and **Edward Teach alias Blackbeard** were feared and famous then, and made the waters between Cuba, Florida and the Bahamas unsafe in the early 18th century. The pirate **Gasparilla** and his crew boarded or sank three dozen galleons from 1784 to 1795.

Treasures at the Bottom of the Sea

It is estimated that **more than 1,000 ships sank off the coast of Florida** from the 16th century. No wonder then that divers from all over the world try their luck in these waters again and again. They use the most modern technology: computers calculate possible locations and the ocean bottom is searched by means of satellite-controlled navigation. New instruments register even small amounts of metal at unexplored depths. Thus there are occasionally spectacular finds that cover the high costs of the equipment.

Risky Business

But treasure hunting is risky and its outcome is uncertain. The professional treasure hunter **Mel Fisher** searched for 16 years for the two **galleons Atocha and Margarita** which sank on that September day in 1622. The search cost him over 8 million dollars, and his son and daughter-in-law lost their lives. No one believed any more that they would be successful when one of the divers in Fisher's crew suddenly swam into a wall of pure silver. Almost 1,000 bars of silver from Atocha were still neatly stacked on the ocean floor after centuries. Fisher also found the wreck of the Margarita in 1980 and salvaged **treasure worth US$ 350 million**; however, only after many days in court could he claim it for himself. The laws on treasure are unclear. Treasures found within the three-mile limit belong to the government.

There are still shipwrecks off the coast of Florida to be explored

Only wrecks that are found outside of the 24-mile limit belong to the finder. Between them there is a grey area in which ownership has to be determined in court. Spectacular finds in Florida did not come to an end with the discovery of Atocha and the Margarita. In 1987 Nuestra Señora de Maravilla, which rammed another ship fully laden in 1659 and sank, was discovered. In 1990 divers near the Dry Tortugas found another ship that had sunk in the 17th century.

Success on the Beach

In the face of competition from the professional treasure hunters, amateurs have hardly any chance of becoming millionaires overnight, since all the easily accessible places have been searched already. It is easier to find a spectacular treasure on the beach than when diving. After almost every hurricane, gold doubloons from colonial times are washed ashore on the beaches of southern Florida. One of the most valuable old pieces of jewellery ever found by treasure hunters turned up not on the ocean floor but on the beach: a **gold necklace** worth US$ 50,000. For those not lucky enough to find treasure themselves, there us plenty to see in museums – for example in Mel Fisher's Museum in Sebastian.

Melbourne

INFORMATION
The Melbourne – Palm Bay Area Chamber of Commerce
1005 E. Strawbridge Ave.
Melbourne, FL 32901-4782
Tel. 1-321-724-5400
www.melpb-chamber.org

WHERE TO EAT
Crossfire Deli & Grill $$
2447 N Wickham Rd..
Tel. 1-321-752-0076
Small but fine restaurant with a large menu of Mediterranean dishes; also with tasty tapas and creatively constructed burgers

WHERE TO STAY
Hampton Inn $$
194 Dike Road
Melbourne, FL 32904
Tel. 1-321-956-6200
www.hampton.com
Well-run inn with 60 nice rooms and suites, and friendly service.

WHAT TO SEE IN AND AROUND MELBOURNE

Melbourne

The **Foosaner Art Museum** has rotating exhibitions of works by famous artists and workshops. The little **Brevard Zoo** has exotic animals including Australian kangaroos, wallabies and emus. **Eau Gallie Fishing Pier** at the end of the causeway of the same name and **Melbourne Beach Fishing Pier** at the end of Ocean Avenue are popular meeting places for anglers.

Foosaner Art Museum: 1463 Highland Ave., Tue – Sat 10am – 5pm, Thu until 7pm, Sun 1pm – 5pm, admission US$5, www.foosanerartmuseum.org

Brevard Zoo: 822 5 N Wickham Rd., daily 9.30am – 5pm, admission US$14.50, www.brevardzoo.org

Merritt Island

Off the coast and beyond the Indian River lies the narrow Merritt Island, which was once inhabited by peaceful Native Americans. Now it is part of a large wildlife preserve that surrounds Kennedy Space Center (►Cape Canaveral) and where more than 1,500 various plants and animals have been counted.

*Beaches

The long and narrow barrier island off the coast is bordered by holiday resorts with romantic names. The resort named **Satellite Beach** is growing in leaps and bounds and has way over 10,000 residents. There are expensive holiday homes, some with yacht moorings, especially in **Indian Harbour Beach**. **Paradise Beach** and also **Melbourne Beach** have especially nice swimming areas. To the south **Melbourne Shores** and **Floridiana Beach** are popular with tourists and locals alike.

Further south Highway A1A crosses Sebastian Inlet. Deep sea fishers can go out to the Atlantic from Indian River since there is a gap here between the barrier islands. The **swimming and surfing beach** is fabulous.

McLarty Museum exhibits treasures salvaged from a Spanish galleon that sank in 1715 (hours: Wed to Sun 9am–5pm).

❶ Sebastian Inlet, daily 10am – 4pm, admission US$2, www.floridastateparks.org/sebastianinlet/

Sebastian Inlet

In Sebastian (between Melbourne and Vero Beach) finds made by **Mel Fisher** (1922–98) are on display. In 1985 the most famous and successful treasure hunter in the world and his team celebrated an outstanding achievement. After searching for years he discovered the **wreck of the Atocha, which sank in 1622**. This legendary ship was on its way back to Spain loaded with gold, silver, coins and jewellery.

❶ 1322 US 1; Mon – Sat 10am – 5pm, Sun 12pm – 5pm, closed Sept, admission US$6.50, www.melfisher.com/treasuresales/locotions.asp

*Mel Fisher's Treasure Museum

The world famous treasure hunter Mel Fisher (1922 – 1998) with a young crew on board his explorer ship

★★ Miami

————————————————— ✦ J 7

Region: South-east
Elevation: 0 – 7m/22ft above sea level
Population: 409,000 (greater metropolitan area: about 5.6 million)

»Welcome to Miami – Bienvenido a Miami!« – with this hit pop-star Will Smith together with Eva Mendes paid homage to Florida's metropolis a few years ago, where the air is scented with orange blossoms and arroz con pollo and where there are more statues of José Marti and Simon Bolivar than of Abraham Lincoln and George Washington. But the Spanish-speaking majority thinks in a thoroughly American way, as the dynamic skyline over the palm trees shows.

»It is my dream to see this wilderness transformed into a prosperous land.« **Julia Tuttle** (1840–98) had big plans for the settlement on Biscayne Bay, but she certainly didn't expect one thing: little more than one hundred years after its incorporation in 1896 Miami (»Maya-mi« meaning »large water« in the Seminole Indian language) is a boomtown bursting with life, which attracts 11 million partygoers and tourists from around the world annually.

Julia Tuttle started it all

It started with a bouquet of orange blossoms. That is what Mrs Julia Tuttle, who had land on the Miami River and wanted a railway connection, sent to the railway magnate **Henry Flagler** in 1895. He had built his East Coast Railway as far as ▶Palm Beach and considered his work to be completed. But then a cold snap destroyed the citrus crops in northern Florida and Julia Tuttle used the chance to advertise her wilderness in the south with blossoming orange branches. Flagler reacted immediately. As early as April 1896 his Florida East Coast Railroad reached Miami. The rest, as they say, is history. Spurred by the development of the sand dunes on the coast (today ▶Miami Beach) Miami was already a popular holiday venue around 1910. It survived both the Florida Land Bust in the 1920s and two catastrophic hurricanes. The city celebrated the end of the depression with hotel architecture that was the most modern of its time. Soon Art Deco buildings were a part of Miami and Miami Beach like the sun, sand and beach.

Orange blossoms, railroaders and Cubans

During World War II shorts were traded in for uniforms. Soldiers were trained and the wounded were cared for in the south of Florida. After the war many GIs returned with their families to Miami to live. National airlines discovered Miami. Miami Beach became the **Amer-**

Miami skyline

Highlights Miami

► **Bayside Marketplace**
Lively rendezvous
►page 243

► **Pérez Art Miami Museum**
Works by leading contemporary
North and South American artists.
►page 247

► **Little Havana/Calle Ocho**
The heart of Spanish-speaking Miami is
Little Havana, especially on Calle Ocho.
►page 249

► **Coconut Grove**
People-watching in one of the street
cafés in »The Grove«.
►page 249

► **Villa Vizcaya**
The winter home of the industrialist
John Deering is simply overwhelming.
►page 249

► **Coral Gables**
A walk through Coral Gables, the
»City Beautiful«, goes by remarkable
buildings like the Venetian Pool and
the Biltmore Hotel.
►page 251

► **Miami Seaquarium**
Sword whales, dolphins and a successful manatee-raising programme
are worth a visit.
►page 255

ican Riviera: between 1945 and 1954 more hotels were built here than in all of the other states together. But Miami attracted not only tourists.

In the 1950s organized crime came to the city. Almost all Mafia families on the east coast used Miami as the base for their activities in the Caribbean and Cuba. Gambling, prostitution, drug dealing – Miami became known as a dangerous place to be.

On 1 January 1959 Miami's future path was reset. The success of Castro's revolution on Cuba brought a flood of exiles to Miami, above all members of the deposed junta and almost the entire conservative upper class. In 1973 300,000 **Cubans** already lived in Miami. They were to change the face of the city for good. In the 1980s Fidel Castro emptied the Cuban prisons and sent another 140,000 compatriots, many of them criminals, to Miami.

During the 1980s Miami's new Downtown was built. Other immigrants came from Latin America and from Cuba; street signs, billboards, displays all became bilingual. For the first time Miami was called »North South America«. Numerous businesses settled in Miami with feelers stretched out towards the markets of Latin America. Film and television discovered Miami. The TV series *Miami Vice* (1984 until 1989) established the city's image as the playground of tough guys and easy girls and reflected its role in international drug dealing. Miami recovered from the activities of the Columbian drug cartel thanks to drastic police measures and to Hurricane Andrew, which blew through the city in 1992.

Today Miami is one of the most important centres of international finance and a wide-open door to Latin America. But from 2007 to 2012 the city was shaken by the worst real estate and financial crisis since after 1929. In hardly any other large city in the USA is the difference between rich and poor as obvious as it is in Miami. Moreover, the percentage of the population in Miami that is Hispanic or Latino, at almost 70 percent, is the largest of any American metropolis.. But the image has remained: chic, cool, hot – and always a bit disreputable.

DOWNTOWN

The tourist focal point is Bayside Marketplace on the **Miamarina**, where mega-expensive yachts crowd in and excursion boats depart for Biscayne Bay. Incidentally: Miamarina includes the former **Pier 5** of the harbour and became known as the mooring of Sonny Krockett's houseboat in the TV series Miami Vice. There is a promenade here, where people go to be seen; the outdoor stage occasionally hosts pop music stars and the best salsa bands perform in the Latino café. In the nearby **Hard Rock Café** there's always something going on. The gallerias offer souvenirs for every taste and strong café Cubano. **Bayfront Park** with the skyscraper backdrop of Biscayne Boulevard has three important monuments: the **Torch of Friendship** symbolizes Miami's variegated relationship to Central and South America; the **World War II Memorial** commemorates the American soldiers who were killed in World War II; the **Challenger Memorial** honours the crew of the Challenger spacecraft that was lost in 1986.

**Bayside Marketplace

Miami's main artery is the southern part of the palm tree-lined Biscayne Boulevard, where the first skyscraper boom began in the 1920s. **Freedom Tower** (600 Biscayne Blvd.), which was built in 1925 and still stands apart, is reminiscent of this time. The richly decorated tower was once the headquarters of the daily newspaper Miami News. Cuban refugees were housed here in the 1960s. A small exhibition on the ground floor depicts the sufferings of Cuban exiles during the Castro regime and their achievements in the USA after fleeing Cuba. In 2000 the modern **American Airlines Arena** was built diagonally opposite as the new home of the »Miami Heat« basketball team. On the southern edge of Bayfront Park unusual skyscrapers characterize the skyline: in 1972 the 139m/456ft-high **One Biscayne Tower** was completed. Next to it is the 55-storey **Southeast Financial Center** (200 S. Biscayne Blvd.), the second highest building in Florida (233m/764ft.)

*Biscayne Boulevard

Miami

INFORMATION
Greater Miami CVB
701 Brickell Avenue, Suite 2700
Miami, FL 33131
Tel. 1-305-539-3000
www.gmcvb.com

AIRPORT
Miami International Airport
Tel. 1-305-876-7000
www.miami-airport.com
Miami International Airport is just a few
miles west of Downtown. There are
good connections to local mass transportation. Hotels, car rental agencies run
shuttle buses to take guests to their destination in comfort. Plenty of taxi companies also serve the airport.

PUBLIC TRANSPORTATION
Tri-Rail
Tel. 1-800-874-7245
www.tri-rail.com
This regional express train runs from
Monday to Saturday several times a day
on the route Miami – Fort Lauderdale –
Palm Beach.

Miami-Dade Transit
Tel. 1-305-891-3131
www.miamidade.gov
Miami's public transportation includes a
dense Metrobus network with 70
routes, which include Miami's suburbs as
well. An elevated railway called the
MetroRail runs through the city on a
22mi/35km long route from North Miami to Dadeland in the south. The trains
run from 5.30am to midnight.
The driverless MetroMover runs on two
circular tracks in downtown Miami and
connects all of the larger hotels, government offices and shopping centres daily
between 5am and midnight. No charge.

CITY TOUR
Miami is not the city to explore on foot.
Public transportation doesn't always
take you where you want to go. Only
the MetroMover (see above), a driverless
elevated train, as well as the MetroRail
and the MetroBus do run to interesting
places in the city. Organized city tours
are recommended, most of which start
from Bayside Marketplace.

SHOPPING/NIGHT LIFE
Bayside Marketplace
3050 Grand Avenue
Mon – Thu 10am – 10pm, Fri, Sat
Miami's most popular venue is on Biscayne Bay and includes more than 150
shops, a food court and entertainment.
The place is lively until late evening. The
drinks are cafe Cubano, mojito or even a
caipirinha.

CocoWalk
Coconut Grove
Sun – Thu 10am – 10pm, Fri, Sat 10am
– 11pm, bars until 3am
CocoWalk is the heart of Coconut
Grove. Enjoy the four dozen shops and
boutiques with tasteful goods on three
storeys or do some people-watching
from one of the numerous restaurants.
Busy until late at night.

Streets of Mayfair
Grand Avenue
In Coconut Grove, be sure to take a look
at the Streets of Mayfair. There's lots to
buy here as well and the southern atmosphere is lively until late.

EVENTS
Coconut Grove Arts Festival
On a weekend in February the first large arts festival of the USA takes place outdoors.

Carnival Miami, *Calle Ocho Festival*
»Little Havana« is especially busy during carnival (Feb/March). There are colourful parades, Caribbean rhythms and salsa music on the streets.

WHERE TO EAT
❶ *Garcia's Seafood Grille & Fish* $$
398 NW North River Drive
Tel. 1-305-375-0765
Red snapper and stone crabs are available in the middle of »Little Havana«.

❷ *Michell's Genuine Kitchen* $$
130 NE 40th Street
Tel. 1-305-573-5550
Modern eatery in the Design District that spoils its guests with fine and unusually creative fusion cuisine. Prices are moderate.

❸ *Atrio*
1395 Brickell Avenue
Tel. 1-305-503-6500
Progressive »American cuisine« on the 25th floor of the Conrad Miami Hotel with a breath-taking view of the skyline of downtown Miami.

❹ *Cheen-Huaye* $$
15400 Biscayne Blvd.
Tel. 1-305-956-2808
Authentic Mexican or Yucatán-cooking, of which Chef Marco is a master.

WHERE TO STAY
❶ *Inter-Continental Miami* $$$
100 Chopin Plaza
Tel. 1-305-577-1000
www.icmiamihotel.com
Post-modern skyscraper (640 rooms and 36 suites) with lots of marble. The lobby holds The Spindle by artist Henry Moore.

❷ *Hyatt Regency Miami* $$$
400 SE 2nd Ave.
Tel. 1-305-358-1234
www.miamiregency.hyatt.com
The 610 tastefully furnished rooms and 50 suites offer a wonderful view of Biscayne Bay and the harbour.

❸ *Hampton Inn Miami – Coconut Grove / Coral Gables* $$$
2800 SW 28th Terrace
Coconut Grove
Tel. 1-305-448-2800
www.hamptoninncoconutgrove.com
The modern mid-range hotel with 136 rooms and suites is only a few steps from the centre of town and a few minutes by car to attractions in Coral Gables.

❹ *Holiday Inn Port of Miami*
340 Biscayne Blvd.
Tel. 1-305-371-4400
www.holidayinn.com
Hotel with 200 rooms and suites right on the harbour in Downtown Miami, outdoor pool and fitness centre.

Miami Downtown

Where to stay
- ❶ Inter-Continental
- ❷ Hyatt Regency
- ❸ Hampton Inn Miami-Coconut Grove/Coral Gables
- ❹ Holiday Inn Port of Miami

Where to eat
- ❶ Garcia's Seafood
- ❷ Michell's Genuine Kitchen
- ❸ Atrio
- ❹ Cheen-Huaye

Loud, lively and multilingual, Flagler Street runs into town from Bay-front Park and gives the best impression of Downtown Miami. Wealthy tourists from Latin America stock up on consumer goods here; European visitors think they are in Caracas. The street first runs to **Guzman Center for the Performing Arts**, which was opened in 1926 as the Olympia Theater and later converted into a cultural centre. On the other side of the street is the **Alfred I. DuPont Building** (169 E. Flagler St.); it was built in 1938 as the headquarters of the Florida National Bank, which was controlled by the DuPont family.

*Flagler Street

The Metro-Dade Cultural Center was built some time ago built around a post-modern piazza; It includes the Pérez Art Museum, the Historical Museum of Southern Florida as well as a library.

*Miami Dade Cultural Center

It offers an exciting dramatization of 10,000 years of history. The exhibition begins with the Indians who built their shell mounds in mangrove swamps. There are treasures of the Spanish galleons, which were salvaged off the coast of Florida. Another topic is the explosive development of the city of Miami. Excellent is the presentation entitled **»Tropical Dreams: A People's History of South Florida«**.
❶ 101 W Flagler St., Tue – Fri 10am – 5pm, Sat, Sun noon – 5pm, admission US$8, www.historymiami.org

*Historical Museum of Southern Florida

It opened in its new location in the new Museum Park in Downtown Miami in 2013. The new building was designed by Swiss architects Herzog and de Meuron and exhibits not only works by renowned US American artists, but also works by Latin American artists since 1940. The highlights include works by **Max Ernst, Jasper Johns, Alexander Calder, Robert Rauschenberg and Cristo**.
❶ 1103 Biscayne Blvd., Tue – Sun 10am – 6pm, Thus 10am – 9pm, admission US$12, www.pamm.org

*Pérez Art Museum Miami

South of Flagler Street is Miami's landmark: Miami Tower, which is illuminated at night. This 52-storey skyscraper was built in 1987 to designs by **I. M. Pei** (in cooperation with Spillis Candela & Partners). The colourful lighting is by **Douglas Leigh**. On St Patrick's Day, for example, the building is bathed in Kelly green and on Valentine's Day in red light.

*Nations-Bank Tower

On N.E.1st Avenue, which runs through the middle of downtown Miami, two buildings are worth mentioning. One is the Catholic **Gesù Church**, which was built in 1925 and has stained glass windows from a workshop in Munich, Germany. The other, not far to the north, is the **U.S. Federal Courthouse** with its Moorish inner courtyard, which was built in 1931. A brilliant mural shows the development of Florida from wild swampland to a progressive civilized state.

N. E. 1st Avenue

Brickell Avenue Biscayne Avenue ends at the **Miami River. In the 1980s impressive high-rise architecture was built here. The bridge across the Miami River connects the busy city centre with the well-to-do residential areas between Biscayne Bay and Brickell Avenue. Brickell Avenue was originally conceived as a residential street for wealthy families; today it is lined with the marble and glass palaces of over 100 financial institutions. The street is called the »**Wall Street of the South**« and not without reason. The futuristic buildings of the architectural cooperative Arquitectonica are remarkable. The best-known is **Atlantis** (2025 Brickell Ave.; photo ▶p.57), which became a sensation for the square hole in its façade – with a palm tree and a red spiral staircase. **Brickell House** (no. 501), which was built in 1871 at Brickell Park, is also noteworthy.

Rickenbacker Causeway From the southern end of Brickell Avenue the Rickenbacker Causeway (toll) runs across the shallow **Biscayne Bay** to **Virginia Key** and further to the island of **Key Biscayne**.

Miami: view of Miami River and Brickell Avenue;
Miami Tower illuminated on the left

LITTLE HAVANA

South-west of downtown Miami there is a neighbourhood populated by many Cuban exiles, who came to Florida in several waves after 1959. Between SW 12th Avenue and SW 27th Avenue there is a colourful, mixture of shops, small markets and friendly restaurants in a relaxed atmosphere; café cubano and mojito are available everywhere and in the evening the rhythmic sounds of salsa and dancon can be heard. This area is now called Little Havana. The street language is Spanish.

Neighbour-hood of Cuban exiles

The busy main street of Little Havana is Calle Ocho (SW 8th St.), the annual scene of the boisterous **Carnaval Miami Festival** with its hours-long parades of salsa bands. Calle Ocho, which starts at the banking palaces of Brickell Avenue as SW 8th Street, runs west through Little Havana and then becomes **Tamiami Trail** (US 41), the main road out of Miami.

**Calle Ocho

There are interesting buildings and monuments along Calle Ocho. The annual »International Hispanic Theater Festival« is held in **Teatro Avante** (774 S. 8th St., www.teatroavante.com), which performs classical and modern Spanish-language dramas. On the little square where SW 13th Street runs into Calle Ocho a marble monument was solemnly unveiled in 1971 with an eternal flame in memory of the members of **Brigade 2506**, who lost their lives in April 1961 during the failed invasion of Cuba. To the west at the intersection of SW 15th Avenue is the park that was originally named after Máximo Gómez, the leader of the Cuban liberation army, but which is now known as **Domino Park**. Older Cuban exiles meet here to play dominoes.

This museum commemorates the failed invasion at the Bay of Pigs on Cuba in 1961.

Bay of Pigs Museum

❶ 1821 SW 9th St., Mon – Fri 10am – 5pm, admission free, www.bayofpigsmuseum.org

COCONUT GROVE

The area of Miami's southern suburbs was established around 1840 by »Conchs«, immigrants from the Bahamas. Later wealthy people from New England came and built their winter homes here. Artists and hippies joined them. Simple half-timbered homes and buildings made of Coquina limestone as well as Mediterranean villas in the middle of profusely blooming gardens give the settlement lots of atmosphere. The heart of the neighbourhood is the intersection of Grand Avenue, Main Highway and McFarlane Road.

Where the rich live

**Villa Vizcaya
Not far south of Rickenbacker Causeway is the beautiful Villa Vizcaya in the middle of classical-style gardens. The building was built from 1912 to 1916 as the winter residence of James Deering, who produced harvesters, and was built in Italian Renaissance style. In the opulently furnished rooms of the palace a collection of French, Spanish and Italian art as well as valuable furnishings, carpets and sculptures – and a collection of old Baedekers – can be admired.

❶ 3251 S. Miami Ave.; daily 9.30am – 4.30pm, admission US$18, www.vizcayamuseum.org

*Miami Museum of Science & Planetarium
North of Villa Vizcaya lies another prestigious building that was built in the first quarter of the 20th century in the Mediterranean style. Today it houses a natural science exhibition as well as a space travel show and a planetarium. In cooperation with the Smithsonian Institution the museum was expanded to a »Science Center of the Americas« (3280 S. Miami Ave.; hours: daily 10am–6pm).
Hinweis: This museum will move to the new Museum Park Downtown in 2015.

❶ 3280 S. Miami Ave., daily 10am– 6pm, admission US$15, www.miamisci.org

Miami City Hall
About 2mi/3km further south-west lies Miami City Hall, a remarkable example of **Art Deco** architecture at Dinner Key. It was built in 1933 as the **terminal for seaplanes**. The last seaplane took off from here in 1945. Nine years later it was converted to City Hall.

**Coconut Grove Village
Westwards toward the centre of town (Grand Ave./Main Hwy.) is the **old town centre** of Coconut Grove. In the 1960s there was a colourful mixture of simple shops, cafés and galleries; in the 1970s and 1980s it mutated to a chic shopping zone. In the 1990s the area was discovered by young people and tourists. The selection in the shops changed with the times. Today there are pretty street cafés, cinemas and shops that sell beach fashions, CDs, DVDs etc. Venues like **CocoWalk**, which was built in 1990, the **Streets of Mayfair** and **Commodore Plaza** have remained popular.

Coconut Grove Playhouse
At the south-western edge of Coconut Grove Village stands the **Coconut Playhouse**, which was built in 1926 in the Moorish style. It became known as the place where Beckett's drama Waiting for Godot was first performed in America. Today cabaret programmes and musicals are performed here, too.

❶ 3500 Main Highway, currently closed

The Barnacle State Historic Site
Nearby at Dinner Key Channel there is a piece of the original Florida. A **wooden house** stands here on stilts; it was built in 1891 by Ralph Munroe, the most famous sailboat builder of his time. He imitated

Villa Vizcaya: Italian flair in Coconut Grove

the building style of the Conchs, who had found an interesting solution to the problem of ventilation in a tropical climate. The rooms and covered verandas are grouped around the »barnacle«, the octagonal living room in the middle. The original furnishings have been preserved, as has the **boathouse with workshop.**

❶ 3485 Main Highway; tours: Fri -- Mon 10am, 11.30am, 1pm, 2.30pm, tickets US$3, www.floridastateparks.com/thebarnacle/

CORAL GABLES

The suburb of Coral Gables sprawls west of Coconut Grove. It was built in 1926 by **George Merrick** to designs by his father as an upper-class residential neighbourhood with generous parks and sports facilities; here too Mediterranean architecture, which was fashionable at that time, was used. Eight city gates were planned originally, but only four were actually built, all of them in the north of the suburb. Anyone driving west on the Tamiami Trail will pass by three of them, the **Douglas Entrance**, the Granada Entrance and the **Prado Entrance**. They were modelled on triumphal arches that can be found

**Mediterranean ambience

in Madrid, Toledo and Seville. The main artery is **Coral Way**, which traverses Coral Gables from east to west. The Spanish Renaissance **Coral Gables City Hall** at the intersection of Coral Way and LeJeune Road is an architectural attraction. Coral Gables is still elegant and beauty-conscious – so much so that not even the residents are allowed to park a pickup truck in their driveway. As an irony of history, today more and more wealthy YUCAs (»Young Urban Cuban Americans«) live on the streets with Spanish names.

*Miracle Mile From City Hall the Miracle Mile, the eastern arm of Coral Way (SW 22nd Ave.), runs towards Miami. After a period of stagnation the broad thoroughfare was revived. Here stands the **Colonnade Building** with its rotunda, wonderful marble interior, beautiful ornamentation and Spanish tile roof; it was designed and used by Merrick. Tthe **Colonnade Hotel** next to it was built in 1985.

Merrick House West of City Hall the childhood home of **George Merrick** is worth noting. It was restored in the style of the 1920s and is a museum today (907 Coral Way; tours: Wed, Sun 1pm–4pm). Two interesting buildings near Merrick House are **Poinciana Place** (937 Coral Way),

Mediterranean atmosphere in Coral Gables

which was built in 1916 as Merrick's honeymoon cottage, and **Casa Azul** (1254 Coral Way) (1924) with its spectacular roof of glazed blue tiles.

Merrick House: 907 Coral Way, tours Wed and Sun 1pm, 2pm, 3pm, ticket US$5, www.coralgables.com

Just before Merrick House DeSoto Boulevard branches off from Coral Way towards the south-west and DeSoto Plaza. On the way is the picturesque Venetian Pool, a very pretty swimming pool that was built in an abandoned coral limestone quarry; films were made here with the Tarzan actor Johnny Weissmuller and the actress Esther Williams. Towering coral limestone constructions, a casino, Venetian-style arched bridges, little **waterfalls** and **artificial caves** attract not only tourists, but also many local people. The artist Denman Fink designed the charming **fountain on DeSoto Plaza** in front of the Venetian Pool in the 1920s.

**Venetian Pool

❶ 2701 DeSoto Blvd., early April – mid June Tue – Fri 11am – 5.30pm, Sat, Sun, 10am – 4.30pm, mid June – mid Aug. Mon – Fri 11am – 6.30pm, Sat, Sun 10am – 4.30pm, mid Aug – early Sept Mon – Fri 11am – 5.30pm, Sat, Sun 10am – 4.30pm, admission US$11, www.coralgables.com

DeSoto Boulevard ends in front of the Biltmore Hotel, which opened in 1926. The centre of the 275-room complex is the 100m/330ft-high tower, which was probably modelled on the Giralda in Spanish Seville. The hotel lobby, with its Italian marble and Spanish tiles, is a feast for the eyes, and has already impressed such guests as **Judy Garland** and **Ginger Rogers**. The luxury hotel was used as a military hospital during World War II and afterwards as a veterans' hospital. It then fell into disuse and deteriorated from 1968 to 1986. It was renovated recently and is now used as a luxury hotel again and as a backdrop for fashion photographers, film makers and bridal couples. Around the hotel there are two golf courses, a polo field and more than a dozen tennis courts. During the hotel's heyday Italian gondoliers brought guests to the beach at Biscayne Bay via a »**Canale**«.

**Biltmore Hotel

The campus of the University of Miami (14,000 students) is located at the southern edge of the Biltmore Hotel property; it was founded in 1926. The art museum here holds outstanding Pueblo and Navajo **Indian arts and crafts**. Another highlight is the **Kress Collection** with works from the Renaissance and the Baroque, including paintings by **Tintoretto** and **Jordaens**. In the Beaux-Arts Gallery works by famous artists of the 19th and 20th century can be seen. Paintings by **Frank Stella** and **Roy Lichtenstein** as well as ceramics by **Pablo Picasso** have pride of place.

*Lowe Art Museum

❶ 1301 Stanford Dr.; Tue -- Sat 10am – 4pm, Sun noon – 5pm, admission US$10, www.miami.edu/lowe

*Fairchild Tropical Gardens

Only a few minutes' drive south of Coral Gables lies Matheson Hammock Park. There are virgin hardwood groves here as well as a beautiful beach. The south-west part of the park has been dedicated to the botanist David Fairchild in the form of the ***Fairchild Tropical Garden**. Thousands of varieties of plants are cultivated here, including more than 100 species of palm tree.

❶ 10901 Old Cutler Rd.; tours: Mon – Fri 9.30am–4.30pm, Sat, Sun 7.30am – 4.30pm, ticket US$25, www.fairchildgardens.org

SOUTH MIAMI

The area south-west of Coral Gables has been developed all the way to the ▶Everglades National Park and consists of residential areas with malls, golf courses and parking lots, petrol stations, used car lots and waterbed dealers. Anyone driving this way should stop at two attractions.

*Miami Metrozoo

The zoo was heavily damaged by hurricane Andrew in August 1992, but afterwards rebuilt according to the most modern scientific standards. More than 100 species of animals live in areas modelled on natural biotopes. The main attractions are the Bengal tigers, koala bears, gorillas, reptiles, a few giant aviaries (more than 300 different kinds of birds) and a petting zoo (12400 SW 152nd St.; hours: daily 9.30am–5.30pm).

❶ 12400 SW 152nd St., daily 9.30am – 5.30pm, admission US$16, www.miamimetrozoo.com

*Gold Coast Railroad Museum

Nearby train lovers will be tempted by the highly polished old locomotives and wagons of the Gold Coast Railroad Museum. The star of the museum is a Pullman wagon that was used by US Presidents Roosevelt, Truman and Eisenhower. »California Zephyr« trains as well as an extra-powerful diesel locomotive that belonged to NASA can be viewed. On weekends rides on steam and diesel engine locomotives are offered.

❶ 12450 SW 152nd St.; Mon – Fri 10am -- 4pm, Sat, Sun 11am – 4pm, admission US$6, www.gcrm.org

KEY BISCAYNE

Exclusive recreational and residential area

Sting in faded shorts, Paris Hilton with or without her lapdog: when Miami's gossip columns reports on celebrities, the name Key Biscayne comes up often. South-east of Miami lies this 7mi/11km-long barrier island with its **beautiful beaches, expansive sports facilities**, most luxurious residences and several gourmet restaurants. Key

Biscayne is known above all to golfers and tennis players as the venue for important tournaments. Get to the island via Brickell Avenue or Bayshore Drive across the Rickenbacker Causeway (toll).

South Florida's largest tropical seawater aquarium is situated at the southern tip of Virginia Key. In the late 1950s numerous episodes of the worldwide popular TV series with the clever **do**lphin Flipper were filmed here. Presently the female orca whale Lolita is the absolute star of the seawater circus. The controversial aquarium holds thousands of sea creatures. The artificial coral reefs and the underwater station, where the feeding of the sharks can be watched, are also worth seeing. In the mangrove forest of **Discovery Bay** endangered species are presented, including several sea turtles.

**Miami Seaquarium

❶ 4400 Rickenbacker Causeway; daily 9.30am – 6pm, admission US$40, www.miamiseaquarium.com

The new nature centre is dedicated to the grand old lady of ecology (▶Famous People) and has interesting aquariums, beautiful walks through almost untouched hammocks and beach tours guided by experts in the field. The writings of Marjorie Stoneman Douglas are also interesting.

*Marjory Stoneman Douglas Biscayne Nature Center

Crandon Park: 8am until sunset, parking fee per vehicle US$5, www.miamidade.gov/parks/parks/crandon_beach.asp
Biscayne Nature Center: 6767 Crandon Blvd. daily 10am – 4pm, free admission, www.biscaynenaturecenter.com

One of the most beautiful beaches in the Sunshine State lies practically at Miami's front door: the 2mi/3km-long beach slopes so gently to the Atlantic that it's possible to walk all the way to the sandbanks far out in the water. With a little luck some dolphins may swim by.

*Crandon Park Beach

❶ 6747 Crandon Blvd., 8am until sunset, parking fee per vehicle US$5, www.miamidade.gov/parks/parks/crandon_beach.asp

On the southern end of Key Biscayne, Crandon Boulevard ends at the entrance to this beautiful nature reserve that protects the **dunes**. No less beautiful than Crandon Beach, the 1.2mi/2km-long **beach** is also the site of Florida's oldest lighthouse. Built in 1825, the **Cape Florida Lighthouse** was besieged by Indians and burned down during the Second Seminole Wars. The 31m/100ft-high lighthouse was rebuilt shortly afterwards and still offers a point of orientation for ships.

*Bill Baggs Cape Florida Recreation Area

Bill Baggs Cape Florida State Park: 1200 S. Crandon Blvd., Key Biscayne, daily 8am until sunset, admission: pedestrians US$2, vehicles US$8, www.floridaparks.org/capeflorida/
Cape Florida Lighthouse: daily 9am – 5pm, tours Thu – Mon 10am and 1pm

Biscayne National Park

ARRIVAL
By car: US-1 to Homestead, then follow SW 328th Street (North Canal Drive) east
By boat: to Herbert Hoover Marina at Homestead Bayfront Park or to the marina in Black Point Park.

INFORMATION
Biscayne National Park
Dante Fascell Visitor Cente
9700 SW 328 St.
Homestead, FL 33033

Tel. 1-305-203-7275
www.nps.gov/bisc

ACTIVITIES
Dante Fascell Visitor Center
Rent canoes and kayaks here or book boat tours

BiscayneUnderwater
Tel. 1-305-230-1100
www.biscayneunderwater.com
Tours with a glass-bottom boat and kayaks, also guided snorkeling adventures.

The underwater world of Key Biscayne shimmers in every imaginable colour

BISCAYNE NATIONAL PARK

Biscayne National Park was established in 1980 and is located about a one-hour drive south of Miami; it is the largest marine nature preserve in the continental USA. It protects an area of 275 sq mi/712 sq km including 44 barrier islands, coral reefs, mangrove forests and costal swamplands. The reef itself is located several miles off the coast and offers refuge to about 50 different types of coral as well as a variety of tropical fish and shellfish.

Largest marine nature reserve of continental USA

Dante Fascell Visitor Center, accessible via North Canal Street (SW 328 Street), is located 9mi/15km east of Homestead on Convey Point. The informative exhibitions are devoted to the complicated natural history of Biscayne Bay (hours: daily 9am–5pm).

Dante Fascell Visitor Center

❶ SW 328 St., daily 9am – 5pm, free admission, www.nps.gov/bisc/

The coral reefs that grew before the Keys in the open sea are a special attraction, but for some time now they have been endangered by environmental pollution. The warm Gulf Stream that flows by here enables various kinds of coral to flourish. The corals are a home to an unbelievable variety of fish. Sponges, shrimps, crayfish and lobsters can also be seen. Moreover sea turtles live in this region as well. Divers explore the **wrecks of ships** that ran aground here on the reefs in the past. In 1733 alone 19 Spanish galleons sank here during a hurricane on their way to Europe. **Mangrove Coast** On the main land the Mangrove Coast is mainly intact. With their tangle of roots the mangroves capture the finest sediment and filter the water. They are the nursery for the fish who live in the bay and offer ideal living conditions for tideland and sea birds. The ****Keys** (Cayos) in the nature preserve have a vegetation that is unique in the USA. The islands bear a variety of tropical hardwoods and bushes that are otherwise only found in the Caribbean. On **Elliott Key** a few miles off the coast there is a dock, a campground and a pretty beach. The ranger station, which has information on the problems of the nature preserve, is only open occasionally in the winter.

**Coral reefs

FLORIDA CITY · HOMESTEAD

The fertile coastal plain on the southern edge of metropolitan Miami is one of the important areas in the USA for cultivating vegetables. The completely frost-free climate allow several harvests every year for lettuce, tomatoes, avocados, onions etc. Recently decorative plants, flowers, herbs and spices have been added.

The East Coast's salad bowl

Andrew was here: In August 1992 the Homestead – Florida City area was devastated by Hurricane Andrew. More than 170,000 people were left homeless, and almost all the crops were destroyed as well as the nearby Homestead Air Force Base. In the meantime life has started up again; all signs of the devastation are gone.

NORTH MIAMI · PORT OF MIAMI · CAUSEWAYS

Opa Locka

Opa Locka in northern Miami was a model of settlement building in the 1920s. At that time the city planner **Glen Curtiss** designed it in Moorish style. The streets are shaped like a sickle and named after characters in Arabian Nights. The **City Hall** and the **Heart Building** (former Opa Locka Hotel) with domes and minarets are worth seeing. In May an Arabian Nights Festival is held here.

*Museum of Contemporary Art

Integrated into the ultra-modern North Miami Civic Complex in the suburb of North Miami to the east this museum attracts friends of contemporary art. Original exhibitions that like to break with conventions are the trademark of the house. They attract visitors from the avant-garde American urban scene. The exhibits include works by **Keith Haring, Jasper Johns, Roy Lichtenstein**, Claes Oldenburg and Robert Rauschenberg.

❶ 770 NE 125th St.; Tue, Thu – Sat 11am – 5pm, Wed 1pm – 9pm, Sun noon – 5pm, admission US$5, www.mocanom.org

Port of Miami

The port of Miami is located on the artificial Dodge Island and Lummus Island and is the most important sea-passage terminal in the world. More than a dozen cruise ships can dock here at one time. About **4 million passengers** pass through every year, most of them to the Bahamas or the Caribbean. The harbour was expanded in the 1990s. Meanwhile giant container ships can dock here as well. A tunnel between Watson Island and the Port providing direct access to the interstate highway system is planned. It will relieve downtown Miami of Port passenger and cargo traffic.

Causeways

North of the harbour »streets on stilts« connect the mainland with the islands and the vacation city of Miami Beach. The **MacArthur Causeway** runs from the mainland to **Watson Island** where the **Japanese Gardens** with pagoda, teahouse and waterfall as well as the **Garden of the Americas** are located. ***Jungle Island** is a special attraction on Watson Island. The nicely arranged park has not only parrots, but also marabous, cockatoos, and many other animals including an albino alligator There are shows with trained animals every day.

The **Miami Children's Museum** is located right on McArthur Causeway and has many activities for children to try out.

About 300m/1,000ft further to the north the **Venetian Causeway**,

Cruise ships line up in the port of Miami

which leads over to Miami Beach, crosses Biscayne Bay and connects the artificially created **Venetian Islands**.

Further to the north is **Julia Tuttle Causeway** (I-195), named after the »mother of Miami«. It connects Miami with Miami Beach. At the western bridgehead of Julia Tuttle Causeway apartment complexes for the well-to-do have been constructed recently.

Japanese Gardens: Mon – Fri 7am – 3.30pm, Sat, Sun 9am – 6pm, free admission, parking fee US$10

Jungle Island: 1111 Parrot Jungle Trail, Mon – Fri 10am – 5pm, Sat, Sun 10am – 6pm, admission US$33, www.jungleisland.com

Miami Childrens Museum: 780 McArthur Causeway, daily 10am – 6pm, admission US$16, www.miamichildrensmuseum.org

** **Miami Beach**

◈ J 7

Region: South-east
Elevation: 0 – 3m/10ft above sea level
Population: 92,000

Before setting the sun illuminates the pastel-coloured houses in the Art Deco district. Inside are the sounds of salsa music, clinking glasses and laughing voices. Miami Beach is Florida's party town, where Jennifer Lopez, Paris Hilton and friends turn night into day and paparazzi lie in wait for hung-over celebrities.

In 1868 the farmer Henry B. Plum saw palms on an island while sailing along Florida's Atlantic coast. He tried his luck with coconuts and built the first house. But the mangrove swamps and the clouds of mosquitoes prevented more than that. In 1894 Plum gave up and sold his land to John Collins, a farmer from New Jersey. He only saw his property two years later when he came to Miami on one of the first trains. But he could not pay for his dream of building a bridge from the mainland to the sandy island. Enter **Carl Fisher**, the owner of the Indiana Speedway. The bridge was built and Collins' property turned into a winter resort with golf course and tennis courts. Miami Beach was born! Meanwhile railway magnate **Henry Flagler** advertised in the cool northern USA for the new winter holiday venue and had the Royal Palm Hotel built. Fisher's advertising campaigns – in cold New York he set up billboards proclaiming »It's June in Miami« and attracted investors and visitors – were also successful.

Stormy beginnings

America's millionaires wanted their place in the sun: in the 1920s the super-rich such as media tsar William Randolph Hearst and the industrialist Alfred DuPont had their winter residences built on »Millionaire's Row«. Real estate prices skyrocketed. While Miami Beach in 1921 had five hotels and nine apartment buildings, four years later it already had 56 hotels, 178 apartment buildings and 858 private homes. The hurricane in 1926 ended the building boom, but Miami Beach stayed in business. In 1928, at the height of prohibition, mafia gangs under Al Capone took over the alcohol business in Miami.

In the 1930s and 1940s the growth continued and Art Deco began to flourish. Architects designed buildings with the forms of eclecticism, Mediterranean architecture and the streamlines of new means of transportation. After the Japanese attack on Pearl Harbor (1941), the Miami Beach hotels were temporarily turned into training camps, military hospitals and private quarters. After the war a broader social spectrum was attracted to Miami Beach.

Art Deco in Miami Beach

Highlights Miami Beach

► **Art Deco Historic District**
The world's largest collection of Art Deco buildings is one of the top attractions in southern Florida.
►page 268

► **South Beach**
Bronzed guys and girls, an electrifying atmosphere: the paths leading to this palm-lined beach are the catwalks of the rich and beautiful.
►page 268

► **Collins Avenue**
Credit cards were never busier: in an Art Deco setting on south Collins Avenue, shopping for clothes is even more fun than usual.
►page 255

► **Ocean Drive**
Scantily dressed Latinas, Latinos wearing gold rings, muscular Afro-Americans and red-faced Yankees in Bermuda shorts: the cafés on Ocean Drive are the place to watch people.
►page 268

In the 1950s and 1960s the city where houses until then barely reached over the palm trees turned into a sub-tropical Manhattan with various skyscrapers. »Millionaire's Row« disappeared, **»Hotel Row«** appeared. But the 1980s saw a crisis in the tourism industry. Not until new tourist markets were opened in Europe, Asia and South America, and southern Florida was discovered by the media did Miami Beach experience another renaissance, which not even the murder of the fashion designer Versace on the steps of his home on Ocean Drive in 1997 could affect.

★★ SOUTH BEACH · ART DECO HISTORIC DISTRICT

Athletic boys, bronzed models, a square mile of colourful houses amongst art and kitsch – and all of it in sensual Caribbean surroundings: visitors don't know where to look first. South Beach, also called »SoBe«, is Miami Beach. The area between Dade Boulevard in the north and 1st Street in the south is to blame for Miami Beach's reputation as a hip party zone. But while it is possible to see enough of scantily clad people, the unique architecture exerts a longer-lasting fascination. South Beach has the largest collection of Art Deco buildings in one place: several hundred of them. It was placed under monument protection in 1979 but in the early 1970s the Art Deco Historic District (►MARCO POLO Insight p.268/270) at 6th Street, Alton Road, Collins Avenue and Dade Boulevard almost disappeared: investors wanted to tear down the entire neighbourhood and build apartment blocks. The

Miami Beach

INFORMATION
Greater Miami CVB
701 Brickell Avenue, Suite 2700
Miami, FL 33131
Tel. 1-305-539-3000
www.miamiandbeaches.com

AIRPORT
Miami's international airport lies about
7mi/11km west of Miami Beach and is
easy to reach with public transport.
Many hotels in Miami Beach run shuttle
buses to bring guests comfortably to
their destination. Plenty of taxi companies also serve the airport.

A bird's eye view of Miami Beach

PUBLIC TRANSPORTATION
Miami-Dade Transit
Miami's public transport runs the dense
MetroBus network with 70 routes,
which also serves Miami Beach.

CITY TOUR
Insider Tip
Art Deco District tour
A walking tour through the Art Deco
District takes about 1.5 hours and is well
worth it. Tickets available at Art Deco
Welcome Center, 1001 Ocean
Drive/10th St., daily 10.30am, Thu also
at 6.30pm, ticket US$20, www.mdpl.
org.

SHOPPING
Collins Avenue
Collins Avenue between 6th Avenue and
8th Avenue is a place for upmarket
shopping. Designer shops here include
Armani, Nike and Polo Sports.

Lincoln Road Mall
Only a few steps further is the bustling
Lincoln Road Mall, where almost anything can be bought. Tourists and locals
alike come here.

Bal Harbour Shops
Luxury by Chanel, Stella McCartney, etc.
is available in this posh shopping centre
with about 100 shops on Collins Avenue
about a 20-minute drive north of South
Beach.

Aventura Mall
One of the largest malls in metropolitan
Miami is in North Miami Beach. More
than 250 shops offer nice things for the
»normal« budget. It's not surprising then
to find department stores like Bloomingdale's, JCPenney and Sears Roebuck
here.

EVENTS
Art Deco Weekend
Held every year on a weekend in January
in Miami Beach's Art Deco District: a
popular festival involving many artists
and musicians.

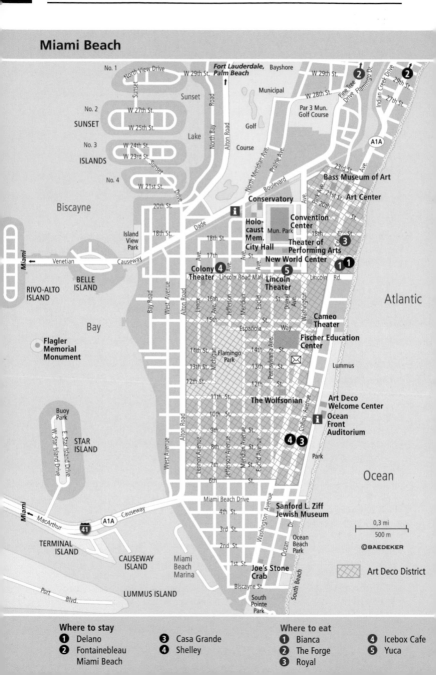

Miami Beach

Fort Lauderdale, Palm Beach
Bayshore

No. 1
North View Drive
W 29th St.
W 29th St.
Pine Tree Drive
Flamingo Dr.
29th St.
Indian Creek Drive
27th St.

Sunset
Sunset
Municipal
W 28th St.

No. 2
SUNSET
W 27th St.
Par 3 Mun. Golf Course
A1A

No. 3
ISLANDS
W 25th St.
North Bay Road
Alton Road
Golf Course

No. 4
W 24th St.
W 23rd St.
23rd St.
Collins Ave.

Biscayne
W 21st St.
Boulevard
21st St.
20th
Park Ave.
Bass Museum of Art
Art Center

20th St.
Conservatory
Dade
Holo-caust Mem. City Hall
Mun. Park
18th St.
Convention Center
Theater of Performing Arts
18th St.
3

Island View Park
18th St.
17th St.
Ave.
Ave.
New World Center
5
1 1

Miami
Venetian Causeway
Colony Theater
4
Lincoln Road Mall
Lincoln Theater
Lincoln Rd.
Atlantic

BELLE ISLAND
Bay Road
West Avenue
Alton Road
Lenox
Ave.
16th
Jefferson
Meridian
15th
Euclid
St.
Drexel Ave.
Washington

RIVO-ALTO ISLAND
Española
Way
Cameo Theater

Bay
14th St.
Michigan
Flamingo Park
14th
Pennsylvania Ave.
St.
Fischer Education Center

Flagler Memorial Monument
13th St.
12th St.
13th
12th
Lummus

Buoy Park
11th St.
The Wolfsonian
Art Deco Welcome Center

STAR ISLAND
E. Star Island Drive
W. Star Island Drive
10th St.
Collins Avenue
i
Ocean Front Auditorium

Alton Road
9th St.
8th St.
7th St.
Lenox Avenue
Jefferson Avenue
Meridian Avenue
Euclid Avenue
4 3
Park

Miami
MacArthur Causeway
A1A
41
6th St.
Ocean

TERMINAL ISLAND
Miami Beach Drive
4th St.
Washington Avenue
Sanford L. Ziff Jewish Museum
0,3 mi
500 m
©BAEDEKER

CAUSEWAY ISLAND
3rd St.
Ocean Dr.
Ocean Beach Park
Art Deco District

Miami Beach Marina
2nd St.
1st St.
Joe's Stone Crab
South Beach

Port Blvd.
LUMMUS ISLAND
Biscayne St.
South Pointe Park

Where to stay

1 Delano
2 Fontainebleau Miami Beach
3 Casa Grande
4 Shelley

Where to eat

1 Bianca
2 The Forge
3 Royal
4 Icebox Cafe
5 Yuca

Miami Boat Show

More than 2,300 exhibitors take part in the world's largest fair of its kind. There is much to see in the Miami Beach Convention Center, in Sealine Marina and in Miamarina (February).

Art Basel Miami Beach

More than 260 galleries from all over the world present masterpieces of the 20th and 21st centuries (early December)

NIGHT LIFE

Miami Beach's nightlife is incomparable, as TV fans know. Collins Avenue throbs, for example at the Rose Bar in the Delano Hotel (1685 Collins Ave), in the Marlin Hotel lounge (1200 Collins Ave) and at the Sky Bar in the Shore Club (1901 Collins Ave). Current hip addresses include the Coral Bar in The Tides hotel (1220 Ocean Drive).

WHERE TO EAT
❶ Bianca $$$$

1685 Collins Ave., tel. 1-305-674-5752
Upmarket Italian restaurant in the Delano Hotel.

❷ The Forge $$$

432 41st St.
Tel. 1-305-538-8533
Evening restaurant with elegant atmosphere; exquisitely prepared food, choice wines.

❸ Royal $$$

1775 Collins Ave.
Tel. 1-305-534-6300
Steaks and fresh oysters served on a romantic terrace.

❹ Icebox Cafe $$$

1657 Michigan Ave.

Tel. 1-305-538-8448
Delicious desserts served here.

❺ Yuca $$$

501 Lincoln Road
Tel. 1-305-532-9822
»New World cuisine« with a Latin American touch, for example a Peruvian tamal verde.

WHERE TO STAY
❶ Delano $$$ *Insider Tip*

1685 Collins Avenue
Tel. 1-305-672-2000
www.delano-hotel.com
An Art Deco jewel that became a society venue after renovation by star designer Philippe Starck (238 rooms and suites).

❷ Fontainebleau Hilton $$$$

4441 Collins Ave.
Tel. 1-305-538-2000
www.fontainebleau.com
Excellently run top-class hotel that is already well-known as a film setting, with every imaginable comfort (846 rooms, 658 suites, spa, marina, golf, 11 restaurants)

❸ Casa Grande $$$

834 Ocean Drive
Tel. 1-305-672-7003
www.casagrandesuitehotel.com
Delightful Art deco hotel with 32 luxury suites on South Beach. Early reservations an absolute must!

㉑ Shelley $$

844 Collins Ave.
Tel. 1-305-531-3341
www.hotelshelley.com
49 units in a renovated hotel from 1931, only one block from Ocean Drive; Happy Hour with free drinks at the bar

fact that this did not happen is mainly due to the Miami Beach Art Deco Preservation League. Under its leadership the aged buildings from the 1930s and 1940s were restored and put to use again as hotels in lemon yellow, Caribbean blue apartment buildings and neon-lit cafés.

Ocean Drive Ocean Drive is the **catwalk of the young, rich and beautiful. 1963 Mustangs and brightly polished Harleys cruise up and down the street; light airplanes trailing advertising banners announce the next party venue. Many of the buildings are pretty street restaurants, chic bars and hotels with lobbies that are worth a look inside. Many have been in the movies and were used as locations for shows such as Miami Vice to CSI Miami. The finest **Art Deco buildings** are the snow-white **Hotel Lord Balfour** (no. 350), the geometrical **Park Central** (no. 640), the **Colony Hotel** with its changing colours from baby blue to flamingo pink (no. 736), the orange **Waldorf Towers** (no. 850) and the white, ivy-covered **Cardozo** (no. 1300) – the latter is the family business of Gloria and Emilio Estefan. There is natural green and blue across the street in **Lummus Park**: the park with its palm trees and paths for strollers and bikes separates Ocean Drive from the popular palm-tree-lined Lummus Park Beach (between 5th Street and 23rd Street).

South Beach South Beach has been »in« for years – for the publicity-hungry, for gays and lesbians as well as for everyone else. The **broad beach is a party venue all year round. The villa of the fashion designer Versace, who was murdered at the height of a wave of violence, is nearby. It is now a private club

Collins Avenue The main axis of Miami Beach is Collins Avenue, often called »The Strip«. It is also flanked by Art Deco buildings. Architect L. Murray Dixon designed **Tiffany (801 Collins Ave.) and **Fairmont** (1000 Collins Ave.). **Essex House** (1001 Collins Ave.) was built in 1938 to plans by Henry Hohauser in the so-called Nautical Modern style. Roy F. France created the skyscraper **St Moritz** (1565 Collins Ave.) in 1939. The apartment building **Surfcomber** (1717 Collins Ave.) was only built after World War II to designs by the architectural office of MacKay & Gibbs. Three of the largest Art Deco hotels are the **National** (1677 Collins Ave.), a lemon yellow dream with an expansive swimming pool, the **Delano** (1685 Collins Ave.), where Sandra Bullock, Dennis Rodman, Will Smith and Barbra Streisand have stayed and the **SLS Hotel** (1701 Collins Ave.), a completely symmetrical construction crowned with towers. Streamlining and construction details are reminiscent of 20th-century means of transportation like airplanes, rockets and submarines.

Art Deco on the world-famous Ocean Drive in Miami Beach

Washington Avenue is Miami Beach's main street and has more Art Deco buildings. Built in 1924, the **George Washington Hotel** (534 Washington Ave.) was one of the first beach hotels in Miami Beach. Further noteworthy buildings include the **Hotel Taft** (1044 Washington Ave.), which was built in 1936 by Henry Hohauser, the **Main Post Office** (1300 Washington Ave.), which was built in 1939 in the so-called Deco Federal Style with a decorated rotunda, as well as the **Old City Hall** (1130 Washington Avenue), which was built in 1927. The **Sanford L. Ziff Jewish Museum** presents Florida's Jewish tradition, which goes back to the 18th century, and is housed in Beth Jacob Synagogue, which was designed in 1936 by architect Henry Hohauser. A warehouse that was built in 1927 with a Moorish façade holds part of the **collection** of the eccentric art lover **Mitchell Wolfson**. Exhibits include decorative art, including posters and advertising from 1880 to 1945.

*Washington Avenue

Jewish Museum of Florida: 301 Washington Ave., Tue – Sun 10am – 5pm, admission US$6, www.jewishmuseum.com

The Wolfsonian: 1001 Washington Ave., Thu -- Tue noon – 6pm, , Fri noon until 9pm, admission US$7, www.wolfsonian.org/visitus

Tropical Architecture

Pastel-coloured houses that seem to swim like a swarm of fish through Florida's shimmering heat: no building style fits the truly relaxed atmosphere of Miami Beach as well as Art Deco. The bright city on the sea has the world's largest collection of these fanciful houses. The Art Deco District of Miami Beach is one of the top attractions of the Sunshine State.

All of it was new: the style, the forms, the colours, even the daring with which all of these contrary elements were combined.

A New Style from Europe

Art deco, which was named after an exhibition held in 1925 in Paris called »Exposition Internationale des Arts Decoratifs et Industriels Modernes«, had a very eclectic approach to past and contemporary forms. It drew equally on the decorative art of Viennese Art Nouveau, the forms of Maya and Aztec

Art Deco façade decoration

architects and the 4,000-year-old ornamentation of Mesopotamia and Egypt. Cubism and Futurism also influenced the concept of these houses. Streamlines and lack of ornaments were the trademarks of this new style. The entrances were emphasized, as were the roofs and roof structures: the houses now got stepped gables inspired by Mesopotamian ziggurats. **Geometrical symmetry** was praised as it had never been before.

Successful Leap to the New World

From Europe, where it had already influenced buildings in Paris around 1900, Art Deco came to America in the 1930s. The USA was pursuing the American dream and developing into an economic super-power, fascinated by everything that symbolized progress. **The Chrysler Building in New York** carried Art Deco to lofty heights; many of the skyscrapers built in Manhattan at this time had Art Deco elements. The new style was novel and exciting. It was inspired by the aerodynamic design of the cars, trains and planes that were coming off the assembly lines by the tens of thousands, promising a new beginning after the dark years of the Depression.

Miami Beach: Capital of Art Deco

Making use of chrome, aluminium and vivid colours, it was not only progressive but also thoroughly humorous – especially in Miami Beach from the mid-1930s. A small group of local architects around Henry Hohauser (1895–1963) created »Miami Beach Art Deco« by adding tropical elements like stylized flamingos, flowers, pelicans, cranes and suns, which at first attracted derision as being kitschy, to the previous form vocabulary of Art Deco. Depending on the ornamentation, variants of the style were known as **»Streamline Moderne«**, **»Tropical Deco«** and **»Depression Moderne«**. How to recognize **»Nautical Deco«**? Correct: round porthole windows, long balconies resembling sundecks on ships and shady »eyebrows« over the windows.

Much-photographed Art Deco building in Miami Beach

Renaissance in the 1980s

By the late 1960s the days of the approximately 400 Art Deco houses in Miami Beach appeared to be numbered. The neighbourhood was run down, its residents aging and poverty-stricken. Profit-oriented investors set their sights on the houses. They were saved in 1976, when concerned residents under the leadership of the feisty Barbara Baer Capitman founded the **Miami Design Preservation League** (MDPL). Their most difficult job was to convince lurking investors and chronically broke home-owners of the potential of the neighbourhood as a tourist attraction. In 1979 the MDPL achieved its aim of having the area added to the National Register of Historic Places. It was the first time that 20th-century objects were listed as historic buildings. In 1980 **Andy Warhol** came. This was a turning point: the world-famous performance artist and collector of Art Deco was guided through the neighbourhood by Barbara Baer Capitman – and followed by a mass of international journalists; he thus brought the work of the MDPL to international attention. Since then the league has watched over the Art Deco Historic District with Argus eyes.

Art Deco District

Nowhere are as many Art Deco buildings found in one place as in Miami Beach, even if the exponents in New York City are far more famous than the tourist inns at the hot and humid South Beach, whose »portholes« and »eyebrows« are illuminated at night by kitschy bright neon tubes.

❶ Vertical lines
often reach to a ziggurat (stepped) or an antenna-shaped peak.

❷ Horizontal lines
follow rows of windows and rounded corners or decorative railings.

❸ Rows of windows

❹ »Eyebrows«
above the windows are intended mainly to give shade.

❺ Fluting
decorative tower (often stepped or ziggurat) is often fluted, that is grooved or riffled.

❻ »Portholes«
characterize the special style of »Nautical Deco«, which imitates the forms of luxury passenger liners.

❼ Frieze
often with stylized tropical plants and animals

❽ Strict geometrical forms
are a must in Miami Beach Art Deco.

❾ Rounded corners
emphasize the streamlines of the new building style.

❿ Decorative tower
Often there are stepped towers modelled on ziggurats from ancient Mesopotamia. Some of the decorative towers are crowned with an antenna-shaped point or »finial«.

⓫ Railing

⓬ Neon lights
At night neon lights emphasize the lines of the window sills, portholes and eyebrows.

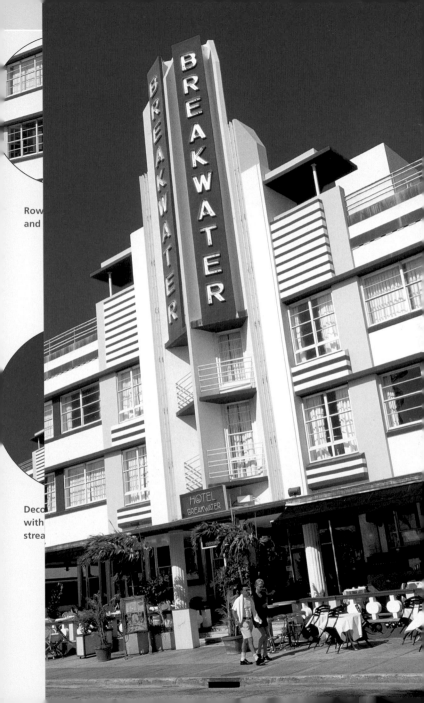

Row
and

Deco
with
strea

*Española Way	Española Way between 14th and 15th Street is also worth a visit. The Spanish-style street was built in 1925 and attracted artists above all. Today small galleries can be found here and a weekend market keeps it lively. At the beginning of Española Way the **Cameo Theater** (1938; architect: Robert Collins) stands out; it is now a popular nightclub.
Euclid Avenue	On Euclid Avenue, note the following Art Deco buildings: The Denis (no. 841; 1938; architect: Arnold Southwell), The Enjoie (no. 928; 1935/1936; architect: Albert Anis and Henry J. Maloney) as well as The Siesta (no. 1110; 1936; architect: Edward A. Nolan).
*21st Street	There are some wonderful Art Deco buildings along this street as well, some of which need renovation. This includes the former luxury hotel Plymouth (no. 226; 1940; architect: Anton Skislewicz) and the adjacent Adam's Hotel (1938; architect: L. Murray Dixon). Henry Hohauser's masterpiece is considered to be Governor (no. 435), built in 1939. The nearby Tyler Apartment Hotel (no. 430; 1937; architect: L. Murray Dixon) also stands out. Abbey (no. 300; 1940; architect: Albert Anis) is also interesting. On the corner of Washington/21st St. is the clubhouse of the Municipal Golf Course by August Geiger (1916).

> **MARCO ☉ POLO TIP**
>
> ! *Winter delicacies* **Insider Tip**
>
> The restaurant Joe's Stone Crab (11 Washington Ave.) is at its busiest from October to March. That's when it serves the delicacy that made it famous: crayfish.
> Reservations:
> Tel. (305) 673-0365

*Bass Museum of Art	The art museum in Collins Park was built in 1930 by Russell T. Pancoast, who used elements of Mayan architecture. The impressive reliefs are by Gustav Bohland. Inside the works of old and new masters are exhibited, including pictures by **Albrecht Dürer** and **Peter Paul Rubens** (The Holy Family) as well as some works by **Impressionists.**

❶ 2121 Park Ave. Wed – Sun noon – 5pm, admission US$8, www.bassmuseum.org

Collins Park Hotel	Offset wings, pilasters and zigzag motifs are the characteristics of the adjacent Collins Park Hotel, which was built in 1939 according to plans by Henry Hohauser.
*Lincoln Road	Two blocks to the north of Española Way is the gallery row of Miami Beach. Artists converted the derelict office buildings on Lincoln Road to workshops and shops with the help of government funding in the 1980s. Today Initiative 52, which is now called **ArtCenter**, has studios and galleries in three buildings (no. 800, 810, 924), which

give an excellent impression of the art scene in Miami Beach. A »studio crawl« is held on the first Saturday of every month, when it is possible to speak personally to the artists.

Colony Theater was designed by R. A. Benjamin in 1934; the theatre is a model of Art Deco in Miami Beach (1040 Lincoln Rd.). It was renovated extensively and reopened in 1976; today it is a focal point of cultural life in the city. Further information: www.colonytheatremiamibeach.com

The **Lincoln Theater**, a utilitarian Art Deco building from 1935–36 designed by Robert E. Collins, is now home to an H & M shop.

ArtCenter: Lincoln Rd. 800, daily 11am – 10pm, Fri, Sat until 11pm, free admission, www.artcentersf.org

The heart of Miami Beach – at least the city fathers see it that way – is the giant Convention Center with its **white Art Deco façade**. Not only conventions and political rallies are held here, but also large-scale sports events. In 1964 the boxer Cassius Clay alias Muhammad Ali won his first world championship here. **Holocaust Memorial** Adjacent to the MBCC on the west is the Holocaust Memorial on Meridian Avenue. It is dedicated to the Jews who were killed during the Third Reich. A lily pond is the foundation for a 14m/46ft-high bronze arm. Life-size figures with fear-stricken faces try to climb up this arm.

Miami Beach Convention Center (MBCC)

On the south side of the convention centre the peach-coloured **Jackie F. Gleason Theater of the Performing Arts** strikes the eye; it was built in 1951 by the architects Dixon, Hohauser and Pancoast. The completely renovated utilitarian building is now called The Fillmore, has 3,000 seats and shows Broadway hits and concerts of all kinds. Further information: www.thefillmore.com

On the plaza before the theatre a **mermaid** by Roy Lichtenstein catches the eye; its shape and colours were inspired by local Art Deco.

OTHER ATTRACTIONS IN MIAMI BEACH

The Fontainebleau Miami Beach on Collins Avenue (no. 4441), which was opened in 1954 and recently renovated for millions of dollars, is an attraction of its own. This **daringly sweeping beach hotel** is a place of superlatives: it not only has more than 1,500 rooms and suites, and the largest ballroom in the area, but also waterfalls in tropical gardens and a wonderful water park. The luxury hotel is also easily recognizable because various US presidents since Dwight D. Eisenhower have slept here; John F. Kennedy celebrated his election here in 1960. The Fontainebleau has also served as the setting for many later Hollywood blockbusters, including a scene of the James Bond thriller *Goldfinger* (1964).

*Fontainebleau Miami Beach

*Beachfront Promenade Between 21st Street and 46th Street there is a long boardwalk with a beautiful view on the narrow strip of dunes between the long row of luxury hotels and the beach. Strollers as well as walkers and joggers keep it lively from early morning to late at night.

Gold Coast, Bal Harbour Follow Highway A1A from the Fontainebleau Hilton north a few miles past modern hotel and apartment buildings along the so-called Gold Coast. Malicious gossip maintains that these buildings were built with ill-gotten gains. The road leads to the beach resort Bal Harbour, where there is a giant and exclusive shopping centre.

*Ancient Spanish Monastery Past Haulover Beach Park and via FL 826 or US 1 the road leads to the Ancient Spanish Monastery, a medieval monastery that media tsar **William Randolph Hearst** had moved to the New World stone by stone from Spain in the 1950s. The monastery was once the home of Cistercian monks and was built in 1141 in Segovia (16711 W. Dixie Highway; hours: Mon–Sat 10am–4pm, Sun 1pm–4pm).
🛈 16711 W. Dixie Hwy., Mon – Sat 10am – 4pm, Sun 11am – 4pm, admission US$8, www.spanishmonastery.com

Well-known from films and television: Miami Beach with its generously proportioned holiday resorts

On the southern tip of Miami Beach a park with a bathing beach, fishing pier and picnic areas is dominated by the post-modern South Pointe Tower.

South Pointe, Miami Beach Marina

At the eastern end of MacArthur Causeway lies the modern Miami Beach Marina. Excursion boats leave from here to take people deep sea fishing and diving.

It lies before South Pointe and opposite the harbour entrance and still belongs to Miami Beach, but for a long time it has been a highly exclusive **refuge for the wealthy**. Anyone who cannot afford his own apartment or villa here can stay in the Fisher Island Resort (www.fisherislandclub.com/hotel). The island is only accessible by boat for residents and their guests.

Fisher Island

The same applies to the artificial islands between MacArthur Causeway and Venetian Causeway called Star Island, Palm Island and Hibiscus Island, where many a celebrity has lived. Al Capone felt just as much at home here as Liz Taylor, Don Johnson and Madonna did later.

Star Island, Palm Island, Hibiscus Island

North of Star Island on a small island an **obelisk** commemorates Henry Morrison Flagler, who was challenged by Julia Tuttle to bring his East Coast Railway to Miami and thus made it a centre of tourism.

Flagler Memorial

★ Mount Dora

✴ H 4

Region: Central
Elevation: 56m/170ft above sea level
Population: 11,000

About an hour's drive north-west of ▶Orlando Florida shows a completely unexpected side to its personality. Forested hills, almost mountains, lakes sparkling in the sunlight and green meadows with grazing cattle and horses, old live oaks make the area »Florida's Switzerland«.

In 1880 the town was founded and named after a certain Dora Ann Drawdy, who lived here with her husband. In the 1920s Mount Dora was a centre of orange cultivation. In 1930 US president Calvin Coolidge spent the winter in the local Lakeside Inn. Then the town sank into oblivion. Only recently has the pretty town on the lakeside been discovered as a weekend refuge by harried city dwellers.

From cultivating oranges to tourism

Mount Dora

INFORMATION
Mount Dora Chamber of Commerce
341 Alexander St.
Tel. 1-352-383-2165
www.mountdora.com

SHOPPING
Village Antique Mall
405 N. Highland Ave.
Daily 9am – 6pm
More than 80 antique dealers under one roof

Renninger's Antique Center
20651 US 41
Sat and Sun 9am – 5pm
180 dealers on the eastern edge of town

Farmer's Market
on US 441 (at the eastern edge of town)
Sat and Sun 8am – 4pm
Regional products available

WHERE TO EAT
The Goblin Market Restaurant $$$
331 N. Donelly St.
Tel. 1-352-735-0059
Creative cooking in an old warehouse

WHERE TO STAY
Heron Cay Lake View B & B $$
495 Old Hwy. 41
Tel. 1-352-383-4050
www.heroncay.com
This Victorian jewel with 7 pretty rooms has a hearty and sumptuous breakfast in the morning.

MOUNT DORA AND SURROUNDINGS

*Victorian architecture

Many of the pretty Victorian buildings have been lovingly restored recently. Some of them now house cafés, snack bars and antique shops. Beautiful houses can be found on **Donelly Street** and **Fifth Avenue.** The 600m/2,000ft-long **Palm Island Boardwalk**, which runs through a sub-tropical swampland and offers nice views of the lake – and with a little luck some alligators – is a nice place to stretch your legs.

*Wekiwa Springs State Park

About 12mi/19km to the south-east, near Apopka, is a bubbling **crystal-clear spring** called Wekiwa Springs; many visitors come to canoe on the Rock Spring Run and the Wekiwa River or just enjoy the beautiful natural setting. Archaeologists have discovered that the Timucuan Indians already lived on the shores of the Wekiwa River 5,000 years ago.

❶ daily 8am until sunset, admission: pedestrians US$2, vehicles US$6, www.floridastateparks.org/wekiwasprings/

Leesburg

The town of Leesburg (population 19,000), site of one of the world's largest cool houses for citrus juice concentrate, lies only a few minutes' drive west of Mount Dora in the lake-rich heart of Florida. It is an excellent place for exploring central Florida on a houseboat. There are hundreds of lakes in the area. East of the town are the more than 30ha/74-acre **Venetian Gardens**, an attractive place for bathing, boating and relaxing.

* Naples

—————————————— ✦ H 6

Region: South-west
Elevation: 0 – 3m/16ft above sea level
Population: 21,000

The most millionaires per capita, the most golf courses, and a biblical average age: this town two hours west of ▶Miami on the Gulf of Mexico has lots of labels. But like everything else, there are two sides to the issue. For some it is a millionaires' row suffering from its own wealth, for others it is an island of civilization light years away from the next large city. Naples has a tradition of dividing opinion.

The town was founded by wealthy real estate speculators in 1886; the first hotel opened before the first rail or even road access was laid. When the railway came (1926) and the Tamiani Trail (1928) was built, Naples became an oceanside resort. While investors advertised in the north with slogans like »This bay is even more beautiful than the one at Naples, Italy« and indirectly gave the town its name, the price of land rose quickly more hotels and homes were built. The »millionaire's row« was built, a series of baronial beach homes, which are part of the old part of town today called »Olde Naples«. Hollywood discovered the new town as a winter residence, especially Greta Garbo, Hedy Lamarr and Gary Cooper, who held wild parties in Club 41. During World War II bomber pilots were trained nearby. In 1960 Hurricane Donna destroyed large parts of town, but then Naples – thanks also to the insurance premiums – began a building boom that still continues and apart from many hotel and apartment blocks on Vanderbilt Beach north of Naples has produced many new villas and industrial parks for high-tech and service industries.

Attractive seaside resort

WHAT TO SEE IN NAPLES

The »old city« of Naples has a grid pattern between the bay and the gulf. The heart of town is at the old docks south of South 5th Avenue. The former site of a fish factory, **Old Marine Marketplace** at Tin City (1200 5th Ave. S) is now a photogenic ensemble of colourful

*Olde Naples

Naples

INFORMATION
Naples Area Visitors Bureau
Horseshoe Drive
Naples, FL 34104
Tel. 1-239-252-2384
www.paradisecoast.com

WHERE TO EAT
❶ *Chop's City Grill* $$$$
837 5th Ave. S.
Tel. 1-239-262-4677
The best steaks far and wide, extensive wine list.

❷ *Yabba Island Grill* $$ **Insider Tip**
711 5th Ave.
Tel. 1-239-262-5787
Tasty Caribbean dishes and wonderful rum cocktails.

WHERE TO STAY
❶ *Ritz-Carlton Vanderbilt Beach* $$$$
280 Vanderbilt Beach Rd.

Tel. 1-239-598-3300
www.ritzcarlton.com
Old-established luxury hotel with 460 rooms and suites, its own beach, golf course, tennis courts, spa etc. and excellent cuisine.

❷ *Hotel Escalante* $$$
290 Fifth Ave. S.
Tel. 1-239-659-3466
www.hotelescalante.com
Cultured Mediterranean-style inn with 71 rooms and suites in a sub-tropical garden; beach and shopping right around the corner.

❸ *Cove Inn* $$
900 Broad Ave. S.
Tel. 1-239-262-7161
www.coveinnnaples.com
Friendly accommodation with 50 pastel-coloured rooms right on Naples Bay and a beautiful view of the bustling yacht harbour.

warehouses with restaurants and souvenir shops, a place for browsing and dining. The 300m/1,000ft-long wooden **Naples Pier**, which stretches out into the Gulf of Mexico and is used by fishers, brown pelicans and sun-worshippers alike. It was built already in 1888–89 and has been renovated several times since then. The area for very elegant and expensive shopping is the up-market 3rd Street and and no less 5th Avenue. The shady side streets are a good place to stroll under palm trees along well-watered lawns and beautiful villas and to work up an appetite for dinner.

Other attractions   North-west of the »old city« the **Naples Zoo at Caribbean Gardens**, a lovingly run zoo whose main attractions are tigers from Indochina, islands inhabited by monkeys and alligator-feedings.
Next to the zoo is **The Conservancy of Southwest Florida.** The long name hides a veritable wilderness. On a boat ride visitors can see many alligators and many kinds of waterfowl up close; exhibitions explain the complicated ecosystem.

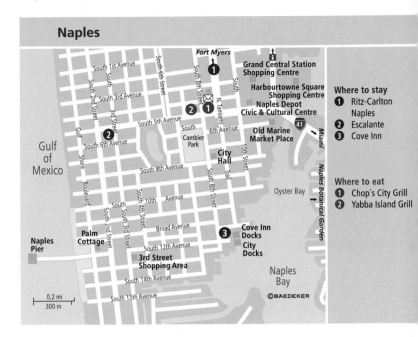

Naples

Fort Myers

Grand Central Station
Shopping Centre

Harbourtowne Square
Shopping Centre
Naples Depot
Civic & Cultural Centre

Old Marine
Market Place

Gulf
of
Mexico

Cambier
Park

City
Hall

Oyster Bay

Cove Inn
Docks
City
Docks

Naples
Pier

Palm
Cottage

Broad Avenue

3rd Street
Shopping Area

Naples
Bay

©BAEDEKER

0,2 mi
300 m

Where to stay
❶ Ritz-Carlton
Naples
❷ Escalante
❸ Cove Inn

Where to eat
❶ Chop`s City Grill
❷ Yabba Island Grill

On the way to Vanderbilt Beach stop at the **Naples Philharmonic
Center** with the attached **Naples Museum of the Arts** (5833 Pelican
Bay Blvd.). Beyond the glass-domed lobby, paintings and sculptures
by contemporary artists are on display.

Naples Zoo at Caribbean Gardens: 1590 Goodlette-Frank Rd., daily 9am
until 5pm, admission US$20, www.napleszoo.com

Conservancy of Southwestern Florida: 1450 Merihue Dr., by appointment only, www.conservancy.org

Naples Museum of the Arts: 5833 Pelican Bay Blvd., Tue – Sat 10am until
4pm, Sun 12noon – 4pm, Jul – Sept closed, admission US$8,
www.thephil.org

**Collier Coun-
ty Museum**

South-east of the city centre on the other side of Naples Bay, this museum illuminates local history from the first period of Indian settlement up to the present. Outside it the typical **Seminole »chickees«**
have been set up.

ⓘ 3301 Tamiami Trail East; Mon – Fri 9am – 5pm, Sat 9am – 4pm, free
admission, www.colliermuseums.com

***Naples
Botanical
Garden**

This wonderful botanical garden south of downtown Naples was reopened in 2009. It has areas called Florida Garden, River of Grass,

Tourists on Naples Pier

Caribbean Garden, Brazilian Garden, Asian Garden and Children's Garden.

❶ Thomasson Dr., Oct – July 9am – 5pm, July – mid Sept daily 8am – 3pm, admission US$13, www.naplesgarden.org

Beaches   Around Naples there are more than 35mi/60km of wonderful beaches. In »Olde Naples« all streets end within sight of **Naples Municipal Beach, as it sparkles between the old villas. To the north lies **Lowdermilk Park** (Banyan Blvd. and Gulf Shore Blvd.). **Clam Pass County Park** consists of a dense mangrove jungle, with a long planked walkway over tideways and marshes to dunes and a wonderful natural beach. Kayaks and canoes are available for renting. To the north **Vanderbilt Beach County Park** adjoins with its luxury hotel. **Delnor Wiggins Pass State Recreation Area** on a barrier island to the north also has wonderful beaches.

❶ all beaches 8am – sunset, admission US$6 – US$8, parking fee US$8

AROUND NAPLES

Bonita Springs   14mi/22km north of Naples and on the north-west edge of Big Cypress Swamp, Bonita Springs (population 14,000) lies on the Imperial River, which has a good reputation among anglers. Right on the Gulf Coast the two holiday resorts Bonita Shores and Bonita Springs attract families with children. The long beach entertains young and old.

Vanderbilt Beach near Naples is one of Florida's best beaches

Corkscrew Swamp Sanctuary lies 10mi/16km east of Bonita Springs is a nature reserve called with **up to 500-year-old swamp cypresses**. The giant trees are densely covered with ferns, orchids and other epiphytes. In the winter endangered American **wood ibis** brood in the trees. The National Audubon Society, which runs the park, had a 2.5mi/4km-long walkway made so that visitors can explore the area without getting their feet wet in this original piece of Florida (access via CR 846, 375 Sanctuary Rd.; hours: Oct–April daily 7am–5.30pm, other times daily 7am–7.30pm).

**Corkscrew Swamp Sanctuary

❶ access via CR 846, 375 Sanctuary Rd., Oct. – early April daily 7am – 5.30pm, otherwise 7am – 7.30, admission US$10, www.corkscrew. audubon.org

The island lies about 20mi/30km south of Naples; bridges connect it with the mainland (US 41 or FL 92 or 951). It is about 10km/6mi long and 6km/3.5mi wide, has a population of about 10,000 and is the northernmost of the Ten Thousand Islands, a **labyrinth of mangrove islands** off the coast of the Everglades. Archaeological excavations have uncovered evidence of a 5,000-year-old Indian settlement. In 1922 an investor named Collier bought a large part of Marco Island in order to build a deep-sea or oil harbour here. Large deposits of oil were expected in this area. Marco Island has been a popular tourist venue since the 1960s. **Wonderful beaches** and excellent **fishing** attract visitors. The interior of the island is criss-crossed by canals bordered by **luxury villas** with private yacht moorings. **Old Marco Village** on the northern end of the island is very nice. Old buildings with friendly shops and

*Marco Island

restaurants make for a lively atmosphere. The harbour is now a shopping centre with an old-world atmosphere. **Beaches** Next to the broad main beach with its fine-grained sand, which is lined by sophisticated hotel and apartment buildings, **Tigertail Beach** in the north-western part of the island is worth a visit; it is best reached via Hernando Drive.

*Collier-Seminole State Park This nature reserve has both cypress swamps and hardwood hammocks with a few royal palms and almost impenetrable mangrove thickets on the coast. Hiking, biking and canoeing trails make it possible to »take only pictures and leave only footprints«. A few nature trails and a 13mi/21km-long canoe trail make exploration possible. The visitor centre has information on the condition of the ecosystem and the local flora and fauna. The Indian settlement history in this area is also part of the exhibition.

❶ daily. 8am until sunset, admission: pedestrians US$2, vehicles US$5, www.floridastateparks.org/collierseminole/

* Ocala

✳ G 3

Region: Central
Elevation: 15m/50ft above sea level
Population: 53,500

Almost everyone drives by and misses a landscape with gentle hills, moss-covered oaks and green pastures where thoroughbred horses graze. The proximity of the entertainment giants in ▶Orlando is both a curse and a blessing to Ocala: around the centre of rural Marion County things still looks as they did before Mickey Mouse arrived.

City of crackers and horses A square surrounded by the tiny »**Ocala Historic District**« and the carefully restored main street, Fort King Street: Ocala wants to appeal not just to tourists but also to its residents. Most of them are descendants of the »Florida Crackers«, the hard-working farmers who made the land arable in the 19th century and who fought in the Seminole Wars. Ocala appears solid and down-to-earth; Timucuan Indians lived here 400 years ago and still do today. The descendants of the Crackers raised cattle on the fertile pastureland that is blessed with clear spring water and when horseback riding became a sport, they added horses. Today Ocala is known as the home of thoroughbred horses and prize-winning racehorses.

Ocala is recommended as the **starting point for excursions** in the area. The city fathers also point to the attractions in the area as an argument for the high quality of life here.

WHAT TO SEE IN OCALA

Next to the old part of town, which is also called »Brick City« because of the brick houses there, Ocala has two museums that could not be more different. On the eastern edge of town **Appleton Museum of Art** holds the art collection of a Chicago industrialist that covers over five millennia. The excellent exhibition ranges from Greek antiquity to ethnological collections from Africa. The southern suburb of Belleview boasts a thoroughly American museum, the **Don Garlits Museum of Drag Racing**, which is dedicated to the patron of this high-speed sport. The most famous dragster pilot in the USA displays his legendary racing cars, the »Swamp Rats«, here. The car with which he drove 323.04mph (520kmh) in 2002 is also exhibited. For lovers of veteran cars, the **Museum of Classic Automobiles** is right next door.

Brick houses, old art and fast cars

Appleton Museum of Art: 4333 E. Silver Springs Blvd., Tue – Sat 10am until 5pm, Sun 12noon – 5pm, Eintritt 6 US$, www.appletonmuseum.org
Don Garlits Museum of Drag Racing & Mus. of Classic Automobiles: 13700 SW 16th Ave.,daily 9am – 5pm, admission US$15, www.garlits.com

Ocala

INFORMATION
Ocala County CVB
112 N. Magnola Ave.
Ocala, FL 34475
Tel. 1-352-438-2800
www.ocalamarion.com

EVENTS WITH HORSES
The horse auctions during Ocala Week (October) in the South-eastern Livestock Pavilion and in the Ocala Breeders Sales Complex attract customers from all over the world. Events related to the »Horse Shows in the Sun« are very popular with spectators.

Ocala County CVB
11008 S. Hwy 475
http://flhorsepark.com

HITS Past Time Farm
13710 Hwy. 27
www.hitsshows.com

WHERE TO EAT
Horse and Hounds $$
6998 NW US 27; tel. 1-352-620-2500
Very English – yes indeed. Fish & chips and ploughman's lunch. But they also serve crab cakes, good salads, soups and steaks from the grill.

WHERE TO STAY
Hampton Inn & Suites $$$
2075 SW Hwy. 484; tel. 1-352-347-1600
Http://hamptoninn3.hilton.com
Part of the Hilton Group; with spacious and well-furnished rooms, pool as well as various fitness facilities

Sleep Inn & Suites $
13600 SW 17th Court
Tel. 1-352-347-8383
www.ocalaflahotel.com
Nice hotel not far from Don Garlits Museum of Drag Racing with comfortable rooms and a small pool

AROUND OCALA

Excursion through horse country to Orange Lake

A charming trip goes from Ocala on CR 475 north of Orange Lake. The route runs through Riddick, the **centre of thoroughbred breeding** in Florida. Rolling hills and many miles of fencing between the roads and the green pastures characterize the countryside, as do the hammocks with centuries-old live oaks covered with Spanish moss. Between them are picturesque farms and studs. The trip ends at **Orange Lake** (19 sq mi/50 sq km), known to fishing fans for its sizeable bass.

*Silver Springs

Silver Springs, a few miles east of Ocala, is one of the most attractive places in the region. Already in the 19th and early 20th centuries when paddle wheelers sailed on the Silver River, this **pond of warm spring water** at 23°C/73°F attracted visitors. On the pond and the Silver River, which is fed by 17 springs, glass-bottom boats allow guests to see the exotic underwater world. Silver Springs has often been used as a film setting. In 1942 several Tarzan movies with Johnny Weissmuller and in 1982–83 the diving scenes from the James Bond movie Never Say Never Again were made here. Around Silver Springs an amusement park has grown up with many attractions. On the **Fort King River Cruise** or the **Wilderness Trail** original Florida landscape can be discovered. Then there is an alligator and snake show, a botanical garden and various rides. For anyone looking for more action there is the nearby **Silver Springs Wild Waters** .

> **?**
>
> MARCO ⊕ POLO INSIGHT
>
> *Did you know?*
>
> With up to 23 cubic m/sec (over 6,000 gal/sec) of water Silver Springs is one of the strongest artesian wells on earth. This amount of water would easily supply all of New York City.

❶ daily 10am – 5pm, longer in the summer, admission US$32, www.silversprings.com
Silver Springs Wild Waters: late March–Labor Day daily 10am–6pm

*Ocala National Forest

East of Silver Springs lies the Ocala National Forest; it has an area of about 500 sq mi/1330 sq km and has been a nature reserve since 1908. A piece of the wooded landscape typical of central Florida has been preserved here. It is characterized by pines on sandy knolls that rise up like islands out of the brush known as **»Big Scrub«**. Swamp cypress dominate in the lowlands. Hardwood tree islands (hammocks) with magnolias, oaks, laurel trees and palm trees enliven the scenery.

The forest is a refuge for many kinds of animals. Apart from snakes, alligators and racoons there are also black bears and **Florida pumas**. Of course, there are also many interesting kinds of birds, including

bald eagles. Because of its many lakes, springs and slowly meandering rivers the forest region is a paradise for campers, canoeists, divers and other outdoor enthusiasts. Seasoned hikers enjoy the approx. 60mi/100km-long **Ocala Hiking Trail**. **Juniper Springs, Alexander Springs and Salt Springs** are wonderful spots which have campgrounds, canoe rentals, nature trails and other tourist facilities.

> **Insider Tip**
>
> *Like Tarzan and Jane...*
>
> MARCO❂POLO TIP
>
> Make your childhood dream come true: swing like Tarzan or Jane on a vine from tree to tree or drop into the water at Juniper Springs in Ocala National Forest. The swimming hole is accessible daily from 8am until sunset, camping is possible. Further information at: www.fs.usda.gov/recmain/ocala/recarea/

** Orlando

———————————— ✦ H 4

Region: Central
Elevation: 32m/100ft above sea level
Population: 238,000 (metropolitan area: over 2 million)

Over 40 million visitors annually, around 450 hotels, about 113,000 rooms and the numbers are growing. Endless queues at the attractions, coupon books as thick as the telephone book with »special offers«. Visitors can be overwhelmed by Orlando. But even if you are allergic to mice, at least make a short stop in the world capital of amusement.

Orlando is a thoroughly American fairy tale. Even those who just drive by on I-4 are not completely immune to its remarkable success story. Office, apartment and hotel towers in all colours line both sides of the multi-lane highways. Digital billboards advertise Disney, Burger King and the dentist. It took just about 4 decades for the city to grow from a rural town in central Florida to a billion dollar a year money-making machine. The end of the boom is not in sight. Even the hurricane year 2004, when Orlando stood in the path of storms, only slowed down business for a couple of days. **American fairy tale**

Not bad then for a city that doesn't even know for sure where it got its pretty name. According to one of the many theories it was named after Orlando Reeves, a corporal who was killed here in 1836 by Seminoles when he woke up his comrades with a warning shot. Later veterans of the Seminole Wars settled down here. In 1843 the brothers Aaron and Isaac Jernigan built a **ranch** and a **trading post** at Lake Holden, which attracted more settlers. In the 1860s the area was already covered with ranches and cotton plantations; in 1872 Orlando was incorporated. A **A billion-dollar money machine** certain William Holden planted the **first orange grove** in 1875, and a little later citrus fruits surpassed cattle as the most important source of income. In 1880 the railway came – and with it the **first tourists**, who stayed in elegant hotels on Orange Avenue and relaxed around the 54 lakes within the city limits. Unimpressed by cold spells – in 1886 and 1894–95 the entire citrus crop was ruined by cold snaps – Orlando continued to grow, but more slowly. In 1929 a fruit fly plague caused the citrus industry to collapse. Then came the Depression. World War II helped the monoculture to diversify and up to the beginning of the 1960s the **space industry** and its suppliers settled in Orlando, spurred on by the Cold War and the nearby space industry in Cape Canaveral. Then Orlando made the most important deal in its history. **Walt Disney** came. The »father« of Donald Duck and Mickey Mouse bought land south-west of Orlando through front men for a new mega-resort. As soon as the transaction became public, real estate prices skyrocketed. Orlando experienced a land boom the likes of which Florida had never even known in the 1920s. On 1 October 1971 ▶**Walt Disney World's Magic Kingdom** opened its doors. The ultra-modern amusement park set new standards in the industry and in the next decades made Orlando the entertainment capital not only of the USA, but of the whole world. Other theme parks came, with Universal Studios leading the way and then SeaWorld Orlando, Disney's biggest competition. The fast pace infected the city of Orlando too. The day when the goings-on around Orange Avenue could be watched from a rocking chair on the porch were over. At the beginning of the third millennium

Highlights in Orlando

▶ **Charles Hosmer Morse Museum of American Art**
Beautiful art nouveau glass and stained glass by Louis Comfort Tiffany and other artists, including work by the artist-poet John LaFarge and the architect Frank Lloyd Wright can be seen in Orlando's Winter Park suburb.
▶page 291

▶ **Discovery Cove**
A trend-setting water theme park with an expansive lagoon and a new kind of dolphin programme.
▶page 292

▶ **SeaWorld Orlando**
Lots of fun for over 30 years with trained dolphins, »killer« whales, sea otters, sea lions etc. Interesting theme areas, including »Manatees – the Last Generation?« and a few wet »thrill rides« attract children and adults.
▶page 293

▶ **Universal Orlando**
Next to Walt Disney World second-to-none high-tech thrills. Successful films like Earthquake, Jurassic Park, Terminator 2 and Spider Man in 3D, also roller coasters and top-class stunt shows.
▶page 295

Orlando is one of the fastest-growing metropolitan areas in the USA. But the financial crisis that started in 2007 stopped the growth. Even without Disney & Co. it is the talk of the nation: as a high-tech centre and as home of the NBA basketball team **Orlando Magic**. The city has kept its love of green spaces. It has 47 parks with old oaks and pretty lakes to help soothe the jangled nerves of residents and visitors.

Orlando

INFORMATION
Orlando Tourism Bureau
8723 International Dr., Suite 101
Orlando, FL 32819
Tel. 1-407-363-5872
www.orlandoinfo.com

AIRPORT
Orlando's international airport is only a few miles east of the city centre. All of the amusement parks, hotels and car rental agencies are easy to reach by shuttle bus. Regular buses run all day at short intervals between the airport and downtown Orlando.

CITY TRANSPORT
Orlando has a well-developed bus network called LYNX, which includes the large amusement parks. Moreover, there are many taxi, minibus or van and limousine services.

PARKS AND PRICES
A visit to a mega-amusement park is not exactly cheap. On the other hand, the admission price includes all the rides, shows and other attractions. The single-day ticket for Aquatica (www.aquatica-byseaworld.com) currently costs US$50 for an adult and US$45 for a child. A day at SeaWorld (www.seaworldparks.com) costs US$85 for an adult and US$77 for a child. Anyone who wants to visit more than one park should buy the

»4 Park Orlando Flex Ticket« (about US$290 for an adult and about US$270 for a child); it is valid for 14 days at Sea-World, Universal Studios/Islands of Adventure, Aquatica and Wet 'n Wild in Tampa. A day at Universal Orlando costs about US$90 for an adult and about US$85 for a child; the 2-day-ticket costs about US$125 (adult) and US$115 for a child. There are different multi-park tickets here as well (www.universalorlando.com).

SHOPPING
As is fitting for a tourist venue of this magnitude, which has a high disposable income among locals as well, there are any number of outlets in Orlando. Here is a selection:

Premium Outlets
4951 International Drive
Mon – Sat 10am – 11pm, Sun 10am – 9pm

Orlando Premium Outlets
8200 Vineland Avenue
Mon – Sat 10am – 11pm, Sun 10am – 9pm

Florida Mall
8001 S Blossom Trail
Mon – Sat 10am – 11pm,
Sun noon – 6pm
www.simon.com

Orlando

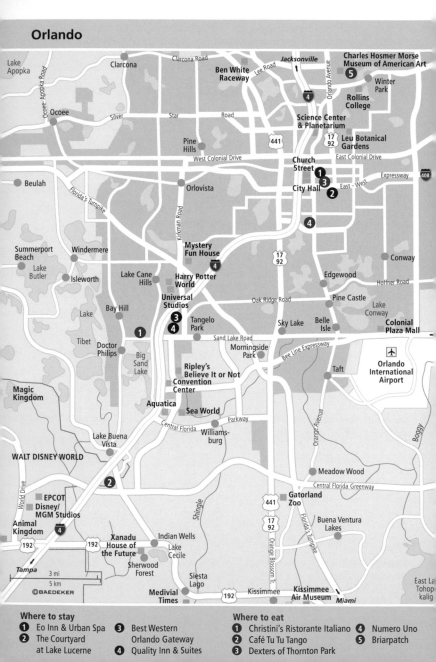

Where to stay
1. Eo Inn & Urban Spa
2. The Courtyard at Lake Lucerne
3. Best Western Orlando Gateway
4. Quality Inn & Suites

Where to eat
1. Christini's Ristorante Italiano
2. Café Tu Tu Tango
3. Dexters of Thornton Park
4. Numero Uno
5. Briarpatch

©BAEDEKER

About 260 specialty shops and one of the best food courts far and wide

Orlando Fashion Square
3201 E Colonial Dr.
Mon -- Sat 10am – 9pm,
Sun 11am – 6pm
www.orlandofashionsquare.com
The widest range of fashion is available here.

WHERE TO EAT
❶ *Christini's Ristorante Italiano* $$$$
7600 Dr. Phillips Blvd.
Tel. 1-407-345-8770
Excellent Italian food. Special tip: pork chops marinated in port wine.

❷ *Café Tu Tu Tango* $$
8625 International Drive
Tel. 1-407-248-2222
Stone-baked pizza, fish, seafood, vegetarian dishes.

❸ *Dexters of Thornton Park* $$
Thornton Park
808 E Washington St.
Tel. 1-407-648-2777
Tortillas, fresh pasta and great sandwiches; pretty decor, often live music.

❹ *Numero Uno* $$
Downtown,
2499 S Orange Ave.
Tel. 1-407-841-7187
Tasty Cuban cooking; try »Moros y Christianos« (black beans with rice).

❺ *The Briarpatch*
Winter Park, 252 Park Ave. N.
Tel. 1-407-628-8651
This place has served homemade breakfast and lunch for a quarter of a century.

An absolute must: eggs Benedict and homemade ice-cream!

Insider Tip

WHERE TO STAY
❶ *Eo Inn*
Thornton Park, 227 N. Eola Drive
Tel. 1-407-481-8485
www.eoinn.com
Elegant boutique hotel (19 rooms) with a wellness area. It also has a pretty view of Lake Eola.

❷ *The Courtyard at Lake Lucerne* $$$
211 N Lucerne Circle E
Tel. 1-407-648-5188
www.orlandohistoricinn.com
In a picturesque garden and still centrally located, a B & B with romantic guestrooms, a veranda and cocktail bar.

❸ *Best Western Orlando Gateway* $$
7299 Universal Blvd.
(east of International Drive)
Tel. 1-407-351-5009
www.bworlando.com
Reasonably priced and clean accommodation with 298 rooms and suites, pool and restaurant near »SeaWorld« or the water park Aquatica

❹ *Quality Inn & Suites* $$
7495 Canada Ave.
(near International Drive)
Tel. 1-407-351-7000
www.qualityinn.com
Clean and modern inn with 133 rooms and 67 suites in a good location; quiet and yet not far from famous attractions. There is room for up to four people in the spacious rooms, small breakfast included.

DOWNTOWN ORLANDO

A young city Orlando's grid-like city centre is small and manageable on foot; tourists generally do not go there since it offers no more than the usual office buildings found in American cities of this size. In recent years downtown Orlando has become noticeably more lively. Tens of thousands have moved into the newly built or restored apartments. Restaurants, cafés, pedestrian zones and cultural attractions have made the once run-down centre attractive again. The fact that there are more than 10,000 students in Orlando and many young people working in the service industry and with modern technology and electronics has practically made it a young city.

The main street, which is filled with office employees around the lunch hour, is still the north-south **Orange Avenue**. Along with a lot of non-descript functional architecture, several buildings nevertheless make their mark, including the post-modern **City Hall**, which was opened in 1992. Near the **First National Bank**, which was inspired by ancient Egyptian architecture, Orange Avenue crosses **Church Street** with its **Church Street Station**, a mini-entertainment zone located around the old railway station.

*Orange County Regional History Center The County Courthouse holds the Orange County Regional History Center. Its outstanding exhibits depict the history of the region. Note especially the documentation of the Afro-American community in Orlando as well as the exhibition »The Day We Changed«, about the changes that Walt Disney brought to the region.

❶ 65 E Central Bld., Mon – Sat 10am – 5pm, Sun noon – 5pm, admission US$9, www.thehistorycenter.org

LOCH HAVEN PARK

Regional cultural centre A few minutes' drive along the I-4, about 3mi/5km north-east of downtown, leads to Loch Haven Park with its three artificial lakes. With three museums and the **Orlando Repertory Theater** (1001 Princeton St.) the park is the cultural centre of the region.

The **Orlando Museum of Art** (2416 N Mills Ave.), which concentrates on American art since the 19th century as well as African art, is considered a gem by insiders.

The **Orlando Science Center** (8777 E Princeton St.) covers scientific topics as diverse as Florida's geography, the canals on Mars and the human body.

The wonderful ***Harry P. Leu Gardens** of the entrepreneur Harry P. Leu are a true oasis of peace. The rose garden has more than 1,000 different varieties that bloom all year. Moreover, the **largest collection**

of camellias in the USA can be admired here as well as magnolias, orchids and azaleas. The **Butterfly Garden** has colourful butterflies from all over the world. Leu House is the place where the »green« businessman worked.

Orlando Museum of Art: 2416 N Mills Ave. Tue – Fri 10am – 4pm, Sat, Sun noon – 4pm, admission US$8, www.omart.org

Orlando Science Center: 8777 E Princeton St.; Sun – Thu 10am – 5pm, Fri, Sat 10am – 10pm, admission US$17, www.osc.org

Harry P. Leu Gardens: 1920 N. Forest Ave.; daily 9am – 5pm, tours daily 10am – 3.30pm, admission US$7, www.leugardens.org

✱ WINTER PARK

The wealthy town of Winter Park borders on the north. This place has not lost any of its relaxed charm since it was founded in 1887 as an artists' colony. The local attractions reflect the residents' lifestyle. The **Albin Polasek Museum & Sculpture Gardens** exhibits the work of this artist of Czech descent in light-flooded rooms and a garden with palm trees. His sculptures made him one of the most important 20th-century American artists. No less inspiring is a stroll through **Kraft Azalea Gardens** (Alabama Drive) on the beautiful **Lake Maitland** with its thousands of azaleas and various types of palm trees.

Albin Polasek Museum & Sculpture Gardens

Albin Polasek Museum & Sculpture Gardens: 633 Osceola Ave., Tue – Sat 10am – 4pm, Sun 1pm – 4pm, admission US$5, www.polasek.org

!	*Practice free falling …*	Insider Tip

MARCO⊕POLO TIP

… at iFly Orlando. After instruction by professional jumpers, practice the proper posture – weightless in indoor wind tunnels.
Address: 6805 Visitors Circle, daily: 10am – 10.30pm,
www.iflyorlando.com

On Winter Park's main boulevard this museum exhibits works by **Louis Comfort Tiffany** (1848–1933), which are among the finest art nouveau works to have been produced. Numerous paintings, stained glass windows, lamps etc. come from Tiffany's earlier house in New York City. Other important artists are also represented, including the art nouveau French glass painter **Emile Gallé**, the American painter and writer **John LaFarge** and the architect **Frank Lloyd Wright**.

**Charles Hosmer Morse Museum of American Art

❶ 445 Park Ave. N., Tue – Sat 9.30am – 4pm, Sun 1pm – 4pm, Nov – April Fri until 8pm, admission US$5, www.morsemuseum.org

The best reason to drive further north past Winter Park is the **Audubon of Florida – National Center for Birds of Prey**. The conservation league, along with an informative visitor centre, has the largest

Maitland

rehabilitation clinic for wounded birds in the eastern USA. Visitors can see birds of prey that are native to Florida like ospreys and bald eagles up close.

❶ 1101 Audubon Way, Tue – Sun 10am – 4pm, admission US$5, http://fl.audubon.org/

✱ INTERNATIONAL DRIVE

Pure energy ...

Begun in the early 1980s and continuously expanded since then, the 4.5mi/7km-long **thoroughfare** south-west of downtown Orlando is so to speak the umbilical cord to which all of the famous theme parks in the area are connected. It has earned its nickname of »Orlando's Most Dynamic Destination«. Its sidewalks and bike paths are lined by more than 100 hotels, some of which have **spectacular architecture**, along with three very big **theme parks** and countless smaller amusements, about 150 restaurants, 500 designer shops, department stores and factory outlets and several entertainment complexes. Spoiled for choice!

✱✱Discovery Cove

One of the most unusual attractions is undoubtedly Discovery Cove, a SeaWorld affiliate. For a fee visitors can swim with the three dozen **dolphins** in the expansive **lagoon**. The visitor limit of only 1,000 a day (the larger neighbouring parks admit to 50,000 a day!) means that you can enjoy the dolphins in peace. Other attractions, including snorkelling in a coral reef and a tropical river half a mile long, both inhabited by swarms of tropical fish, are included in the steep admission fee.

❶ 6000 Discovery Cove Way, admission US$219, admission only by appointment made at least 30 days prior, tel. 1-877-577-7404, www.discoverycove.com

Titanic – The Experience

This park feeds a dark fascination. From the famous staircase where Leonardo DiCaprio alias Jack Dawson walked in the legendary blockbuster film, to the original deckchairs and yellowed photos: Titanic fans will get their money's worth here.

❶ 8445 International Drive; hours: daily 10am–8pm, admission US$25, www.titanictheexperience.com

✱Wet 'n Wild

This water park offers plenty of opportunities to get wet, what with rides like Raging Rapids (rapids with waterfall) and The Surge (one of the longest waterslides in the USA). The giant slide named Stuka is nothing for weak nerves: plummet down the steep 76m/250ft-long slide almost at free fall into a pool. The Black Hole is another white-knuckle experience: a plunge on a small raft into total darkness.

❶ 6200 International Drive; 10am – 8pm, admission US$56, www.wetnwildorlando.com

A superlative among waterparks, made by SeaWorld in 2008: 36 water slides, artificial rivers and lagoons are spread across the 20ha/50 acre grounds. **The Dolphin Plunge** is the most popular attraction with two parallel transparent tubes in which people slide through a lagoon past four Commerson's dolphins, whose dark and light markings make them look like orcas, the SeaWorld trademark. **Tassie Twisters** is an exciting raft ride downhill through rapids into the **Lazy River**.

✱✱Aquatica

❶ 5800 Water Play Way, daily from 9am, closing times vary between 6pm and 10 pm, admission US$50, info tel. 1-407-351-3600, www.aquaticabyseaworld.com

This attraction was founded by Robert L. Ripley. Young and old will be astonished at the most unbelievable exhibits in the crooked »Sinking Building« (8201 International Dr.; hours: daily 9am–11pm).

Ripley's Believe it or not! Museum

❶ 9.30am – midnight, admission US$20, www.ripleys.com/orlando/

✱✱ SEAWORLD ORLANDO

Accessible via International Drive, SeaWorld Orlando lies 10mi/16km south-west of downtown Orlando and is one of the most spectacular theme parks – above and below the water. In 1973 Busch Entertainment, the entertainment branch of the mega-brewery Anheuser-Busch, opened SeaWorld, which has been improved and expanded several times and includes an imposing **sea water aquarium**, an

SeaWorld dolphins are true masters in synchronic swimming

artificial **reef** with swarms of colourful inhabitants, pools for **sting rays**, a **dolphinarium**, and facilities for penguins, seals and otters as well as a **flamingo garden**. The shows with trained **dolphins and orcas** or »killer whales« have always been the public's favourite. The nice thing about this park is that it does not overwhelm the senses: it has a manageable size and everything is easy to see on foot.

In the **dolphin nursery** young dolphins are raised. In the area called **Turtle Trek**, turtles and also manatees can be watched up close. For most tourists in Florida this is one of few chances to take time to observe these endangered animals.

In the **Sea Lion & Otter Stadium** the two sea lions Clyde and Seymore appear as pirates and the agile sea otters play tricks on them. An walrus takes part, too. The **Manta Aquarium** is breath-taking: visitors can walk through the glass tunnel and watch **mantas, barracudas** and other beauties of the deep. But no trip to SeaWorld is complete without a visit to **Shamu Stadium**: the orca whale Shamu and his companions show their acrobatics and make the water splash over the first 14 rows of visitors! And this would not be Orlando, if there were no roller coasters and other »thrill rides«. The most recent attraction is **Explore Antarctica** with an adventurous tour through the world of penguins.

❶ 7007 SeaWorld Drive access via I-4, Exit 72, depending on the season and weekday daily 9am to 7pm or 10pm admission US$82, www.seaworldparks.com

✳✳ UNIVERSAL ORLANDO

Here everything bangs, explodes or takes off. Universal Orlando, an affiliate of Universal Studios in Hollywood, focuses on »action«. It offers some of the best high-tech attractions ever. **Universal Studios** in Orlando opened in 1990. After a rocky start this Hollywood theme park earned its place next to Walt Disney World. With the help of creative minds that switched over from Disney-MGM Studios to Universal Orlando a second theme park was conceived and built a few years later. In 1999 **Universal Islands of Adventure** opened, a tour de force aimed at youths and adults that was inspired by Hollywood blockbusters and features hair-raising roller coasters and the craziest technical effects. With **City Walk**, which was opened the same year, an entertainment zone for adults that connects the two parks, Universal confirmed its interest in older customers.

❶ 6000 Universal Blvd., depending on the season and weekday daily 9am to 7pm or 10pm, on special occasions the park often stays open until midnight, admission US$96, www.universalorlando.com.

Spider Man and Wolverine at Universal Orlando

Universal Studios Look familiar? Famous movie sets await visitors here. Scenes from **Ghostbusters were filmed here, the on-location shots for **Blues Brothers** there, as well as various mafia films. Altogether the sets from about three dozen movies were set up here, including that of the Hitchcock classic **Psycho**, the house of Norman Bates. These areas offer spine-tingling pleasure, and especially on weekends and during the high season the fans form long queues. In **E.T. Adventure** Steven Spielberg's most popular extra-terrestrial needs our help to save his home planet. In **Disaster! – A major motion picture … starring You** visitors can experience in an interactive adventure an earth-quake with a magnitude of 8.3 on the Richter scale while riding a subway in San Francisco: suddenly the earth shakes, subway shafts collapse, masses of water flood the tunnel and a tank explodes. Ultra-modern high-tech effects tests the visitors' perception of reality in computer animated shows. **Terminator 2 3-D** uses three giant screens and live shows on stage to make the audience feel a part of the action. The latest digital technology, high-tech simulators, aroma sprays and shaking seats in **Shrek 4-D** produce an event in which Shrek, Princess Fiona and Donkey start out on new adventures. **Revenge of the Mummy**, also new, plunges visitors into deep darkness at first and then – by means of the latest technology, some of it in-house proprietary technology, and any number of talking mummies and crawling scarabs – takes them on the worst ride of their lives. The live shows are thrilling too. **Men in Black: Alien Attack** is an interactive spectacle, in which the spectators can help fight against aliens. In the **Horror Make-Up Show** the audience gapes while arms are cut off and other »cosmetic surgery« is performed – not for weak nerves! It is no exaggeration to say that this also applies to **Fear Factory live**, where visitors can themselves try out breathtaking stunts – before an audience.

Islands of Adventure Roller coasters rocket, people scream and squeal, and things crash and rattle here as if there was no tomorrow: welcome to Islands of Adventure, the mecca of adrenaline junkies! The park, which no less a person than Steven Spielberg helped design, brings dinosaurs to life and offers the very latest in entertainment in the form of roller coasters, »thrill rides«, that truly deserve respect. These can be tried out in the theme areas **Marvel Super Hero Island and **The Lost Continent**. For example the **Incredible Hulk** Coaster races through corners and loops at a speed of up to 55mph (90kmh). The hanging ride called **Duelling Dragons** consists of two spirals that turn around each other, where two ride constructions repeatedly race at each other at top speed only to miss each other by inches at the last minute. **Doctor Doom's Fearfall** is also not for faint hearts and

High-speed thrills on the Incredible Hulk Coaster

weak stomachs: a rocket-like start »shoots« participants almost 60m/200ft straight up only to bring them back to the starting point in an almost free fall. The latest attraction is **Simpsons – The Ride**: a thrilling roller-coaster trip through the world of yellow-skinned Homer, Marge, Bart. Lisa and Maggie Simpson. The **Amazing Adventures of Spider-Man** is an absolute delight to roller coaster fans. Wearing 3-D eyeglasses the participants' cars first get shaken up only to plunge down a 100m/330ft skyscraper canyon in New York by means of computerized effects and three-dimensional video projections. But Spiderman arrives in the nick of time.

For families whose kids always want dinosaurs the **Jurassic Park** theme area is the highlight of the visit. Here they will meet the dinosaurs that Spielberg taught how to walk in his top-selling movies. The zone is conceived as a tropical jungle and in the Discovery Center similar to the visitors' centre in the movie, visitors can learn everything about the pre-historic beasts. Various dino-relevant attractions await, including Jurassic Park River Adventure, where a gentle raft ride turns into a nightmare when the passengers have to flee a hungry T-Rex by going over the edge of an almost 30m/100m-high waterfall. The latest attraction is **Harry Potter World** with Hogwarts Castle, the village Hogsmeade and the forbidden forest. Of course special restaurants serve magical dishes and shops sell miraculous gifts.

AROUND ORLANDO

Fort Christmas

Follow along FL 50 east towards Titusville for about 25mi/40km to reach Christmas, a town with a reconstructed fort from the time of the **Seminole Wars**. Documents, historic maps, weapons and utensils of the first settlers as well as pictures of the Seminole chiefs depict the time when this land was grabbed by the white people. Incidentally: many visitors mail their Christmas cards from the **post office in Christmas**, Florida.

❶ 1300 Fort Christmas Rd., Tue – Sat 11am – 4pm, free admission, www.nbbd.com/godo/fortchristmas/

Citrus plantations of Clermont

The town, which the founder named after his French hometown, lies 23mi/37km west of Orlando. It was known as a centre for the cultivation of oranges and grapefruits until the 1980s.

Today the hilly countryside with its many lakes around Clermont is becoming more popular as a place to live and to relax.

Two attractions that are interesting for tourists as well are the **Waterfront Park**, which attracts water sports fans and sunbathers, as well as the new **Bike Trail**, which follows an old railway line from Clermont to Ocoee. Clermont is also the venue of an annual **triathlon** that attracts athletes from all over North America (www.triflorida.com).

Sanford, about 20mi/32km north of Orlando, on the road to ▶Daytona Beach, this town of 54,000 lies on the idyllic **Lake Monroe**. It started out in 1837 as a trading post and up to a few years ago it was the centre of a larger fruit and vegetable farming region. Until today it remains the »gateway to southern Florida«, above all for tourists who come to the Sunshine State by auto train.

MARCO ◉ POLO TIP

Fine wine **Insider Tip**

About 7mi/10km north of Clermont on US 27 the Lakeridge Winery & Vineyards is a recommended stop. The personnel inform guests on winegrowing under local conditions, where the grape harvest is usually finished by July or August. The cellar, where good wines can be tasted, is also open for viewing (hours: Mon–Sat 10am – 5pm, Sun 11am – 5pm; www.lakeridgewinery.com).

Monroe Harbor is the base for relaxing **boating excursions** on the lake itself (some with a paddle-wheeler) as well as on the **St John's River**.

★★ **Palm Beach**

✦ J 6

Region: South-east
Elevation: 0 – 5m/16ft above sea level
Population: 8,300

Is Palm Beach in Florida the wealthiest city in the world or is it Malibu in California? One thing is certain: the city fathers watch over their billionaires with Argus eyes. In early 2005 they even refused to give Donald Trump permission to have fireworks at his wedding celebration. Visitors who earn as much in a year as the lady at the next table donates during a charity function can't believe their eyes …

Teenagers in Rolls Royce convertibles, power shopping and a city ordinance that prohibits clothes-lines: located on a palm island off the Gold Coast, Palm Beach with its grandiose villas and its Tiffany, Armani and Gucci shop windows, is the **winter quarters of the American rich and famous** and their equally rich and/or famous friends. From November to April »one« meets in the Palm Beach Polo & Country Club or in the brand-new ballroom of Trump's Mar-a-Lago-Estate on Ocean Boulevard, where the construction magnate likes to have world-famous stars like Céline Dion and Gloria Estefan perform in front of small groups of his friends.

Playground of the jet set

Palm Beach

INFORMATION
Palm Beach CVB
1555 Palm Beach Lakes Blvd. Suite 800
Palm Beach, FL 33401
Tel. 1-800-554-7256
www.palmbeachfl.com

BEACHES
The most beautiful beaches are privately owned and off limits, but that's no reason to do without a swim. Midtown Beach at the east end of Worth Avenue is a public beach. The one in Phipps Ocean Park further to the south is quieter.

SHOPPING
Even by American standards Worth Avenue in Palm Beach is second to none in shopping. Every exclusive label is present. But a bulging wallet or a platinum card is also necessary. This may be hard to believe, but the city of billionaires also has second-hand shops! As an alternative to paying a four-figure sum for a tuxedo, go to Déjà Vu (219 Royal Poinciana Way) or The Church Mouse (374 S County Rd.).

NIGHT LIFE
Palm Beach prefers to keep itself to itself after dark: nightlife generally takes place in the form of private parties, balls and charitable events. For dancing it's best to go to West Palm Beach, where bars, restaurants and music bars around Clematis Street stay open until 4am.

❶ *Respectable Street Café*
518 Clematis St.
Tel. 1-561-832-9999
www.respectablestreet.com

One of the best places in Florida for live music of the last two decades

WHERE TO EAT
❶ *Café l'Europe* $$$$
331 S County Road
Tel. 1-561-655-4020
Elegant French restaurant with Italian and also German culinary accents

❷ *Eau Spa Cuisine at the Ritz-Carlton* $$$
100 S. Ocean Blvd.
Tel. 1-561-533-6000
Chef Ryan Artim creates delicious food. It is served with the best world's wines

❸ *Cucina dell'Arte* $$$
257 Royal Poinciana Way
Tel. 1-561-655-0770
Classic Italian cuisine that values fresh ingredients

❹ *Havana Restaurant* $$
6801 S. Dixie Highway
Tel. 1-561-547-9799
Cuban cooking at affordable prices – from sandwiches to baked fish filet with herbs

WHERE TO STAY
❶ *The Breakers* $$$$
Palm Beach, 1 S. County Road
Tel. 1-561-655-6611
www.thebreakers.com
560 rooms and suites. This traditional luxury hotel with its elegant rooms, contemporary Kid's Club and five heavenly restaurants is and remains the first address in Florida.

❷ *Biba* $$
320 Belvedere Road

West Palm Beach
Tel. 1-561-832-0094
www.hotelbiba.com
43 rooms and suites Chic boutique hotel
with sake bar and zen garden. Room interiors with clear lines and warm colours.

❸ *The Colony Hotel* $$$

Palm Beach 155 Hammon Ave.
Tel. 1-561-655-5430
www.thecolonypalmbeach.com
83 rooms and suites Good accommodation between the Atlantic and Worth
Avenue with friendly and obliging
service.

Palm Beach

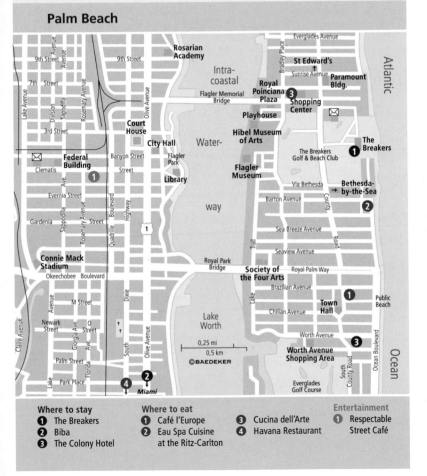

Where to stay
❶ The Breakers
❷ Biba
❸ The Colony Hotel

Where to eat
❶ Café l'Europe
❷ Eau Spa Cuisine
  at the Ritz-Carlton
❸ Cucina dell'Arte
❹ Havana Restaurant

Entertainment
❶ Respectable
  Street Café

Highlights Palm Beach/West Palm Beach

▶ **The Breakers**

The unchallenged flagship of the hotel trade in Florida is also the place where old and new money meet.
▶page 303

▶ **Whitehall**

Today the winter palace of the restless railway magnate Flagler is a museum.
▶page 303

▶ **Worth Avenue**

»It's worth it« – the motto of one of the most exclusive shopping streets in the world where all of the labels are also exclusive.
▶page 307

▶ **Norton Museum of Art**

Art lovers consider this to be the »first address«: paintings by impressionists like Gauguin and Matisse as well as modern American artists, including Edward Hopper and Andy Warhol.
▶page 308

This is a busy time too on exclusive Worth Avenue, where the architect **Addison Mizner** (▶Famous People) made his mark with Mediterranean houses, arcades and inner courtyards. Then there are the many gourmet restaurants and hotels right on the beach, neighbours to the Kennedys, Rockefellers and Vanderbilts.

History Yes, you guessed right: Palm Beach has always been rich. It all began when the Spanish freighter Providentia, loaded with coconuts from the Caribbean, ran aground in 1878 off the coast of the 22km/13mi-long and only 1km/0.6mi-wide island. **Railway magnate Henry M. Flagler**, who explored the area in the early 1890s, saw the potential of the palm-tree covered island bordered by the deep blue and turquoise Atlantic. In 1894 he had his Florida East Coast Railroad extended to Lake Worth and built the legendary Royal Poinciana Hotel on Palm Beach. A year later the Palm Beach Inn was added, later to be known as Breakers. As could be expected, the elegant hotels attracted an illustrious clientele. John D. Rockefeller stopped here, the newspaper tsar Randolph Hearst and US President Harding as well. In 1918 **Addison Mizner** stepped off the train and gave the city its Mediterranean appearance. At that time the service personnel lived

! Insider Tip

Cycling through paradise

The best way to experience Palm Beach with its people, dogs and cars is on a bike and on Lake Trail. The most beautiful villas and yachts can be admired at leisure this way. Bike rental: Palm Beach Bicycle Trail Shop, 233 Sunrise Ave., tel. (561) 659-4583.

MARCO ⊕ POLO TIP

Whitehall – the magnificent palace built by the railway magnate Henry M. Flagler

beyond Lake Worth in West Palm Beach on the mainland. Meanwhile the former suburb has developed into the 80,000-strong centre of Palm Beach County. Electronics companies have settled here, as have tax accountants and real estate agents who control their territory in Palm Beach from here.

WHAT TO SEE IN PALM BEACH

Since 1926 this beautiful palace has been **Palm Beach's landmark** and its calling card! It is a luxury hotel with 540 rooms in the style of an Italian palazzo which is located right on the water and despite its size does not appear ostentatious. It is still the place where the city's old and new money meet. It has the number of golf courses, spa clubs and beauty salons appropriate to a hotel of its class. With the **Flagler Club** on the top two floors of the seven floors it has an even more elegant hotel in a hotel: for guests in the 28 suites, 28 butlers stand ready to redefine the word »service«.

**The Breakers

On the west side of the island railway magnate Henry M. Flagler (►Famous People) had a 55-room palace built in the Beaux-Arts style with the lyrical name of **Whitehall** as a wedding present for his third wife. The couple lived here every winter from 1902 until Flagler's death in 1913 and thus inaugurated high society here. As was customary for the »Gilded Age« around 1900, every room was decorated extravagantly along a different historical theme. Thus there is a **Louis XV ballroom**, a **Swiss billiard salon** and a **Louis XIV concert hall**.

**Whitehall (Flagler Museum)

Pointsmen for the Economy

Florida would never be what it is today had not three men and one woman set a new course in the 19th century. By building the railway they created the necessary conditions for turning the swampy peninsula into a tourist paradise.

The idea came from US Senator Yulee: before the American Civil War he built the first railway from the Atlantic port Fernandina straight across north Florida to the Gulf Coast port of Cedar Key in order to transport cedarwood, sugar cane and cotton. Smaller businessmen joined in and laid their own tracks, which however were not connected to each other.

Henry M. Flagler

When the businessman Henry M. Flagler visited Florida in 1879 – his ailing wife came here to recuperate – he saw a market opportunity. At that time Florida was already an insider's tip among wealthy convalescents, but getting there was still

Henry M. Flagler

difficult and there was no appropriate accommodation. Flagler, who had become wealthy in the oil business with **John D. Rockefeller**, had the financial means to develop Florida. He bought up existing train lines and connected them. He created a consolidated rail network along the east coast of the USA. At especially beautiful locations, like St Augustine, he had elegant Mediterranean-style luxury hotels built. In 1894 Flagler's railway builders constructed the enchanting Palm Beach. Flagler bought a hotel there and converted it into the legendary The Breakers. Flagler's ideas bore fruit. The wealthy from the cold north-east USA came to Florida by the thousands.

Julia Tuttle Attracted Flagler

The winter of 1895 set Florida tourism back. Cold spells not only destroyed the citrus crops but also drove away the tourists. This was Julia Tuttle's hour. She owned a plantation in southern Florida on the Miami River and had already asked Flagler several times to extend his railway to the south, but without success. Now she sent him a branch of blooming orange blossoms – which convinced him. Julia Tuttle and Henry M. Flagler became business partners. In April 1896 the first train reached the then quite small settlement of Miami. This was the start of its uninterrupted rise to Florida's metropolis. But Flagler's rise, too, was unstoppable: he pushed his East Cost Railroad south as the Overseas Railroad over the Keys to Key West by building bridges at great expense. On 22 January 1912 Flagler took the first train to Key West. This enterprise cost several millions and 700 workers their lives, but now it was possible to take the **train from New York to Key West**. Then, on Labor Day 1935, a hurricane destroyed the tracks over the Keys and blew a train filled with passengers into the sea. The railway was not reconstructed.

Henry B. Plant

What Flagler did successfully on the East Coast, Henry B. Plant did on the **Gulf Coast**. Like Flagler he recognized Florida's tourist potential when his wife came here to convalesce. He developed southwest Florida and from Tampa expedited freight to Key West and Cuba. He attracted many tourists to Florida's Gulf Coast, which was known for its wonderful beaches and sunny weather, with his comfortable trains and hotels. In 1895 already he had a railway network of over 1,400 miles (2,400 kilometres).

And today?

The heyday of the railway is history now. Trains still run from New York or Washington to Orlando and Miami, but now most tourists travel by air or in their own cars to the »Sunshine State«. A few shorter sections have been reactivated recently as museum trains for leisure trips through the countryside.

22 January 1912: Flaglers train arrives at Key West

After Flagler's death Whitehall changed hands several times and in 1959 was even scheduled to be torn down. Today the building is a protected monument that gives the visitor an impressive picture of the restless builder.

In the expansive garden, which is separated from the street by a beautiful wrought iron fence, in a newly built **Flagler Pavilion** stands **The Rambler**, Flagler's private railway coach, in which he made the first train trip to Key West in 1912.

❶ Whitehall Way, Coconut Row; Tue – Sat 10am – 5pm, Sun noon – 5pm, admission US$18, www.flagler.org

A few minutes' walk further south, along the Intracoastal Waterway, are – in sub-tropical vegetation – the stucco buildings of this non-profit organization. It was founded in 1936 by wealthy art-loving residents in order to satisfy the community's cultural needs; the facility was designed by the famous architect Mizner and houses a worthwhile **library**, interesting **rotating exhibitions** and beautiful **sculpture gardens** with samples of all the varieties of plants that flourish in southern Florida.

*Society of the Four Arts

❶ 2 Four Arts Plaza; daily 10am – 5pm shorter hours in winter, admission US$5, www.fourarts.org

»It's worth it!« – the 200 exclusive shops on this **most elegant shopping street** hope to attract their wealthy clientele with this motto. And since they know that billionaires can't resist a bargain, they offered reduced parking rates – »no matter if you spend one or a hundred thousand dollars ...«.

**Worth Avenue

All famous labels are represented here: Tiffany, Armani, Louis Vuitton etc. Some of the newer trendy labels like Jimmy Choo and Juicy Couture have sneaked in, too. Fine restaurants and a Mediterranean atmosphere, for which **Addison Mizner** was once again responsible, make a shopping trip along this astronomically expensive street, from which small diversions lead into quiet inner courtyards, an almost obscene pleasure.

Some of the most beautiful villas from the 1920s were also designed by Addison Mizner. Especially fine examples can be seen on South Ocean Boulevard, including the villa of the cosmetics queen **Estée Lauder** (no. 126), a house built in 1919 where ex-Beatle **John Lennon** relaxed decades later (no. 720), and not least the castle-like Villa Mar-a-lago (no. 1100), which was built by the Cornflakes heiress Marjorie Merriweather Post and bought in 1985 for the bargain price of 8 million dollars by the billionaire Donald Trump.

**Luxury villas

Tiffany, 259 Worth Avenue: the world famous purveyor of glass art and jewelry resides here in suitable ambience

WHAT TO SEE IN WEST PALM BEACH

*Raymond F. Kravis Center for the Performing Arts

The focal point of the old centre of West Palm Beach is the Raymond F. Kravis Center for the Performing Arts (701 Okeechobee Blvd.), which was completed in 1992, with its generously proportioned **theatre and concert hall**. The architecturally very attractive cultural centre was designed by the Canadian-German architect **Eberhard Zeidler**. The **Palm Beach Symphony** and the Philharmonic Orchestra of Florida regularly perform here.

❶ 701 Okeechobee Blvd., tel. 1 561 8 33 06 91, www.kravis.org

**Norton Museum of Art

In 1941 an industrialist from Chicago founded the Norton Museum, considered by art lovers to be an extremely high-class address. Its collection includes important works by French impressionists like **Gauguin, Matisse and Monet**. The American collection includes such heavyweights as **Edward Hopper, Jackson Pollock, Georgia O'Keeffe and Andy Warhol**.

❶ 1451 S Olive Ave.;Tue – Sat 10am – 5pm, Thu until 9pm, Sun 1pm – 5pm, admission US$12, www.norton.org

South Florida Science Museum, Planetarium & Aquarium

In this museum in the charming **Dreher Park** technical and natural phenomena can be explored. In the **Native Plant Center** almost all of the local flora is represented, and in the **Aquarium** Florida's aquatic fauna can be seen (feedings Tue, Thu, Sat 1pm). For anyone who wants to take a look at the universe there is a planetarium or **observatory** with a large telescope.

❶ 4801 Dreher Trail; Mon – Fri 10am – 5pm, Sat 10am – 6pm, Sun noon until 6pm, admission US$12, www.sfsm.org

Palm Beach Zoo

The Palm Beach Zoo with its native and exotic animals is also popular. Some can be even be petted. The stars in this zoo are the Florida panthers, which now are rarely found in the wild.

❶ 1301 Summit Blvd.; daily 9am – 5pm, admission US$19, www.palmbeachzoo.org

AROUND PALM BEACH

*Lion Country Safari

15mi/24km to the west lies a **safari and amusement park** where lions roam around free. Visitors drive their cars through the grounds. Keep windows and doors closed for safety reasons! In Safari Village there is a **petting zoo** as well as a **dinosaur and reptile park**.

❶ 2003 Lion Country Safari Rd., Loxahatchee; mid Dec – Aug Mon – Fri 10am – 5pm, Sat, Sun 9.30am – 5.30pm, Sept – mid Dec daily 9.30am – 5.30pm, admission US$27.50, www.lioncountrysafari.com

Sea turtles lay their eggs at Juno Beach

North of Palm Beach the metropolitan area of ►Miami and the so-called Gold Coast ends. On the next 80mi/130km of coast there are surprisingly large stretches of open land between individual towns, seaside resorts and brand-new retirement communities. The boom that rolled over the Gold Coast in the last decades has reached this Treasure Coast only in greatly reduced form.

Treasure Coast

Singer Island, unfortunately an almost completely built-up barrier island, still has the **John D. MacArthur Beach State Park** hidden away behind sand dunes; it offers good swimming and hiking as well as a nature centre with information on the highly sensitive ecological system.

Singer Island

❶ 10900 Jack Nicklas Drive, daily 8am until sunset, admission pedestrians US$2, vehicles US$, www.floridastateparks.org/macarthurbeach/

Juno Beach (population 3,400) is a typical retirement community: during the winter months the population triples. This settlement with

*Juno Beach

its beautiful beach was bypassed by Flagler's railway because the railway magnate could not come to an agreement with the owners of the local railway line. Thus Juno Beach missed its chance to become a millionaires' row.

Between May and September the excellent **Marine Life Center of Juno Beach** conducts tours to the nesting places of the sea turtles in **Loggerhead Park**. These primeval-looking animals come on land here in June and July in order to bury up to 100 eggs in the sand.

❶ 14200 US 1, Mon – Sat 10am – 5pm, Sun 11am – 5pm, free admission, www.marinelife.org; Turtle Walks: June/July Wed – Sat 9pm on appointment tel. 1-561-627-8280, ticket US$ 20

*Jupiter

The seaside resort of Jupiter is located about 7mi/11km further to the north (population 55,000). Its prominent landmark is the red brick **Jupiter Lighthouse**. It was built in 1860 and is considered to be the town's birthplace.

The historic building is also the home of the **Loxahatchee River Historical Museum**, which has the hard life of the early white settlers and the living conditions of the Native Americans as its main topic, is worth a visit.

But some stop here for only one reason: Burt Reynolds! The **Burt Reynolds & Friends Museum** was founded in 1999 on the ranch of the popular Hollywood actor; it has memorabilia on Burt Reynolds' films, including the canoe from Deliverance, as well as »holy relics« of famous Reynolds associates, like baseballs signed by the legendary Mickey Mantle and Muhammad Ali's boxing gloves.

Jupiter Lighthouse, Loxahatchee River Historical Museum: 500 Captain Arrows Way, Jan – April daily, otherwise Tue – Sun 10am – 5pm, admission US$9, www.jupiterlighthouse.org

Burt Reynolds & Friends Museum: 100 N. US 1, Thu – Sun 11am – 4pm, admission US$5, www.brift.org

Jupiter Island

Beyond Jupiter Inlet, on the beautiful barrier island Jupiter Island, a visit to **Blowing Rocks Preserve** is worthwhile. This section of coast consists of porous coral limestone. High tides or high seas force sea water through holes and pipes in the stone and cause fountains to spray up to 15m/50ft high.

❶ 574 S. Beach Rd., daily 9am – 4.30pm, admission US$2, www.nature.org

*Hobe Sound National Wildlife Refuge

About 7mi/11km further to the north is the wonderful nature reserve on Hobe Sound. Apart from a magnificent beach and imposing dunes there are also several square miles of sea-water marsh in its original state. Every year in the summer many sea turtles come to the nature reserve in order to lay their eggs on land undisturbed.

❶ Hobe Sound Nature Center: 13640 SE Federal Hwy. (US 1) Mon – Sat 9am until 3pm, free admission, http://hobesoundnaturecenter.com

A few miles further inland the Jonathan Dickinson State Park (16450 SE Federal Highway; hours: daily 8am–sunset) offers a completely different picture. From **Hobe Mountain**, a giant sand dune, there is a view of uninterrupted thicket made up of cedar and palmetto. The course of the **Loxahatchee River** is lined by mangrove forests and cypress swamps. The reserve is a refuge for numerous endangered species, especially manatees and sea turtles. These gentle creatures can best be watched from a canoe (canoe rental in the park).
❶ 16450 SE Federal Hwy., daily 8am until sunset, admission: pedestrians US$2, vehicles US$6, www.floridastateparks.org/jonathandickinson/

*Jonathan Dickinson State Park

* Panama City · Panama City Beach
——————————— ✦ D 2

Region: North-west
Elevation: 0 – 9m/30ft above sea level
Population: 36,500

Anyone who asks about museums and art galleries here will usually be rewarded with an amused look. In Panama City Beach, the centre of the 18mi/30km long »Redneck Riviera«, everything revolves around having fun on the white sand beach and in the warm blue waters. The endless rows of faceless hotels make no apology for being there. The oil spill in the Gulf of Mexico did not change anything either.

But there's one thing to be said about Panama City Beach: it never tried to be anything else. With its twin, Panama City on the other side of St Andrews Bay, it has been the venue for millions of holiday makers from Alabama, Mississippi and Georgia ever since beach holidays were invented. The families of Southerners relaxed on the indisputably beautiful beaches. For a long time it was contemptuously called »Baja Georgia« or even the »Redneck Riviera«, because of the predominance of people from the Deep South on the beaches. In spring tens of thousands of college students invaded, ready for anything. The **rowdy beach parties** were broadcast live by radio stations from all over North America.
Panama City Beach consists of sports bars with dozens of TV screens and old-fashioned motels, go-cart tracks, minogolf courses and hotels that look like they were built in a day. Highway US 98, which is called **»Front Beach Road«** within the city limits, is the main drag day and night where everything happens.

Redneck Riviera

WHAT TO SEE IN PANAMA CITY & BEACH

Downtown Panama City
In the centre of this bustling port and industrial city some historical buildings have been nicely restored. There are good restaurants here too. The marina at the end of Harrison Avenue has room for more than 400 yachts and fishing boats.

In the **Science & Discovery Center of Northwest Florida** young visitors are introduced to natural phenomena.

❶ 308 Airport Rd., Panama City, Tue – Sat 10am – 5pm, admission US$, http://scienceanddiscoverycenter.org

*Miracle Strip
The Miracle Strip of Panama City Beach hops day and night with its many amusement parks, bars, discos and other attractions. Tourism began to develop here in the 20th century. Above all during »spring break« thousands of young people from Alabama, Georgia and other states come here to party. There are several amusement parks, including Miracle Strip Amusement Park, the largest of its kind in northern Florida, and **Shipwreck Island**

Springtime on the »Redneck Riviera«

Water Park, a combination of amusement park and fun swimming pool attract young and old. When visitors tire of giant water slides, bungee jumping and roller coasters, the long **City Pier** or one of the walkways that run into the dunes are great places to enjoy the sunset.

Shipwreck Island Water Park: 12201 Hutchinson Blvd., May – early Sept daily 10.30am – 4.30pm, admission US$33, http://shipwreckisland.com

Gulf World Marine Park

The aqua park is arranged like a sub-tropical garden and shows **dolphins, sea lions, sea otters and sharks** in their natural element. The dolphin shows always attract large crowds. Anyone can go into the water with the playful animals, for a fee of course.

❶ 15412 Front Beach Rd. summer daily 9am – 7pm, otherwise 9.30am – 5pm, admission US$28, www.gulfworldmarinepark.com???

Museum of Man in the Sea

It's interesting to speculate on how strong the nerves of early divers were while viewing this museum! From the **old diving bells** to **diving helmets** from the 18th century and claustrophobic diving suits from the time of World War II, this exhibition run by the Institute of Diving documents man's early efforts to live and work under water.

❶ 17314 Panama City Beach Parkway, Tue – Sat 10am – 5pm, admission US$5, www.maninthesea.org

*St Andrew's State Park

The nature reserve at the east end of Panama City Beach has the most beautiful stretch of sand (2.5mi/4km long) on the Redneck Riviera. It was founded in 1951 and was military property before that. Today it shows what this section of coast looked like before mass tourism developed here. Walk through dunes and sea water marshes on the **Heron Pond Trail** and watch cranes and ibis.

❶ 4607 State Park Lane; daily 8am – sunset, admission: pedestrians US$2, vehicles US$8, www.floridastateparks.org/standrews/

*Shell Island

Nothing but the sun on this 6mi/10km-long beach on Shell Island, a delightful little island in St Andrew's Bay. Get there by boat from St Andrew's State Park.

Shell Island Shuttle: Spring – fall daily 10am – 5pm every 30 minutes, www.shellislandshuttle.com

AROUND PANAMA CITY BEACH

There are charming and easily accessible places for excursions nearby, for example the seaside resorts to the north-west, **Seaside** and **Grayton Beach** (▶Fort Walton Beach, Around), **Florida Caverns** (▶Marianna) one hour's drive north-east and the historic town of ▶**Apalachicola** to the south-east.

Panama City

INFORMATION
Panama City Beach CVB
17001 Panama City Beach Parkway
Panama City Beach, FL 32413
Tel. 1-850-233-5070
www.thebeachloversbeach.com

WHERE TO EAT
❶ *Firefly $$$*
535 Richard Jackson Blvd.
Tel. 1-850-249-3359
Well-prepared food, well-selected wine list as well as tasty sushi in the Firefly Bar next door attracts many guests.

❷ *Boars Head $$$*
17290 Front Beach Rd.
Tel. 1-850-234-6628
The traditional restaurant is popular for its good steaks and excellent wine list.

WHERE TO STAY
❶ *Edgewater Beach Resort $$$$*
11212 Front Beach Rd.
Tel.1-850-235-4044
www.edgewaterbeachresort.com
520 apartments This is the place to relax; it has its own swimming facilities, spa zone and golf course.

❷ *Quality Inn & Suites $*
3602 West Hwy. 98, tel. 1-805-522-5200
www.qualityinn.com
52 rooms. Orderly modern inn in Panama City, not far from the university campus

❸ *Sunset Inn $$*
8109 Surf Drive, tel. 1-850-234-7370
www.gulfcrestbeachresort.com
Friendly accommodation on a broad beach, yet not right in the centre of activity.

Panama City

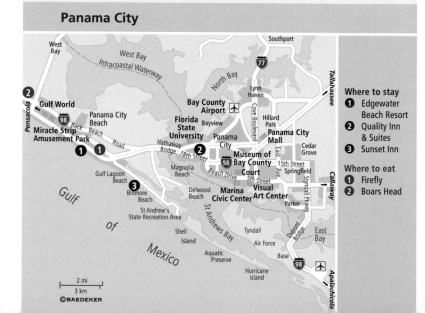

Where to stay
❶ Edgewater Beach Resort
❷ Quality Inn & Suites
❸ Sunset Inn

Where to eat
❶ Firefly
❷ Boars Head

©BAEDEKER

★★ **Pensacola**

✦ **B 2**

Region: North-west
Elevation: 0 – 12m/40ft above sea level
Population: 52,000

White beaches, pleasant temperatures and hospitable south-ern atmosphere are the attractions of this city at the extreme end of the Florida Panhandle. Since the old town has been restored, tourists are discovering that Pensacola is more than an air force base on the Gulf of Mexico.

Pensacola – and not ▶St Augustine or Jamestown (Virginia) – very nearly became the oldest city in the USA. **Spanish conquistadors** knew and appreciated the natural harbour of Pensacola Bay, which is protected by the barrier islands Perdido Key and Santa Rosa Island, in the 16th century. In 1559 Don Tristan de Luna went ashore with soldiers and colonists near the present air base. Three years later a hurricane destroyed the settlement, which was never rebuilt. Colonization only began seriously in the early 18th century when the Spaniards arrived on the **Castillo San Carlos de Austria**.

During the Spanish-French War Pensacola was fought over and changed hands several times. In 1763, at the end of the Seven Years' War it went to the British, but reverted to Spain in 1781 already. Then Pensacola became a safe haven for pirates, runaway slaves and Indians. In 1821 Pensacola briefly felt the hand of history as the place where Florida was turned over to the USA.

The United States expanded the harbour into a **navy base**. During the Civil War the fort was held by Union troops and played an im-portant role in the blockade of the Confederate states. Reconstruc-tion after the Civil War was made easier by a lumber boom, which was however already over in 1900. Then came commercial fishing and carried the economy for a while until the US navy set the course for modern urban development by building a naval air base.

Today Pensacola is the **economic centre of the region** and thanks to its location and cultural heritage a rising holiday venue. In this it profits from the nearby Gulf Islands National Seashore with its great beaches, which however suffered the effects of the Deepwater Hori-zon oil spill in 2010.

PENSACOLA

INFORMATION
Pensacola Visitor Information Center
1401 E. Gregory Street
Pensacola, FL 32502
Tel. 1-850-434-1234
www.visitpensacola.com

CITY TOUR
A trip on the trolleybus which leaves from the Visitor Center for the local tourist sites explains why Pensacola is often called »Five Flags City« (daily 1pm, ticket US$16, www.americanheritage towns.com

EVENT
Fiesta of the Five Flags **Insider Tip**
Every year at the end of May an extravagant celebration is held in every neigh-bourhood of the city. The highlight of the festival is the re-enactment of the landing of the city's founder Don Tristán de Luna on the white Pensacola Beach to be met by the Indian chief Mayoki. Infos: www.fiestaoffiveflags.org

WHERE TO EAT
Jackson's Steakhouse $$$$
400 S. Palafox St.
Tel. 1-850-469-9898
Presently the best restaurant in town, it serves innovative »Southern cuisine«.

Dharma Blue $$$
300 S. Alcaniz St.
Tel. 1-850-433-1275
Light »fusion cuisine« and excellent sushi on Seville Square. The terrace is especially nice.

Spanish colonial architecture on Seville Square in Pensacola

Insider Tip

Flounder's Chowder House $$
800 Quietwater Beach Rd.
Tel. 1-850-932-2003
Fresh fish and seafood – and the brilliant sunset from the terrace is for free.

WHERE TO STAY
The Portofino $$$$
10 Portofino Dr., Pensacola Beach
Tel. 1-877-484-3405
www.portofinoisland.com
The 150 living units, which are spread over several high-rises on the beach, are furnished with all the creature comforts. On the more than 100 ha/250 acres of grounds there are gardens, sporting facilities, restaurants and cafés.

Pensacola Grand Hotel $$$
200 E. Gregory Street
Tel. 1-850-433-3336
www.pensacolagrandhotel.com
A 15-storey building with 212 spacious rooms and suites, and a unique past: the lobby was originally a railway depot.

Solé Inn & Suites $$
200 N Palafox Street
Tel. 1-850-470-9298
www.soleinnandsuites.com
Unadorned hotel complex, but with surprisingly elegant rooms in downtown Pensacola.

WHAT TO SEE IN PENSACOLA

What a conglomeration of people! When Pensacola began to grow up at the end of the 17th century it was the meeting place of Indians, freed slaves, white settlers from the most varied backgrounds and all sorts of seafarers from the Caribbean. They plied their trades at the harbour jetties of Seville District east of Palafox Street. The most successful then settled in ostentatious residences in the quarter bordered by Government Street, Adams Street, Tarragona Street and Alcanz Street.

*Seville District

About two dozen restored buildings today form Historic Pensacola Village, the city's largest attraction. The village is characterized by Spanish, Creole and British colonial architecture. **Dorr House** (311 Adams St.) was built in 1871 and is a rare example of the Greek Revival style in Florida. Lavalle House (205 E Church St.) was built in 1805 by Carlos Lavalle in the so-called French Creole style and has furnishings from this period. **Julee Cottage** (210 E Zaragoza St.), a modest, leaning wooden house dating from 1804 belonged to Julee Panton, a freed black slave. A few steps further the **Museum of Industry** (120 E Church St.), housed in an old railway car, is dedicated to the development of industry in this part of Florida. Right next door in an old warehouse the **Museum of Commerce** (201 E. Zaragoza St.) presents the development of transportation by means of a reconstructed street scene from 1890. **Lear-Rocheblave House** (214 E. Zaragoza St.), also nearby, dates

*Historic Pensacola Village

from 1890; it is a beautiful Victorian house surrounded by a veranda. A few blocks away the **Pensacola Historical Museum** is dedicated to the eventful history of the city. There is also a **Children's Museum**.

Historic Pensacola Village: Tivoli High House, 205 E Zaragoza St, Tue – Sat 10am – 4pm, tours 11am, 1pm, 2.30pm, ticket US$6, www.historicpensacola.org

Pensacola's Children's Museum: 111 E Zaragoza St. Tue – Sat 10am – 4pm, admission US$3, www.pensacolawithkids.com

*Palafox Historic Business District

The historic business district of Pensacola runs from the harbour to Wright Street. Many of the beautiful houses are reminiscent of New Orleans: wrought-iron balconies decorate the façades, pedestrians stroll under shady arcades. Spanish neo-Renaissance and Mediterranean styles predominate, especially at **Palafox Square**, the heart of the old city centre.

The **Saenger Theater** (118 Palafox St.), which opened in 1925, is worth a visit. Its opulent terracotta ornaments are a beautiful example of Spanish neo-Baroque. Along with well-known plays many concerts are held here – from classical to rock and pop music

The **T.T. Wentworth Jr. Florida State Museum** was built on Plaza Ferdinand in 1907 as a neo-Renaissance palace with red roof tiles. It is devoted to the history of the Florida Panhandle.

Saenger Theater: 118 Palafox St., tickets tel. 1-850-595-3880, www.pensacolasaenger.com

Wentworth Museum: Plaza Ferdinand, Tue – 10am – 4pm, free admission, www.historicpensacola.org

AROUND PENSACOLA

**National Museum of Naval Aviation

You can't help but be impressed: this is one of the largest and most interesting air and space museums in the world. The halls and hangars on the grounds of the **Naval Air Station** (NAS) a few miles south-west of the city centre display more than 100 aircraft from almost 100 years of American naval flying. The exhibits range from **biplanes** from World War I to **Hornet fighters** that were used only recently in the Near East. Sea planes, the bridge of an aircraft carrier, the deep-blue jets of the famous **aerobatic and formation team Blue Angels** and the **command capsule of the space lab Skylab**, which was flown by navy pilots, are highlights of the exhibition.

The **IMAX cinema** screens films including ones on the everyday life of a jet pilot.

❶ 1750 Radford Blvd.; daily 9am – 5pm, www.navalaviationmuseum.org

Legendary Blue Angels jets on display at the
National Museum of Naval Aviation

Pensacola's natural harbour was so important to the city fathers that they had four forts built to protect it from enemy attacks. Fort Barrancas, on a cliff at the harbour entrance which looks across to Perdido Key and Santa Rosa Island, was built between 1834 and 1844 by US troops on the foundations of British and Spanish forts and is open to the public today in conjunction with a visit to the National Museum of Naval Aviation.

*Fort Barrancas

ⓘ Mar – Oct. daily 9.30am – 4.45pm, Nov – Feb daily 8.30am – 3.45pm, free admission, www.nps.gov/guis/

Right in front of Pensacola are the fine white to shimmering silver sandy beaches of two barrier islands – Perdido Key and Santa Rosa Island, which is only a few hundred yards wide but about 50mi/80km long, extending all the way to ►Fort Walton. Sections of special historical or ecological interest are part of the **Gulf Islands National Seashore**. The beaches were seriously affected by the Deepwater Horizon oil spill in 2010, but meanwhile they are accessible again.

**Santa Rosa Island, Perdido Key

ⓘ admission US$8 (vaild for one week), more information: www.nps.gov/guis/

From Pensacola drive across the 3mi/5km-long **Pensacola Bridge** to the suburb of Gulf Breeze on the spit of land between the bay and the gulf. From there a short bridge connects to Santa Rosa Island. Right behind this bridge lies the seaside resort of Pensacola Beach; along the white beach the chain of snack bars, restaurants, taverns, hotels,

*Pensacola Beach

motels, giant apartment blocks, t-shirt stands as well as bike and surfboard rentals seems endless. The 400m/1,300ft-long pier is one of a kind.

*Fort Pickens At the western end of Santa Rosa Island the imposing Fort Pickens stands guard on the white sand. Built in 1834, the **fortress** defended the entrance to the harbour along with Fort McRee on Perdido Island opposite and Fort Barrancas on the mainland. The massive ruins, especially the dark corridors and courtyards deserve a closer look. A small museum is dedicated to the most famous prisoner at Fort Pickens: from 1886 to 1888 the **Apache chief Geronimo** was imprisoned here with 17 of his braves.

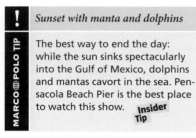

MARCO ● POLO TIP

Sunset with manta and dolphins

The best way to end the day: while the sun sinks spectacularly into the Gulf of Mexico, dolphins and mantas cavort in the sea. Pensacola Beach Pier is the best place to watch this show. **Insider Tip**

*Blackwater River State Forest Only a 20-minute drive north-east of Pensacola, this forest is famous for its rivers Juniper Creek, Sweetwater Creek, Coldwater River and Blackwater River. The town of **Milton** on the southern edge of the forest took advantage of this by calling itself the »**canoeing capital of Florida**«. Indeed, canoeing tours on the rivers meandering through untouched forests are a delight. In Milton several tour organizers rent canoes and kayaks, and also offer day trips or longer tours.

* Perry

⭐ F 2

Region: North Central
Elevation: 13m/42ft above sea level
Population: 7,000

An old part of Florida lies on the route to the Panhandle. This land was not developed by railway barons and their friends but by farmers and day-labourers, the so-called Florida Crackers. In Perry a museum is dedicated to the people who helped make the land of Florida cultivable.

The city fathers have proudly named their town the »Tree Capital of the South«. In this way they commemorate Perry's role in the lumber boom around 1900. The region's wealth of lumber was recognized at the end of the 19th century; the settlement that was founded in 1857 became the centre of the industry. The production of turpentine was

Perry

INFORMATION
Perry-Taylor County Chamber of Commerce
428 N. Jefferson Street
Perry, FL 32347
Tel. 1-850-584-5366
www.taylorcountychamber.com

EVENT
In October the Florida Forest Festival takes place with various events related to forestry (like sawing contests), exhibitions and music.

WHERE TO EAT
Roy's Restaurant $$
100 1st Ave SW, Steinhatchee
Tel. 1-352-498-5000
Popular venue for locals and tourists.

It has a giant salad bar and good fish dishes.

WHERE TO STAY
Steinhatchee Landing Resort $$$
203 Ryland Circle
Steinhatchee, FL 32359 **Insider Tip**
Tel. 1-352-498-3513
www.steinhatcheelanding.com
29 cosy Cracker-style cottages.

Days Inn Perry $
2277 S. Byron Butler Parkway
Perry, FL 32348
Tel. 1-850-584-5311
www.daysinn.com
Centrally located motel with 60 spacious and well furnished rooms as well as a nice outdoor swimming pool.

another important forest industry, but by the end of the 1930s large parts of the region were deforested. Sawmills and paper factories had to close, and many people moved away. Today US 98 keeps the place alive: with its motels along the highway Perry is a welcome break for tourists on the way south.

WHAT TO SEE IN AND AROUND PERRY

The museum was opened in 1973 in fragrant woods south of town and gives an impression of the development of forestry and the lumber industry in Florida. The most important types of trees are presented, as well as a broad selection of products made from wood fibre or tree sap. The exhibition focuses on the history of local forestry and the production of turpentine. Next to the museum there is a **reconstructed Cracker homestead** with its outbuildings. In 1863 a pioneer family settled here and earned their living from the forest industry typical to the area. The main house is a simple log cabin with the veranda and outside kitchen typical of the South. The entire farmstead is surrounded by a log fence.

*Forest Capital State Museum & Cracker Homestead

❶ 204 Forest Park Dr., US 19/27A/98; Thu – Mon 9am – noon and 1pm – 5pm, admission US$2, www.floridastateparks.com/forestcapital/

*Keaton Beach, Steinhatchee A charming side trip goes via CR-361 south to the Gulf Coast, which is still largely undeveloped here and thus called the Lost Coast. A drive of about 20mi/35km leads to the beautiful Keaton Beach, site of a very popular restaurant. 20mi/35km further on the somewhat dusty lumber and fishing settlement of Steinhatchee (population 800) at the mouth of the river of the same name, which is a **centre of sports fishing**. Steinhatchee was founded in the 1870s, as the first settlers brought cedars that had been cut down in the hinterland to the coast, tied them into rafts and floated them along the coast to ▶Cedar Key. Meanwhile tourism has arrived.

** St Augustine

✳ H 3

Region: North-east
Elevation: 0 – 10m/30ft above sea level
Population: 13,000

This beautifully tended settlement on Matanzas Bay welcomes visitors with open arms. European guests especially find this to be true. They feel at home immediately under the palm trees of the old town, which could easily be in Spain or Mexico. No wonder: St Augustine is the oldest city in North America, and its residents are the most history-conscious of Floridans.

Oldest city in the USA Narrow, winding alleys, Spanish houses with wrought-iron gates that lead to shady inner courtyards, romantic balconies and expansive plazas with palmettos and trees covered in Spanish moss: St Augustine is a trip through time. It started in 1513 with Ponce de León. In that year the Spanish seafarer arrived – supposedly, since there is no evidence to sustain the claim – here on »pascua florida« (Easter Sunday) and claimed it for his king, naming it »Florida«. However, only when the French settled further north near today's ▶Jacksonville did the Spanish government remember what it had. With orders to kill all Protestants in the New World, General **Don Pedro Menéndez de Avíles** landed here in 1565 with 600 soldiers.

After founding the Castillo de San Augustín he led his army northwards, burned down the French Fort Caroline and annihilated everyone in the fort.

Then the Spanish settlement of St Augustine developed into the administrative base for about 30 Spanish bases on the Florida peninsula. The settlement was attacked repeatedly by pirates looking for booty. One of the most famous buccaneers, **Sir Francis Drake**, plundered the growing colonial city in 1586. John Davis, another pirate,

Highlights in St Augustine

► **Castillo de San Marcos**
This masterpiece of Spanish colonial fortification protected the city and secured the sea passages for Spanish ships returning home.
►page 325

► **Old Town**
The historic old city of St Augustine has been restored and maintained beautifully; several very interesting museums attract visitors.
►page 328

► **Dow Museum of Historic Houses**
Do not miss this museum. It comprises a whole block of historic buildings from various periods of city history.
►page 329

► **Anastasia Island**
From St Augustine cross the Bridge of Lions to the barrier island with its brilliant beaches.
►page 331

The most popular attraction in St. Augustine is Castillo de San Marcos

St Augustine

INFORMATION
St. Augustine Visitor Center
10 Castillo Drive
daily 8.30am – 5.30pm

St Augustine

Where to stay
1. Casa Monica
2. BW Spanish Quarter Inn
3. Ramada Inn

Where to eat
1. Harry's
2. OC White's
3. Spanish Bakery

St Augustine, Ponte Vedra & The Beaches VCB
29 Old Mission Ave.
St Augustine, FL 32084
Tel. 1-904-829-1711
www.floridahistoriccoast.com

PARKING
Parking space is extremely rare in St Augustine. It is best to park in the garage with Spanish colonial-style architecture on the northern edge of the old city (6 S. Castillo Drive).

CITY TOUR
The old town can easily be explored on foot. The visitor centre (see above) at the large parking lot on the northern edge of the old city and at Castillo de San Marcos provide maps of the town. »Sightseeing trains« and horse-drawn carriages start from there.

WHERE TO EAT
Insider Tip
❶ *Harry's Seafood Bar & Grill*
46 Av. Menendez, tel. 1-904-824-7765
Hearty and spicy southern specialties and wonderful fish dishes – including lobster and shrimps – are served here.

❷ *O. C. White's* $$$
118 Av. Menendez
Tel. 1-904-824-0808
Popular venue for local people and tourists, who enjoy the coconut shrimps, Caribbean chicken or even a Porterhouse steak.

❸ *Spanish Bakery* $
42½ St George Street, St Augustine Beach
Tel. 1-904-471-3046
Tasty snacks and good lunches.

WHERE TO STAY

❶ Casa Monica $$$$
95 Cordova Street, tel. 1-904-827-1888
www.casamonica.com
138 rooms and suites The castle-like hotel was built in 1888 and re-opened a few years ago after comprehensive renovation and modernization. Spanish colonial ambience, first-class service.

❷ Best Western Spanish Quarter Inn $$
6 Castillo Drive
Tel. 1-904-824-4457
www.bestwestern.com
Comfortable accommodation (40 rooms and suites) near Castillo de San Marcos. The old town is within walking distance.

❸ Ramada Inn $$
116 San Marco Avenue
Tel. 1-904-824-4352
www.ramadainnhistoric.com
This well-run modern house has 100 comfortably furnished rooms is located at the edge of the old town.

killed about five dozen of the residents of St Augustine in 1668. When the English expanded their settlements in Virginia to the south in the 17th century, the Spanish in St Augustine responded by building Castillo San Marcos. The fortress withstood several English sieges. In 1763 Florida temporarily came under British control. St Augustine, now the **capital of the British colony of East Florida**, experienced the arrival of British loyalists, who had fled the American Revolution and gone south. In 1783 Florida reverted to Spain. Attracted by generous awards of land, US American settlers now took over the lands left by the English who remained loyal to the king. In 1821 Florida became part of the United States and ▶Tallahassee was made the new capital. St Augustine was forgotten. Only the arrival of the East Coast Railroad of the railway magnate **Henry Flagler** woke the city from its sleep. In 1883 Flagler visited the city and recognized its tourist potential immediately: a little while later the railway arrived, luxury hotels mushroomed, and the beaches on Anastasia Island were developed. In 1887 and 1914 city fires destroyed many historic buildings, but the tourist future was already determined. Today tourism is the most important source of income in the city, and preserving the Spanish heritage is its most important endeavour.

WHAT TO SEE IN THE OLD TOWN OF ST AUGUSTINE

The view over the cannons on to Matanzas Bay includes sails appearing on the horizon and daring characters jumping ashore: the garrison of this **coastal fortress** that was built in 1672 to protect the city and the gold fleet that returned to Spain from the Antilles saw a great deal of action.

**Castillo de San Marcos

** *Castillo de San Marcos*

This massive fortress has guarded the oldest continuously settled city in the USA for more than 300 years. It was built from 1672 to 1695 by the Spanish to protect the city and the gold and silver transports that returned from the Caribbean to Spain. It offered protection against pirates and the attacks of enemy troops with its 13-foot-thick (four metres) walls made of durable local Coquina limestone, and its cannon and mortar decks.

❶ daily 8.45am – 5.15pm
admission US$7,
www.nps.gov/casa/

❶ Quay wall
at the harbour entry
(Matanzas River)

❷ Ravelin
This triangular barbican was supposed to protect the entrance area.

❸ Moat
It was usually dry but could be flooded in times of danger.

❹ Outer drawbridge
This bridge leads to the barbican of the fortress. It was raised every evening.

❺ Inner drawbridge
Only entrance to the fortress, with portcullis

❻ South-west bastion
(San Pedro Bastion) with watchtower and cannon deck

❼ South-east bastion
(San Agustin Bastion) with watchtower, flagpole and cannon deck

❽ Cannon and mortar deck
Heavy iron and bronze cannons and mortars stood here.

❾ North-east bastion
(San Carlos Bastion) with high watch and bell tower

❿ Plaza de Armas
Inner courtyard; armaments and drill ground

⓫ Fortress chapel
To the west is the »British Room«.

⓬ Powder store
Later it was also used as a regular storeroom and prison.

North-west bastion (San Pablo Bastion) with watchtower

St George Street ends at Plaza de la Constitución. The plaza opens to the bay and is a nice place to relax on park benches under shady trees. In 1598 it was built according to a model used everywhere in the Spanish world, where a new city was always planned around a central plaza. The monument in the middle of the plaza was only unveiled in 1813. The west side is dominated by **Government House**. This former palace of the Spanish colonial government has a display in the ground floor on the history of the city and its various phases of restoration. The Cathedral Basilica of St Augustine, the seat of the oldest Roman Catholic diocese in North America, was also restored and reconstructed several times. The beautiful Spanish-Moorish church was built in 1797 and takes up the north side of the plaza.

❶ 48 King St., Thu – Mon 10am – 4pm, free admission, www.staugustine.ufl.edu

*Plaza de la Constitución

The Cathedral-Basilica of St. Augustine, the **episcopate of the oldest Roman Catholic diocese in North America**, was also restored and reconstructed several times. The beautiful Spanish-Moorish church was built in 1797 and takes up the north side of the plaza.

❶ 38 Cathedral Place, daily 7am – 5pm, free admission, donations requested, www.thefirstparish.org

*Cathedral-Basilica of St Augustine

The Old St Augustine Village Museum consists of ten historic buildings in their original locations. They were built between the late 18th century to the early 20th century and thus represent some of the important periods of city history. The oldest building is also the most interesting: built in 1790, the Prince Murat House was the home of Achille Murat, Napoléon's nephew and Prince of Naples. Exiled from post-Napoleonic France, the prince occupied the house in 1824 and then stayed here several times thereafter. A small exhibitions displays correspondence between Murat and Napoleon Bonaparte as well as some nice reports on the prince's charismatic personality.

❶ 149 Cordova St., Mon – Sat 10am – 5pm, Sun 11am – 5pm, admission US$8.95, www.moas.org/dowmuseum

** Dow Museum of Historic Houses

The two stone lions that guard the photogenic Bridge of Lions can be seen from the cathedral. The Spanish-Moorish style **drawbridge over the bay** has connected the old city with the beaches on Anastasia Island since 1927. It is presently being restored thoroughly.

*Bridge of Lions

South of the plaza there are more attractions for visitors. The Spanish **Military Hospital**, however, is no for the faint-hearted. Guides full of anecdotes describe the military hospital from the second Spanish colonial period and tell grisly stories about each of the surgical instruments.

❶ 3 Aviles St.; Mon – Sat 10am – 6pm, admission US$8, www.spanishmilitaryhospitalmuseum.com

Spanish Military Hospital

*Oldest House – Casa González-Alvarez

The »oldest house« in St Augustine is easy to recognize by the four flags hanging outside, which flew over the city in the last 400 years. The complex consists of several buildings and is named **Casa González-Alvarez** after its two owners, whose beginnings go back to 1702, as well as a house that now holds the **Manucy Museum of St Augustine History**. It exhibits old maps and photos and various items from the Spanish colonial period.

❶ 14 St Frances St.; daily 9am–5pm every 30 minutes, ticket US$8, www.staugustinehistoricalsociety.org/

*Lightner Museum

From the southern edge of the Plaza de la Constitución King Street leads out of the Spanish colonial centre of St Augustine towards the west. A few minutes' walk behind Government House is the Lightner Museum. It is housed in the **luxurious Alcazar Hotel**, which was built in the flamboyant style of the railway magnate Flagler and then went broke during the Depression in the 1920s. The representative building holds the collections of the **Chicago publisher Otto Lightner**, who bought the empty hotel in 1948. Several floors hold everything from Egyptian mummies to stuffed birds, rare minerals, historic steam engines and automatic musical instruments.

❶ 75 King St.; daily 9am – 5pm, admission US$10, www.lightnermuseum.org

Flagler College

Once there do not miss the artistic **Tiffany stained-glass windows** of Flagler College with its towers, diagonally opposite. This building was once the legendary Ponce de León Hotel.

Zorayda Castle

Also on the south side of King St, but beyond Granada Street, a large **palace was built in the Moorish style** in 1883. It is modelled after the Alhambra in Granada. Antiquities are exhibited here, including a more than 2,000-year-old Egyptian carpet with a cat pattern.

❶ 83 King St.; Mon – Sat 10am – 5pm, Sun 11am – 4pm, admission US$10, www.villazorayda.com

WHAT TO SEE OUTSIDE THE OLD TOWN

Fountain of Youth Archeological Park

In 1513 – as far as the legend and the local advertising goes – Ponce de León landed here, north of today's Castillo, in order to search for the **mythical fountain of youth**. He did not find it, but archaeologists found the remains of a pre-Columbian Timuacan Indian village. A guided tour shows gardens, excavations and the fountain, whose story was just too good for it not to be »reconstructed«. The place has all the marks of a tourist trap, but despite the kitsch it also possesses charm.

❶ 11 Magnolia Ave.; daily 9am – 5pm, admission US$12, www.fountainofyouthflorida.com

Casa González-Alvarez is the oldest house in Florida

The grounds of the **first mission station** in North America are a nice place to relax. In 1565 Pedro de Menéndez de Avíles is supposed to have landed and celebrated the first mass in America with his priests here. Along with the church and a 63m/210ft cross the little chapel of **Our Lady of La Leche** is worth looking at. It is the oldest church in the USA dedicated to the Virgin.

Mission of Nombre de Dios

❶ 27 Ocean Ave.; Thu, Fri, Sat 10am – 6pm, Sun 12noon – 4pm, free admission, donation requested, www.missionandshrine.org

AROUND ST AUGUSTINE

From St Augustine highway A1A crosses the Bridge of Lions to a narrow barrier island off the coast. Anastasia Island is known for its enchanting beaches and high dunes. The nicest is St Augustine Beach in Anastasia State Recreational Area. Unfortunately large parts of the dunes are now covered with holiday houses, but there are regular gaps that make the beaches accessible.

**Anastasia Island

Insider Tip

Just a few miles beyond the bridge there is an alligator farm. **Large reptiles** have been raised here since 1893. The unchallenged star is Maximo, an Australian crocodile almost six metres (20 feet) long. Lateste attraction is the ZIP line, where you can swing high above alligators and crocodiles along 50 different obstacles.

St Augustine Alligator Farm Zoological Park

❶ 999 Anastasia Blvd.; hours: daily 9am–5pm, summer until 6pm, admission US$22,95, ZIPline US$65, www.alligatorfarm.com

***St Augus-
tine Light-
house &
Museum**

Not far from the alligator farm is a 50m/165ft-high lighthouse built in 1874 on the foundations of the previous lighthouse; its black and white spiral motif makes it a popular photo motif and its observation platform offers a wonderful panoramic view. But be warned: 219 steps have to be climbed to get to the top! The lovingly restored light-house-keeper's house has a little exhibition on the hard life of the lighthouse-keeper.

❶ 81 Lighthouse Ave.; daily 9am – 6pm, admission US$9.50,
www.staugustinelighthouse.com

***Fort
Matanzas**

About 14mi/22km south of St Augustine lies a small Spanish fort that was built in the entry to the Intracoastal Waterway. In 1565 the slaughter of the French Huguenots by the Spanish took place here; the French had built Fort Caroline further to the north at the mouth of the St John's River. From the visitor centre on the A1A a park rang-er takes visitors to the fort by boat.

❶ daily 9am – 530pm, accessible by boat and free admission, donation requested, www.nps.gov/foma/

A relic from Spanish colonial times: Fort Matanzas

About 20mi/32km south of St Augustine, on the other side of the Matanzas Inlet, highway A1A runs to the **Dolphin Conservation Center at Marineland**, which was renovated thoroughly in 2005. This tourist attraction originally opened in the 1930s and is thus one of the oldest of its kind. The park stages **programmes with dolphins**. Every effort is made to offer ecology-friendly tourism.

*Marineland

❶ 9600 Oceanshore Blvd., daily 9am – 4.30pm, admission US$8.50, programmes with dolphins in various price ranges, www.marineland.net

A few miles to the south lies the superb, largely undeveloped Flagler Beach with its dunes, a good place for recreation. In the summer **sea turtles** lay their eggs in protected areas.

*Flagler Beach

About 12mi/20km north of St Augustine a super-modern golfing mecca was opened in 1998 right on the I-95. The core of the facility with two 18-hole golf courses is a luxury hotel and the Golf Hall of Fame with a museum and an IMAX cinema. The most famous golfers of all time are commemorated and the development of the sport with the little white ball is presented.

*World Golf Village & Hall of Fame

❶ Mon – Sat 12noon – 6pm, admission US$20, www.worldofgolffoundation.org

★★ St Petersburg

✦ G 5

Region: Central West
Elevation: 0 – 14m/46ft above sea level
Population: 245,000

Juan Ponce de León would probably turn over in his grave: the fountain of youth that the Spanish sea-farer searched for in vain is in St Petersburg. Florida's most famous residence for senior citizens? Yes, since the residents have gotten 10 years younger in the last three decades; the average age now is 39.

Of course, St Petersburg cheated a bit. Since there was no spring that promises eternal youth, it began to attract high-tech businesses in the 1990s. The young hardware and software developers stirred up the nightlife in the otherwise quiet pensioners' colony. New trend hotels, gourmet restaurants and bistros accelerated the rejuvenation. The skyline grew, too.

Successful rejuvenation- Castle

Since 1998 the city has invested 1.5 billion dollars in apartment and office buildings. It added new concert arenas, a modernized event calendar with top-class events and a dozen new art galleries. Today

History

One of St. Petersburg's landmarks is the »upside down pyramid« on the pier that reaches 400m/1,300ft into Tampa Bay

senior citizens with grey and white hair enjoy »**St Pete**« just like punks with rainbow-coloured hair. But St Petersburg has kept its unique charm despite changing its appearance: downtown its palm tree-lined streets open to Tampa Bay and still have the aura of a seaside resort. The pelicans still sit in a line along the pier and in the yacht harbour; sailboats anchor off shore, and dolphins play in the surf.

In 1875 General John Williams from Detroit bought about 700ha/1,700acres of land on the Pinellas Peninsula in order to build a holiday resort with beautiful parks and broad boulevards. 13 years later his vision grew with the arrival of the Orange Belt Railway of the Russian entrepreneur Peter Demens. The Russian named the city after his hometown: St Petersburg. The invention of air conditioning in the 1950s made the city more attractive to seniors and it soon became a pensioners' colony.

But since the 1990s the city on Tampa Bay has worked successfully on changing its image. The weather helped. The sun shines here almost every day, a fact that earned St Petersburg an entry into the Guinness Book of Records.

WHAT TO SEE IN ST PETERSBURG

The **landmark of St Petersburg** – and the best place for people-watching – reaches 730m/2,400ft into Tampa Bay. Something is always going on here. It starts at the five-storey **pyramid** with various restaurants and shops with a selection geared toward cruise ship tourists and others who stop for short visits. Its observation terrace offers a good view of the city skyline.

❶ 800 2nd Ave. NE; Mon – Thu 10am – 8pm, Fri, Sat 10am – 9pm, Sun 11am – 7pm, free admission (except for special events), http://stpetepier.com

**The Pier

How old – and yet young – the city is can be seen in the permanent and the rotating exhibitions. The people who made »St Pete« can be seen here: the first citrus farmers, angry creditors chasing the highly indebted Peter Demens, the seaplane that began commercial flight here in 1914 (at the beginning of the pier, 335 2nd Ave.; hours: Mon noon–7pm, Tue–Sat 10am–5pm, Sun 1pm–5.30pm).

❶ 335 2nd Ave. (at the beginning of the sea bridge), Tue – Sat 10am – 5pm, Sun 1pm – 5pm, admission US$12, www.spmoh.org

*St Petersburg Museum of History

One block north of the pier a neo-classical villa holds an exquisite art collection. It covers works from antiquity to items from pre-Columbian America, Far Eastern art, famous French impressionists and modern American artists like Georgia O`Keeffe.

❶ 255 Beach Dr. NE; Mon – Sat 10am – 5pm, Thu until 6pm, Sun 12noon – 5pm, admission US$17, www.fine-arts.org

*Museum of Fine Arts

South of downtown a modern gallery has dedicated itself since 1982 to the work of the **Catalan Surrealist** Salvador Dalí (1904–89). The exhibition shows 95 oil paintings, more than 100 drawings and water colours, prints and sculptures by Salvador Dalí from 1914 to 1980. These include several masterpieces like his self-portrait (Figueres), The Persistence of Memory (»melting clocks«) as well as the large painting The First Days of Spring. A large library with publications on Dali and Surrealism is attached to the museum.

❶ 1 Dali Blvd., Mon – Sat 10am – 5.30pm, Thu 10am – 8pm, Sun 12noon until 5.30pm, admission US$21, www.thedali.org

**Salvador Dalí Museum

PINELLAS SUNCOAST

St Petersburg Beaches, Pinellas County Beaches, Holiday Islands: there are various names for the 50km/30mi-long Gulf Coast of the Pinellas Peninsula's barrier islands. With **361 sunny days a year** and snow-white endless beaches their future was determined: the leisure

Holiday paradise

St Petersburg

INFORMATION
St Petersburg/Clearwater Area Convention & Visitors Bureau
13805 58th St. N., Suite 2-200
Clearwater, FL 33760
Tel. 1-727-464-7200
www.visitpeteclearwater.com

DOLPHIN WATCHING
Hubbard's Marina
Madeira Beach, 150 John's Pass
Tel. 1-727-393-1947
www.hubbardsmarina.com
The best dolphin-watching tours around.

NIGHT LIFE
❶ *BayWalk*
153 2nd Avenue North
The BayWalk Entertainment Center gave the somewhat quiet city centre the necessary vitamin shot a few years ago. Apart from trend boutiques the shopping centre, built in the Californian mission style, also has restaurants, bars and cinemas as well as beautiful courtyards for relaxing. BayWalk is a good choice for evenings and nights, too, because of its restaurants, bars and cinemas.

❷ *Jannus Landing Courtyard*
16 2nd Street North
Tel. 1-727-896-2276
Famous musicians appear all year round in this wonderful outdoor arena in St Petersburg.

❸ *Coliseum Ballroom*
535 4th Avenue
Tel. 1-727-892-5202
This wonderfully old-fashioned ballroom is where St Petersburg's seniors dance and young people rock.

WHERE TO EAT
❶ *Marchland's Grill $$$$*
(in the Renaissance Vinoy Resort)
501 5th Ave. NE St Petersburg
Tel. 1-727-824-8072
Nostalgic elegance and French-Mediterranean inspired cuisine: the pasta with forest mushrooms and the steaks are especially to be recommended.

❷ *Lobster Pot $$* **Insider Tip**
17814 Gulf Blvd., Redington Shores
Tel. 1-727-391-8592
The best lobster as well as tasty fish and clam dishes.

❸ *Hellas $$$*
785 Dodecanese Blvd., Tarpon Springs
Tel. 1-727-934-2400
Probably the best Greek restaurant in the old sponge diver town

❹ *PG's Oyster Bar $*
7500 Gulf Blvd., St. Petersburg Beach
Tel. 1-727-367-3309
Oysters, clams, crawfish and fried fish, good and cheap. There's another one in Indian Rocks Beach.

WHERE TO STAY
❶ *Renaissance Vinoy Resort $$$$*
St Petersburg 501 5th Ave. NE
Tel. 1-727-894-1000
www.marriott.com
360 rooms and suites. The best inn downtown with its own golf course tempts guest with Mediterranean elegance. Many VIPs have stayed here.

❷ *The Don CeSar Beach Resort & Spa $$$$*
St Petersburg Beach, 3400 Gulf Blvd.

Tel. 1-727-360-1881
www.loewshotels.com
350 rooms and suites. Cool marble
floors and elegant stucco ceilings: the
landmark of St Pete Beach offers pure
luxury with lots of culture.

❸ *Hotel Indigo* $$
St. Petersburg, 234 3rd Ave. N
Tel. 1-727-822-4814
www.stpeteflhotel.com

80 rooms. The former Martha Washington Hotel has been able to keep its old-fashioned charm until today.

❹ *Beach Heaven* $$
4980 Gulf Blvd., St Petersburg Beach
Tel. 1-727-367-8642
www.beachhavenvillas.com
18 nicely furnished rooms and suites.
Pink and turquoise Art Deco inn on the
beach.

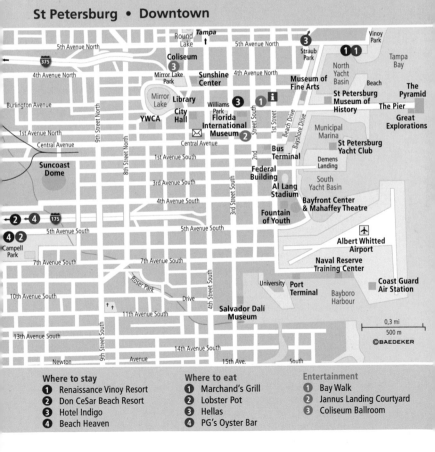

St Petersburg • Downtown

Where to stay
❶ Renaissance Vinoy Resort
❷ Don CeSar Beach Resort
❸ Hotel Indigo
❹ Beach Heaven

Where to eat
❶ Marchand's Grill
❷ Lobster Pot
❸ Hellas
❹ PG's Oyster Bar

Entertainment
❶ Bay Walk
❷ Jannus Landing Courtyard
❸ Coliseum Ballroom

Masterpieces by Salvador Dalí in St Petersburg

industry has covered them with hotels, restaurants, marinas, diving, fishing and other water sports facilities, so much so that the communities merge with each other. American families and European package-tour travellers are the target audience of all this, since they appreciate the proximity of Florida's top amusement parks. The atmosphere is accordingly noisy and informal. Many beaches are so full in the winter that traffic moves at a snail's pace. But there are also quieter and less developed parts.

*St Pete Beach
It all started in St Petersburg's resort. Tourists bathed here in the bath-water warm Gulf of Mexico as much as one hundred years ago. Several causeways lead across **Boca de Ciega Bay** to the six-mile-long beaches of the traditional resort town. Watersports lovers are spoiled for choice here: everything goes! The landmark is the pink **Don CeSar Resort** (3400 Gulf Blvd., ▶photo p.67) on the beach. This luxury hotel is decorated with Moorish elements and slender towers; a few years ago it was renovated at a cost of millions and is now once again resplendent in the atmosphere of the 1920s.

Pass-a-Grille is adjacent to the south on a small spit of land. This beach belonging to a French fishing town that was founded in 1911 is a bit quieter and has an undisturbed view of the islands in Tampa Bay.

*Fort DeSoto Park
South of Pass-a-Grille lies **Mullet Key**, an island that guards the entrance to Tampa Bay. The nature reserve for birds and plants is named after the massive **Fort DeSoto**, which was built here in 1898 at the time of the Spanish-American War. However it was spared its baptism of fire since the war was ended before the fort was completed.

North of St Pete Beach lies **Treasure Island**, a 3.5/6km mi-long barrier island that is connected to the mainland by two bridges. The name is reminiscent of earlier times when pirates hid here; settlers dug up almost the whole island looking for buried pirate treasure. Here, as on the neighbouring Madeira Beach, beach tourism is important. **Madeira Beach** also has **St John's Pass Village**, a fishing village built in early 20th-century style, where a creaking wooden sidewalk leads to pretty little shops, pleasant fish restaurants and bars. Boating trips and dolphin-watching tours can be undertaken from here, too.

*From
**St Pete Beach
to Sand Key**

Family oriented attractions lie to the north: **Reddington Beach**, North Reddington Beach and Reddington Shores.

A change from sunbathing can be found in **Indian Shores** at the **Suncoast Seabird Sanctuary** (18328 Gulf Blvd.; hours: daily 9am–sunset), which opened in 1971. It is the largest clinic for wounded birds in the USA, caring for cranes, pelicans and ibis as well as seabirds. Most of the injuries are caused by direct or indirect contact with people: pollution and fishing lines are the most common culprits.

! *Bikers and skaters watch out!*

Insider Tip

MARCO ⊕ POLO TIP

Instead of driving along the »Sun Coast« in stop-and-go traffic, try a bike or even roller skates on the 50m/80km long Pinellas Trail. This paved bicycle path follows an old railway line and connects St Petersburg with Tarpon Springs. It isn't that busy yet either.

The next of the barrier islands is **Sand Key**, the longest on this section of coastline, where an incredibly beautiful beach surrounded by palm groves, **Sand Key Park** (1060 Gulf Blvd.), makes a dive into the surf irresistible.

Suncoast Seabird Sanctuary: 18328 Gulf Blvd., daily 9am until sunset, free admission, www.seabirdsanctuary.com

Opposite Sand Key Park lies Clearwater Beach, the next holiday island that is completely dedicated to sun-worshippers. Several miles of the **finest sand beaches** are bordered by hotels, motels, restaurants and organizers of all sorts of fun sports. The seaside resort of the same name, which lies on a narrow stretch of sand between the Gulf and Clearwater Harbor, appears much more relaxed with its quiet side streets than the neighbouring communities. Locals and tourists meet at Clearwater Public Beach with its 330m/1,100ft-long pier. The sunsets here are fabulous.

*Clearwater
Beach

The Clearwater Marine Aquarium is worth seeing. Injured dolphins, sea lions and sea otters are cared for here . During a »Sea Life Safari« to Shell Island dolphins, various sea birds and other animals can be seen along the coast.

❶ 249 Windward Passage, daily 9am – 6pm, admission US$20, http//:seewinter.com

*Caladesi & Honeymoon Islands The island hopping ends in Clearwater Beach. Cross **Memorial Causeway** to get back to the mainland and continue north. Just before Dunedin there is an unusual sight: undeveloped, natural islands! In 1921 Caladesi Island and Honeymoon Island were torn apart by a hurricane and then made into state parks. They show what the barrier islands looked like 120 years ago. Honeymoon Island can be reached via Causeway Boulevard (toll) and has **wonderful beaches** with showers and changing rooms. A boat runs to Caladesi Island, which is also one of the places in Florida where **sea turtles** can lay their eggs undisturbed on the beach on summer nights.

*Tarpon Springs Tarpon Springs (population 24,000) at the northern end of the Pinellas Suncoast, with its Greek flair, is the most unusual site on the Suncoast. Canals called »bayous« wind through the town. Restau-

Natural sponges of all sizes can be bought in Tarpon Springs

rants and bakeries have Greek names, and Greek music spills out of the dark kafenions. One third of the population is of Greek origin, and descended from the Greek sponge divers who came here around 1900 from Key West. They began to harvest natural sponges from the sponge reefs on a large scale using the know-how that they brought along from the Aegean. But in 1940 bacteria attacked the sponge reefs

Sundance Insider Tip

Every evening people from Clearwater Beach meet two hours before sunset at Pier 60 Park, in order to celebrate the colourful sunset. Lively music from the Pier 60 Pavilion and street artists help pass the time.

and at the same time the production of synthetic sponges ruined the market for natural sponges. Only recently has the demand for natural sponges revived the business.

A stroll along ***Dodecanes Boulevard** is charming. In the old Sponge Docks natural sponges are for sale. Spongeorama's Sponge Factory also informs on the local sponge industry and about the Greek immigration one hundred years ago. There are also sponges for sale.

St Nicholas Boat Line offers half-hour boat tours and explains everything about the local sponge industry.

In the **Konger Tarpon Springs Sea Aquarium** divers can be watched feeding sharks and tarpons several times a day.

*St Nicholas Orthodox Cathedral was dedicated in 1943 and copies Hagia Sophia in Constantinople; it is worth a stop. It is decorated with icons and Greek marble.

St Nicholas Boat Line: 693 Dodecanese Blvd., daily 10am – 4.30pm, tel. 1-727-942-6425, tickets at various prices, www.visitstpeteclearwater.com
Spongeorama's Sponge Factory: 510 Dodecanes Blvd., hours vary, free admission, www.spongeorama.com
Konger Tarpon Springs Sea Aquarium: 850 Dodecanese Blvd., Mon – Sat 10am – 5pm, Sun 12noon – 5pm, admission US$7, www.tarponspringsaquarium.com
St. Nicholas Orthodox Cathedral: Pinellas Ave./Orange St., daily 10am – 4pm, free admission, donations requested

This masterpiece of engineering, a 20km/12mi-long **highway on stilts** (I-275/US 19; toll; ▶photo p.110), curves elegantly across the entrance to Tampa Bay. The core is a 7km/4mi-long bridge whose centre is suspended from two giant pylons, which allow ocean-going ships to pass.   `

*Sunshine Skyway

The old bridge was rammed in 1980 by a freighter and collapsed partially. Several cars plunged into the water and more than 30 people were killed. Today parts of the old bridge serve as a fishing pier for passionate anglers.

★★ Sanibel & Captiva Islands

─────────────── ✦ **G 6**

Region: South-west
Elevation: 0 – 2m/7ft above sea level
Population: 6,000

No house is higher than the palm trees. In view of the wonderful beaches, this might suggest that the islanders are insular and unwelcoming. In fact they took revenge in the 1970s for the bridge that was built from the mainland in 1963 against their will with the strictest land-use laws in Florida. Thus there are no hotel or apartment blocks here, but only smiling and mostly very wealthy people.

Natural beauty   Not even Hurricane Charley, which uprooted most of the cedars on Periwinkle Way, the main street on Sanibel Island, and tore the rest of the place apart in August 2004, could mar the natural beauty of the islands for good. There are no forests of billboards or neon lights on these two barrier islands that are connected by a bridge. Everything

The shell-covered beaches of Sanibel are world-famous

revolves around peace and quiet on this part of the southern Gulf Coast. It is not therefore not surprising if the residents might occasionally be unfriendly to tourists. In the winter months, especially, their paradise is full to bursting.

The two islands that are separated by the narrow Blind Pass were discovered early. Juan Ponce de León supposedly named the larger island Sanibel, after his queen San Ybel. No one really knows where the other name comes from. But this area used to be a popular **refuge for pirates**. It is said that José Gaspár, the most fearful of them, held kidnapped women captive on Captiva Island. Toward the end of the 19th century a few »Crackers« settled on the islands and tried to raise limes and coconuts, but without success. Then they tried tourism: in 1938 the first holiday resort opened.

History

Blue, yellow and green, and every shade between can be found on the island beaches. Sanibel Island has four public beaches, all of them on the Gulf side – five, counting the thoroughly acceptable Causeway Beaches by the bridge. Lighthouse Beach is at the east end of the island and also has a l**ighthouse** of 1884 that can be viewed, a pretty pier and a **board walkway** through the neighbouring wetlands. Gulfside City Park, accessible via Algiers Lane, has nice picnic benches under shady gnarled cedars and wonderful sand. Tarpon Bay Beach at the end of Tarpon Bay Rd. is a short walk away from the parking lot. Bowman's Beach, the quietest of the four, can be reached via Bowman's Beach Rd. and is the only beach with picnic grills.

**Beaches

WHAT TO SEE ON SANIBEL

Very interesting for nature lovers. More than 30,000 **shells from all over the world** and all the types that wash up on the beaches here are displayed. Crafts using shells are also on show, including some from Barbados and Mexico. Shell-collecting novices can have their finds identified (3075 Sanibel-Captiva Rd.; hours: daily 10am–5pm).
❶ 3075 Sanibel-Captiva Rd., daily 10am – 5pm, admission US$9, www. shellmuseum.org

**Bailey-Matthews Shell Museum

Everyday life on the island 100 years ago is the subject of this open-air museum, which is made up of several buildings. A stroll through the palm-shaded grounds leads to the **Rutland Home**, a settler's house from 1913, to **Bailey's General Store** with an old gasoline pump and to **Miss Charlotta's Tea Room**.
❶ 950 Dunlop Rd., Nov. – Apr. Wed – Sat 10am – 4pm, May – mid Aug. Wed – Sat 10am –.1pm, admission US$5, www.sanibelmuseum.org

*Sanibel Historical Village & Museum

Sanibel and Captiva

INFORMATION
Sanibel & Captiva Islands Chamber of Commerce
1159 Causeway Rd.
Sanibel Island, FL 33957
Tel. 1-239-472-1080
www.sanibel-captiva.org

Lee County CVB
12800 University Dr.
Fort Myers, FL 33907
Tel. 1-239-338-3500
www.fortmyers-sanibel.com

PARKING
Parking spaces are scarce on the two islands.

BIKING
Probably the best way to get around on the two islands is on a bike. Sanibel alone has about 20mi/32km of bike paths. All of the attractions can be reached by bike from Periwinkle Way (main street on the island).

SHELL COLLECTING
The magic word here is »shelling«: every high tides brings new shells to the beaches of Sanibel and Captiva. They come in all shapes and colours. Empty shells may be taken along without restrictions, but living shells may not and the fines if caught are high. The best time to collect shells is from **Insider** February to April. **Tip**

BOATING EXCURSIONS
From the dock of the South Seas Plantation, excursion boats run to the neighbouring uninhabited and paradise-like islands Cabbage Key, Useppa Island,

Boca Grande and Cayo Costa. Dolphins can be seen on such a tour as they play in front of the boat's bow.

WHERE TO EAT
Mad Hatter $$$
Sanibel Island
6467 Sanibel-Captiva Rd.
Tel. 1-239-472-0033
Romantic restaurant with a view of the Gulf of Mexico. Creative »fusion cuisine«, inspired by recipes from all over the world.

Mucky Duck $$$
Captiva Island
11546 Andy Rosse Lane
Tel. 1-239-472-3434
English pub right on the beach. Great atmosphere, great sunsets.

Hungry Heron $$
Sanibel Island
2330 Palm Ridge Rd.
(in Palm Ridge Place)
Tel. 1-239-395-2300
Popular venue for locals.

WHERE TO STAY
Casa Ybel Resort $$$$
Sanibel Island
2255 W Gulf Drive
Tel. 1-239-472-3145
www.casaybelresort.com
This holiday heaven (114 suites) right on the beach with its excellent restaurant is one of the best of its kind in the Sunshine State.

West Wind Inn $$$
Sanibel Island
3345 West Gulf Drive

Tel. 1-239-472-1541
www.westwindinn.com
Beautiful resort on the beach; many of
the 103 rooms have an enchanting view
of the beach. Nice pool bar.

Kona Kai Motel **$$**
Sanibel Island
1539 Periwinkle Way
Tel. 1-239-472-1001
www.konakaimotel.com
Comfortable Polynesian-style motel with
13 rooms and a large pool.

This reserve, named after the popular caricaturist J. N. »Ding« Darling, protects 2,000ha/5,000 acres of untouched mangrove, marsh and swamp area on the side of the island facing the mainland.

**»Ding« Darling National Wildlife Refuge

On the 5mi/8km-long **Wildlife Drive** tourists can watch countless migratory birds from their cars in the winter, and in the summer ibis, roseate spoonbill, grey heron as well as the almost-extinct white heron. A 2mi/3km-long walkway leads to observation points from where alligators and sea otters can be seen. In the modern visitor centre there is information on the nature preserve (1 Wildlife Drive; hours: daily 8am–sunset). A paddling tour through the mangrove wilderness of the »Ding« Darling NWR is an authentic Florida experience. The visitor centre rents canoes.

❶ Jan – April daily 9am – 5pm, May – Dec Sat – Thu. 9am – 4pm, admission per car US$5, www.fws.gov/dingdarling

WHAT TO SEE ON CAPTIVA

Captiva, five miles (8km) long and half a mile wide, is Sanibel's little sister. The few residents of the island mainly live from tourism. **Turner Beach** at Blind Pass is the main reason for day visitors to come here: some come only because of the spectacular sunsets. The northern tip of the island is taken up by the luxurious **South Seas Island Resort**. On the grounds of a former copra plantation surrounded by thick mangrove forests, it is one of the best venues for tennis-playing visitors to Florida.

From the South Seas Island Resort boats sail north to the neighbouring Cabbage Key, where there are neither streets nor cars, but only a pier and **Cabbage Key Inn** (6 rooms, 7 cottages and a restaurant). **Jimmy Buffett** ("Famous People) is supposed to have been inspired by the cheeseburgers made here to compose his hit Cheeseburger in Paradise. The restaurant also has the most expensive wallpaper around: diners glue dollar bills to the wall. There are supposed to be about 25,000 dollars there now!

Excursion to Cabbage Key

★★ **Sarasota**

━━━━━━━━━━━━━━━━━━━ ✦ **G 5**

Region: Central West
Elevation: 0 – 9m/30ft above sea level
Population: 52,000

Before World War I wealthy visitors discovered what was then a sleepy fishing village with beautiful beaches. Since then Sarasota has evolved into one of the most attractive recreational resorts on Florida's Gulf Coast.

Refuge for the wealthy and art lovers

The white beaches on the offshore islands of Lido Key, Siesta Key and Longboat Key, which stretches northwards towards Bradenton, a year-round mild sub-tropical climate, a relaxed southern lifestyle and excellent recreational opportunities are the factors that attract pensioners and a growing number of people looking for relaxation. The first white settler came in 1842. In the 1880s a large number of Scottish immigrants came, but in 1910 Sarasota was still a sleepy fishing village. Only a little later wealthy people from the east coast discovered Sarasota Bay. It got its nickname **»City of the Arts«** from the circus impresario and art collector John Ringling and his wife Mable. Their art collection is one of Florida's main attractions. Since 1959 Sarasota has had an opera house with its own opera company and its own orchestra. Asolo State Theater has made a name for itself far beyond Florida's borders, as has the opera, and famous performers of modern and classical music often appear in Van Wezel Performing Arts Hall.

> **?**
>
> MARCO ⊕ POLO INSIGHT
>
> *Father of Golf*
>
> Among the Scottish immigrants of the 1880s there was a certain J. Hamilton Gillespie, who built the first golf course here and thus introduced this sport to America.

WHAT TO SEE IN SARASOTA

*Downtown

The old city centre was built in the 1920s in the Mediterranean style and has recently been regenerated. Expensive jewellery and antique shops, art galleries etc., which confirm Sarasota's reputation as a city with money, can be found in the exclusive **Palm Avenue**, and on western **Main Street** the shopping centre **Kress International Plaza** is worth a look. In the 1930s it was built in Art Deco style and today holds boutiques, a food court and a permanent exhibition featuring local artists. The Sarasota Opera Association is at home in the restored **Sarasota Opera House** (Pineapple Ave./First Street).

Sarasota

INFORMATION
Sarasota Visitor Information Center
655 N. Tamiami Trail
Sarasota, FL 34236
Tel. 1-941-957-1877
www.sarasotafl.org

EVENTS
Sarasota Music Festival
This top-class music festival takes place in May or June.
www.sarasotaorchestra.org/sarasota
musicfestival/festival.cfm

WHERE TO EAT
Moore's Stone Crab **Insider Tip**
Restaurant $$
Longboat Key
Tel. 1-941-383-1748
Old favourite address for fresh fish and seafood, but especially for tasty stone crab dishes. Moore's Crab Cakes are practically world famous.

Bijou Café $$
1287 1st Street
Tel. 1-941-366-8111
J. P. Knagg's popular restaurant serves delicious crab cakes and great pepper steaks.

WHERE TO STAY
Hyatt Sarasota $$$
1000 Blvd. of the Arts
Tel. 1-941-953-1234
www.sarasota.hyatt.com
High-class accommodation (300 rooms and suites) with its own marina and a wonderful lagoon-like swimming pool.

Golden Host Resort $$
4675 Tamiami Trail
Tel. 1-941-355-5141
www.goldenhostresort.com
Centrally located accommodation with 80 rooms and suites as well as a pool in the middle of a fragrant garden. Families with children feel at home here.

Van Wezel Performing Arts Hall (777 N. Tamiami Trail, info: www. vanwezel.org), a modern functional building with a pink, shell-shaped roof, catches the eye on the attractive Bayfront. It is the venue for theatre performances, concerts etc. At the end of Main Street the city **marina** and **Island Park** are located right on the bay. Boat excursions start from here.

*Bayfront

Lavish sub-tropical vegetation and many exotic animals can be found south of town. There are shows every day with **parrots** as well as an exciting **reptile show** with snakes and alligators. On the jungle-like grounds the **Kiddy Jungle** caters for the little ones.
● 3701 Bayshore Rd., daily 10am – 5pm, admission US$15, www. sarasotajunglegardens.com

Sarasota Jungle Gardens

Since 1975 botanists from this organization in the southern part of Sarasota have undertaken expeditions into tropical rainforests and put together a large collection of **epiphytes and orchids**. The bo-

MMarie Selby Botanical Gardens

tanical garden is also home to two models of elegant southern architecture: the former Selby family residence and Christy Payne Mansion, which now holds the **Museum of Botany & Art**.

❶ 811 S. Palm Ave., daily 10am – 5pm, admission US$17, www.selby.org

Mote Marine Aquarium

The work of a research station is presented to the public here. Many forms of life that occur in the Gulf of Mexico can be observed, including seahorses and squids. The shark aquarium attracts many visitors.

❶ 1600 Ken Thompson Parkway, daily 10am – 5pm, admission US$17, www.mote.org

✶✶ RINGLING CENTER FOR THE CULTURAL ARTS

✶✶John & Mable Ringling Museum of Art

Sarasota's main attraction is the museum of the circus king John Ringling , about 3mi/5km north of the city centre on Bayshore Road. Ringling gave it to the state of Florida in 1936. The **neo-Renaissance** style complex was built from 1927 to 1930 and stands in the middle of well-tended gardens with wonderful views of Sarasota Bay.

The art museum holds not only an important collection of **ancient Cypriot art**, but also an excellent display of European masters of

The residence of the circus king looks like it should be in Italy

the 16th, 17th and 18th centuries, including famous works by **Lukas Cranach, Peter Paul Rubens, Anthony van Dyck** and others. Replicas of famous statues, like Michelangelo's David adorn the inner courtyard. The museum annex has rotating exhibitions of contemporary art (hours: daily 10am–5.30pm, Thu– 10pm).

❶ N Tamiami Trail/US 41, daily 10am until 5pm, Wed until 8pm, admission US$ 25, www.ringling.org

John and Mable Ringling Collection

In the year 1950 the Ringling Museum acquired the beautiful interior of the Baroque theatre in Asolo, Italy. It was transported to Florida and rebuilt at great cost. Even after the completion of the new Asolo Center for the Performing Arts it is still being used as a theatre.

*Asolo Theater

The extensive exhibition contains articles reminiscent of the heyday of John Ringling's circus. Along with old circus wagons, costumes and posters there is also a pretty miniature circus. Special exhibitions are dedicated to famous artists and clowns.

*Circus Museum

Located right on Sarasota Bay, Ca' d' Zan is the baronial winter residence of John and Mable Ringling. »John's House«, a very luxurious 30-room villa, was built in 1926 in the style of a Venetian Renaissance palace. It is an **especially beautiful example of historicist architecture** of the 1920s. The old tiles for the roof and the 30m/100ft-high tower were imported from Barcelona. The windows are glazed with Venetian glass. From the terrace marble steps lead down to the water, where Mable Ringling's Venetian gondola was tied up.

**Ca' d' Zan

Directly opposite the Ringling museums, this museum invites a visit. Highly polished **antique cars**, including Paul McCartney's Mini Cooper, John Lennon's Mercedes roadster and a dragster from Don Garlit's workshop and another 100 vehicles are waiting to be admired.

❶ 5500 N. Tamiami Trail/US 41, daily 9am – 6pm, admission US$10, www.sarasotacarmuseum.org

Classic Car Museum

AROUND SARASOTA

The **Ringling Causeway** connects St Armands Key and Lido Key with the mainland. St Armands Keywas bought in the 1920s by the circus magnate John Ringling and is known today for its exquisite

*St Armands Key

shops and restaurants. The **Circus Ring of Fame** was built in 1988 and is dedicated to famous circus artists. **Lido Beach** is one of the most popular beaches in Sarasota; it is about half a mile long and has picnic areas and playgrounds.

Siesta Key **Crescent Beach** is one of the most beautiful beaches in Florida. Large parts of the island are occupied by fine residential estates today. Some of the older houses hidden in luxurious gardens were built in the »Sarasota Style«, which was created by the architects Ralph Twitchell and Paul Rudolph in the 1920s.

Myakka River State Park The nature reserve is located about 19mi/30km south-east of Sarasota on FL 72. The ecosystem on the Myakka River is still intact for the most part. Open land, broad expanses of water, swamps with hammocks (tree islands), large cedar forests and palmetto prairie make for a varied landscape. The area is known for its wealth of deer, wild turkeys, alligators and aquatic birds. Bald eagles, herons and cranes are common. The visitor centre at the park entrance has information on the area. Park rangers offer bird-watching tours and campfire programmes. Hiking trails, including the wonderful **Myakka Trail, and canoe trails cover the State Park.

❶ FL 72, Jun – mid Dec Mon – Fri 10am – 4pm, Sat, Sun 8.30am – 5pm, mid Dec – May Mon – Fri 9am – 5pm, Sat, Sun 8.30am – 5pm, admission: US$6 per car, www.floridastateparks.org/myakkariver/

> **! MARCO POLO TIP**
>
> *Airboat to wild animals* **Insider Tip**
>
> An airboat leaves from the Visitor Center of Myakka River State Park on wilderness tours into the nature reserve. En route wild turkeys and of course alligators might appear. Information: tel. 1-941-365-0100, www.myakkawildlife.com

*Venice South of Sarasota lies the town of Venice (population 17,000). The former fishing village began to flourish in the 1920s when a colony for pensioners was built here. The stock market crash in 1929 brought the boom to an abrupt end, and the community did not flourish again until the 1960s, when the **Ringling Bros., Barnum and Bailey** circus set up its winter base here. Today Venice is a popular holiday site with beautiful beaches.

*Bradenton Bradenton, founded in 1878 by Dr. Joseph Braden, today it numbers 50,000 residents and is located a short drive north of Sarasota at the delta of the **Manatee River**. It is a commercial centre and also a popular place for fishing expeditions out into the Gulf of Mexico or on the Manatee River. **Bradenton Beach** is great for beach holidays. The fortress-like building of the city founder is in the eastern part of town; for the early European immigrants it served as a refuge against Indian attacks. **Manatee Village**, located between 6th Ave. E and 15th St. E, includes the old church (1887), the old court house (1860), Wiggins Store (1903) and the old school house (1908) as well as Stephen's House, built in 1912 in the typical Cracker style.

The natural and cultural history of the region is explained in the ***South Florida Museum**. Indian artefacts are on display, as are Spanish colonial relics. There is a special exhibition on the manatees that live in the local waters (201 10th St. W.; hours: Mon–Sat 10am–5pm, Sun noon–5pm).

❶ 201 10th St. W, Tue – Sat 10am – 5pm, Sun 12noon – 5pm, admission US$16, www.southfloridamuseum.org

North-west of Bradenton, at the mouth of the Manatee River in Tampa Bay, the Spanish conquistador **Hernando De Soto** is commemorated; he is supposed to have landed in this area with an army in May 1539. De Soto led the first expedition of Europeans to explore the south-east of what is now the USA up to the Mississippi River.

De Soto National Memorial

Gamble Plantation, north-east of Bradenton on the northern banks of the Manatee River delta, is a protected monument. It is the only remaining plantation house in southern Florida. Robert Gamble, a major of the Confederate army, had a **sugar cane plantation** here in the mid-19th century; it was operated by about 200 slaves. The manor house of 1844 has been restored.

Gamble Plantation

❶ 3708 Patten Ave./US 301, tours Thu – Mon 9.30am – 4pm, ticket US$6, www.floridastateparks.org/gambleplantation

West of Bradenton the two islands Longboat Key and Anna Maria Island have beautiful seashell sand beaches, where the modern holiday colonies **Bradenton Beach, Holmes Beach** and **Anna Maria** have grown up. The best-known addresses are the Longboat Key Club with its championship gold courses and Colony Beach & Tennis Resort.

*Longboat Key, Anna Maria Island

Sebring

✦ H 5

Region: Central
Elevation: 40m/130ft above sea level
Population: 10,000

Anyone interested in auto racing knows Sebring, since Grand Prix races take place here every year on the third weekend in March.

Sebring

INFORMATION
Greater Sebring Chamber
227 US 27 N
Sebring, FL 33870
Tel. 1-863-385-8448
www.sebringflchamber.com

Sebring International Raceway
113 Midway Drive, Sebring, FL 33870
Tel. 1-863-655-1442
http://sebringraceway.com

AUTO RACING
12 Hours of Sebring
Top-class Grand Prix auto race for sports cars in March.

Historic Fall Classic
In October veteran sports cars race for points.

EVENT
Roaring Twenties Festival
In May the city revives the Roaring Twenties. One of the highlights is the Twenties-style street market.

WHERE TO EAT
Chicanes $$
(in the »Inn on the Lakes«)
3100 Golfview Road
Tel. 1-863-471-9400
Wonderful fresh fish and other tasty dishes are prepared by the innovative kitchen staff. The beautiful view of the lake is free.

WHERE TO STAY
Inn on the Lakes $$$
3100 Golfview Road
Tel. 1-863-471-9400
www.innonthelakes.com
Elegant and traditional house with a spa, pool and 160 spacious rooms and suites.

Kenilworth Lodge
1610 Lakeview Drive
Tel. 1-863-385-0111
www.kenilworthlodge.com
107 rooms and suites. This luxurious and well-run hotel on Lake Jackson was opened in 1916.

Comfortable elevation Sebring is located in the fertile hills of central Florida, where **citrus fruits and avocados** are cultivated. The elevation as well as lakes and waterways keep the climate pleasant.

History Sebring was only founded in 1911. The railway arrived shortly afterwards, and it developed into a winter resort in the 1920s. During World War II an air base was built near Sebring. After the war the city acquired the land and built the **racetrack** for auto races there.

WHAT TO SEE IN AND AROUND SEBRING

*Sebring International Raceway Sebring International Raceway is located south-east of town on the grounds of the former military airport; it is a 4mi/6.5km-long circuit on which important races have been held here since 1950. The high-

At the 12 Hours of Sebring

lights are the »12 Hours of Sebring« in March and the »Sebring Historic Fall Classic« in October. After Indianapolis and ▶Daytona Sebring is the third most important address for thousands of auto racing fans.

Downtown

The **historic centre** has an attractive appearance with its brick houses around Circle Park, Main Street and Commerce Avenue. From **City Pier** there is a beautiful view of Lake Jackson.
The **Cultural Center Complex** houses a theatre and the Highlands Museum of Arts with its interesting art collection.

Lake Jackson

Lake Jackson is very busy in the summer thanks to several beautiful and well-tended beaches. Not just swimmers, but sailors, paragliders and water-skiers find the right facilities here.

*Highlands Hammock State Park The **oldest State Park in Florida** lies a few miles to the west of Sebring is; it was opened in 1931 and can best be reacheddvia US 27 and CR 634. The nature reserve has an almost untouched and typical hammock flora with hardwoods and palms on areas that look like geological upheavals and are surrounded by cypress swamps and cedar forests. Deer, racoons, alligators and many kinds of birds (including bald eagles) populate the area, which can be explored on several nature trails. In the **interpretive centre** there is information on flora and fauna; register for guided nature walks here (hours: daily 8am–5pm).

❶ 5931 Hammock Rd., daily 8am until sunset, admission: pedestrians US$2, vehicles US$6, www.floridastateparks.org/highlandshammock/

** Tallahassee

✳ E 2

Region: North Central
Elevation: 58m/200ft above sea level
Population: 181,000

The city is only a half-hour drive from the coast and has succeeded in preserving some of the charm of the Old South. Old oaks, densely covered with Spanish moss, tidy lawns and pretty 19th-century houses characterize the »biggest small town in Florida«.

Florida's capital The tranquil capital of the »Sunshine State« is located in northern Florida at the beginning of the Panhandle. The »old fields« – the meaning of the Indian name of the settlement – are spread out over several hills and surrounded by cedar forests and lakes. Before the Europeans arrived there was already a flourishing settlement of agrarian Indians. In 1528 the Spanish first moved through the region, and eleven years later the conquistador **Hernando de Soto** spent the winter here. In the 16th century Franciscans founded San Luis Mission, which was at times the central Spanish settlement of the Apalachee region. Conflicts between the rival colonial powers Spain, France and Great Britain led to attacks by the English at the beginning of the 18th century. Many Spanish settlements were destroyed at the time and the native **Apalachee Indians** were driven away. A little while later the unpopulated territory was settled by other Indians, who were then driven out during the Seminole Wars. White settlers came in increasing numbers. They started cotton and sugar cane plantations. In 1824 Tallahassee became the capital of Florida, which led to more people moving in. A city fire in 1843 decimated the city and a yellow fever epidemic slowed the development of the city. Tallahassee only recovered around the turn of the last century. Since the

What a contrast: the old and the new state capitol in Tallahassee

1940s the enormous migration to Florida has also reached the capital of the state.

WHAT TO SEE IN TALLAHASSEE

Florida's capital is known for its beautiful »canopy roads«, avenues that are lined by broadly spreading, live oaks covered in Spanish moss, whose tops spread above the streets. The first avenue, **Old St Augustine Road**, was built already in the 16th century and connected San Luis Mission with the capital at that time, St Augustine. Other pretty canopy roads are Miccosukee Road, Centerville Road, Meridian Road and Old Bainbridge Road.

**Canopy Roads

The old capitol of Florida with its gleaming white façade and conspicuous red and white striped canopies over the windows stands on the highest hill in downtown Tallahassee. It was built in 1839 and renovated in the style of the late 19th century. The **governor's room** as well as the **assembly halls** of the state Supreme Court, the state senate and the state house of representatives are open to the public.

**Old State Capitol

❶ 400 S. Monroe St./Apalachee Pkwy., Mon – Fri 9am – 4.30pm, Sat 10am until 4.30pm, Sun 12noon – 4.30pm, free admission, www.flhistoriccapital.gov

New State Capitol

The new capitol was inaugurated in 1978. This 22-storey building is still the tallest building in Tallahassee and a symbol for the dynamic economic development of the »Sunshine State«. In the entry hall is the large bronze seal of the state of Florida. The **observation gallery** offers a wonderful panoramic view.

❶ S. Duval St., tours: Mon – Fri 8am – 5pm, free admission, www.myfloridacapitol.com

Union Bank

In front of the Old Capitol stands the Union Bank, which was built in 1841. It was at one time the most important bank for the plantation owners. It is part of the Black Archives (▶p. 358).

❶ 219 Apalachee Pkwy., Mon – Fri 9am – 5pm, free admission, www.famu.edu/index.cfm?blackarchives.

Adam's Street Commons

North of the two capitol buildings two city blocks of old Tallahassee have been restored. Cobblestone streets, restaurants, bars, boutiques and **Gallie's Hall**, which was the city theatre at the end of the 19th century, make Adam's Street Commons a popular venue.

*Museum of Florida History

Two blocks to the west the R. A. Gray Building, which was built in 1976, holds the **state archives**, a library and above all an excellent **exhibition on the state**. The almost 3m/10ft-high skeleton of a mastodon that was found in Florida is impressive (500 South Bronough St.; hours: Mon–Fri 9am–4.30pm, Sat 10am–4.30pm, Sun noon to 4.30pm).

❶ 500 S. Bronough St., Mon – Fri 9am– 4.30pm, Sat 10am – 4.30pm, Sun 12noon – 4.30pm, free admission, www.museumoffloridahistory.com

*Park Avenue Historic District

From the museum follow Bronough Street north to Park Avenue with its old trees and several historic buildings. On the corner of Bronough St./Park Ave. a formal columned building named **The Columns** attracts attention. It is one of the oldest buildings in the city and was built in 1830 by the president of the Bank of Florida. Today it is the seat of the Tallahassee Chamber of Commerce. Only a few steps above it is the **First Presbyterian Church**, the oldest church in the city. The population took shelter in this neo-Classical style brick building, which was built in 1838, during the Seminole Wars. Until the Civil War the gallery was reserved for slaves. On the other side of **Monroe Street**, Tallahassee's main north-south axis, lies the pretty **Lewis Park**. Here there are several typical southern-style villas with verandas and columned porticoes, which were built before the Civil War. Lewis House, which belonged to a wealthy banker's family from 1850 to 1993 is an especially impressive example of southern architecture (316 E. Park Ave.).

Insider Tip

Knott House opposite is also open to visitors. It was the residence of the Union General Edward McCook, built in 1843 and bought in 1928 by William Knott, Florida's secretary of the treasury. He had the

Tallahassee

INFORMATION
Tallahassee Area Visitor Information Center
106 E. Jefferson St.
Tallahassee, FL 32301
Tel. 1-850-606-2305
www.visittallahassee.com

EVENT
Market Days
The popular market days are held on the first weekend in December and offer beautiful works of art for sale.

WHERE TO EAT
❶ *Barnacle Bill's* $$
1830 N. Monroe St.
Tel. 1-850-385-8734
Informal restaurant with excellent fish cuisine.

WHERE TO STAY
❶ *Governor's Inn*   Insider Tip
209 S. Adam Street
Tel. 1-850) 681-6855

www.thegovinn.com
This elegant hotel (40 rooms, 8 suites; protected monument!) is in the centre of town. Mahogany furniture embellish the tasteful rooms.

❷ *Best Western Pride Inn & Suites* $$
2016 Apalachee Parkway
Tel. 1-850-365-6312
www.bestwestern.com
Cheerfully furnished rooms, a small fitness room and a pool, full breakfast included.

❸ *Doubletree Hotel Tallahassee*
101 S. Adam Street
Tel. 1-850-224-5000
www.doubletree.com
Modern hotel in the heart of downtown with 240 well-equipped rooms and suites, a restaurant and a bar. Many of the journalists who reported on the irregularities of George W. Bush's election in 2000 stayed in this hotel.

Tallahassee • Downtown

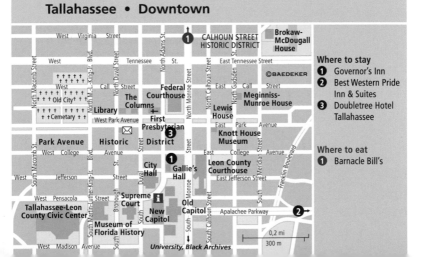

Where to stay
❶ Governor's Inn
❷ Best Western Pride Inn & Suites
❸ Doubletree Hotel Tallahassee

Where to eat
❶ Barnacle Bill's

imposing portico added and furnished the house with valuable Victorian furnishings.

❶ 301 E. Park Ave., Wed – Fri 1pm, 2pm, 3pm, Sat 10am until 3pm on the hour, free admission, donations requested, www.museumoffloridahistory.com

*Calhoun Street Historic District
It is worth taking a stroll through the upper-class neighbourhood on northern **Calhoun Street**. Wealthy citizens lived here during the 19th century. Thus there are some fine examples of the **Greek Revival** and neo-classical styles.
Brokaw-McDougall House, which was built in 1856 at the southwestern edge of the neighbourhood, is only accessible during special events. Sometimes it is used by the government of the state of Florida for special events (329 North Meridian Street).

Governor's Mansion
North-west of Calhoun Street Historic District is the residence of the governor of Florida in a formal park. The building with its entry flanked by Corinthian columns is open for viewing (700 N. Adam St.; tours: March–mid-May Mon, Wed, Fri 10am–noon).

❶ 700 N. Adam St., Mon – Fri 10am – 4pm by appointment, free admission, www.floridagovernorsmansion.com

WHAT TO SEE IN THE OUTER DISTRICTS OF TALLAHASSEE

*Maclay State Gardens
In 1923 a New York financier laid out wonderful gardens about 5mi/8km north of the city centre. His widow turned them over to the state of Florida. In the winter when the **camellias** are in flower it is beautiful here, but also in the spring when **azaleas** and **magnolias** bloom. A look inside Maclay House, which was built in 1905, is also worthwhile.

❶ 3540 Thomasville Rd., daily 9am – 5pm, admission: US$6 per car, Jan. until April additional admission fee for the gardens in bloom: US$6, www.floridastateparks.org/maclaygardens/

DeSoto Archaeological & Historic Site
When undeveloped land was being prepared for building in 1987, the remains of the Spanish conquistador **Hernando de Soto**'s camp from 1539 were found quite by accident east of the town centre (Goodbody Lane/Lafayette Street).

Black Archives Research Center & Museum
On the campus of Florida Agricultural & Mechanical University at the southern edge of town, an exhibition focuses on the history of Afro-Americans with documents on slavery as well as testimonies to the cultural contributions of black Americans (hours: Mon–Fri 9am to 4pm).

❶ Martin Luther King Jr. Blvd./Gamble St., Florida A&M University Campus, Mon – Fri 9am – 5pm, free admission, www.famu.edu

This museum with an aquarium and Discovery Center is located in the western part of town near the airport and shows what rural Florida was like in the 19th century, for example on **Big Bend Farm**. The elegant **Maison Bellevue** was once occupied by the widow of Napoleon I's nephew, who went to America after the Battle of Waterloo and settled as a plantation owner near Tallahassee.

Tallahassee Museum of History & Natural Science

❶ 3945 Museum Dr., Mon – Sat 9am – 5pm, Sun 11am – 5pm admission US$9, www.tallahasseemuseum.org

On a hill in the western part of town traces of the settlement of Apalachee Indians were found, as well as the remains of a **mission station** founded in 1656 by Franciscans and a late 17th-century Spanish **fort**. During the heyday of the settlement (around 1670) more than 1,400 people lived here together – Indians and Spaniards. After English attacks the settlement was abandoned. Presently there is an **outdoor museum** here with replicas of the mission church and the Franciscan priory, an Indian meeting house and the house of the Apalachee chief. Reconstruction of the Spanish fort is planned. The visitor centre is located in a typical southern-style house of the 1930s.

**San Luis Archeological & Historical Site

❶ 2020 Mission Rd., Tue – Sun 10am – 4pm, admission US$5, www.missionsanluis.org

About 6mi/10km north-west of the city centre, at the southern end of Lake Jackson, there is a field of mounds. It is assumed that from about 1200 to 1500 there was an **Indian chief's residence** or a cult centre here. At least one of the mounds was a grave. The high quality of the burial goods indicates close relations with other pre-Columbian cultures in south-east USA.

Lake Jackson Indian Mounds

❶ 3600 Indian Mounds Drive, daily 8am until sunset, admission pedestrians US$2, vehicles US$3, www.floridastateparks.org/lakejackson/

AROUND TALLAHASSEE

The drive from Tallahassee on US 319 north-east into the state of Georgia is an opportunity to get to know at least a bit of **plantation America**.
About 20mi/32km north of Florida's capital, the giant Pebble Hill Plantation and its castle-like manor are open to the public. Pebble Hill was built in the 1820s. Later it was the winter home of a wealthy family from Cleveland, Ohio. In the extravagantly furnished manor house the aristocratic lifestyle of the former plantation owners can be seen up close (.

*Pebble Hill Plantation

❶ tours: Tue – Sat 10am – 5pm, Sun 1pm –5pm, ticket US$5, www.pebblehill.com

Gracious southern architecture: the palatial manor house of Pebble Hill Plantation

Thomasville (Georgia)

About 12mi/20km further to the north-east, the city of Thomasville (population 18,000) has beautiful 19th-century buildings. The city used to be known for its pleasant climate and had elegant hotels. Even American presidents came here to hunt quail and play golf. The **Historic District** has been restored to its former Victorian glory. The shops on the former Main Street (now Broad Street/Jackson Street) look like they did in the late 19th century.

Monticello

From Tallahassee follow US 90 east for 26mi/42km to Monticello (population 3,000), where time really seems to have stood still. Cotton brought prosperity to this town, which was founded in 1827. A massive city hall and beautiful **antebellum houses** testify to this today.

**Wakulla Springs

A side trip 16mi/26km south of Tallahassee to Wakulla Springs is worthwhile, either via US 319 or Woodville Highway (FL 363) and FL 267. The most copious **karst springs** in Florida spill over 54,000 litres per second through a widely spread cave system and into a spring pond. The area around Wakulla Springs, a state park, is a small piece of the original Florida landscape. Crystal-clear water, lush vegetation, and exotic animals like alligators, sea turtles and anhingas (birds) were captured in the 1930s and 1940s by cameras for films. The area was used as the **location of Tarzan films** with the actor Johnny Weissmuller and for other jungle movies. Today it is a popular recreational site. Swimming and trips in glass-bottom boats are possible here. In 1937 **Wakulla Springs Lodge** was built on the shore; in the entryway »Old Joe« is the first thing that everyone looks

Once the setting for Tarzan films: Wakulla Springs

at. This stuffed alligator lived in Wakulla pond until the ripe old age of 200, when he was shot in 1966 by an unknown person.

❶ 465 Wakulla Park Drive, daily 8am until sunset, admission: pedestrians US$2, vehicles US$6, www.floridastateparks.org/wakullasprings/

26mi/42km south of Tallahassee, on Apalachee Bay, the Spanish built a **fortress** in 1679, which was bitterly contested later. In May 1800 the fort was taken by W. A. Bowles, a former British officer, and 400 Indians. Bowles declared himself to be the king of Florida. But he only reigned a few weeks until the Spanish re-took the fort. In 1818 General Andrew Jackson took the fort. After Florida joined the USA, the fort was abandoned. From 1861 to 1865 Confederate troops occupied it in order to blockade the mouth of the St Marks River. There is a **museum** here.

*San Marcos de Apalache State Historic Site

❶ 148 Old Fort Rd., St. Marks, Thu − Mon 9am − 5pm, admission: pedestrians US$2, vehicles US$6, www.floridastateparks.org/sanmarcos/

The mouth of the St Marks River is the core of a nature reserve with an area of 263 sq km/101 sq mi. The marshes and swamps of Apalachee Bay is characterized by swampy **bayous**, hammocks, and oak and cedar woods. Many aquatic birds and alligators live here. Bald eagles and sea hawks can also be seen. About 3mi/5km south of the turnoff of FL 267 from US 98 there is a **nature centre**. **St Marks Lighthouse** A road leads through the nature reserve to the lighthouse of St Marks, which was built in 1831. From the observation platform and several **trails** that run through the grounds many varieties of animals can be seen.

*St Marks National Wildlife Refuge

St. Marks NWR Nature Center: Mon − Fri 8am − 4pm, Sat, Sun 10am − 5pm, admission: per vehicle US$5, www.fws,gov/saintmarks/

** Tampa

—————————— ⟡ G 4/5

Region: Central West
Elevation: 0 – 17m/55ft above sea level
Population: 335,000 (Tampa Bay area: 3.4 million)

Many drive by – to Busch Gardens, which is mentioned in the same breath with Tampa, or across Tampa Bay to the fabulous beaches on Pinellas Peninsula. Too bad. They miss the mightily pulsating heart of the booming Tampa Bay Area.

Bustling port city
The port city at the mouth of the Hillsborough River has lots to offer. The city centre, with its sparkling office buildings, is the result of a building boom in the 1980s and 1990s. It has several important art and cultural sites. Historic areas like Ybor City and Old Hyde Park with their shops and restaurants are attractive places to stroll.

Young and dynamic
It's hard to believe that this dynamically growing port and industrial city – the gateway to the fabulous beaches on the Gulf of Mexico – is less than 100 years old. Spanish conquistadors were the first white people in Tampa Bay, but the systematic development of the area only started 300 years later. In 1824 US Americans built **Fort Brooke** at the mouth of the Hillborough River in order to keep the Seminole Indians under control.

A little fishing village named Tampa developed in the shadow of this fort, but it remained unimportant until the South Florida Railroad of the railway magnate **Henry B. Plant** came in 1885 and the mouth of

Highlights in Tampa

▶ **Former Tampa Bay Hotel**
Built by railway magnate Plant for the high society, the former luxury hotel is now a museum.
▶page 366

▶ **Florida Aquarium**
This informative facility for old and young is one of the best of its kind. The highlight is an artificial coral reef.
▶page 366

▶ **Ybor City**
In this historic quarter, people think that they are on Cuba; it was built by a cigar manufacturer in the 19th century.
▶page 367

▶ **Busch Gardens**
This combination of a large amusement park and zoo is really worth a visit!
▶page 368

the Hillsborough River was developed into a deep-sea harbour. Then things happened quickly. In 1886 the Spanish cigar manufacturer **Vicente Martínez Ybor** moved his production from Cuba and Key West to Tampa. Thousands of Cuban workers came. After the luxurious Tampa Bay Hotel opened in 1891, Tampa became fashionable as a winter residence. Phosphate mining in the interior also added to the development. Tampa's port and the shipping industry also added to its prosperity.

DOWNTOWN TAMPA

Compact, easy of orientation and above all the result of dramatically growth, the city centre focuses on business and is thus as good as dead after hours. But during business hours **Franklin Street Mall**, a

City centre transformed

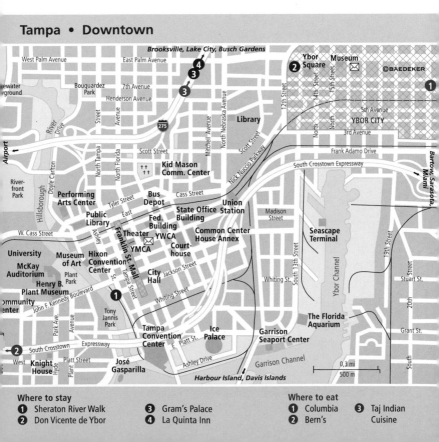

Tampa • Downtown

Where to stay
1 Sheraton River Walk
2 Don Vicente de Ybor
3 Gram's Palace
4 La Quinta Inn

Where to eat
1 Columbia
2 Bern's
3 Taj Indian Cuisine

Tampa

INFORMATION
Tampa Bay Company Visitor Center
615 Channelside Drive, Suite 108 A
Tampa, FL 33602
Tel. 1-813-223-2752
www.visittampabay.com

CITY TRANSPORT
Buses of the Hillsborough Area Transit (HART) operate in the city. The old-time railway wagons of the TECO Line run between the Cruise Ship Terminal and Ybor City.

AIRPORT
The international airport is located 5mi/8km north-west of downtown on Tampa Bay. Buses and taxis run into the city. Information: tel. 1-813-870-8700, www.tampaairport.com

EVENT
Gasparilla Festival
On the first Saturday in February the legendary pirate José Ga**Insider**.ho
Tip
terrorized the settlers on Florida's Gulf Coast in the 18th century, is remembered in a colourful festival.

SHOPPING
Relaxed shopping – without stress and hassle – is possible at Old Hyde Park Village south of downtown around Swan Street and Dakota Street. Several dozen good shops have opened here, selling pretty fashions and other quality products. The best cigars are available in Ybor City at Tampa Rico Cigar Co. on Ybor Square as well as King Corona Cigars at 1523 E. 7th Avenue.

WHERE TO EAT
❶ *Columbia* $$$$
Ybor City 2117 E 7th Avenue

View over Hillsborough Bay to Tampa's modern skyline

Tel. 1-813-248-4961
This restaurant, which opened its doors in 1905, serves tasty Spanish-Cuban dishes. The paella a la Valenciana and la completa Cubana (with **Insider Tip** patatas and black beans) are wonderful. There is also a great Flamenco show almost every evening.

❷ *Bern's Steakhouse* $$$$
Hyde Park District
1208 S. Howard Ave.
Tel. 1-813-251-2421
For 40 years some of the best steaks on the Gulf of Mexico have been grilled here in an overpowering, kitschy ambience.

❸ *Taj Indian Cuisine* $$
2734 E. Fowler Ave.
Tel. 1-813-971-8483
The chicken, especially chicken tikka and tandoori chicken, here is especially delicious.

WHERE TO STAY
❶ *Sheraton Riverwalk Hotel* $$$
200 N. Ashley Drive

Tel. 1-813-223-2222
www.starwoodhotels.com
Well-run establishment of a luxury hotel chain with 282 beautiful rooms and suites overlooking the Hillsborough River.

❷ *Don Vincente de Ybor Historic Inn* $$$
Ybor City 1915 Avenida República de Cuba
Tel. 1-813-241-4545
www.donvincenteinn.com
The best accommodation in Ybor City is in colonial style and has 16 roomy suites as well as a cigar and martini bar.

❸ *Gram's Place* $
3109 N. Ola Avenue
Tel. 1-813-221-0596
www.grams-inn-tampa.com
Simple accommodation with eight clean rooms.

❹ *La Quinta Inn* $$
3701 E. Fowler Avenue
Tel. 1-813-910-7500
www.lq.com
Well-furnished house close to Busch Gardens.

green pedestrian zone between glistening office towers, is by far the liveliest part of the centre. The opulent **Tampa Theater** (711 Franklin St.) of 1926 is worth seeing. It was once the most modern cinema in the USA and today is certainly one of the most beautiful. On Wednesdays, Saturdays and Sundays backstage tours of this Andalusian-style palace are offered, along with a chance to hear the giant Wurlitzer theatre organ.

A few minutes' walk further to the west, on the banks of the Hillsborough River, there is a collection of ancient Greek and Roman art that is, for America, simply magnificent. **20th-century American art** is also exhibited.

*Tampa Museum of Art

❶ 120 Gasparilla Plaza, Mon – Thu 11am – 7pm, Fri 11am – 8pm, Sat, Sun 11am – 5pm, admission US$10, www.tampamuseum.org

UNIVERSITY OF TAMPA · HYDE PARK

**Former Tampa Bay Hotel
On the opposite bank of the Hillsborough River the minaret-like towers of the former Tampa Bay Hotel stand out. The railway magnate Henry B. Plant had this ostentatious building constructed in 1891. With 511 rooms it was the accommodation for high society from the cold north-east USA. Today the former luxury hotel is the main building of the renowned **University of Tampa**.

The south wing of this Oriental-style complex still has its original interior and is now the **Henry B. Plant Museum**, which is dedicated to the life and work of the railway tycoon.

❶ 401 W. Kennedy Blvd., Tue – Sat 10am – 5pm, Sun 12noon – 5pm, admission US$10, www.plantmuseum.org

*Hyde Park
From the former Tampa Bay Hotel South Hyde Park Avenue runs to Tampa's most refined historic residential neighbourhood. The Victorian buildings still reflect some of the elegance of the time around 1900. A drive down **Bayshore Boulevard** presents a wonderful view of the skyline of downtown Tampa.

Near Beach Place the **three-masted José Gasparilla** is anchored; in February it is more or less the epicentre of the city's biggest festival. **Old Hyde Park Village** (1602 W. Swan Ave.) tries to revive the atmosphere of past times. Here there are fashion boutiques, galleries, fine restaurants and nice jazz clubs.

CHANNELSIDE

*Harbour-front on Garrison Channel
The waterside area of downtown Tampa has changed its face completely in the past years. On the north side of the Garrison Channel modern concrete complexes have sprung up, including the **Tampa Convention Center**, **Tampa Bay Times Forum**, the multifunctional **Garrison Seaport Center** and the Florida Aquarium, which has become a top tourist attraction.

Thousands of plants and animals native to the waters of Florida can be observed here under a remarkable green dome. The facility is divided into several ecosystems. In Cypress Wetlands there are not only ibis and owls, but also snakes and other reptiles. The stars in Bays &

**Florida Aquarium
Beaches are the stingrays. But the absolute highlight is the artificial coral reef with its many colourful fish, which is explained in detail

> **!** *Dive with the sharks!* **Insider Tip**
>
> MARCO ⊕ POLO TIP
>
> The most popular attraction in the Florida Aquarium is »Dive with the Sharks«. Interested and especially brave visitors can dive down to sharks from all over the world, accompanied by experienced divers. A diving permit is required.

daily at 11am, 1pm and 3pm by a diver. In Off Shore **sharks** and many other kinds of marine life can be seen.

❶ 701 Channelside Dr. daily 9.30am – 5pm, admission US$22, www.flaquarium.org

YBOR CITY

In the year 1886 the **cigar king Don Vincente Martínez Ybor** established an eleven-block quarter in northern downtown Tampa. For four decades this was the source of the best hand-made cigars in the USA. The quarter went through all the ups and downs of life and today still has a Latin American atmosphere. The descendants of the Cubans who came to Tampa at that time still sell cigars, but they also run restaurants, music shops and hotels. **»La Setima«** – the name for 7th Avenue – is reminiscent of the French Quarter in New Orleans: old buildings of wood and brick characterize the street, traffic is watched from wrought-iron balconies, pedestrians stroll along under **arcades**, the sounds of son and salsa spill out of the dark street cafés. Depression and mass production put an end to hand-rolled cigars, but since the 1990s Ybor City has been experiencing a real renaissance and thanks to its good restaurants and bars has become the popular goal of night owls.

**Historic industrial quarter

Tobacco processing in Ybor City

The daytime attraction is the **Ybor City State Museum**, which is devoted to the role Ybor City played in Tampa's development as the »Cigar Capital of the World. On weekends there is »living history«. In 2014 the **Tampa Baseball Museum** opened here.

❶ 1818 9th Ave., daily 9am –5pm, cigar rolling Fri, Sat, Sun 9.30am – 1pm, admission US$4, www.ybormuseum.org

Ybor Square On this pretty square various shops and restaurants the **Tampa Rico Cigar Company** lets visitors watch cigars being rolled by hand. Not far to the north is the legendary **Café Creole** (currently closed), which opened in 1888, and the no less historic **Cuban Club**, which opened in 1917.

Cigar Museum The Centro Ybor Museum and Visitor Information Cente in old Centro Español houses a Cigar Museum which informs about the once importance of the local cigar industry. Of course visitors can here also watch how cigars are rolled by hand.

❶ 1600 E 8th Ave., Mon – Sat 10am –5pm, Sun 12am – 5pm, free admission

*La Setima Don't miss a stroll down 7th Avenue, called »La Setima«in Spanish. The **Ritz Theater** with its magnificent Art Deco lobby opened in 1917; there are various **»social clubs«** here, too. At one time the various social and ethnic groups in this quarter belonged to societies that represented their interests.

NORTH TAMPA

Busch Gardens Tigers stalk through the »Congo«, orang-utans live in an African village, but who cares about the details? The theme park of the megabrewery Anheuser-Busch north of Tampa is one of the most popular in Florida and presents itself as a one-of-a-kind combination of **zoo, adventure park and amusement park. The fact that Busch Gardens is one of the largest zoos in America and that it has made contributions to the preservation of endangered species usually gets forgotten in the face of the numerous roller coasters and other attractions. But the zoo has had remarkable success at breeding the rare black rhinoceros, koalas and panda bears. The main theme is Africa.

> **!** *First come ...* **Insider Tip**
>
> **MARCO ⬤ POLO TIP**
>
> Avoid long lines at the roller coasters by arriving at Busch Gardens by 9am. The gates open at 9.30am. This way you can enjoy up to 4 »thrill rides« in the first hour. Later you might have to wait up to three quarters of an hour at each ride.

Thousands of animals from the »dark continent« live in appropriate quarters. This includes an artificial savannah where zebras, giraffes

Thrills in Busch Gardens

and gnus feel just as much at home as in their earlier native land. Busch Gardens is divided into eight areas. Each one presents a different part of Africa, whereby »correctness« is less important than entertainment value. Thus **Morocco** has not only snake charmers and fire-eaters behind its high fortress-like walls, but also an ice skating revue. In **Egypt** a copy of the **tomb of Pharaoh Tut-Ankh-Amun** is open to amateur treasure hunters, and the **Montu roller coaster** has hair-raising loops for the unsuspecting. In Congo, Timbuktu and Stanleyville there are more stomach-turning rides. In **Edge of Africa** there is a copy of a **Massai village** and a **safari camp**. **Wildlife Tours** with expert guides are also available. Nairobi has a **rain forest** called **Myombe Reserve**. The chimpanzees and gorillas who live there apparently enjoy it. The **Sesame Street Safari of Fun** is aimed at the smallest visitors and has carousels and a tree house.

One of the latest attractions in Busch Gardens is called **Sheikra** and is one of the steepest roller coasters in the world; it has a loop where passengers plunge down twice practically in free fall only to be shot straight up again. Latest attraction: Falcon's Fury, the tallest free fall drop tower in North America, 102m/335ft high.

❶ 10165 McKinley Dr., daily 10am – 6pm, in summer somesdays until 10pm, admission US$82, www.buschgardens.com

*Adventure Island Water park

This fun park near Busch Gardens is the best way to recover from adventures in the African savannah. **Mega-waterslides** with inspiring names like »Tampa Typhoon« and »Gulf Scream« and **wave pools** promise truly drenching fun (10001 Malcom McKinley Drive; hours: 10am–5pm).

❶ 10001 Malcolm McKinley Drive, late Mar – Aug daily 10am – until at least 5pm, Sept./Oct. only on weekends, admission US$40, http://adventureisland.com

*Museum of Science & Industry (MOSI)

Anyone who has ever wanted to ride a bike on a high wire or experience a hurricane is in the right place here. This museum in north Tampa offers **hands-on and understandable technology and natural science**. Don't miss the detailed exhibition on climate and weather in Florida, which also covers the consequences of global climate change.

❶ 4801 E. Fowler Ave., Mon – Fri 9am – 5pm, Sat, Sun 9am – 6pm, admission US$21, www.mosi.org

*Lowry Park Zoo

This zoo lies about 6mi/10km north of downtown Tampa. Located on the Hillsborough River, it is much quieter than Busch Gardens. Several endangered species can be seen here, like **Florida pumas**, Persian leopards and Sumatra tigers. In the Manatee & Aquatic Center injured **manatees** are nursed back to health.

❶ 1101 W Sligh Ave., 9.30am – 5pm, admission US$24, www.lowryparkzoo.com

AROUND TAMPA

Manatees near Big Bend Power Station

South of Tampa, at the entrance to Hillsborough Bay, the Tampa Electric Company runs **Big Bend Power Station**, in whose warm waste water dozens of manatees spend the winter months.
The power company has meanwhile built a Manatee Viewing Center, from where the endearing animals can be watched, and where there is more information on manatees.

❶ Big Bend Rd./Dickman Rd., Nov – mid April daily 10am – 5pm, free admission, www.tampaelectric.com/manatee

Seminole Hard Rock Café Hotel & Casino

On the eastern edge of Tampa and north of Interstate 4 is the amusement centre of the Seminole Indian tribe with a **casino**, deluxe hotel, several restaurants, food market, pool bar, various night clubs, Hard Rock shop and many other attractions. Or relax for a few days in one of several original Seminole **chickees**. They are furnished quite comfortably. The **Body Rock Spa** is also available for guests.

❶ 5223 N. Orient Rd., open 'round the clock, info-tel. 1-866-502-7529, www.seminolehardrocktampa.com

The nature reserve 20mi/32km north-east of Tampa has the only rapids in Florida outside a water park. However, that is not the only reason to go there. The river landscape here is original and quite lush, with several **walkways and trails** running through it. Canoes and kayaks to explore the river bends can be rented from the park administration. The rapids are somewhat disappointing since they are only knee-deep.

*Hillsborough River State Park

❶ 15402 US 301 N., Thonotosassa, daily 8am until sunset, admission US$6 per car, www.floridastateparks.org/hillsboroughriver/

At least on a weekend a reconstructed stockade fort can be viewed here; the original kept the Indians at bay during the Second Seminole War.

Fort Foster State Historic Site

❶ 15402 US 301 N, Thonotosassa, tours Thu, Sat 2pm, Sun 11am, admission US$5 per car, www.floridastateparks.org/fortfoster/

Dade City lies 27mi/44km north-east of Tampa in hill country that is characterized by spacious horse pastures and dense citrus farms. The main attraction is the **Pioneer Florida Museum**, an outdoor museum on the early settlers in Florida. It has a 19th-century church, an old schoolhouse, a private home furnished in the style of the 1860s, an old railway station with locomotives and railway cars, and various agricultural implements.

Dade City

❶ 15602 Pioneer Museum Rd., Tue – Sat 10am – 5pm, admission US$6, www.pioneerfloridamuseum.org

Manatees in the warm water near Big Bend Power Station

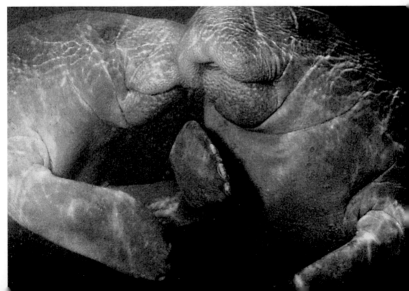

✶✶ Walt Disney World

✦ H 4

Region: Central
Elevation: 28m/100ft above sea level

Around 40 million guests every year! Walt Disney World with its meanwhile four large theme areas is »the mother of the mega-theme parks«. And that's only the beginning: only around one quarter of the land that was acquired by the Walt Disney Company near Orlando has been developed.

The goal of every child's dreams lies only a half-hour drive southwest of ▶Orlando on Lake Buena Vista. Here **Walt Disney** (▶MARCO POLO Insight p. 376) found land in 1963 where he could make his dream of the perfect amusement park come true: a broad expanse of undeveloped land, not far from booming holiday sites on the Atlantic and Gulf Coasts, with good travel connections and a good climate all year round. In fall of 1971 Magic Kingdom, the first part of Walt Disney World, opened its doors. What started as a giant but manageable amusement park has become a gigantic entertainment machine, which covers well over than 100 sq km/40 sq mi. On the grounds, where the Walt Disney Company is practically king, there are today no less than **four theme parks**, dozens of »smaller« attractions, TV studios, a sports centre with vacation classes, more than two dozen hotels and resorts as well as a complete village with shopping and nightlife.

Highlights in Walt Disney World

▶ **Magic Kingdom**
The oldest part of Disneyworld has 60 attractions on offer.
▶page 373

▶ **EPCOT**
Is the name of the popular science exploration park.
▶page 378

▶ **Disney – Hollywood Studios**
The brilliant shows in this unique combination of amusement park and film studios enthral young and old.
▶page 380

▶ **Animal Kingdom**
A combination of recreation and »real« wilderness!
▶page 381

▶ **Typhoon Lagoon · Blizzard Beach**
Top class water park
▶page 383

Every day at 3pm Mickey Mouse, along with many children, leads the parade

More than 50,000 employees see to it that everything runs smoothly every day, and above all that everything is clean, for the empire of the mouse welcomes up to 150,000 guests!

✴✴ MAGIC KINGDOM

The landmark of Magic Kingdom is the fairy-tale **Cinderella's Castle**, modelled after the castle of Neuschwanstein in Bavaria. Seven »countries« with about **60 attractions** as well as fast-food restaurants and ice cream stands are grouped around the castle. **Main Street USA** is the entrance to fun. Horse-drawn carriages and antique omnibuses move up and down this American main street that recreates the atmosphere of the year 1900. **Adventureland** Cross the bridge to Adventureland to go on a **Jungle Cruise** through the jungles of Central Africa and the Amazon, past the Egyptian pyramids and even to pirates of the Caribbean.

In **Frontierland** the **Big Thunder Mountain Railroad** races over mountains and through valleys and dark tunnels. The highlight of the Wild West area is **Splash Mountain**, where guests ride rafts through bayous and swamps and shoot over a waterfall.

Liberty Square revives the period of colonial America and the **Hall of Presidents** introduces all of the presidents of the United States. Right next door – by coincidence? – is the **Haunted Mansion**. Ghosts haunt this run-down house and unearthly musicians play.

In **Fantasyland**, the littlest Disney World visitors will find old friends. **Peter Pan** and Capt´n Hook shake many little hands, **Snow White** jokes with the seven dwarfs and **Dumbo**, the flying elephant, trips over his ears. At **Mickey's Toontown Fair** the world is child-size. Here children meet their TV heroes, especially **Mickey Mouse, Donald Duck and Goofy**.

Things are bit more serious in **Tomorrowland**: with **Buzz Lightyear** and high-tech the universe is saved. **Space Mountain**, a racing roller-coaster, takes guests into orbit. The evening in the Magic Kingdom ends with the show **Wishes**, though not every day during the low season. Mike and Roz, the stars from the Pixar film entertain in the show **Monsters, Inc. Laugh Floor**.

Walt Disney World

INFORMATION
Walt Disney World
Lake Buena Vista, FL 32830
Tel. 1-407-939-6244
www.disneyworld.disney.go.com

ARRIVAL
By air
The two closest international airports are in Orlando and Tampa. Shuttle buses run regularly to Disney World. Shuttle buses also run to Disneyworld from Miami's international airport.

By car
Disney World can best be reached by car from Orlando via Irlo Bronson Highway (US 192) as well as Interstate I-4, which connects Tampa and Orlando. From Miami – Fort Lauderdale the quickest way is on the toll road called »Florida's Turnpike« to Orlando.

HOURS
Opening hours vary, but lie mostly be-

tween 9am and 7pm. During the high season as well as on weekends and holidays hours may be extended due to the crowds. It is wise to be at the gates very early since queues form quickly. Allow for queues in the parks, too. At the most popular rides the wait may be up to two hours.

COST
Presently the price of a day for each one of the four theme parks is US$ 99 (adult) or US$ 93 (child). Add parking fees for US$20, shuttle bus transfer between the various amusement parks as well as food and drinks. Staying several days in Walt Disney World is a better deal. A 4-day pass (Four-Day Park Hopper Pass), with four days of unlimited access to all four parks, presently costs US$ 294 (adult) or US$ 274 (child). The Five-Day Pass (US$ 304 per adult, US$ 284 per child) a are even better value. Anyone who stays in one of the many Disney hotels has even more deals available. European tour op-

erators offer package deals including flights, accommodation and entry to Disney World.

EVENTS
A Dream Come True Parade
Every day at 3pm Mickey Mouse, Goofy and friends hold their parade in the Magic Kingdom. From Main Street to Frontierland they dance through the streets and wave to their thousands-strong fan club. At the end a colourful show is staged in front of Cinderella's Castle. The parade is also held late in the evening. To end the day there is also a brilliant fireworks display.

IllumiNations Insider Tip
This laser and light show with fireworks can be enjoyed to the fullest in the EPCOT Centre at the World Showcase Lagoon.

WHERE TO EAT
❶ *Les Chefs de France* $$$$
EPCOT, French Pavilion
Tel. 1-409-939-3463
The signature of the French chefs Paul Bocuse, Gaston Lenôtre and Roger Vergé cannot be missed here. The restaurant is probably the best in Walt Disney World.

❷ *Coral Reef* $$$
EPCOT, The Living Sea
Tel. 1-409-939-3463
Tastefully prepared fish, lobster and other seafood, also grilled sausages made of alligator meat, are served here. There is also a view of the Living Seas Aquarium free of charge.

❸ *House of Blues* $$
Downtown Disney West Side

Tel. 1-409-934-2583
Tasty Cajun cuisine and Creole specialties are served here with live music. Sunday Gospel Brunch is also popular.

WHERE TO STAY
❶ *Walt Disney World's Dolphin Resort* $$$
1500 Epcot Resorts Blvd.
(via Buena Vista Drive)
Tel. 1-407-934-4000
No less than 1509 rooms and suites, 17 restaurants, five pools, two health clubs, tennis and golf are available at this luxury hotel; it is also a highlight of modern architecture.

❷ *Disney's Polynesian Resort* $$$$
Magic Kingdom, tel. 1-407-934-7639
847 rooms and suites. It really looks as if you are in the South Seas: waterfalls splash, palms and banana plants sway in the breeze, orchids show all their glory. It includes two pools, a health club and various sports programmes.

❸ *Disney's Port Orleans Resort* $$$
Lake Buena Vista, 2201 Orleans Drive
Tel. 1-407-934-7639
This accommodation with 1,008 rooms is modelled on the harbour of New Orleans around 1900. There are 2 restaurants, several shops and 6 pools.

❹ *Disney's Pop Century Resort* $$
1050 Century Drive
(via Osceola Parkway)
Tel. 1-407-934-7639
Bright decoration and symbols of pop culture make this reasonably priced Disney hotel with its 2,800 rooms an attractive option.

Father of the Mouse

Anyone can turn a fly into an elephant. But the graphic artist Walt Disney did more than that: he turned a mouse into a giant, even an international star who has been fighting evil for more than 70 years and who made his creator a billionaire.

Walter Elias Disney was born in 1901 in Chicago. He started working as a graphic artist at the age of 18. At first he could hardly live on what he made. A job as a **cartoonist** did not help much either, even though Disney developed a new process: instead of drawing figures with movable parts and photographing them in different positions, he redrew each new position completely. That made the movements more life-like. In 1922 Disney went into business for himself and made commercials with his brother Roy.

The Mouse is Born

Disney's breakthrough came in **1927** when he drew a precocious mouse with giant ears, which he called Mortimer. On his wife's suggestion he renamed it, and **Mickey Mouse's** career took off. In 1933 already Walt Disney had made about 5 million dollars with Mickey and his friends. Two years later his first movie-length **cartoon, Snow White**, earned 45 million dollars. Other successes followed, like Pinocchio (1938) and Bambi (1942). Adventure films like Treasure Island and documentaries like The Living Desert (1953) made Disney successful in other fields as well. Walt Disney's Wonderful World of Colour, produced in 1961, was the first colour television series ever.

New Horizons

Already in **1955** Disney opened his first amusement park in **Anaheim**, California. Mickey, Goofy and Donald, larger than life and up close – the idea took off. But soon Disneyland was too small for its creator. Disney sent people out to find the right place to realize his dream. He

Walt Disney at work

found it in Florida. Disney's dream was to build a larger amusement park near **Orlando**, a **model city** without economic and social problems. He had the land bought up at rock-bottom prices by front companies. Thus Disney got possession of 43 sq miles (113 sq km) of land.

Creation of a Kingdom

The **400-million-dollar project** was supported by the state of Florida. In view of the revenue that Disney promised the region, he did not have to abide by any building regulations and was able to build roads and hotels as he wanted. He did not live to see the **Magic Kingdom open in 1971**, dying in 1966. But his life's work flourished.

Legendary Success

Already in the first 15 years more than 240 million visitors flooded into Disney's new world of wonders. The Disney corporation itself was surprised by the success and expanded continuously to become one of the **largest entertainment companies in the world**. Walt Disney Company (WDC) today includes the American Broadcasting Company (ABC), Walt Disney Studios, three cartoon TV channels and interests in various other television channels, among other things. WDC made headlines when Roy Disney, the nephew of Walt Disney, left the company after a conflict with the CEO Michael Eisner. But stockholders rallied behind Disney, who was reinstated. Eisner was forced to leave. The firing of several hundred employees when the cartoon branch of the

A world-famous mouse

company was closed in the face of digital competition also caused concern.

Enormous Economic Power

Walt Disney's world of wonders – today the entertainment capital of the world – proved to be a **powerful catalyst for development** for the state of Florida and especially for the Orlando area. Other amusement parks and hotels – whole settlements – sprouted like mushrooms, new highways criss-crossed the landscape, tens of thousands sought and found work here. Disneyworld's success made the population of the Orlando area explode, which is hardly surprising in view of the fact that the Walt Disney Company created over **40,000 jobs in Florida**. Accusations by ecologists that WDC's land use was irresponsible were met with references to the company's environmental policy. Hardly any petrol is used on the property, energy is won by recycling trash left behind by the visitors and waste water is purified organically.

Walt Disney World Florida

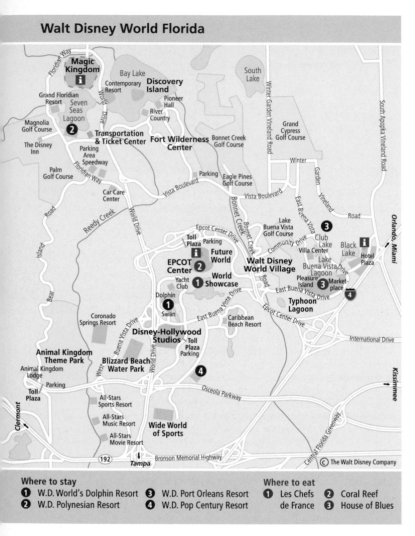

Where to stay

❶ W.D. World's Dolphin Resort   ❸ W.D. Port Orleans Resort

❷ W.D. Polynesian Resort   ❹ W.D. Pop Century Resort

Where to eat

❶ Les Chefs de France   ❷ Coral Reef   ❸ House of Blues

✷✷ EPCOT

The **Experimental Prototype Community of Tomorrow** (EPCOT) is so to speak the scientific counterpart of the Magic Kingdom. It emerged from Walt Disney's dream of a perfect paradise and opened its doors in 1982, the second theme park on the site. Interactive un-

EPCOT, Spaceship Earth

derstanding and learning scientific relationships and the latest technologies is fun here. EPCOT has two parts: **Future World** and **World Showcase**. **Spaceship Earth**, a giant, gleaming silver globe that looks like a giant golf ball is the trademark of Future World. Around this globe global US companies – including AT & T, Kodak and General Motors – present the latest information on research and technology.

On the **Test Track** guests ride in an open car at breath-taking speeds around curves and just miss hitting various obstacles. Not for those of a nervous disposition! **Mission: Space** is the most popular and at the same time most controversial attraction of the entire Walt Disney World. A rocket trip to the moon and to Mars is simulated whereby the guests experience a gravity force of two Gs.

For visitors with health issues there is a tamer version. **Honey, I shrunk the audience** is the interactive version of the popular film with (almost) the same name: by means of sophisticated special effects and optical tricks dogs appear as giants on the screen and jump into the audience, as do mice and a rowdy five-year-old. **The Land** offers a 15-minute hang-glider ride through California. **The Seas** with Captain Nemo and his friends takes visitors into the mysteries of the ocean deep.

»Mission Space« is Disney's latest attraction

World Showcase

On an artificial lagoon in the southern part of the park a **world exhibition** presents eleven countries of the world with their characteristics, which here means no more than that »clichés abound!«. »Germany«, for instance is a naïve ensemble of leather pants, beer mugs and medieval half-timbered houses. France and Italy don't get off any easier. The presentation of Canada is worth seeing: in a round cinema **Oh Canada** presents wonderful pictures from the Pacific over the Rocky Mountains to the lighthouses on the Atlantic.

** DISNEY – HOLLYWOOD STUDIOS

Mixture of amusement park and film studios

Opened in 1990, this theme park is an exciting combination of real film settings, amusements; stage shows and breath-taking rides. Famous film themes were used as a background for the »thrill rides« through well-known film settings, while films and popular game shows are actually made nearby.

Toy Story Mania reveals itself to be a breathless 3D adventure in which the audience appears to shrink to the size of toys.

The stage show **The world of East High** revolves around songs from the Disney film High School Musical. The show **American Idol** is like the famous TV production. Another highlight is **Lights, Motors, Action**, in which seemingly suicidal stuntmen perform terrifying stunts. The **Rock´n Roller Coaster** accelerates guests in 2.8 seconds from 0 to 60mph (0 to 100kph) and throws them into five curves accompanied by the rock'n'roll band Aerosmith's guitar riffs. The **Twilight Zone Tower of Terror** is a second-to-none chamber of horrors. With the help of the latest in computer animation effects are created that could make the hair of the toughest guys stand on end. For example: anyone who would like to know what it's like inside a falling elevator can find out here.

** ANIMAL KINGDOM

Truly a kingdom of animals: the open areas are so big that visitors sometimes have to search for the animals. This area was created to be as much like the natural habitat of these mostly African animals as possible. Animal Kingdom was opened in 1998 and consists of five areas. The transition from artificial amusement park to a »real« wilderness with live animals is often so smooth that it is easy to imagine an African springbok behind the nearby vending machine.

Mixture of amusement park and wilderness

The **Tree of Life** on Discovery Island is the trademark of this part of the park. More than 300 reliefs of animals have been carved into the trunk and branches of the 44m/144ft-high tree. All of the animals that are mentioned in the song The Circle of Life – from the film The Lion King – can be seen here. Children love the 3-D film **It's Tough to be a Bug**, which is shown daily at the roots of the Tree of Life. In the film children meet termites that exude liquids, bad-smelling dung beetles and many other kind of creepy-crawlies.

But the many well-known Disney figures that can be seen in **Camp Minnie-Mickey** are cuddly. In the **Lion King Theater** the thrilling **Festival of the Lion King** takes place, both on the stage and in the audience.

In **Africa** guests can take part in the **Kilimanjaro Safari**. Ride in an open safari truck through an expertly built artificial savannah. On this Game Drive see all the well-known African animals, giraffes, antelopes, gnus, zebras, rhinos and elephants. The **Pangani Forest Exploration Trail**, with hippos and – obviously contented – gorillas, is particularly exciting.

Bengal tigers and many other animals populate the **Asia** area. On the **Maharaja Jungle Trek** admire the endangered predatory cats in an area similar to their north Indian habitat. There's water fun here too:

the **Kali River Rapids** are a raft ride through a foaming inferno of a river – on a hot day a refreshing experience.

Dinoland USA remains a sensation. In the **Fossil Preparation Lab** the skeleton of a Tyrannosaurus Rex called **Dino Sue** has been erected. On the **Cretaceous Trail** plants and animals can be seen that survived the catastrophe 65 million years ago that killed off the dinosaurs. In **Dinosaur** go on a virtual trip through time in the **Time Rover** back to the Cretaceous period, meeting eerie pre-historic creatures on the way. The **Primeval Whirl**, which races around tight curves until everything goes black, is a top-class »thrill ride«. Due to open in 2016 is **Avatar Land**, inspired by James Cameron's film, where you can explore planet »Pandora«.

✱✱ TYPHOON LAGOON · BLIZZARD BEACH

These two Disney fun pools are – even sceptics agree – the absolute top! **Wave pools** and **water slides** like the **Crush'n'Gusher** in a wonderful South Seas world dominated by the 30m/100ft-high **Mount Mayday** are the special attractions of **Typhoon Lagoon**. This resort is more for families. **Blizzard Beach**, on the other hand, is for the young and fit (and athletic adults!). The truly breath-taking water slides have all sorts of twists and turns. The absolute highlight is the **Summit Plummet**: those who dare slide down from a height of 40m/130ft at break-neck speeds and splash into the pool at the bottom at a speed of 55mph/90kmh.

Disney nostalgia in front of Cinderella Castle

PRACTICAL INFORMATION

Which documents are necessary for entry? When is the best time to go? Which currency? Credit card, cash or traveller's cheques? And what in the world is a »GATOR XING«? Look it up here – preferably before the trip!

Arrival · Before the Journey

By air The popularity of Florida as a holiday destination means that there are **daily scheduled and charter flights** from major airports in Britain and other European countries Florida. The domestic flights from other parts of the USA are numerous. The most important airports for non-stop and direct flights to Florida are Miami, Orlando, Fort Lauderdale, Fort Myers, and Tampa. **Non-stop flights from Europe to Florida take about eight or nine hours.** Refer to the address list opposite for affordable non-stop, direct and transfer connections.

> ! **MARCO ◈ POLO TIP**
>
> *Air Pass* **Insider Tip**
>
> Make the trans-Atlantic flight on a US carrier (i.e. American, Delta, United) and take advantage of special savings local and excursion flights. An Air Pass or multiple coupons make it possible to visit other parts of the United States

Some **cruise ships** that operate between Europe and America stop regularly in Miami, the busiest cruise ship port in the world. Many tourists begin and end their ocean trip here. Other cruises destinations in Florida are Port Everglades (Fort Lauderdale), Port Canaveral (near the space centre) and Tampa on the Gulf of Mexico.

By freighter A **trans-Atlantic crossing by freighter** with private cabins for passengers and the appropriate service is becoming more and more popular, for example to the American ports Miami, Savannah (Georgia) and New Orleans. Contact a travel agent for further information.

By train There are only limited train services to Florida from other parts of the USA. Express trains **Silver Star** and **Silver Meteor** run daily from New York via Jacksonville, Palatka, Deland, Winter Park, Orlando, Kissimmee Tampa, Lakeland, Winter Haven, Sebring, Okeechobee, West Palm Beach, Delray Beach, Deerfield Beach, Fort Lauderdale, Hollywood and Miami. **Car trains** run several times a week between Lorton, VA (Washington, DC) and Sanford, FL (Orlando).

By bus Florida is of course included in the US network of **Greyhound buses**, which are useful for reaching Florida from other states and for travelling within Florida (details: p. 105–106). Depending on the distance involved and the special offers available, this is not necessarily cheaper than flying or renting a car. Reserve in advance to get cheaper tickets.

EUROPEAN AIRLINES

Air France
Tel. (0870) 142 43 43 (GB), tel. 1-800-237-2747 (USA), www.airfrance.com

Alitalia
Tel. (0870) 544 82 59 (GB), tel. 1-800-223-5730 (USA), www.alitalia.it

British Airways
Tel. (0870) 850 98 50 (GB), tel. 1-800-847-9297 (USA),
www.britishairways.com

Deutsche Lufthansa
Tel. (0845) 773 77 47 (GB), tel. 1- 800-645-3880 (USA), www.lufthansa.com

Iberia
Tel. (0845) 601 28 54 (GB), tel. 1-800-772-4642 (USA), www.iberia.com

KLM
Tel. (0870) 507 40 74 (GB), tel. 1-800-618-0104 (USA), www.klm.com,
www.nwa.com

Virgin Atlantic
Tel. (0870) 574 77 47 (GB), tel. 1-800-862-8621 (USA), www.virginatlantic.com

US AND OTHER AIRLINES

Air New Zealand
Tel. (0800) 028 41 49 (GB), tel. 1-800-262-1234 (USA), www.airnz.co.nz

American Airlines
Tel. (0845) 778 9789 (GB), tel. 1-800-433-7300 (USA), www.aa.com

Continental
Tel. (0800) 77 64 64 (GB), tel. 1-800-231-0856 (USA), www.continental.com

Delta Air Lines
Tel. (0800) 41 47 67 (GB), tel. 1-800-241-4141 (USA), www.delta.com

Qantas
Tel. (0845) 774 7767 (GB), tel. 1-800-227-4500 (USA), www.qantasusa.com.au

United
Tel. (0845) 844 47 77 (GB), tel. 1-800-538-2929 (USA), www.united.com

BY TRAIN
Amtrak
Tel. 1-800-USA-RAIL (USA), tel. 1-800-872-7245 (USA), www.amtrak.com

ARRIVAL AND DEPARTURE REGULATIONS

Anyone planning a trip to the USA should absolutely get up-to-date information from the US embassy at home (►Information, embassies). **Pre-Information**

A passport and, for the citizens of most countries, a visa are necessary to travel to the USA. By the terms of the **Visa Waiver Program (VWP)** citizens of the United Kingdom, Ireland and many other EU countries, as well as Australians and New Zealanders, can normally enter **without a visa for a 90-day stay** for business or holiday, provided they arrive with a recognized airline or shipping company and have a return or onward ticket that is valid for the period of 90 **Travel documents** days after the date of entering the USA. If you are unsure of your eligibility for the VWP, refer to the website www.travel.state.gov. It is advisable to take care on this point, as the regulations are liable to change. All travellers must have their own machine-readable passport when entering the USA. This applies to children as well. Children's entries in their parents' passports will not be accepted.

Upon entering a digital fingerprint of the index finger and a digital photo will be taken of everyone. Upon leaving the same procedure is followed in order to compare and make sure that the same person is leaving.

The actual **length of stay** will be determined individually and should be appropriate to the purpose of the trip. Only people who have entered with a valid visa can extend their stay. The latest possible departure date will be stamped into the passport upon arrival.

US authorities only accept **machine-readable passports** for visa-free entry. **Children** must have their own passport; children's identity cards or entries in their parents' passports will not be recognized. Citizens of countries that participate in the Visa Waiver Programme must have an **electronic entry permits (ESTA)**. These can be obtained before travelling for a fee (currently US $14 per application) online under **https://esta.cbp.dhs.gov** and are valid for unlimited entries in a period of two years.

Visas required
In many cases a **visa** will be required to enter the USA for people from countries where a visa is not normally required for a tourist trip. This includes: people who do not enter with a regular means of transportation, people who want to study, exchange students, people who want to work in the USA (even if only temporarily; this includes journalists and au-pairs!), people who want to conduct research, people who want to get married in the USA and to stay there.

Adequate finances
Adequate finances must be proven when entering. They must be enough to cover the cost of the stay and a return or continuing ticket.

Vaccinations
A vaccination record will only be requested from persons who arrive from an endangered area. It is advisable in any case to get information on the latest requirements from the nearest consulate.

Pets
Anyone who wants to take his **dog** along to the USA has to show a veterinary health and rabies vaccination record, which was produced at least one month and no more than twelve months before travelling and that is valid for no more than one year. All other pets require a veterinary health record. US embassies have the details.

National driving licence
Anyone who wants to drive in the United States has to have a valid national driving licence. An international driving licence is not

necessary and only recognized in connection with a valid national driving licence.

Extremely thorough security checks are carried out in air and sea travel. It is important, therefore, to plan enough time to be able to pass through the checks before departure.

Security checks

DUTY REGULATIONS

When arriving fill out the **immigration card** as well as a **customs declaration**. Duty free goods include personal belongings (including clothing, toilet articles), jewellery, cameras and video cameras, film or binoculars, sporting goods, for adults over 21 years old 1 quart (1.1 litres) of alcoholic beverages, 200 cigarettes or 50 cigars or 3 US pounds (lbs; about 1350 g) of tobacco. In addition gifts worth US$ 100 (excluding alcohol and cigarettes) per person may be brought in. Groceries, plants, sweets or fruit are **strictly forbidden**.

Arriving in the USA

In general the customs regulations of the country of destination apply. As a member of the EU, the following may be brought into the UK (from the age of 17 upwards): tobacco (200 cigarettes, 100 cigarillos, 50 cigars, 250g of loose tobacco), alcohol (1 litre of high-proof spirits), coffee (500g of coffee and 200g of instant coffee), scent (60g of perfume and 250g of eau de toilette), medicines for personal use and all other goods up to a value of £ 390, excluding articles for personal use.

Return to UK

TRAVEL INSURANCE

The cost of medical treatment can be a problem for tourists. A stay in hospital can be extremely expensive. Treatments must be paid for in advance or in cash on the spot. Medical insurance that includes coverage in the USA is strongly recommended, as is a credit card with an adequate line of credit. In many cases it is even cheaper to go back home and to be treated there. Before travelling to the USA it is absolutely necessary to consult your medical and accident insurance company to see to what extent you are covered. In most cases it will be necessary to buy additional **travel medical insurance**.

In the USA auto insurance is compulsory. However, **auto insurance from the UK** is not valid in the USA. Before travelling to the USA it is advisable to make sure that you are covered by an auto insurance that is valid in the USA. Travel agents, insurance agents and auto clubs will have more information.

Third party auto insurance

Cruises

Cruises   Many visitors to Florida do not want to miss out on a short cruise to the Bahamas or to Key West, or a longer one through the Caribbean. Boating excursions for several hours start from many places along the coast as well. They offer sumptuous meals, duty-free shopping and sometimes gambling.

The port of **Miami** rightly deserves the title of »Cruise Capital of the World«: About 4 million cruise ship passengers pass through here every year. It is also the home port of several large cruise ship lines. **Port Everglades** outside of Fort Lauderdale is also a busy port. The third-largest port for cruise ships is **Port Canaveral** near the space centre Cape Canaveral. Cruises leave for the Bahamas from **Palm Beach**. From **Tampa** on the Gulf coast luxury liners leave for Key West or Mexico and the Caribbean. **Key West**, the southernmost port in mainland USA, has an almost Caribbean atmosphere, and a growing number of cruise ships stop there.

Cruise ships leave Miami for the Bahamas and the Caribbean

CRUISE PORTS
Port of Miami
Tel. 1-305-371-7678
www.miamidade.gov

Port Canaveral
Tel. 1-321-783-7831
www.portcanaveral.org

Port Everglades
Tel. 1-954-523-3404
www.porteverglades.org

Port of Key West
Tel. 1-305-294-37 90
www.keywestcity.com

Port of Palm Beach
Tel. 1-561-842-4100
www.portofpalmbeach.com

Port of Tampa
Tel. 1-813-905-7678
www.tampaport.com

CRUISE SHIP LINES
Carnival Cruise Line
Tel. 1-888-227-6482
www.carnival.com

Celebrity
Tel. 1-800-647-2251
www.celebrity.com

Cunard
Tel. 1-800-772-6273
www.cunard.com

Norwegian
Tel. 1-866-234-7350
www.ncl.com

Princess
Tel. 1-800-PRINCESS
www.princess.com

Royal Caribbean
Tel. 1-866-562-7625
www.royalcaribbean.com

Electricity

The mains supply is **110 Volts AC**. Those bringing European norm **110 Volts AC**
(set switch to 110!) electrical appliances need an **adapter** which can
be purchased at the airport or department stores.

Emergency

EMERGENCY TELEPHONES
There are emergency telephones along
many of the interstate highways.

EMEREGENCY NUMBERS
IN FLORIDA
Police, ambulance, fire department
Tel. 911 (if no one answers dial 0 for the
telephone operator.

Florida Highway Patrol Tel. FHP	*US Auto Club AAA* Tel. 1-800-AAA-HELP
Tourist emergency number Tel. 1-800-656-8777	*ADAC emergency centre Orlando* Tel. 1-888-222-1373

Etiquette and Customs

Strict rules for alcohol consumption The laws and standards on the consumption of alcohol are regulated at the state level in the USA (sometimes even in individual counties) and thus vary greatly. The **legal drinking age** in Florida is 21 years; that means that anyone younger can neither buy alcohol nor get it in restaurants. Wine, beer and spirits are only available in **liquor stores**. On Sundays alcoholic products can only be bought after 1pm. The consumption of alcohol is prohibited in public areas (administrative buildings, railway stations, beaches). The consumption of alcohol is even prohibited in parked cars. Driving under the influence of alcohol is prosecuted severely. The allowed **blood alcohol level is 0.0**. Moreover the transport of opened bottles or cans of alcoholic beverages is prohibited in cars (not even in the boot!).

Smoking not tolerated The tolerance of smoking has been low for some time in the USA. None of the airlines allow smoking, nor is it allowed in public buildings. Restaurants only have small smoking areas. Meanwhile anyone smoking around children risks a public confrontation.

Greetings Greetings in Florida are informal. First names are used commonly, although older people are often alert to whether they are addressed as »Mr« or »Mrs«. By the way, using first names does not imply familiarity. Americans do keep strangers at a distance, but they are usually polite.

Smalltalk »It's a fine day, isn't it?« No matter whether they are in an elevator or a queue: when Americans are present for anything more than a short time, they often make small talk. This does not mean that they want to start a conversation, but only that this is polite. Not speaking or turning away is considered to be rude.

Invitations »Come and see us some time!« After a meeting and an animated conversation, friendly Americans often leave with this phrase. Do not take this invitation literally; it's only a polite expression. Americans would be very surprised if someone actually did turn up without first reconfirming the invitation by telephone.

The belief that Americans are naïve and uneducated persists because of cliché Americans who appear in public regularly. Most US citizens do know something about the rest of the world and also that they do not live in paradise. Visitors from »old Europe« who criticize American problems like racial issues, immigration policies, the school system, arms control and foreign affairs could be seen as rude. It's better to wait until your opinion is asked for. Then you will notice that Americans are also interested and expressive conversationalists.

Discussions

In the USA tips are not included in the bill and are thus given separately. This is not required, but the personnel in restaurants and hotels are not paid well and genuinely depend on their tips. 15% of the bill before tax is usual. Leave the tip in the restaurant on the table.
Hotel pages expect $1 per bag. Maids get $2 per day. It's OK to leave the tip in the room in an envelope when checking out. If a hotel or restaurant offers valet parking, the valet gets $1 (when taking the car away and when returning it).

Tipping

Health

In the USA a distinction is made between drugstores and pharmacies. Prescription medicines are available at the latter. In Florida there are numerous branches of Eckerd's drugstores. Every Winn-Dixie supermarket also has a drugstore.

Drugstore, pharmacy

Drugstores or pharmacies are mostly open from 9am to 6pm. Some are even open until 9pm. The pharmacies in 24-hour supermarkets are open around the clock.

Hours

There are no special emergency services outside of the regular opening hours. It might be necessary to go to the closest emergency room, ER, in a hospital. Hospitals are also open around the clock and have their own pharmacies.

Emergencies

Medical care is good. This applies not only to doctors in private practice and dentists, but also to the hospitals. Tourists who take medications regularly should take along a copy of the prescription in case an American doctor needs to write a new one.

Medical care

A hospital stay or even just a visit to the emergency room can break the holiday budget. So it is advisable to **get travel insurance for the USA before travelling**.

Medical care is expensive

Medical emergency service Doctors in private practice and hospitals are listed in the Yellow Pages of local telephone books. In case of emergency **dial 911 or 0 for the operator**, who can connect you to the nearest emergency room.

Health risks Personal negligence is the greatest health risk factor. It is easy to underestimate Florida's **sun and heat** and forget head covering and water bottles when going out, which can have disastrous consequences. The sun is at its most intense between 11am and 3pm. People with sensitive skin should stay out of the sun during this time. Along with a good **sunscreen**, a very good **insect repellent** is indispensable since mosquitoes are always present near water – which makes them all the more common in the swamps and wetlands of Florida. **Mosquito season is from June to November**. At this time long sleeves and long trousers are recommended.

Information

The U.S. no longer operates national tourist offices in other countries, and the U.S. Travel & Tourism Administration in Washington has also ceased to exist. In a number of countries the Visit USA Association provides information and literature (see addresses below). A number of American tourist destinations have representation abroad: see below for phone numbers in the UK. For visa information refer to US embassies and their websites.

IN FLORIDA
Visit Florida
661 E. Jefferson Street
Tallahassee, FL 32301
Tel. 1-850-488-5607
www.visitflorida.com

VISIT AMERICA
Australia
www.visitusa.org.au

Canada
6519B Mississauga Road Mississauga,
ON L5N 1A6
Tel/fax (416) 352-5567
www.seeamerica.ca

Ireland
60 Merrion Square, Dublin 2
Tel. 01-890-29-63
www.visitusa.ie

New Zealand
www.visitusa.co.nz

UK
US Embassy, 24 Grosvenor Square,
London, W1A 1AE
Tel. 0870 777 2213
Fax: 0207 495 4851
www.visitusa.org.uk

FLORIDA DESTINATIONS: UK CONTACT

UK representations of cities and areas in Florida
Central Florida: tel. 01373-466707
Daytona Beach: tel. 020-7932 2471
Florida: tel. 020-7932 2406
Keys & Key West: tel. 01564-794555
Space Coast: tel. 01293-449145
Fort Lauderdale: tel. 01628-778863
Kissimmee-St. Cloud Tel. 01732-875722
Miami: tel. 01444-443355
Sarasota: tel. 020-7257 8858
St Petersburg/Clearwater:
Tel. 020-8339 6121

US EMBASSIES
In Australia
Moonah Place
Yarralumla, ACT 2600
Tel. (02) 6214-5600
Fax (02) 6214-5970
http://canberra.usembassy.gov

In Canada
490 Sussex Drive
Ottawa, Ontario K1N 1G8
Tel. 613-688-5335
Fax 613.688.3082
http://canada.usembassy.gov

In Republic of Ireland
42 Elgin Road, Ballsbridge, Dublin 4
Tel. +353 1 668-8777
Fax +353 1 668-9946
http://dublin.usembassy.gov

In UK
24 Grosvenor Square
London, W1A 1AE
Tel. (0)20 7499-9000
http://london.usembassy.gov
US Consulates General in Cardiff,
Edinburgh and Belfast.

EMBASSIES IN USA
Australia
1601 Massachusetts Ave N.W.
Washington DC 20036
Tel. 1-202-797-3000
www.austemb.org

Canada
501 Pennsylvania Avenue N.W.
Washington, D.C. 20001
Tel.1-202-682-1740, fax: -682-7619
www.canadianembassy.org

Ireland
2234 Massachusetts Ave NW
Washington DC 20008
Tel.1-202-462-3939, -232-5993
www.irelandemb.org

New Zealand
37 Observatory Cir NW
Washington, DC 20008
Tel. 1-202-328-4800, -667-5227
www.nzembassy.com

UK
3100 Massachusetts Avenue,
Washington DC, 20008
Tel. 1-202-588-7800, fax -588 -7850
Emergency tel.: 1-202-588-6500
www.britainusa.com

CONSULATES IN FLORIDA
Australia
Contact British or Canadian consulate

Canada
200 S. Biscayne Boulevard Suite 1600,
Miami
Tel. 1-305-579-1600
http://can-am.gc.ca/miami/

New Zealand
Contact British or Canadian consulate

Consulates:
UK
1001 Brickell Bay Drive Suite 2800,
Miami, FL 33131
Tel. 1-305-374-1522
www.britainusa.com/miami

OTHER SOURCES
US Government Official Website
http://www.firstgov.gov

USA Weather Information
http://www.weather.com/

Recreation Services
http://www.recreation.gov/

Literature

Novels, prose **Max A. Collins:** *CSI: Miami, Heat Wave.* Simon & Schuster, 2004. Florida's »Crime Scene Investigation« (CSI) dominates the TV channels around the world. Now also in book form.

Ernest Hemingway: *Islands in the Stream.* The Florida classic – not just for deep sea fishermen.

Ernest Hemingway: *To Have and Have Not.* A turbulent story about a boat owner with a dubious reputation who is killed in a battle with Cuban bank robbers.

Carl Hiaasen: *Stormy Weather.* The Miami Herald columnist's novel on profiteers who tried to take advantage of the chaos caused by Hurricane Andrew.

Zora Neale Hurston: *Their Eyes were Watching God.* About a black woman in rural Florida.

Marjorie Kinnan Rawlings: *Cross Creek. My Planting Experiences in Florida.* The author is famous for her beautiful accounts of rural life.

Peter Matthiessen: *Killing Mister Watson.* Historical novel about Ed Watson, an Everglades pioneer.

Marjorie Stoneman Douglas: *The Everglades – River of Grass.* Sarasota: Pineapple Press, 1988. One of the most sensitive books on the fragile landscape of the American south-east.

Tennessee Williams: *Memoirs.* There is a generous chapter on his time in Key West in his memoirs.

Michael Gannon: *The New History of Florida*, 1996. A weighty and scholarly but readable work.   Non-fiction

Laura Cerwinske and David Kaminsky: *Tropical Deco: The Architecture and Design of Old Miami Beach*, 1991. An informative and well-illustrated survey.

Stuart McIver: *Dreamers, Schemers and Scalawags: The Florida Chronicle*s. About the gangsters and millionaires who shaped the Sunshine State.

Diane Roberts: *Dream State*. The author is a native of Florida and radio journalist who knows her subject well and can write interestingly about politicians, money-makers and rogues past and present

John Rothchild: *Up for Grabs*. An entertaining journey around Florida that takes a look at the deal-making in the history of the state.

Jeanne Voltz and Caroline Stuart: The Florida Cookbook: From   Cookbook
Gulf Coast Gumbo to Key Lime Pie. Traditional and modern recipes.

Herbert W. Kale, David S. Maehr and Karl Karalus: *Florida's Birds:*   Nature
A Handbook and Reference. The ideal companion for bird-watchers.

Kevin McCarthy: *Alligator Tales*. Lots of stories by alligator hunters, but also the arguments for protecting the animals.

Media

There is a television in every hotel room. The main television   TV
channels are free. Beyond that there are many **TV** programmes on private channels that sometimes charge quite steep fees (pay TV).

American radio stations can be heard on **medium wave (AM)**. They   Radio
give the most up-to-date information on weather, traffic, events etc. **FM** carries stations with local information from individual towns, national parks etc. In sparsely populated areas fewer radio stations can be heard and more in more populated areas.

A broad palette of daily newspapers and periodicals to suit every   Newspapers
taste is available. Florida's leading daily is the **Miami Herald**. There   and
are also several regionally important newspapers.   magazines

UK and Irish newspapers

Newsstands sell papers from the UK and Republic of Ireland, but they are normally a day old. Some publications, such as the UK paper The Times, are available in a US edition the same day.

Money

Currency

The US monetary unit is the dollar (US$), colloquially called the »buck«. Apart from notes, or bills, worth $1, 2, 5, 10, 20, 50 and 100 (there are also larger notes for bank business), there are coins worth 1 (penny), 5 (nickel), 10 (dime), 25 (quarter) cents, and more rarely 50 cents (half-dollar) and 1 dollar in circulation.

The **exchange rate of the US dollar** varies against other rates. It is better to exchange money in your home country – part of it into traveller's cheques, which are accepted almost everywhere, since the exchange rates will be better there. Up to $10,000 may be brought into or taken out of the country freely. Larger amounts must be declared in the customs declaration form which non-residents are required to complete on the plane.

Traveller's cheques

Traveller's cheques and major foreign currencies can be exchanged without difficulty in banks or in branches of Thomas Cook or American Express. It is much more convenient when changing to have traveller's cheques that were issued in dollars.

❶ Opening times of banks: Mon–Thu 9am–3.30pm, Fri until 4.30pm

Credit cards

The most common method of payment is the **credit card**; Euro/MasterCard and Visa are the most common. When renting a car, a credit card is required for the deposit; most hotels require them as well. ATMs (automatic teller machines) are available at many locations around the clock.

Most international bank cards enable the holder to withdraw money from ATMs in the USA, though there will probably be a charge incurred and the exchange rate is likely to be less advantageous than offered by banks and bureaux de change at home. Of course, the PIN is necessary for withdrawals.

EXCHANGE RATE
1 US$ = 0.61 GBP
1 GBP = 1.63 US$
Current exchange rates:
www.oanda.com

LOST CREDIT CARD
MasterCard: Tel. 1-800-627-8372 (USA)
VISA: Tel. 1-800-847-2911 (USA)
American Express: Tel. 1-800-327-2177 (USA)

Personal Safety

Thanks to Al Capone, Miami Vice and a few spectacular murders in the 1990s Florida has been considered to be the backyard of thieves. This applies especially to the metropolitan Miami – Fort Lauderdale – Palm Beach area. **The social gap is very large here**. Crimes involving drugs cause the police problems. The relatively long coastline and the proximity of the Central and South American drug production have turned Miami into a dangerous drug transhipment centre.

Crime

Even though the situation has calmed down since the tourist murders of the 1990s, be careful in the Sunshine State. A good rule is to apply common sense. Avoid parks, unlit areas, dark streets etc. after dark and do not go out alone. If you become involved in an accident that took place under strange circumstances, stay in the car and wait before getting out until the circumstances are clearer. Keep valuables and large amounts of money in the hotel safe. When travelling keep everything that might look attractive to thieves in the boot. But if something does happen, do not resist the thieves. Heroism has had a high price before now in a number of cases. In case of an emergency contact the police immediately: **Emergency number 911**.

Be careful

Post · Telecommunications

The **U. S. Mail** is only responsible for mailing letters and packages (also for wiring money). Telephone and telegram services are in private hands. **Stamps** are available in post offices as well as from machines in airports, railway stations, bus stations, hotel lobbies and drug stores.

U. S. Mail

US flags fly **outside post offices,** which have the following hours: Mon–Fri 9am–5pm or 6pm, Sat 8am–12noon. Smaller post offices close over lunch.

Mailboxes are painted blue and have »US Mail« written on them in white, and a stylized eagle.

? *Postage*

MARCO ⊕ POLOINSIGHT

Postcard within the USA: 32 cents every ounce/28 g
Letter within the USA: 45 cents
Postcard to Europe: $1.05
Airmail letter (maximal 1 ounce/28 g) to Europe: $1.05

TELECOMMUNICATIONS

Letters The telephone dials also have letters on them, which are often used to help remember numbers (national breakdown service: tel. 1-800-AAA-HELP).

Public Most public phones only operate on calling card or credit cards.
telephones There are still a few coin-operated phones around for local calls.

? *MARCO ⊕ POLO INSIGHT*	*Telephone services*
	Information inland: Tel. 411
	Information overseas:
	Tel. 1-555-1212
	Collect calls: Tel. 0
	Country codes from the USA
	to UK: 0 11 44
	to Republic of Ireland:
	0 11 353
	to Australia: 0 11 61
	to Canada: 1 (North American
	Numbering Plan)
	Country code to the USA:
	from UK and Republic of Ireland:
	00 1
	from Australia: 0011 1
	from Canada: 1

Numbers with 800 or 888 can only be called within the USA and are **toll free**. Do not confuse them with 900 numbers, which usually connect to quite expensive commercial services.

For **local calls** dial 1 and then the telephone number. For calls within the USA dial 1, then the area code and then the telephone number.

For **international calls** dial 011, then the country code, then the area code without the 0 and then the telephone number from private telephones. From public telephones dial 0. The operator will answer and give instructions.

Collect calls To place a collect call dial 0 and then the telephone number. When the operator answers tell him to place a collect call.

Telephone Prepaid **phone cards** with often quite reasonable rates are
charges recommended for international calls; they can be bought in shopping centres, at airports, at petrol stations etc.

Mobile Mobile telephones are also called cell phones in the USA, or just cells.
telephones The use of quad-band phones, which work both in the USA and Europe, is recommended.
Smartphones can be used without limitations in the USA. High roaming rates can be avoided by using a Cellion USA SIM card (Info: www.cellion.de).
The UniversalCard can be used from a Cellion mobile phone account as well as from a US landline and every US call box.

There are only a few business left that still send telegrammes. Addresses of business offices that specialize in sending telegrammes overseas (i.e. Western Union) can be found in local telephone books.

Telegrammes

Internet cafés can be found in all larger towns. »Hot spots« in airports or other public places, often also in hotels or cafés, make it possible to go online without a cable if the laptop in question is equipped with mobile technology (WLAN, Wi-Fi). Copy shops like FedEx Kinko's also offer internet – often around the clock. This makes it possible for people to check their emails while on holiday in the USA, surf the net or telephone via Skype.

Internet

Prices · Discounts

Many hotels, restaurants, amusements parks etc. adjust their prices to the season. The rates are higher during the high season and summer vacations as well as around the main holidays. But prices could be reduced by half during the low season, when hotels and amusement parks have attractive special rates.

Seasonal prices

Marked prices are net prices without sales tax. Most items are charged with a state sales tax of currently 6%. Some cities, communities and counties also charge a general sales tax (usually 1%). Some towns also have a tourism development tax.

Children, students and senior citizens benefit especially from discounts. The spectrum covers everything from airline and railway tickets to special rates in hotels, amusement parks, national and state parks. It is worthwhile in any case to ask all tourist facilities about discounts when planning the trip.

> **?** | *What does it cost?*
>
> MARCO ⊕ POLO INSIGHT
>
> Cup of coffee: from $1.50
> Pint of beer: from $5
> Simple meal: from $8
> 3-course menu: from $20
> Simple accommodation: from $40
> Moderate accommodation: from $80
> 1 gallon (3.8 l) petrol: c. $3,90
> 1 gallon (3.8 l) diesel: c. $3.60

Some tourist organizations publish brochures that can be found in various places including tourist offices, visitor centres, hotel receptions, petrol stations and supermarkets. Many of the businesses that place ads in these brochures also have coupons with many discounts, ranging from reduced hotel rates to super deals in the local factory outlet.

Collect coupons!

Time Zones in the USA

Alaska Time
GMT -9

Pacific Time
GMT -8

Mountain Time
GMT -7

Central Time
GMT -6

Eastern Time
GMT -5

Atlantic Time
GMT -4

Hawaii Time
GMT -10

C A N A D A

©BAEDEKER

M E X I C O

Pacific Ocean

Atlantic Ocean

Florida

Gulf of Mexico

Difference to
Greenwich Mean Time
(GMT)

200 mi
400 km

Time

Eastern Time Zones Most of Florida is in the Eastern Time Zone, 5 hours behind Greenwich Mean Time.

Central Time Zones The western Panhandle is in the Central Time Zone and is one hour behind the rest of Florida.

Daylight saving time Zones Daylight saving time, when the clocks are set ahead one hour for the summer, runs from the first Sunday in April to the last Sunday in October.

Transport

Airports The two most important **air traffic hubs** in Florida are Miami and Orlando, followed by Fort Lauderdale, Daytona, Tampa, Fort Myers, Jacksonville and Tallahassee. From these airports there are daily flights to many small airports in Florida and also to other destinations in the USA. Moreover many small landing strips in Florida are used on demand.

All larger airports are well-connected to regional roads. Moreover there are **good local connections** to the city centres or important locations further away. Many of the larger hotels, car rental agencies etc. have an **airport shuttle service** for their guests and customers. All of the larger car rental agencies are present in the larger airports so that there is no problem picking up a car.

Local travel connections

Passenger travel by rail is organized by **Amtrak**, which is responsible for passenger service and train schedules. The rails themselves and the train cars are owned and serviced by various companies. Amtrak trains run daily on the routes New York – Jacksonville – Miami or Tampa (Silver Service/Palmetto) as well as New Orleans – Pensacola – Orlando (Sunset Limited). The **Auto Train**, a comfortable car transport train, runs from Lorton (Virginia) – Sanford (Florida). Amtrak offers various rail passes, which can however only be bought outside the USA at reasonable rates. These rail passes are valid for 15 or 30 days. The **USA Rail Pass** is valid for the entire USA and of course also for Amtrak routes in Florida with unrestricted stopping.
The **Tri-Rail** passenger trains run daily between Miami, Fort Lauderdale and Palm Beach. This city express is an economical way to visit the holiday resorts on the south-east Atlantic coast. Occasionally local tour guides offer accompanied Tri-Rail sightseeing tours.

Amtrak trains

> **Insider Tip**
>
> **MARCO ❂ POLO TIP**
>
> **❗ Murder on the Mystery Train**
>
> Fort Myers has an attraction for Agatha Christie fans. On five evenings a week (Wed–Sat 6.30pm, Sun 5.30pm) the Murder Mystery Train leaves from Colonial Station for an unknown destination. En route the unbelievable happens: murder. The passengers then are asked to help hunt for the murderer. More information: tel. 1-800-736-4853, www.semgulf.com

Excursion trains by **Seminole Gulf Passenger Service** run daily at least once on the route Naples – Fort Myers – Punta Gorda – Fort Ogden– Arcadia during the high season. On set dates there is also a **Dinner Train** in the evening, where a set dinner is offered to passengers.

Seminole Gulf Railway

Many European travel companies include organised bus trips through Florida in their catalogue. Travel agents have more information.

Organised bus trips

Buses of the Greyhound Inc. company are generally well-equipped and offer a comfortable trip. Greyhound buses cover routes between all important cities and tourist centres in Florida. The most important stops are Miami, Miami Beach, Orlando, Jacksonville, Tallahassee, Daytona Beach, Fort Lauderdale, West Palm Beach, Sarasota, Tampa and Key West.

Bus travel by Greyhound

The **Greyhound AmeriPass**, available for 7-60 days, and the **Greyhound DiscoveryPass** can also be recommended for tours of Florida. However these passes can only be bought outside of the USA. Ask a travel agents for information.

Cabs There is an ample number of taxis (cabs) in cities and major tourist centres. They can be stopped anywhere on the street by waving at them. Since the distances in the cities and tourist centres along the coast are often long, the fares can be quite high. The trip from Miami International Airport to Miami Beach, for example, costs at least US $50 (without a tip)!

Public transport In the larger cities public transport services are good. **Buses** run along set routes in many towns. In Miami there is also **Metrorail**, a commuter train. Moreover downtown Miami has a completely automatic elevated railway called the **Metromover**, which can be used free of charge. Public transport fares are relatively reasonable and comparable to central European standards. Local transport buses generally only accept exact change. The bus drivers do not sell tickets or give change.

TRAVELLING BY CAR

Every US state, along with the federal laws, has its own traffic regulations. Visitors from Europe will notice some differences. The following regulations should be observed:

Right of way At unmarked intersections the one who gets there first has the right of way. Drivers may have to use hand signals.
At many intersections all lanes have stop signs, called **4-way stop**. Every driver must stop here. The first one at the intersection may then proceed.

Seatbelts Seatbelts are required in Florida. Children under four years old may only ride in a children's seat.

Speed limits In cities and residential areas the speed limits are between 20mph/32kph and 35mph/56kph; if there is a school, nursing home or hospital nearby the speed limit might even be only 15mph/24kph! On roads leading out of town and country roads with two-way traffic speed limits are 45mph/72kph. If the road runs through areas with wild animals, then the speed limit at night is only 35mph/56kph. On multi-lane roads and motorways (highways) speed limits are 55mph/88kph. On highways with little traffic the speed limit is 70mph/112kph.

No blood alcohol is allowed for drivers (**0.0 per mille**). »Driving under the influence« is punished severely. Opened liquor bottles may not be transported in cars, not even in the boot.
people under 21 years old may not have any alcoholic products at all with them.

Blood alcohol

On a street with two-way traffic, always stop when a school bus is dropping off or picking up passengers. If a school bus stops on a divided roadway then only the traffic flowing in the same direction as the bus must stop.

School buses

In the USA **traffic lights come after (!) the intersection**. Right turns on red are allowed after stopping and checking traffic. Right turn on red is not allowed when the sign »No turn on red« is present. When the sun is low, when visibility is less than 300m/1,000ft, in rain and on long straight roads with oncoming traffic, **low beam lights must be switched on.**

Traffic lights, right turns

Parking: parking is not allowed on country roads or motorways outside of towns as well as on many streets within towns (►MARCO POLO Insight, right). If a stop is necessary, pull over onto the shoulder of the road. Also parking is not allowed in front of fire hydrants and in bus stops. Anyone who parks in a **no-parking zone** or blocks a driveway can count on getting towed away for a high towing fee.

? *Kerbstone colours*

Red: no parking
Yellow: general loading zone
Yellow/black: truck loading zone
Blue: handicapped parking
Green: max. parking 10 minutes
White: max. parking 5 minutes
during business hours
No colour: unlimited parking

U-turns are generally not allowed and marked by the sign **No U Turns.**

U-turns

Passing on the right is allowed on multi-lane roads (interstates, many highways). When changing lanes to the right, it is advisable to be just as careful as when changing to the left.

Passing on the right

Solid double lines may not be crossed, nor single lines on the driver's side. Many streets having turning lanes that can only be entered when the line is broken.

Solid line

Multi-lane streets in metropolitan areas (especially around Miami – Fort Lauderdale) have lanes in areas where traffic can back up, which can be used during rush hour by cars with more than one occupant. Violations will be prosecuted by the police.

Rush hour lanes

INLAND FLIGHTS
American Airlines
Tel. 1-800-433-7300
www.aa.com

Delta Air Lines
Tel. 1-800-221-1212
www.delta.com

United
Tel. 1-800-864-8331
www.united.com

US Airways
Tel. 1-800-428-4322
www.usairways.com

RAIL TRAVEL
Amtrak
Tel. 1-800-USA-RAIL
www.amtrak.com

Tri-Rail
Tel. 1-800-TRI-RAIL
www.tri-rail.com

Seminole & Gulf
Tel. 1-800-SEM-GULF
www.semgulf.com

BUS TRIPS
Greyhound
Tel. 1-800-231-2222
www.greyhound.com

RENTAL CARS
Alamo
Tel. 1-800-GO-ALAMO
www.alamo.com

Avis
Tel. 1-800-331-1212
www.avis.com

Budget
Tel. 1-800-527-0700
www.budget.com

Hertz
Tel. 1-800-654-3131
www.hertz.com

»Xing« The English word »crossing« is often shortened to »Xing« in the USA. The traffic sign marked »Ped Xing« refers to a pedestrian crossing. The sign »Gator Xing« means that alligators are likely to cross the road.

Hitchhiking Hitchhiking is allowed in the USA but not on Interstates and on- and off-ramps. It should be noted that hitchhiking is considered to be dangerous by Americans – for drivers and hitchhikers.

Police stop When the police stop your car, remain seated in the car, open the window and leave your hands in sight on the wheel. Then wait for instructions from the officers.

Interstates Interstates are like motorways and are recognizable by the blue-white-red signs. Interstates with two-digit even numbers run east-west, and those with two-digit odd numbers run north-south. Three-digit numbers refer to beltways around cities.

Highways are basically multi-lane country roads. The white signs mark them as national (for example US 1) or state roads (for example SR 84 or FL 84). Their numbers also roughly correspond to the compass direction. ALT (alternative) or BUS (business) refers to bypasses.

Highways

The most important difference between highways and interstates is the fact that highways are not limited access roads. Be careful at junctions and when turning left.

Toll refers to road use fees, which are charged on certain interstates and highways as well as for the use of some bridges, causeways and tunnels or underpasses. Keep some loose change in the car to avoid long lines at the manned booths.

Toll

On divided roadways the off-ramps or exits are usually on the right, but when there is no room the exit may be placed on the left.

Off-ramps

Petrol stations are usually located in populated areas, near on- and off-ramps for highways and at intersections on country roads. **Unleaded gas** is sold in the categories **regular** and **super (premium)** as well as **diesel**. In order to start the pump turn the lever or lift the handle. Many petrol stations especially in the evening and at night require payment in advance. Often there are full service and self-service pumps.

Petrol stations

RENTAL CARS

Florida is best explored in a rental car, which can used to reach attractions that are off the beaten track. Some rental agencies have good deals, and the weekly packages are especially reasonable. But don't let the very low basic rates fool you. Instead watch out for adequate insurance rates (collision, third-party, deductible). Insurance packages can be expensive. Then state taxes are added and maybe even airport taxes, the latter only if an airport shuttle is used from the airport to the rental agency.

Preferred means of transport

Anyone who wants to rent a car must present a national or internationally recognized driver's licence and generally must be at least 21 years old. Some agencies allow people to drive from the age of 18, but charge a correspondingly expensive »underage« rate.

Driving licence, minimum age

Claiming a car Every rental agency has a counter at the airport, but the cars are claimed elsewhere. A shuttle bus will take you from the airport to the car depot. If the reserved car is not available, a car from the next higher category is made available for the same price. This can also be done with »upgrade coupons«, which some travel agencies and airlines give away. Before leaving the agency's grounds check the car for defects and point them out immediately.

Rental agencies require a **security deposit** to rent a car, but most of them will accept a credit card instead.

Insurance The agencies offer a confusing array of different policies, not all of which are necessary. Here is a short explanation: **CDW** (Collision Damage Waiver), damage waiver for damage to the car (highly recommended); **LDW** (Loss Damage Waiver), damage waiver in case the car is lost or stolen; **PAI** (Personal Accident Insurance), accident insurance for occupants; **PEC** (Personal Effect Coverage), insurance for baggage; **LIS** or **SLI**: supplemental liability insurance to raise the liability level above the legal minimum.

Travellers with Disabilities

Disability-friendly Florida's building regulations are very friendly to the disabled. Public buildings, airports, ports, hotels and restaurants are equipped for the handicapped. Even the sidewalks are made for the handicapped. There are parking places for the disabled everywhere. The many attractions also offer aids for the handicapped. The large amusement parks have wheelchairs to rent. Many of the beaches have **surf chairs** which allow people who have difficulty walking to enjoy beach life.

TRAVEL AGENTS IN THE USA
Flying Wheels Travel
Tel. 1-507-451-5005
www.flyingwheelstravel.com
This agent offers guided tours and excursions in minivans equipped for the disabled.

Accessible Journeys
Tel. 1-610-521-0339
www.disabilitytravel.com
This agency serves mainly people with walking disabilities and wheelchairs.

ORGANIZATIONS FOR THE HANDICAPPED
Florida Disabled Outdoor Association (FDOA)
Tel. 1-850-201-2944
www.fdoa.org
This organisation offers especially helpful information and internet links.

Society for Accessible Travel and Hospitality (SATH)
Tel. 1-212-447-7284
www.sath.org

Information and recommendations for people with all kinds of handicaps are available at this organisation. They also publish Open World Magazine. Their website has a list of web addresses for individual attractions and travel agents along with general information.

American Foundation for the Blind
Tel. 1-212-502-76 00
www.afb.org
People with visual impairments will get help from this foundation.

RENTAL CARS
Wheelchair Getaways
Tel. 1-425-253-8213
www.wheelchair-getaways.com
They rent vehicles equipped for the disabled. Agencies in West Palm Beach, Fort Lauderdale, Miami, Naples, Fort Myers and Jacksonville. The vehicles can be picked up at the airports of the above mentioned cities as well.

HELP IN UK
RADAR
12 City Forum, 250 City Road,
London EC1V 8AF
Tel. (020) 72 50 32 22
www.radar.org.uk

HOTEL/TRAVEL ADVICE
Metro-Dade Disability Services
1335 N.W. Street Miami, FL 33125
Tel. 1-305-547-5445
They have a free guidebook for physically disabled people entitled »Directory of Services for the Physically Disabled in Dade County«.

Weights, Measures, Temperatures

1 inch (in;) = 2.54 cm	1 mm = 0.03937 in	**Linear**
1 foot (ft;)= 12 in = 30.48 cm	1 cm = 0.033 ft	
1 yard (yd;) = 3 ft = 91.44 cm	1 m = 1.09 yd	
1 mile (mi;) = 1.61 km	1 km = 0.62 mi	
1 square inch (in²) = 6.45 cm²	1 cm² = 0.155 in²	**Square**
1 square foot (ft²) = 9.288 dm²	1 dm² = 0.108 ft²	**measures**
1 square yard (yd²) = 0.836 m²	1 m² = 1.196 yd²	
1 square mile (mi²) = 2.589 km²	1 km² = 0.386 mi²	
1 acre = 0.405 ha	1 ha = 2.471 acres	
1 cubic inch (in³) = 16.386 cm³	1 cm³ = 0.061 in³	**Cubic**
1 cubic foot (ft³) = 28.32 dm³	1 dm³ = 0.035 ft³	**measures**
1 cubic yard (yd³) = 0.765 m³	1 m³ = 1.308 yd³	
1 gill = 0.118 l 1 l = 8.747 gills		**Liquid**
1 pint (pt)= 4 gills = 0.473 l 1 l = 2.114 pt		**measures**

1 quart (qt)= 2 pt = 0.946 l 1 l = 1.057 qt
1 gallon (gal) = 4 qt = 3.787 l
1 l = 0.264 gal

Weights

1 ounce (oz;) = 28.365 g

1 pound (lb;) = 453.59 g

1 cental (cwt;.) = 45.359 kg

100 g = 2.527 oz

1 kg = 2.206 lb

100 kg = 2.205 cwt

Temperature Celsius = 5/9 (Fahrenheit - 32)

Fahrenheit = 1.8 x Celsius + 32

When to Go

In the north four seasons, in the south two

North Florida has four seasons. Rain falls at all times of the year here. South Florida is different; it actually only has two seasons. The warm waters around Florida, high humidity and high evaporation make the weather summer-like and humid, from May to October extremely so. From November to April the weather is cooler and dry for three to five months.

Temperatures

From June to September the weather is quite hot. The highest **temperatures** can be found around the Keys and inland, where daytime temperatures during hot periods are frequently over 40°C/104°F. In the summer there are also severe thunderstorms with hail and tornados. The months of March, April and May as well as October and November are comfortable. The weather is mostly

A thunderstorm over the beach at Miami Beach

sunny then with summer-like temperatures. From December to February the weather in northern and central Florida can get quite cool. There can even be frost, which damages the citrus and vegetable crops severely.

Rain

The Florida Panhandle has the greatest amount of **rain**, more than 1,500mm/59in fall annually. The Keys are dry and get only two thirds of the rain measured in the north, 1,000mm/39in.

Hurricane season

Every year Florida has to face several tropical cyclones which either hit land or pass by, most of them **between June and October**. A hurricane can not only reach gigantic proportions, it also has massive destructive potential. In a six-week period in late summer 2004 no less than nine hurricanes wreaked havoc around Florida.

The news programmes on the **radio** and **TV** broadcast weather reports regularly. The **NOAA Weather Radio Network** gives up-to-date information on the most recent developments in the weather over Florida, the Gulf of Mexico, the west Atlantic and the Caribbean Sea.

? MARCO ⊕ POLO INSIGHT

NOAA Weather reports

- 162.400 MHz
  Daytona, Key West, Pensacolaj
- 162.475 MHz
  Fort Myers, Gainesvolle,
  Orlando, Palm Beach)
- 162.550 MHz
  Jacksonville, Miami, Panama
  City, Tampa

High season for north Florida is May to September. But in the subtropical south the high season is from mid-December until mid-April. The months of April and May as well as September, October and November are **low season** in all of Florida. **Important holidays** Hotels, amusement parks etc. are full and expensive on the weekends of President's Day, Easter, Memorial Day, 4th of July, Labor Day, Thanksgiving, Christmas, New Year's Eve and New Year.

Index

List of Maps and Illustrations

Photo Credits

Publisher's Information

1st Edition 2015
Worldwide Distribution: Marco Polo
Travel Publishing Ltd
Pinewood, Chineham Business Park
Crockford Lane, Chineham
Basingstoke, Hampshire RG24 8AL,
United Kingdom

Photos, illlustrations, maps::
171 photos , 34 maps and illustrations,
one large map
Text:
Inge Scherm, Annette Bickel, Helmut
Linde, Andrea Mecke, Axel Pinck
Editing:
John Sykes, Rainer Eisenschmid
Translation: Barbara-Schmidt-Runkel
Cartography:
Christoph Gallus, Hohberg;
MAIRDUMONT Ostfildern (map)
3D illustrations:
jangled nerves, Stuttgart
Infographics:
Golden Section Graphics GmbH, Berlin
Design:
independent Medien-Design, Munich
Editor-in-chief:
Rainer Eisenschmid, Mairdumont
Ostfildern

Printed in China

Despite all of our authors' thorough
research, errors can creep in. The pub-
lishers do not accept any liability for thi
Whether you want to praise, alert us to
errors or give us a personal tip Please
contact us by email or post:

MARCO POLO Travel Publishing Ltd
Pinewood, Chineham Business Park
Crockford Lane, Chineham
Basingstoke, Hampshire RG24 8AL
United Kingdom
Email: sales@marcopolouk.com

FSC
www.fsc.org
MIX
Paper from
responsible sources
FSC® C011918

MARCO ⊕ POLO

HANDBOOKS

MARCO ⊕ POLO
TRAVEL HANDBOOK
ANDALUCÍA
INFOGRAPHICS · 3D ILLUSTRATIONS · PULL-OUT MAP
Insider Tips
NEW

MARCO ⊕ POLO
TRAVEL HANDBOOK
BARCELONA
INFOGRAPHICS · 3D ILLUSTRATIONS · PULL-OUT MAP
Insider Tips
NEW

MARCO ⊕ POLO
TRAVEL HANDBOOK
BERLIN
INFOGRAPHICS · 3D ILLUSTRATIONS · PULL-OUT MAP
Insider Tips
NEW

MARCO ⊕ POLO
TRAVEL HANDBOOK
DRESDEN
INFOGRAPHICS · 3D ILLUSTRATIONS · PULL-OUT MAP
Insider Tips
NEW

MARCO ⊕ POLO
TRAVEL HANDBOOK
FLORIDA
INFOGRAPHICS · 3D ILLUSTRATIONS · PULL-OUT MAP
Insider Tips
NEW

MARCO ⊕ POLO
TRAVEL HANDBOOK
GRAN CANARIA
INFOGRAPHICS · 3D ILLUSTRATIONS
Insider Tips
NEW

MARCO ⊕ POLO
TRAVEL HANDBOOK
ICELAND
INFOGRAPHICS · 3D ILLUSTRATIONS · PULL-OUT MAP
Insider Tips
NEW

MARCO ⊕ POLO
TRAVEL HANDBOOK
LONDON
INFOGRAPHICS · 3D ILLUSTRATIONS · PULL-OUT MAP
Insider Tips

MARCO ⊕ POLO
TRAVEL HANDBOOK
NEW YORK
INFOGRAPHICS · PULL-OUT MAP
Insider Tips
NEW

MARCO ⊕ POLO
TRAVEL HANDBOOK
PARIS
INFOGRAPHICS · 3D ILLUSTRATIONS · PULL-OUT MAP
Insider Tips
NEW

MARCO ⊕ POLO
TRAVEL HANDBOOK
ROME
INFOGRAPHICS · 3D ILLUSTRATIONS · PULL-OUT MAP
Insider Tips
NEW

MARCO ⊕ POLO
TRAVEL HANDBOOK
VENICE
INFOGRAPHICS · 3D ILLUSTRATIONS · PULL-OUT MAP
Insider Tips
NEW

www.marco-polo.com

Florida Curiosities

The world's first scheduled airplane flight, the world's first refrigerator and then the world's first sunscreen, and women who are not allowed to skydive – Florida has lots of oddities and curiosities.

►Deepest south
Florida is the southernmost US state on the North American continent. Only Hawaii in the Pacific Ocean lies further south.

►First scheduled airline flight in the world
On January 1, 1914 for the first time a flight was carried out according to a fixed flight schedule, by a pontoon airplane from St Petersburg to Tampa.

►The first refrigerator
The physician Dr John Gorrie invented the first mechanical cooling system in 1851 for his patients in Apalachicola.

►The first sunscreen
The chemist Benjamin Green developed the first sunscreen in Miami Beach in 1944 when he experimented in his own kitchen with cocoa butter.

►Problem for couples
Co-habitation by unmarried couples is officially not allowed in Florida and can be punished by up to 60 days in jail.

►US city with the largest area
With more than 1963 square kilometres (758 square miles) Jacksonville is the largest city in the 48 contiguous US states.

►Would you believe it?
Unmarried women are not allowed to skydive on Sundays.